AMERICAN
POWER &
LIBERAL
ORDER

AMERICAN POWER & LIBERAL ORDER

A CONSERVATIVE INTERNATIONALIST GRAND STRATEGY

PAUL D. MILLER

Georgetown University Press / Washington, DC

Library of Congress Cataloging-in-Publication Data

Names: Miller, Paul D., author.
Title: American power and liberal order : a conservative internationalist grand strategy / Paul D. Miller.
Description: Washington, D.C. : Georgetown University Press, 2016. | Includes bibliographical references and index.
Identifiers: LCCN 2016019988 (print) | LCCN 2016024344 (ebook) | ISBN 9781626163423 (hc : alk. paper) | ISBN 9781626163430 (eb)
Subjects: LCSH: United States—Foreign relations—21st century. | Security, International. | National security—United States.
Classification: LCC JZ1480 .M553 2016 (print) | LCC JZ1480 (ebook) | DDC 327.73—dc23
LC record available at https://lccn.loc.gov/2016019988

♾ This book is printed on acid-free paper meeting the requirements of the American National Standard for Permanence in Paper for Printed Library Materials.

17 16   9 8 7 6 5 4 3 2 First printing

Printed in the United States of America

Cover design by Jen Huppert.

CONTENTS

ILLUSTRATIONS

Figure

Tables

ACKNOWLEDGMENTS

I would like to thank William Inboden, George Seay, and the board of the Clements Center for National Security at the University of Texas at Austin for giving me the place, time, and funding to write this book. Dr. Inboden has been an exemplary mentor and friend. I hope this book honors the legacy of Bill Clements—former governor of Texas, deputy defense secretary, and confidant to President Ronald Reagan—whose family foundation created the Clements Center and helps fund my position there.

Many thanks to Nina Silove, Josh Busby, Josh Eisenman, Eugene Gholz, Patrick McDonald, Sharyl Cross, Megan Reiss, Ben Griffin, Larry O'Bryon, and especially Anna Scanlon, who provided comments on earlier drafts of this book.

I'd like to thank Klon Kitchen, whose office at the National Defense University was down the hall from mine. Much of this book originated in our arguments over lunch; Klon's was the voice of persistent, nagging, and often persuasive disagreement in my head as I tried to refine ideas over the years. I suspect Klon will find more in this book that he disagrees with than otherwise, which is why he was such a helpful foil, spur, and debating partner. "Better is open rebuke than hidden love. Faithful are the wounds of a friend; profuse are the kisses of an enemy" (Proverbs 27:5–6).

Thank you to my children, Liam, Lily, and Lydia, for their laughter and smiles. Finally, thank you to my long-suffering wife, who showed saintly patience as she lived with this book and my preoccupation with it for many months.

This book is inspired in part on ideas I first explored in "American Grand Strategy and the Democratic Peace," *Survival*, vol. 54, issue 2, April/May 2012, pp. 49–76, and "Five Pillars of U.S. Grand Strategy," *Survival*, vol. 54, issue 5, October/November 2012, pp. 7–44. These articles have been copyrighted by the International Institute for Strategic Studies and are used with permission.

The views in this book and any errors are my own. All statements of fact, opinion, or analysis expressed are mine and do not reflect the official positions of the US government, any of its departments or agencies, either administration for which I worked, the Clements Center, or the University of Texas at Austin. Nothing in the contents should be construed as asserting or implying US government authentication of information or endorsement of the author's views. This material has been reviewed by the Central Intelligence Agency's Publications Review Board to prevent the disclosure of classified information.

INTRODUCTION

In 1994, President Bill Clinton asked Deputy Secretary of State Strobe Talbott to come up with a pithy catchphrase to summarize his grand strategy, akin to "containment" during the Cold War. Talbott and his boss, Secretary of State Warren Christopher, mentioned their effort to the author of containment, George F. Kennan, a chief architect of US Cold War strategy. Kennan scoffed at the idea. "'Containment' had been a misleading oversimplification; strategy could not be made to fit on a 'bumper sticker,'" Kennan believed.[1] It is better to focus on articulating the strategy than its nickname.

Kennan's advice has been ignored for the last quarter-century by scholars and policymakers, many of whom have raced to coin easy-to-remember phrases—*retrenchment*,[2] *strategic restraint*,[3] *"restrainment*,"[4] *off-shore balancing*,[5] *cooperative security*,[6] *selective engagement*,[7] *competitive engagement*,[8] *deep engagement*,[9] *sustainment*,[10] *responsible sovereignty*,[11] *forward partnership*,[12] *democratic internationalism*,[13] *transformation*,[14] and, naturally, *new containment*[15]—summarizing sweeping concepts and abstract theories of international relations. In practice, it has sometimes been difficult to differentiate between them. In reaction, as advocates for each strive to stand out, they inevitably caricature their rivals—accusations of imperialism, primacy, preponderance, and hegemony, on the one hand, and isolationism and pacifism on the other, are common—leading to a cheapened debate. More troubling, one gets the impression that the main difference among the options is simply a matter of degree, as if US foreign policy options could be presented as a spectrum of how involved America ought to be in the world: grand strategy reduced to a choice between "less" versus "more."[16] Some scholars have explicitly tried to frame grand strategy as a question of "whether the nation has expanded or contracted its strategic commitments as a whole."[17] Considering the broad array of issues, challenges, and opportunities with which foreign policy must concern itself, answering them all with "more" or "less" is unsatisfying.

These intellectual shortcuts leave unanswered more fundamental questions. What reasons—what *interests*—does the United States have that would impel it to be involved in the world in the first place? What threats and opportunities exist, in which regions of the world? What kind of "engagement" are we talking about—trade, diplomacy, war, or something else? What tools does the United States have with which to engage other states? How can the United States go about securing its varied interests? What does the United States stand to gain by being more involved in the world—or less? What should America's grand strategy be?

In the search to articulate America's grand strategy, "containment" has been strategists' worst enemy. By sloganizing a broad approach to the world and summing it up so concisely that it could fit on a bumper sticker, it implies that all grand strategies should have similarly short and catchy titles. Simple labels lead to simplistic foreign policy. Coining the term "containment" was a rhetorical strategy that helped sell American efforts during the Cold War—essential in a democracy[18]—but, with hindsight, the United States was probably *too* single-minded during the Cold War—something Kennan himself came to believe. The weaknesses of Cold War foreign policy—the failure to understand the nature of the Vietnam War, the open-ended support for right-wing dictatorships, and the failure to recognize the rise of jihadist movements—stemmed in part from the United States' sole focus on the Soviet Union. Kennan's criticism of his own strategic catchphrase was apt.

Today the strategic environment is even more complex, making it much harder to articulate even what US interests and goals are, let alone devise a plan for accomplishing them—*and* to summarize that plan in a single catchphrase. The search today for a pithy mantra is intellectually limiting. American foreign policy must be more nuanced and multifaceted than that. Identifying interests and developing plans are the work of foreign policy and are the aim of this book. Sloganeering is the work of advertising, at which this book makes no attempt.

What Is Grand Strategy?

This is a book about American grand strategy. The very concept of grand strategy has come under fire by some scholars and policymakers who believe it is too amorphous or impractical. By some definitions it is. The more expansive conceptions of grand strategy demand that it be an all-encompassing idea for coordinating the resources of an entire nation to achieve its ultimate goals. This is a staggeringly ambitious and ultimately unworkable concept because of the limitations of human knowledge and because governments cannot control everything. Grand strategy cannot be a plan to coordinate "whole-of-nation" efforts, a notion that seems fanciful, and we should not expect grand strategy to be a master concept that explains everything yet that simultaneously can be summarized by a simple label.[19]

But these criticisms do not invalidate the concept of grand strategy altogether. Strategy, both grand and humble, is inescapable and even inevitable. Strategy is, at the very least, implicit in the choices statesmen make in their budgetary and deployment decisions. Unless such choices are done by coin flip, policymakers are making deliberate choices and trade-offs and thus are operating off of some sense of relative priorities, toward some goals and not others. Even if they do not articulate it as such, this is a strategy. Strategies can be made better and more consistent if they are thought through, articulated, and tested, but even those that are not are still strategies. And policymakers are better off trying to do strategy because other states are trying to operate strategically: Whoever is successful will enjoy a competitive advantage over other states and adversaries in the international system. More positively, grand strategy operates as a conceptual center of gravity that orders, prioritizes, and focuses—even simplifies—foreign policy efforts. It is an effort to impose intellectual order on the chaos of world events and the chaos of one's own bureaucracies. Such intellectual shortcuts are impossible to avoid. Policymakers cannot know everything or even, in a time-constrained environment, all of the most important things; they cannot spend all their time immersed in the minutiae of data about the entire world every day.

Grand strategy, then, is useful as the "intellectual architecture that gives form and structure to foreign policy"[20] or as "a nation-state's theory about how to produce security for itself."[21] However, grand strategy is more than a set of ideas. Many states do not publish grand strategy documents, yet they have strategies whether they know it or not. Their behavior, unless purely random, is strategy in action. This notion—of strategy as the observed patterns of state behavior and, therefore, the inferred goals toward which the state is moving—has some advantages to it. One can observe a state's grand strategy by examining patterns in its behavior. Grand strategy can be conceived of as "the long-term pattern in a state's distribution and employment of its diplomatic/political, military and economic means toward its overall ends."[22] Grand strategy, then, has two aspects—as organizing concept and as pattern of behavior—both of which are essential.

The Organization of This Book

This book weaves several related arguments throughout the ensuing chapters. I make a historical argument that an understanding of the mutually reinforcing nature of American power and liberal order has animated US grand strategy for more than a century. I advance a set of theoretical arguments: American power and liberal order are mutually constitutive, the balance of power and the spread of democracy are complementary objectives, and kinetic operations against terrorists and stability operations in failed states are mutually reinforcing. I advance a normative argument that this approach to US grand strategy is just (or more just than the alternatives). Finally, I offer policy prescriptions, tweaks to adapt US grand strategy to the contemporary security environment.

This book begins with an argument that American power and liberal order are mutually reinforcing. It is followed by a chapter on the history of American foreign policy to illustrate the blend of power and liberalism that have animated US diplomacy for most of its existence (chapter 2). I then describe the twenty-first-century security environment (chapter 3). Contrary to scholars who believe the end of the Cold War ushered in an era of relative peace and stability, I argue that the contemporary environment is highly unstable. In chapters 4 and 5, I lay out the theoretical groundwork for four of the United States' five strategic courses of action (no such discussion is necessary for homeland defense). In chapter 4, I describe how the balance of power and the democratic peace are mutually reinforcing and complementary. I advance a similar argument in chapter 5 regarding kinetic operations against nonstate actors and investing in good governance abroad.

I then describe how the United States should apply this grand strategy to each geopolitical theater around the world (chapters 6 through 9). Finally, I describe how the United States should organize itself and what resources it should use to implement its grand strategy, including homeland defense (chapter 10), diplomacy and development assistance (chapter 11), and the military and intelligence communities (chapter 12). This step is often absent from discussion of grand strategy, which tends to focus on big ideas and organizing concepts. Unfortunately, that leaves policymakers and officials charged with the implementation of strategy without concrete guidance, and it ensures the academic research has little relevance. The oversight is understandable: Planning for implementation requires command of a vast, complex, and sometimes classified array of minute details. I offer only the beginnings of a thought process that could guide planning regarding US diplomacy, development strategy, and military and intelligence policy. I conclude with a brief chapter that summarizes my argument and describes how all five pillars of American grand strategy must work together in the United States' war against jihadist groups.

A note on terminology: In this book I use "grand strategy" and "national security strategy" (and sometimes just "strategy") interchangeably. Some scholars prefer to make fine distinctions between these terms, reserving "grand strategy" for military affairs and "national security" for all policy, foreign and domestic, aimed at protecting the United States and enhancing its power. I prefer to use both terms to refer to civilian and military policies and programs about international affairs because, in practice, that is how soldiers, diplomats, intelligence professionals, and others conventionally use them. There is little use in employing narrow technical definitions that are unused and, possibly, unrecognized by the audience at which this book is primarily aimed. I also find it useful to avoid the broader definition of "national security strategy." Under that sweeping definition, virtually every realm of human life could be considered part of "national security," from education to anti-poverty programs to environmental policy. Addressing some of these issues from a national security standpoint is much in vogue in security studies. But if everything is national security, the term has lost all meaning; lines must be drawn. And there is something to be said for avoiding the securitization of all of human life. Cleaning up the schools and the environment is surely the right thing to do—because they are intrinsic goods, not primarily because they contribute to America's national power.[23]

Notes

1. Gaddis, *George F. Kennan*, chap. 25.
2. MacDonald and Parent, "Graceful Decline?"
3. Gholz, Press, and Sapolsky, "Come Home America"; Posen, *Restraint*; Cronin, *Restraint*.
4. Martel, "Grand Strategy of 'Restrainment.'"
5. Walt, "In the National Interest"; Layne, "From Preponderance to Offshore Balancing."
6. Carter and Perry, *New Concept of Cooperative Security*.
7. Art, *Grand Strategy for America*.
8. Schadlow, "Competitive Engagement."
9. Brooks, Ikenberry, and Wohlforth, "Don't Come Home America."
10. Porter and Mykleby, *National Strategic Narrative*.
11. Krasner, "Orienting Principle for Foreign Policy."
12. Hoffman, "Forward Partnership."
13. Deudney and Ikenberry, *Democratic Internationalism*.
14. Gaddis, "Grand Strategy of Transformation."
15. Herberg-Rothe, "New Containment Policy."
16. As, for example, the options presented in Posen and Ross, "Competing Visions for U.S. Grand Strategy."
17. Dueck, *Reluctant Crusaders*, 12.
18. Freedman, *Strategy*, 336ff.
19. See Miller, "On Strategy, Grand and Mundane," for a more in-depth discussion of the nature of strategy.
20. Brands, *What Good Is Grand Strategy?*, 3.
21. Posen, *Restraint*, 1.

22. Silove, "Beyond the Buzzword."
23. See Strachan, "Lost Meaning of Strategy," and Elkus, "Must American Strategy Be Grand?" for a similar critique. Strachan notes of security studies that "by being inclusive they end up by being nothing." Posen, similarly, argues that including everything would "dilute the most important purpose of grand strategy" (*Restraint*, 2).

PART I

A FRAMEWORK FOR THINKING ABOUT US GRAND STRATEGY

1

In Search of a Twenty-First-Century Grand Strategy

It is commonplace to lament the United States' lack of a coherent grand strategy. Cold War historian John Lewis Gaddis argued in 2009 that the United States suffered from a "grand strategic deficit" that went back two decades to the fall of the Soviet Union. One scholar recently wrote that America "is squandering the moment" because "it has no grand strategy," has been "floundering," and is "a great power adrift."[1] Another wrote, "The absence of even an incomplete grand strategy means that all foreign and security policy issues are treated in virtually an ad hoc fashion."[2] Yet another: "During the span of two decades American foreign policy has swung between the extremes [because of] the failure to develop a new national strategy for dealing with fundamental changes in the international system."[3] Ike Skelton, then chairman of the House Armed Services Committee, held hearings on American grand strategy in 2008 because, as he told the committee,

> there does not seem to be a comprehensive strategy for advancing United States' interests. This strategy is void, and it detracts from almost every policy effort advanced by the United States Government. Our international actions can be likened to a pick-up sandlot baseball game, rather than a solid course of action. Major policies are sometimes inconsistent and contradictory, and so we sometimes suffer from a splintering of national power and an inability to coherently address threats and reassure and cooperate with allies around the world.[4]

There is much truth to these criticisms. The American foreign policy establishment has not covered itself in glory in the recent past. Its record of failure and scandal includes the terrorist attacks of 2001; the intelligence failure surrounding Iraq's alleged weapons of mass destruction; the botched execution of postwar reconstruction in Iraq; the irresponsible exits from Iraq, Afghanistan, and Libya; ineffective responses to Iran's nuclear program, Russia's aggression, and China's assertiveness; and fears that the government's war powers, allegedly including targeted killings, indefinite detentions, and overbearing surveillance, have grown beyond oversight and accountability. After two difficult wars, the failed Arab Spring, and decades of China's rise, US policymakers are scrambling to respond. There is no consensus about America's role in the world, and we still lack a strategy for using American leadership to invest in liberal order. The first and biggest problem this book addresses is the need to rethink America's grand strategy and its role in the world.

Paradoxically, one of the best ways to rethink American foreign policy is to relearn the history of what is, in fact, a remarkably successful record. Despite the litany of failures above, the United States has a much longer, and startlingly impressive, record of foreign policy—from achieving independence and securing continental hegemony to emerging victorious in three world wars in the twentieth century. This past provides us a useful trove of wisdom from which we can rethink the present and plan for the future. But "our national ignorance of our own past successes impoverishes our foreign policy process today."[5] A second problem this book addresses is our tendency to forget our past, exaggerate discontinuities, and focus on our failures. I take a historical approach to articulating a grand strategy for America, seeking to understand where we have come from in order to chart a course for the future because "most grand strategies begin with a look backward before they look forward."[6]

A third problem is a tendency to misunderstand what *strategy* is and, thus, to misdiagnose the problems in US foreign policy. The standard complaints against US foreign policy are often fair criticisms of its day-to-day management, but they can obscure a deeper and longer consistency to US strategic goals and success in pursuing them. Many recent failings of US foreign policy were failures of management, oversight, and implementation. Strategy is not management; poor management does not necessarily suggest the absence of a strategy meant to guide implementation. Blaming every failure on poor strategy can cause some policymakers to question a good strategy that had the misfortune of being poorly implemented and others to question the idea of strategy altogether. During Skelton's hearings on US grand strategy, several witnesses expressed skepticism that the United States has had a grand strategy or that having one was even possible, and one member suggested the United States give up on "fuzzy Grand Strategy stuff."[7] It also encourages a perennial search for the next grand strategy every four or eight years that, its advocates hope, will cut the Gordian knot of all US foreign policy problems. Such a search is unrealistic. As Sarah Kreps has rightly argued, "one individual, even the most powerful, may be unequipped to change a country's grand strategy. American interests, threats, and capabilities do not change on Inauguration Day. Grand strategies are characterized by their longevity, often spanning many years, with little more than minor tweaks around the margins."[8] Rather than proposing an ambitious and entirely new grand strategy out of whole cloth, I suggest "tweaks" to what I argue is already established strategy. In doing so, I attempt to clarify what strategy is, and what it means to think strategically, by concrete example.

A final problem is that scholars and policymakers have not come to a consensus about America's role in the world or the relationship between American security and world order. Some have suggested that the United States is a state like any other and, since the collapse of the Soviet Union, faces few things that truly qualify as threats to its national security. In this view, the United States can afford to retrench from its various commitments abroad. Others argue that the United States is exceptional because of the extent of its power and appeal of its values, which is how the United States became the leader and architect of liberal order. They are apt to argue that there is no end to threats facing the United States, including nonstate groups, failed states, and even environmental collapse, and thus the United States should expand its international role. Each camp's preferred grand strategy differs from the others because of the different threats it believes the United States should guard against. At root of this disagreement is a tendency to overemphasize the extent to which the security environment has changed and thus to exaggerate the extent to which the United States needs to change its grand strategy. In fact, there is a greater degree of continuity in the security environment, and thus in the United States' ideal grand strategy, than is widely appreciated. This book's historical approach attempts to correct for that.

The Post–Cold War Debate

The post–Cold War debate over US grand strategy, which has unfolded in three phases, has failed to resolve these problems. First, in the years after the end of the Cold War, scholars and policymakers debated whether the fall of the Soviet Union fundamentally changed the international system and whether the United States could or should sustain its uniquely powerful "unipolar" position within it.[9] Liberal internationalists argued that the appeal of liberalism and international institutions had largely replaced the need to engage in the balance of power.[10] Advocates of "restraint" argued that the United States could now afford to retrench in the face of diminished threats abroad and adopt a more hands-off strategy of "off-shore balancing."[11] The liberal internationalists largely won the policy debate. The United States cut its military budget and reduced its overseas military presence, as both camps wanted, but did not pare back its international commitments. It sustained its ambition to lead and expand the community of democratic states, defended access to the global commons and the principle of nonaggression, and even increased its interventions abroad for peacekeeping and humanitarian causes.

In retrospect, the debate over unipolarity seems misguided. The true unipolar moment dawned in 1945, when the United States produced almost half of world gross domestic product (GDP) and had a monopoly on nuclear weapons, a moment that passed quickly. By 1989, the United States' economic unipolarity had ebbed considerably; by 2015, China and the European Union (EU) were peer competitors. Militarily the United States spends more than most of the world combined, but the spread of nuclear weapons created a crude sort of equality, limiting the United States' ability to *use* its vastly greater military power, while terrorism and insurgency proved partially effective at playing to the US military's weaknesses. The mischaracterization of America's power position, coupled with liberal internationalist assumptions about the end of great power balancing, led policymakers to believe they could wield American power at will even while cutting its budget and disregarding the shifts in power among and between other states and the rise of unconventional threats. As a result, the United States allowed an unacknowledged gap to grow between its decreasing military, diplomatic, and intelligence capabilities and its continued global ambitions, reflecting a naive underappreciation for the continued realities of power in the post–Cold War world.

In the second phase of debate, after the terrorist attacks of 2001, scholars debated the rise of failed states, terrorists, and other nonstate actors and argued how best the United States should organize its grand strategy to construct a new global order to respond to the apparently growing chaos.[12] Some characterized the United States' conflict with al-Qaida and its sympathizers as an ideological struggle on par with the struggles against fascism and communism, which demanded a similarly ambitious grand-strategic response from the United States.[13] Others, who took the rhetoric of the "War on Terror" at face value and sidestepped the question of jihadist ideology, focused only on the question of how to thwart terrorist tactics and argued that the United States had overreacted to the attacks of 2001.[14] Scholars also argued over whether or not reconstruction and stabilization operations were necessary (or possible) to drain the swamp from which jihadist groups grew.

It is not clear that a consensus position ever emerged in these years. Scholars and policymakers remained divided sharply over whether or not the war in Iraq was a useful exercise of US power, how it related to the war against al-Qaida, and how important traditional security concerns, such as great power politics, remained in the post-9/11 era. The conceptual clutter was matched by policy failure. The United States never fully committed to either a lean and surgical counterterrorism approach nor to fully resourced and competently executed counterinsurgency, reconstruction, and stabilization operations. The muddle achieved neither the economy of the first option nor the ambition of the second.[15] And the United States remained distracted while traditional rivals proved increasingly assertive. China embarked on a markedly more assertive foreign policy after 2008, North Korea tested nuclear weapons for the first time in 2006, Russia invaded Georgia in 2008 and Ukraine in 2014, and Iran resisted efforts to halt its nuclear program.

Third and most recently, since the United States began to wind down its long wars in Iraq and Afghanistan and, simultaneously, suffered a contraction in its fiscal situation, scholars and policymakers have debated whether the United States is now facing an unprecedented limitation on its freedom of action and whether it needs to begin limiting its commitments abroad in line with a new and emerging world order in which it will play a diminished role. Advocates of restraint have become even more vocal than in the aftermath of the Cold War.[16] Other scholars have sought to find ways of preserving America's influence through greater reliance on allies and partners abroad or better use of diplomacy and development assistance.[17]

A major problem with the post–Cold War debate on grand strategy from both realists and liberal internationalists is that their arguments tended to take an insufficiently short-term view of events. Neither the terrorist attacks of 2001 nor the war in Iraq, nor even the fall of the Soviet Union, were events of sufficient magnitude to fundamentally alter the United States' century-old strategic courses of action. It was in the United States' interest to protect itself and maintain a favorable balance of power both before and after the fall of the Soviet Union. These events altered the global strategic context (or reflected underlying changes that had been developing for some time), and consequently they certainly required the United States to adapt the means it used to pursue its ends. However, there seems to be a tendency for scholars and policymakers to overreact and treat the most recent past as the most important facts—an example of "recency bias" in international relations. That is why some scholars and policymakers were attracted to the concept of "unipolarity" in the immediate aftermath of the Cold War, why the Clinton administration was drawn to the spread of democracy, and why George W. Bush made the War on Terror the centerpiece of his foreign policy. Individually, they were all imbalanced overreactions to recent events, part of the reason post–Cold War administrations have failed to articulate a coherent grand strategy.[18]

Against Restraint

But a larger problem is the rise of restraint as a school of thought among American scholars and policymakers after the Cold War and, even more dramatically, after the Iraq War. Eugene Gholz, Daryl G. Press, and Harvey M. Sapolsky argued that the United States can and should withdraw most of its military forces deployed abroad and pull out of the North Atlantic Treaty Alliance (NATO) and other alliances, and need not be concerned about the success or failure of democracy in other countries because "America faces almost no discernable security threats."[19] Their argument has gained ground since the failure of US efforts in Iraq. Micah Zenko and Michael Cohen argued in *Foreign Affairs* more recently that the United States is actually very safe because it faces no "existential" threat, great power war is unlikely, democracy, prosperity, and public health are all on the rise, and the international challenges today are unlikely to kill many American citizens. Considering these developments, in their view, the United States is certainly safer today than it was during the Cold War and does not need to continue investing in its military establishment at current levels.[20] Similarly, Barry Posen in his recent book *Restraint* distrusts hypothetical causal chains that purport to explain how small incidents would lead to major threats: "The United States should focus on a small number of threats. . . . It can do that because the United States is economically and militarily strong, well-endowed and well-defended by nature, and possessed of an enormous ability to regenerate itself." Posen believes that the United States can choose the threats it focuses on because they are small enough compared to its strength and argues that the United States should redeploy its military forces homeward and withdraw from most alliance commitments.[21]

There are major problems with restraint. First, even if the assumptions that undergird the policy recommendations were true, withdrawing military forces and ending alliances would still be inappropriate. Even if territorial defense were the extent of American security, the United States would still require a more forward presence around the world than advocates of restraint understand. Advocates of this view rightly argue that the United States is one of the few large countries in the world that never has to worry about a land invasion from a hostile power. Since Canada's independence from the British Empire and Mexico's loss in the Mexican–American War, neither country has, nor ever will, pose a significant threat to the United States. A hostile Eurasian hegemon, like the Soviet Union, Nazi Germany, or Imperial Japan, might dominate the wealth and power of much of the globe but even then would find it almost insurmountably difficult to project power across the Atlantic and Pacific, storm the beaches of California or Virginia, defeat the

US military in open battle on its home turf, and subdue the best-armed partisan resistance in history—short of annihilating the country altogether with an indiscriminate nuclear attack.

This is, I think, true but myopic. Japan was able to launch a surprise attack in 1941 because the United States lacked a worldwide network of reconnaissance and surveillance assets to notice a fleet including six aircraft carriers crossing the Pacific. Today, the United States would be able to see a large naval task force heading for American waters because it has intelligence, surveillance, and reconnaissance assets based around the world. But many of these assets are ground-based systems located on foreign soil; overhead satellites and US-based systems by themselves do not provide a flexible, reliable, and redundant warning system with full global coverage. Google Earth and international media cannot fill the gap: They are unreliable and cannot be tasked or redirected at will by US personnel in times of crisis. Even accomplishing the barest minimum of security requires US intelligence and military assets, facilities, and personnel deployed to overseas locations (albeit fewer than at present) to keep an eye on the movement of foreign navies and air and space assets—and that means bilateral security agreements with foreign countries.

A second problem with the school of restraint is the term's use as a rhetorical device. Advocates of restraint regularly argued against a strategy of "preponderance," "dominance," or "extraregional hegemony," which, they claimed, had characterized America's grand strategy since the end of the Cold War or even since World War II. Yet it is unclear who is supposed to have advocated these positions. The labels "preponderance," "geopolitical dominance," and "hegemony" were used almost exclusively by critics of those positions (another scholar coined "muscular dominance" to describe the position he disagreed with).[22] But opponents of restraint typically described their position as "liberal internationalism," defended the United States' "unipolar" status or its role as "leader" or the "indispensable nation," and called for a strategy of "deep engagement."[23] There is an important difference between "dominance" and "leadership" that advocates of restraint wrongly elide. Nor has the United States' behavior since the Cold War— cutting its military, intelligence, and foreign aid budget, reducing the size of its armed forces, and redeploying more than half of its troops abroad back home—been consistent with a strategy of "primacy" or "hegemony." Far from pursuing a strategy of hegemony, the United States has, in fact, retrenched in hard-power terms.

Advocates of restraint are arguing against a position no one holds and no one has implemented. Their use of the label "restraint" functions more as rhetorical strategy to suggest that their opponents are in favor of "unrestrained" grand strategy—which, of course, no one has ever been but makes restraint look moderate by comparison. The subtle denigration of foreign policy initiatives they dislike with prejudicial labeling enables advocates of restraint to influence the debate often without engaging their opponents on the merits. Instead, they resort to caricatures—often thinly veiled ideological attacks— that policymakers believe "that the United States is so powerful and virtuous that it can pretty much remake the world on its own terms," as one scholar claimed.[24] No policymaker or scholar is on record as having said such a thing. The war in Iraq obviously hovers in the background of these criticisms. Critics betray a troubling tendency to overinterpret that war as a morality play in which American hubris led to a just and tragic fall—a simplistic reading of history and an unhelpful approach to learning its lessons and applying them to future policymaking. Moreover, advocates of restraint sometimes overgeneralize from Iraq as if it were the paradigmatic case of the United States' role in the world. But Iraq was a single outlier, not a representative sample of US foreign policy.[25] Recognizing the failures of the Iraq War does not require opposition to a broad role for the United States in the world. Further, advocates of restraint do not have a monopoly on recognizing restraints in US grand strategy. In fact, every proposed grand strategy recognizes limits and the need for restraint at some point; the disagreement is over where those limits lie. I generally disagree with restraint as a label and a school of thought, but, because any grand strategy must identify priorities and recommend where to allocate resources, the strategy outlined in this book also recommends where *not* to allocate resources. I necessarily advocate restraint in certain regions, in response to certain issues, and under certain conditions.

The Argument of This Book: American Security and World Order

The third and most serious problem with restraint is that it rests on an overly narrow conception of "security" and a misunderstanding of the relationship between American security and world order. Advocates of restraint argue that the two are separable: America might be safe even in a hostile, unstable, illiberal world and therefore can safely look to its own shores and remain relatively uninvolved in developments abroad. These scholars are correct that at the most basic level, security is the protection of American lives and territory from immediate physical harm and the perpetuation of America's political independence. And if that were the full extent of America's security concerns, a radical reduction in America's military budget and overseas presence would be appropriate: Restraint would be "America's best option today because of the paucity of international threats."[26]

But defining security *exclusively* as protection against invasion and conquest is an overly narrow and provincial conception of security. Robert Art
rightly notes that "America's purpose in the world cannot be reduced simply
to self-protection."[27] There are other forms of insecurity. "Invasion is not the
only form of coercion," according to Nicholas Spykman, because, at the most
obvious level, in a world dominated by a hostile, illiberal power, America
would be vulnerable to "economic strangulation" and blackmail.[28] A world
economic order dominated by mercantilism, autarky, or imperialism would
make Americans, along with everyone else, poorer and less economically
free. The United States is more integrated with the world economy now than
in decades: Trade as a percentage of US GDP rose from less than 10 percent
in 1960 to 30 percent in 2013, according to the World Bank. Sustaining a
relatively open global trading regime is essential to American prosperity and,
thus, national security. That is why policymakers regularly see "security" in
broader terms—rightly, in my view—seeking to build a favorable international environment.

Nor is this simply about trade. The trading regime is only the most concrete example of a much broader phenomenon that is central to US national
security. The United States exists in a social system comprising patterned
interrelationships among 193 sovereign states, scores of intergovernmental
organizations, and hundreds of multinational corporations, regulated by
thousands of treaties and centuries of precedent. The international social system—or "world order" for short—is defined by its most powerful members,
articulated in norms and ideologies, embodied in institutions, and gives rise
to a discernable *culture* in which states operate. World order is "a political formation in which settled rules and arrangements exist between states to guide
their interaction" and, I would add, a cultural formation as well.[29] "Rules and
institutions"—and the norms they embody—"alter the environment in which
states operate."[30] The culture of world order shapes how states treat each other,
what expectations policymakers have of other states, whether a given treaty
or initiative is considered politically feasible, what states believe is "normal,"
and what counts as "aggressive."[31] In this view, American national security is
linked to the growth of a favorable culture of world order—which implies a
much greater and more expansive American role in the world.

Put another way, academic realists and advocates of restraint fail to appreciate the reality of norms, institutions, ideology, and culture in constructing
security. Their focus on the formal structure of the international system—
anarchy, sovereign statehood, and the distribution of power[32]—leads them
to argue that all states are guided by a similar logic according to a rational-
actor model, regardless of their domestic political makeup, the beliefs of their
policymakers, the dominant norms in the world, the presence or absence of

democracy, and other factors. This is surely wrong. In a real sense, the world is not anarchic and states are not "like units." Realists' focus on structure has obscured the importance of other factors shaping state behavior. While there is no *legal* authority, there are *norms* that guide behavior and set expectations and function like an informal "constitution" for world order.[33] States differ from each other by their position in the international system, their ideologies, their strategic cultures and histories, their capabilities, and their beliefs about the justice or injustice of world order.[34] International politics is thus not the product of a one-dimensional pursuit of power by all states under uniform conditions; it is a response by different kinds of states to an environment of power, as perceived through the lens of different identities and ideologies. The distribution of such norms and identities matters as much as the distribution of power.[35]

The culture of world order is relevant for US national security. Illiberal norms and hostile ideologies abroad do not simply cause "psychological discomfort" for Americans.[36] If the narrower, territorial conception of security focuses on whether there is a bigger fish in the ocean, the broader conception worries about poison in the water. It matters that much of the world, including its legal regime, trading institutions, and efforts at arms control, is informed and guided by liberal norms. Liberal norms make up the atmosphere in which American research, innovation, learning, exploration, discovery, production, trade, entrepreneurship, discovery, travel, humanitarianism, proselytism, tourism, diplomacy, and more take place: It is where the nations live, move, and have their being. A world of liberal norms makes it easier to do all these things. A world of illiberal norms makes it harder, costlier, riskier, and, in some cases, illegal or impossible.

The dominance of liberal norms and the prevalence of democracy and free-market capitalism around the world have direct, practical, and positive security implications for the United States. "Today, the world's great industrial powers share similar democratic national identities and appear to eliminate the balancing of military power from their relationships altogether," according to Henry Nau.[37] Similarly, John Ikenberry argued that, as the hegemonic power of the liberal system, the United States "can identify its own national interest with the openness and stability of the larger system."[38] Threats to this system are threats to the United States; sustaining the health of this system is a vital national security interest of the United States.[39] The great twentieth-century theologian, writer, and polemicist Reinhold Niebuhr was partly right that "our sense of responsibility to a world community beyond our own borders is a virtue, even though it is partly derived from the prudent understanding of our own interests."[40] He would be nearer the mark if, instead of "even though," he had said "because": Maintaining liberal order is a virtue *because* it is a national security interest. As Nau argued, "converging identities safe-guard national security just as surely as dominant military power."[41] Narrowly focusing on the territorial security of the United States while neglecting the nature of world order (Is it healthy or anemic? Hostile or friendly? Stable or unstable?) is shortsighted. In brief, liberal order is the outer perimeter of American security. This becomes even more important if America's relative power declines. The incentive to invest in liberal order as an extension of American influence rises if the United States' ability to rely on its raw power advantage declines.[42]

The current distribution of norms is highly favorable to the United States. It has not always been so. World order has changed and evolved over millen-nia—but not randomly. The culture of world politics is largely the creation of its most powerful members—sometimes as a conscious construction, some-times as an unintended emergent property of their patterned interactions—which is why realists are right to stress the enduring importance of power in world politics. For the past three hundred years, the most powerful states in the international system have been the United Kingdom, the United States, and, since World War II, the liberal democratic states of Western Europe and Japan.[43] Powerful, illiberal states have launched repeated challenges to liberal ascendancy; all have failed. At present, the international order is "a hierarchi-cal order with liberal characteristics . . . built on both American power domi-nance and liberal principles of governance."[44] Scholars and policymakers have called this, variously, the "maritime system," the "Open Door," the "demo-cratic community," and a strategy of "deep engagement" to sustain the "free world," or "liberal order" (the phrase I use in this book). Politically, liberal order favors liberal democracies, the rule of law, and civil liberties. Economi-cally, liberal order means capitalism, relatively free trade and low trade barri-ers, freedom of the seas, neutral rights, the sanctity of contract, and peaceful rule-based dispute adjudication. Internationally, liberal order means nonag-gression and territorial inviolability—with limited exceptions for humani-tarian intervention—and favors intergovernmental cooperation on issues of global concern. Liberal order does not encompass the whole world and is not evenly distributed around the world. Scholars have defined its boundar-ies differently and categorized its various members in different ways, some viewing it as a worldwide order with liberal democracies constituting its core, others viewing it as an order that only exists among democracies and high-lighting how the distribution of power creates different relations—hierarchy and community—among its members.[45]

Under this broader understanding of American security, the definition of "threat" used by advocates of restraint is too narrow. Zenko and Cohen's threshold of threat—situations that pose an "existential" danger or that cause immediate bodily harm and death to American citizens—is shortsighted. Almost no dangers in American history have been literally existential in the sense of actually threatening to end the continued physical existence or political independence of the United States. By that standard, only the Confederacy's secession and the Soviet Union's nuclear arsenal were true threats to the United States. Similarly, Posen's distrust of hypothetical causal chains seems shortsighted. The outbreak of World War I, the Bolshevik Revolution of 1917, the German invasion of Poland in 1939, North Korea's invasion of the South in 1950, the Islamic Revolution of 1979, and a host of other international incidents were not threats to the United States, by Posen's or Zenko and Cohen's standards. None of these events killed a single American, and none of them threatened the physical existence or political independence of the United States. Yet it was easy to see how these developments threatened liberal order and would eventually materialize into threats against the American homeland, US prosperity, or the American way of life without a proactive response. Posen's response—"we know that everything is related to everything else, but this insight is not useful in the real world of strategy"[46]— is dismissive beyond warrant and reflects an underappreciation for strategic forecasting. Just because policymakers are not prescient does not mean forecasting is futile. Events that threaten liberal order are threats to the United States, even if indirect.

Christopher Layne has criticized this view on the grounds that it leads to overextension: "By definition, any strategy that equates security with the defense of de-territorialized 'milieu goals'—like openness—rather than with tangible strategic factors—like geography and the distribution of power—is open ended, because it is impossible to fix a point beyond which America's security interests are not implicated."[47] This is unpersuasive. It *is* possible to fix limits (although US policymakers have sometimes failed to do so). The "milieu" is not undefined and featureless, requiring an all-or-nothing defense: It is made of up specific things such as the presence or absence of pirates in strategic waterways, the proportion of power possessed by a state expressing a hostile ideology, the efficiency and competence of liberal institutions, and more. Layne is right that variables such as power and geography play a role; he is wrong that they matter only in material terms. Power and geography affect how order is constructed and where it is most important to the United States. Fiji's autocracy is irrelevant to the survival of liberal order; Pakistan's is not. The Convention on the Rights of the Child is dispensable; the Nuclear Non-Proliferation Treaty is not. The United States' efforts to sustain a favorable milieu can and should be strategic and selective, largely by focusing on regions with the greatest concentration of wealth, power, and danger. I describe and apply the process of prioritization in chapters 6 through 9.

Another objection to this view of American security and world order is that it is unsustainable. Liberal order depends on American power, in this view, and it was only built because of the historically unprecedented disparity of power the United States found itself in possession of after 1945 within the Western bloc and after 1989 globally. As China and other developing countries close the gap between themselves and the developed world, America's relative power will decline (even if its economy and military spending grow in absolute terms), and the United States' ability to sustain liberal hegemony will erode. This is especially true, according to some scholars, as hegemonic powers are virtually guaranteed to decline as spending on military power and system maintenance crowds out investment, slows long-term growth, and undercuts competitiveness. If true, grand strategies that aim at the continuation of liberal order are expensive projects in proving the futility of working against the grain of history.[48]

This objection depends on two premises: that liberal order depends on American hegemony and that American power is inevitably declining. Both are contestable. First, liberal order is much older than American hegemony, having antecedents in the Pax Britannica of the nineteenth century and perhaps earlier. It does not depend on unipolarity or hegemony: The British built their version of liberal order within a multipolar balance-of-power system, and the United States within the bipolar Cold War. Today, the rise of China or a belligerent Russia *might* end American hegemony (and might not), but liberal order could nonetheless live on. The rise of India and the enduring prosperity of liberal democratic Europe and Japan suggest liberal order has many pillars to stand on.[49]

Second, while American relative power has declined if measured in crude material terms such as America's share of global GDP, that is not a very full measure of the United States' ability to secure its interests. The United States has arguably *increased* its ability to achieve its goals by fostering a favorable international environment. Liberal order is an extension of American—and other democracies'—power. By entrenching liberal norms, it gives them a life beyond the fiat of any single liberal state. Liberal norms and institutions are an "invest[ment] in its future power position" because they "can both conserve and prolong the power advantages of the leading state."[50] The system is self-reinforcing: Liberal states uphold liberal order, which in turn enhances their power to defend and extend the system. Whether American unipolarity lasts, there is ample reason to believe that American influence and liberal order are sustainable. Unipolarity is a tool or, better yet, an opportunity. The important question is what America should *do* with its unipolarity while it lasts. Using it to build liberal order enhances American security and extends American influence even if America's relative material power declines.

Abstract as it may seem, this broader conception of security appears to be instinctive for policymakers. American statesmen faced with crises abroad, including Presidents Woodrow Wilson, Franklin D. Roosevelt, and Harry Truman, rightly took the larger view that because the United States was a primary beneficiary, participant, and (later) architect of liberal order, a threat to liberal order was a threat to the United States itself. FDR's famous analogy about lending his garden hose to a neighbor whose house is aflame worked because of Americans' instinctive understanding that their individual safety was inextricably entwined with their neighbors': A fire next door might spread. The same logic, FDR argued, works in the neighborhood of nations.[51] So too, today, there are major challenges to liberal order that should be understood as threats to US national security—even when they are not immediate or "existential."

Another way of framing the argument is that Zenko and Cohen are mistaken to define "threat" exclusively as "danger"—physical harm or injury—at the expense of "risk" or "uncertainty." The Soviet nuclear arsenal was probably the greatest "danger" there will ever be against the United States. It is difficult to imagine a greater danger than the complete nuclear eradication of the United States. But strategic planning does not (or should not) concern itself only with danger. It should also concern itself with risk and uncertainty. Although nuclear war would be dangerous, during most of the Cold War there was probably a low risk of it actually happening (except during the Cuban Missile Crisis and the war scare of 1983).

Today, mass-casualty terrorism is not as dangerous as nuclear war, but there is a higher risk of it actually happening—terrorism has killed more Americans than nuclear weapons have. The same is true of a wide range of lower-level dangers. Many lesser dangers are actually happening, and more likely to happen, than previously, making the world a more *risky* place, despite a lower level of *danger* from any single threat. In addition, the presence of many different risks, any of which may come to pass and interact in unpredictable ways, collectively increase the uncertainty in world affairs. The Cold War seemed stable because there was one controlling dynamic that planners war-gamed over and over again; there seemed to be few scenarios they had not imagined or planned for. Today it is nearly impossible to imagine all possible future scenarios that could result from the complex dynamics at play in the contemporary security environment. That surely includes some scenarios in which the physical safety of the United States is not so assured as it seems today. The apparent physical safety of America in the post–Cold War period has blinded some scholars and policymakers to the uncomfortable fact that we live in a far riskier, less predictable world. That is why "the ultimate case for some type of American overseas military presence is a preventive one," a form of "insurance" against the uncertainties of the future.[52]

All things equal, both the narrow and the broad conceptions of security are important for developing grand strategy. The existence of liberal order is an opportunity for the United States: Continuing to invest in its upkeep is a cost-effective strategy for producing an outer ring of security for itself. Advocates of restraint are wrong to neglect this opportunity and their view illustrates the weakness of an exclusively threat-centric and reactive grand strategy. Liberal order already exists over much of the globe. It would be a foolish waste to walk away from it. At the same time, because the United States' perception of its national security interests has expanded to include the upkeep of world order, its perception of threats has also expanded. Advocates of internationalism have sometimes done a poor job of prioritizing which among the dizzying array of threats are most pressing. The narrower conception of security can help focus policymakers' minds and provide criteria for prioritizing which threats to liberal order are most relevant to American security.

But all things are not equal. Today, scholars and policymakers are in greater danger of underestimating threats to American security than overestimating them: We are more prone to undervalue the importance of liberal order to American security than overinvest in it. In the aftermath of Iraq and Afghanistan, policymakers in both parties have suggested the United States needs to pare back its international commitments, avoid interventionism, exercise a restrained version of American leadership—or even pass the baton of leadership altogether—and turn aside from ambitious efforts to champion liberalism abroad. Because this seems to be the prevailing wisdom of the moment, I intend to stress the opposite. The foundational argument of this book is that American security and liberal order are mutually constitutive: Liberal order is the outer perimeter of American security, and American power upholds liberal order. Policymakers should understand threats to liberal order to be indirect threats to the United States itself. Because of this relationship, the United States is right to include championing liberalism and investing in good governance abroad as parts of its grand strategy.

American Grand Strategy

I argue that, contrary to widespread belief, the United States has been pursuing a fairly consistent set of strategic courses of action at least since its emergence as a great power in the late nineteenth century: defend the US homeland from attack, maintain a favorable balance of power among the great powers, champion liberalism, punish nonstate actors, and invest in good governance and allied capabilities abroad. Homeland defense, great power diplomacy, and kinetic operations against terrorists and other nonstate actors support the narrower conception of security. Failure to pursue these courses of action puts the United States in danger of immediate physical harm. Championing liberalism and investing in good governance abroad support the broader conception of security and the construction of liberal order abroad. Failure in these courses of action introduces more risk and unpredictability in the international system.

These courses of action are a coherent response to the contemporary security environment. The security environment is dominated by states, some of which are large, powerful, and hostile to the United States. But the security environment is also populated by a range of nonstate actors, such as terrorists and drug traffickers, who collectively raise the cost of doing business and weaken the foundations of liberal order. Third, there is a unique security challenge posed by jihadist groups, which are a decentralized blend of state and nonstate actors who share broad aspirations motivated by a common ideology. In response to these different threats,[53] the United States has developed both an offensive and a defensive course of action, roughly corresponding to its alternating realist and liberal inclinations.[54]

Against the great powers, the United States seeks to deter war by adopting countervailing strategies against them, as realists counsel, while seeking to *change* the balance of power in its favor by championing liberalism, as liberal internationalists prefer. The idea is not to "contain" the nuclear autocracies: The United States should welcome their legitimate engagement with the world through trade and diplomacy. Rather, the United States aims to deny them the ability to expand their influence and increase their power through illegitimate means, including invasion, conquest, annexation, coercion, subversion, blackmail, extortion, and terrorism. Simultaneously, the United States seeks to create an environment fundamentally favorable to liberalism and unfavorable to aggression by increasing the proportion of global power under democratic control.[55] In other words, the United States uses means that realists favor (power politics) and means that liberals favor (ideological promotion) because the two are, in fact, mutually reinforcing.

Against hostile nonstate actors, the United States similarly pursues two courses of action. It takes direct military and law enforcement action against them where possible and seeks to shrink their operational space and redress the conditions of state failure that enable their growth by investing in good governance where necessary. By combating nonstate threats directly, the United States provides short-term security and buys time for longer-term solutions to take shape. By selectively investing in the capacity of partner nations to secure their own borders, uphold security, prosecute criminals,

Table 1.1. Pillars of US Grand Strategy

	State-centric Threats	Nonstate Threats
Defensive/realist	Balance power	Punish nonstate actors
Offensive/liberal	Champion liberalism	Invest in good governance

and combat terrorists and drug cartels, the United States works toward the resolution of the underlying conditions that enable armed nonstate groups to take root in the first place. This approach again combines the insights of opposing schools of thought, seeking to avoid the moral problems of endless war and the expense and naiveté of indiscriminate nation-building.

US efforts to combat jihadist groups and governments are especially complex. This conception of grand strategy helps us understand why. It requires the implementation of all five of the United States' grand strategic courses of action. It must protect the homeland, work against jihadist elements in Iran's and Pakistan's governments, directly combat the few jihadist groups that threaten the United States, provide security assistance to allies and partners threatened by local jihadist franchises around the world, and hold out the ideal of accountable, representative government as an alternative to jihadist ideology. I explore this challenge in the conclusion.

The tools and resources available to counter nuclear autocracies and increase democratic power are a dominant military capability; collective security agreements—that is, alliances—with other states, especially powerful democracies; investments in other democracies through trade, aid, weapon sales, and security assistance; and leadership of institutions of global governance, especially those that foster liberal trade. Combating armed nonstate groups involves deploying an array of tailored military and law enforcement tools. Investing in good governance involves, in permissive environments, economic aid, security assistance, and weapon sales. In less permissive environments it involves all of the above, plus what the military calls stability operations.

Many of these tools overlap, and the five courses of action reinforce one another—which is another way of saying that United States has gravitated toward an economical grand strategy. Its globally deployed military power is an important part of balancing against the nuclear autocracies but also gives it advance positions from which to stage kinetic operations against terrorists and other nonstate actors and to undertake a stability operation in a fast-moving crisis. Similarly, stability operations almost always pursue democratization as part of their mandate, supporting the goal of increasing democratic power. Economic aid, security assistance, and weapon sales to poor democracies or partial democracies, especially those under threat from terrorists or autocracies, are effective ways of pursuing almost all courses of action simultaneously. That is why the instruments of national power are so important but also why justifying each tool individually can be so difficult: The United States' alliances, military power, participation in international institutions, foreign aid, and other instruments of national power serve multiple purposes. Figure 1.1 illustrates the relationship between the ends, ways, and means of US grand strategy.

The diversity within this grand strategy is unsurprising considering the complexity of the world and the intellectual background of American foreign policy. As Walter Russell Mead has rightly pointed out, "American foreign policy does not proceed out of a single, unified worldview."[56] I argue that this matrix of offensive and defensive (or realist and liberal) actions against conventional and unconventional threats—alongside homeland defense—constitutes the best shorthand description of US grand strategy; it is the most concise expression of how the United States understands threats and expects to provide security for itself. This is the "intellectual architecture" of US grand strategy at its simplest and most general. Its simplicity can help scholars and policymakers categorize different initiatives, tools, and undertakings.

Like any matrix, it is also simplistic and should not be taken too rigidly. For example, championing liberalism and investing in good governance obviously blur together: Weak states lack the capacity to protect human rights, so investing in their capacity is one of the best ways to champion liberalism in the developing world.[57] In addition, great powers often employ nonstate actors as proxies; defeating the proxies is a part of balancing power (a particularly acute challenge in the war against jihadist groups, some of which enjoy state sponsorship). Because of its generality, this matrix by itself is not a fully articulated grand strategy. It is merely a "master concept" that needs to be unpacked and applied to specific problems to be a useful grand strategy. The question remains, How should the United States pursue each of these strategic goals given the specific threats and opportunities of the twenty-first-century security environment? The answer to that question is the remainder of this book.[58]

This argument is both descriptive and prescriptive. I argue that this conception of US grand strategy is a broadly accurate description of the long-term pattern of behavior of US foreign policy since at least 1898, with traces stretching back even further. These broad goals are well within the mainstream of US foreign policy, they enjoy bipartisan support, and they have been remarkably consistent for decades. Nor do I claim that this is a wholly original insight; other scholars have noted that "American thinking about foreign policy has been relatively stable over the centuries" and have developed schema of schools of thought on American foreign policy from which I have

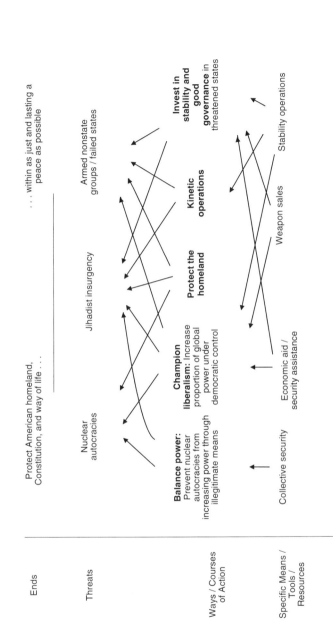

Figure 1.1. US Grand Strategy

benefited.[59] However, it is important to note that I do *not* claim that any particular US president or secretary of state has explicitly articulated American grand strategy this way. Grand strategies do not need to be articulated to be real, and US grand strategy is less the product of an "auteur" and more a "group effort"[60] that has evolved over decades.[61] Nonetheless, the historical record of past policymakers' efforts suggests a continuity to the US foreign policy tradition that is often overlooked and that can and should offer guidance today.

But this is not primarily a work of history—it is a work of policy prescription. By arguing from history I do not mean to suggest that whatever happened in history was the best possible outcome or that policymakers can relax and let historical inertia guide the ship of state. Policymakers do not always adapt quickly or thoroughly enough to changing circumstances, nor do they always pursue all five pillars in balance. The weaknesses of containment can be understood as a consequence of the single-minded focus on balancing against the Soviet Union, and one problem with the War on Terror was the single-minded focus on punishing nonstate actors. American foreign policy is strongest when the United States pursues the full range of objectives relevant to US national security interests and tailors its strategy to the unique security challenges of each era. The five strategic objectives of US grand strategy complement and reinforce one another. Indeed, they must work together to work at all; too much emphasis on one at the expense of others will result in a lopsided and ineffective foreign policy. Focusing only on state-centric threats and the balance of power risks allowing nonstate actors to penetrate American defenses and inflict catastrophic harm on American lives and territory, as al-Qaida did in 2001. Focusing only on nonstate actors to the neglect of great power diplomacy, on the other hand, allows great powers to expand their influence, as Russia did in 2014. Spreading liberalism without balancing power is naive and dangerous; the opposite is shortsighted and morally questionable. And military strikes against nonstate actors without addressing state failure are simply an endless succession of tactical operations without an overarching strategy to solve the problem that enables nonstate actors to operate in the first place.

Today we do not need to invent a new grand strategy out of whole cloth, but neither should we be captive to bureaucratic inertia. We need to take a fresh look at the security environment, think anew about how to apply the United States' tools of national power to produce security for itself, and suggest a series of tweaks to US grand strategy in the twenty-first century. I recommend a variety of tweaks throughout this book, such as adopting a framework for better prioritizing regions, issues, and problems around the world that emphasizes power, wealth, and democracy; forming a Pacific

Alliance; creating a South Asia Command; deemphasizing the Middle East; establishing an MI5-like domestic intelligence agency; shifting overseas military deployments away from large, conventional bases toward the maintenance of platforms of access in each region of the world; institutionalizing stability operations as a core mission for the US military; and vastly increasing foreign aid and civilian assistance. These are, I argue, logical extensions of the United States' existing grand strategy.

Realism and Liberalism

This approach to US grand strategy implies syntheses that have not always been well coordinated in past practice: between the balance of power and the promotion of democracy and between kinetic operations against nonstate actors and, in areas where they operate, reconstruction and stabilization operations. These are specific applications of a broader synthesis between realism and liberal internationalism. In the very long run, the United States has undertaken each of these policies in a way that can appear, in retrospect, to be part of a coherent whole. When considered at the level of separate presidential administrations or individual policymakers, US grand strategy has often been piecemeal and reactionary, oscillating between opposing tendencies.

Realists rightly understand that US foreign policy is, first and foremost, *American* policy. It rightly aims at protecting American interests and promoting American goals. It is orchestrated by American officials, funded with American tax dollars, and implemented by the all-volunteer American diplomatic corps and armed forces. The United States is not a world government and does not have infinite resources. There are many evils in the world that Americans rightly condemn but that are beyond the reach or jurisdiction of their government. American foreign policy should not aim to protect human rights for every human being, provide relief after every natural disaster, or broker peace in every armed conflict. American foreign policy rightly prioritizes the physical safety, territorial integrity, and political independence of the United States.

But liberal internationalists rightly respond that American security is often best served by taking a larger view of the international order in which the United States exists. If, in fact, liberal order is real and makes self-government, civil liberties, free trade, the rule of law, and collective security increasingly normal, that can only be good for the United States and the world. More, creating such a world may actually be "cheaper" than retrenchment because it is the ultimate preventative medicine, keeping the global body politic healthy instead of waiting for catastrophe and dealing with the costs of major surgery later. While advocates of retrenchment count the savings from cutting the defense budget, they neglect the cost of reduced trade and difficult conflicts that are likely to spring up in the wake of American withdrawal from world leadership.

Second, liberal internationalists—and common sense—rightly argue that national security must be embedded in a just and lasting peace among nations to the extent achievable in this flawed world. If the American way of life included, as a matter of necessity, massive injustice, oppression, or violence elsewhere in the world, it would provoke resentment and revolt and would rightly be counted a failure. While the American government rightly puts American interests first, US officials should still be cognizant of how the United States affects others throughout the world and try, where possible, to use US power for the benefit of others. And as the United States is the most powerful nation on earth, its actions often have dramatic consequences for the rest of the world. As Niebuhr said, "a preoccupation with our own interests must lead to an illegitimate indifference toward the interests of others, even when modesty prompts the preoccupation. [The solution is] a concern for both the self and the other in which the self, whether individual or collective, preserves a 'decent respect for the opinions of mankind.'"[62]

The tension between these two poles—protect America, advance liberal order—is often expressed in international relations scholarship, and in American history, as the tension between our interests and our ideals, between realism and liberalism. In US grand strategy, this tension is most visibly evident between the balance of power and the spread of democracy. It is also reflected in the United States' different responses to the challenges of nonstate actors and failed states, alternating between narrow efforts aimed only at punishing nonstate actors and more ambitious efforts to invest in stability abroad. (For example, it was reflected in the debate over the relative merits of counterterrorism against counterinsurgency in Iraq and Afghanistan.) I argue that, in the long run, pursuing either without the other is folly; pursued together, there is a surprising amount of harmony. Fostering democracy and balancing power together is the best way—the best *strategy*—for protecting America against great powers within a stable and nearly just world order, as is investing in stability while conducting kinetic operations against nonstate actors. As Niebuhr said, "every nation is caught in the moral paradox of refusing to go to war unless it can be proved that the national interest is imperiled, and of continuing in the war only by proving that something much more than national interest is at stake."[63] American power should be employed for American ends and, where possible (but only where possible), for higher purposes as well.

The two goals have become so closely related, in fact, that there is an effective identity between the interests of the United States and the interests of liberal order. The United States was a primary architect of the global liberal order and remains one of its chief beneficiaries. The global order of inter-dependent, open societies tied together by networks of trade and alliance mediated through a host of international institutions—underpinned by American power—is an effective tool for the advancement of security for the United States and the free world.

Normative Frameworks

Instead of realism or liberal internationalism, this book is informed by three other frameworks: just war, Christian Realism, and conservative interna-tionalism. The just war tradition is a body of thought and argument about the restrictions that should be placed on the use of lethal force in light of ethical considerations. It addresses itself to the question, When is it just to kill people? It stands in distinction to both pacifism, according to which it is never just to kill, and realism, according to which killing needs no justifica-tion other than raison d'état. Just warriors believe that killing is a morally serious act that needs special justification—but also that some circumstances give that justification.

Important for our discussion, the question of when it is just to kill neces-sarily must invoke or rest upon a broader idea of justice before it can sub-sequently address the problem of the just use of lethal force. I find just war thinking profoundly helpful for thinking about statecraft because the state is, at heart, a coercive instrument. All state behavior—and that means all foreign policy—carries with it the implicit possibility of the use of force. This is sim-ply the implication of sovereignty: In the absence of any superior authority, any state can resort to force to pursue its ends. The normative framework developed for thinking about the application of coercive force thus applies to a far broader range of state behavior than formal interstate war. We could, in fact, talk of *just force* and relate its insights to virtually any field of policy.

Norms are relevant for the second intellectual paradigm that informs this work: Christian Realism. This was the name Niebuhr gave to his political theory and represents his effort to reconcile the insights of realism with the tenets of his Christian faith, which I share. Niebuhr tried to steer a middle course between what he believed was the naive utopianism of Wilson and the cynical realpolitik of Europe, based on his belief in both the dignity and depravity of human nature. He believed the United States should never stop trying to work for a more just, peaceful, and stable world but also that it needed to do so with open eyes, a healthy suspicion of one's own motives, and a clear understanding of how the world actually works. The relationship between his theological beliefs and political convictions is complex but at least involves a biblical understanding of human sinfulness and human potential, of the imperative to pursue justice while recognizing our own contribution to injustice.

If there is a hard core to Christian Realism, it is contained in several related antitheses. We have a responsibility to confront evil in the world, even as we recognize that we are not immune from it ourselves. We have a responsibility to aspire to justice in the world, even as we must maintain a suspicion of our own motives and our own conception of justice. We have a responsibility to work for both justice and order, understanding that there are unavoidable trade-offs between them that make our pursuit of both destined to be imperfect. We must approach political affairs realistically: The *means* by which we work for justice and order must make use of the tools shown to be effective in the fallen and fallible world we actually inhabit. Naiveté about what it takes to get things done is a form of moral irresponsibility. Even as we must retain some germ or seed of idealism and hope to work for justice, we must be aware of the temptation toward crusading idealism, utopianism, and messianism that can infect any idealistic endeavor.

The third intellectual paradigm that informs this work is what Nau has dubbed "conservative internationalism," another tradition in American foreign policy that attempts to blend the strengths of realism and liberal internationalism. He argues that, in the vein of Presidents Truman and Reagan, the United States should remain engaged in a leading role abroad and continue to foster democracy where possible but should be more prudent and realistic in its understanding of how the world works and not put too much trust in global institutions or the good faith of other states.[64]

A common thread runs through these paradigms: moderation. Just war thinking steers a middle course between pacifism and realpolitik. Christian Realism aims to avoid both naive utopianism and cynical realism. Conservative internationalism seeks to combine the insights of realism and liberal internationalism. As Aristotle argued, "virtue is a kind of mean" or intermediate path between extremes.[65] I draw inspiration from these paradigms but avoid slavish replication. Because this is mostly a work of policy analysis and application, not theory, my own interpretation of, use of, and departure from these paradigms is mostly implicit.

Notes

1. Kupchan, *End of the American Era*, 12.
2. Fingar, "Intelligence and Grand Strategy," 124.

3. Martel, "Grand Strategy of 'Restrainment,'" 359.

4. *Considerations for an American Grand Strategy.*

5. Mead, *Special Providence*, 8.

6. Peter Feaver, "Eight Myths about American Grand Strategy," in Ronis, *Forging an American Grand Strategy*, 42.

7. *Considerations for an American Grand Strategy.*

8. Kreps, "American Grand Strategy after Iraq," 633.

9. Wohlforth, "Stability of a Unipolar World"; Layne, "Unipolar Illusion"; Kupchan, "After Pax Americana"; Mastanduno, "Preserving the Unipolar Moment"; Finnemore, "Legitimacy, Hypocrisy, and the Social Structure of Unipolarity."

10. Ikenberry, *After Victory.*

11. Layne, "From Preponderance to Offshore Balancing."

12. Gaddis, "Grand Strategy of Transformation"; Biddle, "American Grand Strategy after 9/11"; Cronin, *Attacking Terrorism*; Ikenberry, "American Grand Strategy in the Age of Terror"; Kagan, "One Year After."

13. Podhoretz, *World War IV*; Woolsey, "At War for Freedom."

14. Boyle, "War on Terror and American Grand Strategy"; Schwenninger, "Revamping American Grand Strategy."

15. Biddle, *American Grand Strategy after 9/11.*

16. Posen, *Restraint*; Cronin, *Restraint*; Milevski, "Collective Failure of Grand Strategy"; Walt, "In the National Interest"; Layne, *Peace of Illusions.*

17. Schadlow, "Competitive Engagement"; Hoffman, "Forward Partnership."

18. Suri, "American Grand Strategy."

19. Gholz, Press, and Sapolsky, "Come Home, America," 8. They repeated their argument in 2009. See Sapolsky et al., "Restraining Order."

20. See Zenko and Cohen, "Clear and Present Safety," and my response in Miller, "National Insecurity."

21. Posen, *Restraint*, 3, xii.

22. Schwenninger, "Revamping American Grand Strategy."

23. Ikenberry comes closest to using and endorsing the label of liberal hegemony, but his position, which does not emphasize military dominance, is not the one being criticized. Edelman used "primacy" favorably in *Understanding America's Contested Primacy* in 2010, long after the label was coined and criticized by its opponents.

24. Schwenninger, "Revamping American Grand Strategy," 32.

25. Brooks, Ikenberry, and Wohlforth, "Don't Come Home, America," 31–33.

26. Gholz, Press, and Sapolsky, "Come Home America," 6.

27. Art, *Grand Strategy for America*, 3.

28. Nicholas Spykman, quoted in Art, "Defensible Defense," 16.

29. Ikenberry, *Liberal Leviathan,* 36.

30. Ibid., 91.

31. For elaborations of these ideas, see Ruggie, *Constructing the World Polity*; Wendt, *Social Theory of International Politics*; and Katzenstein, *Culture of National Security.* The grounding of my argument in a constructivist paradigm distinguishes it

from both Art's "selective engagement" and Ikenberry's liberal internationalism, with which it otherwise shares some similarities. The constructivist paradigm, in my view, provides a fuller rebuttal to the advocates of restraint and a better foundation for an internationalist, engaged grand strategy.

32. Waltz, *Theory of International Politics*.

33. Ikenberry, "Constitutional Politics in International Relations."

34. Martel, *Grand Strategy in Theory and Practice*, emphasizes differences among states. The most obvious difference among types of states is that among great powers, normal states, and microsovereignties. They also differ by their degree of freedom; i.e., between liberal and autocratic states. Finally, they differ in how they perceive the international system, as the debate over "revisionist" states attest. On this last distinction, see Schweller, "Bandwagoning for Profit." It would be possible to develop a typology of statehood differentiating states by their power, freedom, and posture toward the system.

35. Nau, *At Home Abroad*.

36. Art, "Defensible Defense."

37. Nau, *At Home Abroad*, 6.

38. Ikenberry, *Liberal Leviathan*, 70.

39. Threats to liberal order are not threats to the United States just because the United States built it; the fact that the United States deliberately set out to build liberal order doesn't necessarily mean the system served US security. It might have been a foolish waste of power to build world liberal order, in which case threats to liberal order would simply expose the United States' wastefulness, as Layne seems to believe. As it happens, I argue the United States was wise to invest its power in building liberal order.

40. Niebuhr, *Irony of American History*, 7.

41. Nau, *At Home Abroad*, 7.

42. Ikenberry, *Liberal Leviathan*, 152–53, 156.

43. Mead, *God and Gold*.

44. Ikenberry, *Liberal Leviathan*, 7.

45. Ikenberry views the liberal democracies as the center of a worldwide liberal system and autocracies as peripheral members. Nau views liberal order more narrowly, a view I agree with.

46. Posen, *Restraint*, 3.

47. Layne, *Peace of Illusions*, 119.

48. Gilpin, *War and Change*, Kupchan, *End of the American Era*, and Layne, *Peace of Illusions*, make versions of this argument.

49. In other words, the US grand strategy outlined here does not depend on hegemonic stability theory. Hegemons help reduce transaction costs and facilitate communication and thus may make liberal order easier to achieve, but they are probably not strictly necessary. I suggest an oligarchic stability theory, wherein a small group of rich and powerful states collectively perform the function usually assigned to a single hegemon. See Snidal, "Limits of Hegemonic Stability Theory," and Webb and Krasner, "Hegemonic Stability Theory."

50. Ikenberry, *Liberal Leviathan*, 107.

51. Roosevelt, "Press Conference."

52. Art, "Defensible Defense," 50.

53. Feaver is wrong that "Grand Strategy requires a Grand Threat," (see "Debating American Grand Strategy after Major War," 550). It is possible to formulate strategy against a range of diverse threats.

54. To stretch analogies, it also roughly corresponds to Walter Russell Mead's "Jacksonian" and "Wilsonian/Hamiltonian" traditions in American foreign policy. The entire formulation, and my recommendation for how to implement it, is, I hope, Jeffersonian in its economy. See Mead, *Special Providence*.

55. This is a slight reformulation of Nau's first principal in *Conservative Internationalism*. He focuses on increasing the number of democratic states; I focus instead on the proportion of global power under democratic control.

56. Mead, *Special Providence*, 54.

57. Englehart, "State Capacity, State Failure, and Human Rights."

58. I am tempted to label this approach "balanced restrained realistic liberal forward sustainable engagement," but, sadly, it won't fit on a bumper sticker.

59. Mead, *Special Providence*, xvi. See also McDougall's scheme in *Promised Land, Crusader State*.

60. Mead, *Special Providence*, 39–40.

61. See Brands, *What Good Is Grand Strategy?*, for an excellent example of tracing the evolution of grand strategy in different administrations.

62. Niebuhr, *Irony*, 148.

63. Ibid., 36.

64. Nau, *Conservative Internationalism*. Neither Nau nor I use the term "neoconservatism." The term has lost all meaning, having degenerated into a term of denigration to use against anyone whose foreign policy one finds distasteful. To the extent that neoconservatism means the employment of American hard power for forceful democracy promotion abroad, I reject it. As I make clear in chapters 11 and 12, I call for vastly increased foreign aid and civilian democracy assistance, but, compared with some hawkish policymakers, I am relatively less concerned about the size of the United States' overseas military presence.

65. Aristotle, *Nicomachean Ethics*, book II, chap. 6.

2

Power and Liberty in US Diplomatic History

I begin with a brief review of the history of American foreign policy.[1] The purpose is, first, to demonstrate that the mixture of advancing American power and championing liberalism is deeply rooted in the American foreign policy tradition; they constitute America's "strategic culture" or "operational code." This is unlikely to be a controversial claim except among structural realists who dismiss ideology as epiphenomenal. Most critics acknowledge that central to America's foreign policy ideology is the "quest for national greatness closely coupled to the promotion of liberty."[2] Put another way, "the promotion of a more liberal international order, broadly speaking, has always been a central goal of American grand strategy"—central, but not sole, for it is "one factor among many in the decision-making process."[3] This explains why support for liberalism has ebbed and flowed over time, shaped and sometimes overridden by pragmatic concerns. As Henry Kissinger explains, "no nation has been more pragmatic in the day-to-day conduct of its diplomacy, or more ideological in the pursuit of its historic moral convictions."[4] This two-pronged approach to the world has made the United States a formidable power in the world and a "dangerous nation" to its foes.[5]

Second, the purpose is to learn from and respond to this history: to examine its successes and failures, to evaluate when policymakers got the blend of projecting power and championing liberty right and when they got it wrong, to develop a common frame of reference, and to understand the antecedent narrative so policymakers today can learn how best to carry the story forward. This enables us to establish a basis from which normative judgments and policy prescriptions can be made. This is not a comprehensive diplomatic history of the United States but an illustrative narrative demonstrating how pursuing power and championing freedom are both part of the United States' long-term pattern of behavior.

The history of American diplomacy has been told in different ways. An early postwar school held that America was traditionally isolationist until

Europe's inability to manage its affairs became so dire that America was compelled to step in to sort things out, twice, after which it found itself in command of unsought power and influence on a global scale and could not but use its newfound position to spread the blessings of liberty. This view—what Walter Russell Mead calls the "Cold War myth"—has little basis in history and more often obscures than illuminates the history of America's role in the world.

A revisionist school in the 1960s and 1970s rightly argued that the United States consciously sought and successfully achieved its position of power and influence through deliberate effort and planning, motivated by a commitment to political and economic liberalism. However, in developing its corrective view, it introduced two other flaws: It tended to overemphasize the economic dimensions of American diplomacy, treating nearly every initiative as part of a master plan to increase American exports, and it developed a nearly paranoid interpretation of American policymakers' motives, painting them as a cabal of scheming Machiavels wholly driven by greed, imperialism, and the will to power.[6] No doubt they sometimes are, but even Niebuhr balanced his assessment of policymakers' innate selfishness with a healthy regard for their occasionally sincere efforts to act rationally and with goodwill.

There is another way of relating the same story that some "postrevisionists," such as John Lewis Gaddis, have pioneered.[7] The revisionists are right that American policymakers deliberately sought to increase the United States' power and influence in the world, motivated by their commitment to liberal ideology. But this view does not require us to understand the project of liberal expansion as inherently unjust or imperialistic. The justice of the liberal ascendency is an empirical question, not a theoretical one: Sometimes it has indeed been cruel and unjust, but not always. More to the point, it is *effective strategy*: It is a smart way of using limited resources to produce security for the United States. Great power rivalry is an enduring feature of world politics and American foreign policy, and American policymakers consistently use liberalism as an ideological weapon to balance power. The use of power and the fate of liberty go together. The United States "promotes its national interests both by pursuing power and by drawing other states toward its national identity."[8]

Foundations: 1776–1815

The United States was never isolated from the world, and there is no tradition of pure isolationism in American foreign policy. From 1776, it was energetically engaged in securing recognition of its independence, finding new markets, fighting for its trading rights, and securing hegemony over the North American continent—all aspects of an active foreign policy. The United States was not, however, a great power. It was a middling power with widely recognized potential for tremendous future growth. Its poverty of power relative to the European great powers limited America's foreign policy options and explains why American foreign policy choices in the nineteenth century looked different from those in the twentieth. American grand strategy from independence to Reconstruction was an extended, massive act of internal balancing, of building up its inner resources of power to close the gap between itself and the powers most capable of destroying the new republic. American policymakers rightly understood the country to be too weak to challenge the European powers directly and generally believed its resources were too scarce to be spent on exporting the American Revolution abroad. They also recognized that time was on their side: The United States, by dint of demographic and territorial expansion and industrialization, grew stronger more quickly than its European rivals. Finally, the Founders, influenced by the earlier tradition of Puritanism, had an instinctively realist view of human nature, a lower expectation of what government could accomplish, and less expansive ambitions for foreign policy.[9]

In the United States' first decades of existence, it pursued a balance between the great powers of the day, the British and French empires (which were not liberal states at the time). The United States allied with France against Britain to gain independence but negotiated with the British separately at the war's end in violation of its prior agreement with France. Presidents George Washington and John Adams then distanced the country from France by issuing the Proclamation of Neutrality (1793), signing the Jay Treaty with the British (1794), and fighting a small naval "quasi-war" with France (1798–1800) to assert its right to neutrality. Presidents Thomas Jefferson, James Madison, and James Monroe then tilted back toward France; Jefferson embargoed British trade (1807) in a dispute over neutral rights, which contributed to another short war under Madison (1812–15) with the United Kingdom over the latter's impressment of American sailors. Domestic politics also played a role in the United States' vacillation between the two European powers,[10] but for three decades the consistent pattern of US foreign policy was to prevent either France or the United Kingdom from gaining unacceptable leverage over American interests and independence. This was obviously crucial to the survival of the American experiment in self-government.

Nonetheless, the ideology of liberalism, with which Americans justified their revolution and defined their nation, had an inner logic that was not completely smothered by realpolitik. The American Founders, in their defense of self-government and civil liberties, appealed to principles they claimed were universal. The same Puritanism that made the Founders realists also gave them a sense of being agents of divine favor, commissioned by God to establish a model of self-government on behalf of all humanity. They spoke of "self-evident" truths and made universal declarations that government—any government, without qualification—"derives its just powers from the consent of the governed." John Quincy Adams said that the United States "is the well-wisher to the freedom and independence of all," though was careful to add "the champion and vindicator only of her own." President Monroe, in the declaration of his doctrine, shared that "the citizens of the United States cherish sentiments the most friendly, in favor of the liberty and happiness of their fellow men on that side of the Atlantic" (that is, Europe) and in an earlier draft had wanted to make sweeping statements of solidarity with embattled liberals in Spain, Greece, and Latin America. Jefferson even expounded an early version of the democratic peace theory.[11]

The implication was that self-government was appropriate for all peoples and all nations, and thus should rightly be the aspiration of the world, and that America's role was to be the exemplar, spectator, and cheerleader of global liberalism. If anything, the Founders were even more explicit about the universal applicability of their principles than contemporary policymakers, who are often at pains to emphasize the legitimacy of cultural differences in other states. But by and large, in America's earliest days, liberalism was not for export—it was too precious for that. Power and liberty went hand in hand, but the logic worked in reverse from what came later. The United States did not export liberalism to increase its power; it increased its power to protect liberty at home.

Hemispherical Hegemony: 1815–77

If there was ever an era in which American grand strategy was marked by a conscious pursuit of "primacy" or "hegemony," it was from 1815 to 1877. It was directed at North America, not the world, and it was completely successful—a chapter that is often wrongly filed under domestic policy in Americans' memory. The United States explicitly sought to eliminate all external influence on the continent and become the sole major power over the entire landmass. It used a variety of means, including purchase (the Louisiana Territory, from France, in 1803; the Gadsden Purchase, from Mexico, in 1853; and Alaska, from Russia, in 1867), conquest and annexation (West Florida, from Spain, in 1810; Texas, in 1845; and the Mexican Cession in 1848), and coercive bargaining (East Florida, from Spain, in 1819; the Oregon Territory, from Great Britain, in 1846)—and, of course, it used a mix of all three in dealing with Native American tribes. The territorial expansion of the United States was the result of the projection of hard power across the continent—soldiers, explorers, and a tidal wave of immigrants. The US government buttressed these acquisitions with a foreign policy proclamation in 1823—the Monroe Doctrine—that "the American continents, by the free and independent condition which they have assumed and maintain, are henceforth not to be considered as subjects for future colonization by any European powers" and that "we should consider any attempt on their part to extend their system to any portion of this hemisphere as dangerous to our peace and safety."[12] Since the achievement of continental hegemony, the United States has never been in serious danger of invasion and conquest.

But the American pursuit of continental hegemony was not simply history's greatest landgrab. It was cast in terms of the expansion of freedom: "For the leaders and citizens of the new republic, in fact, the nation's foreign policy and its liberal 'ideology' were in many respects indistinguishable. . . . Liberalism in the eighteenth century, and for the next two hundred years, was the main engine of American expansion."[13] Jefferson described American expansion as the extension of an "Empire of Liberty"—better the free rule of American republicanism over the continent than the rule of autocratic European empires.[14] "Expansion derived from the primordial, exceptional American commitment to liberty," according to historian Walter McDougall,[15] or, as Michael Hunt argued, "just as essential to expansion" as hard power was "a guiding vision"—namely, that "the fate of liberty and the mission of the United States had become intertwined."[16] "Manifest Destiny" was a crucial part of the successful nineteenth-century American foreign policy. Americans believed that their continental primacy was both morally good and preordained, the spread of liberty justifying their expansion across the continent. As the leading, and perhaps only, free people in the world, they believed their rise to power could only be a blessing to the world; the expansion of their free institutions and the increase of their power would be a strong example to the rest of the world and an encouragement to aspiring reformers.

Americans' first steps outward are the easiest in which to see self-interest corrupting their sense of justice. The "Empire of Liberty" trampled over Indians and Mexicans to make way for slaveholders; racism was also part of America's foreign policy ideology in the nineteenth century.[17] Americans' self-serving ideological justification for their continental conquest was rife with hypocrisy and outright pretense—which, at least, is the compliment vice pays to virtue. "Hypocrisy and pretension are the inevitable concomitants of the engagement between morals and politics. But they do not arise where no effort is made to bring the power impulse of politics under the control of conscience," as Niebuhr said.[18] By cloaking continental conquest with liberal ideals, Americans gave their harshest critics—which, usually, were other Americans—powerful weapons with which to push for more principled conduct in the future. The effort itself is sound in principle: Better to be a failed idealist than a successful cynic. The opposite reaction—using past failures to lower our moral ambition in the present and future—is exactly wrong.

During the American pursuit of continental hegemony, its relationships with the great powers, especially the United Kingdom, gradually changed. Relations between the United States and the European powers were not uniform. The United States grew more powerful and more liberal at the same time that the United Kingdom was also liberalizing, which influenced how the two states perceived each other and how they treated one another. By century's end they had reached a historic rapprochement.

What became the Monroe Doctrine illustrates the unique dynamics of the Anglo–American relationship in the early nineteenth century. After the War of 1812, the two powers were wary, even hostile, though they continued to benefit from deep trade ties. American and British policymakers alike were alarmed by the Holy Alliance's reactionary moves to crush liberalism in Spain and Italy and wanted to forestall their intervention in the newly independent Latin American countries. Neither country wanted to see Spain reestablish rule over its lost colonies in the Western Hemisphere. That would potentially enrich Spain, upset the balance of power in Europe, and endanger the United States' ambition to keep the New World apart from European imperialism. But British overtures for a joint declaration against European intervention in Latin America was rebuffed by American policymakers interested in pursuing the same goal without drawing too close to a British Empire they still did not trust. The result was a unilateral declaration by the United States that the United Kingdom was bound to support anyway because of its common interests. The Monroe Doctrine was, in part, "a tacit agreement between the United States and Great Britain to maintain the balance of power" between them and in Europe and a "recognition that American safety depended on the balance of power in Europe."[19] But it was a balance they could agree on because it protected liberal forces they both wanted to nurture, albeit to different ends. The Monroe Doctrine had the effect of protecting the independence of the new Latin American republics, enabling the growth of a uniquely American system of international diplomacy, bolstering America's negotiating position with other European powers, and clearing the path for American trade in the Western Hemisphere and later American territorial expansion.

The United States and the United Kingdom came close to war in 1837 over unrest in Canada, in 1844–46 over Oregon, and in 1861–63 as Britain teetered on the brink of recognizing the Confederacy. Notably, however, both countries had grown more explicitly liberal by the time of the Civil War. Britain's Reform Act of 1832 had expanded the franchise, and the Chartist Movement had mobilized Britain's working class behind demands for further reform, changes similar to what the "Jacksonian" movement in the United

States had earlier accomplished. According to McDougall, "the liberal ideology that dominated British policy after 1832 [reduced] the possible sources of friction with an essentially like-minded United States."[20] Most important, the evolution of Abraham Lincoln's war aims from restoring the Union to abolishing slavery significantly influenced the British decision not to intervene: Shared liberal ideology helped bring the two countries together and avert war at a crucial juncture.[21] The Anglo–American rapprochement in the nineteenth century, eventually solidified in the Treaty of Washington (1871), may thus be the greatest early example of US national security directly benefiting from the growth of liberalism at home and abroad. It also laid the foundations of today's "special relationship." Theodore Roosevelt would later carry this further, aligning with the United Kingdom against Germany during a crisis over Morocco in 1905—laying the groundwork for the impending wartime alliance—because he believed "the British were kinfolk who shared a devotion to ordered liberty, free trade, and international progress and stability."[22]

In its first century, the United States was prudently concerned with growing and protecting its power—only secondarily, indirectly, and inconsistently with spreading liberty. Liberalism defined the nation at home, not its foreign policy. But the universal language of liberalism continued to creep into American thinking about the world and yielded direct benefits for US national security as the century wore on. A few—including Thomas Paine—were more ambitious and hoped the United States might proactively lead the world toward liberty. Jeffersonians believed the French Revolution was an echo of America's own, which they were duty-bound to support and encourage, and "what we would now call Wilsonian voices called for intervention in the Latin American, Greek, Polish, Hungarian, and Cuban wars for independence,"[23] but their influence was limited. Until the war in Cuba, America supported liberty abroad rhetorically and by example. In the century to come, it continued to speak the language of liberty but now began to give weight to its words.

Liberal Imperialism: 1877–1939

America's foreign policy in its second century was not a radical departure but a natural evolution, a "derivative and fulfillment,"[24] in response to changing circumstances. With the end of Reconstruction in 1877 and the closing of the frontier, America began to look outward—and took its concern for liberty with it. America's power had grown: By century's end it was indisputably one of the great powers of the world. Domestically, the rise of progressivism and the Social Gospel, inspired by the older Puritan sense of divine mission but shorn of its pessimistic view of human nature, brought a new sense of mission to all aspects of public policy.[25] And the world had shrunk. The railroad, telegraph, telephone, automobile, and airplane made the vast distances of the world easier and cheaper for people, goods, and information to traverse, ending the New World's inaccessibility from the Old. New powers were rising. The unification of Italy and, especially, Germany in 1871 altered Europe's balance of power, while Japan's defeat of Russia in the Russo–Japanese War (1905) heralded its arrival on the world stage. Improvements in naval technology made transpacific travel and commerce faster and cheaper.

How would America use its new power? How would it cope with the new-found proximity of the outside world? How would it respond to the changing balance of power in Europe and new opportunities in the Pacific? As during its first century, the United States responded by enhancing its power and championing liberty, now confident enough in its power to bring the latter fully into its foreign policy. The liberal imperialism of William McKinley, Theodore Roosevelt, and William Howard Taft, the internationalism of Woodrow Wilson and Franklin Roosevelt, and the Cold War consensus of containment reflected the synthesis of power and liberty.

In fact, it is easier to see the liberal than the realist strain in America's early forays beyond its shores as a great power. It went to war against Spain to help Cuban rebels achieve independence in 1898. After the war, President McKinley told Congress, "It should be our duty to assist in every proper way to build up the waste places of the island, encourage the industry of the people, and assist them to form a government which shall be free and independent, thus realizing the best aspirations of the Cuban people."[26] Nor was that mere rhetorical window dressing. Under McKinley and Roosevelt, the United States oversaw four elections in four years, granted Cuban independence, and left— the first example of an American stability operation to help fix a failed state and export democracy. But it failed: Cuba collapsed three years later, and the United States intervened again (and failed again). Liberal imperialism proved naive in its expectations about what American power could achieve.

But McKinley did not know how difficult fixing failed states would prove to be. He used much the same language in describing the United States' occupation of the Philippines the same year:

> No effort will be spared to build up the waste places desolated by war and by long years of misgovernment. . . . We shall continue, as we have begun, to open the schools and the churches, to set the courts in operation, to foster industry and trade and agriculture, and in every way in our power to make these people whom Providence has brought within our jurisdiction feel that it is their liberty and not our power, their welfare and not our gain, we are seeking to enhance.[27]

But the American administration faced a proindependence insurgency, to which it responded with effective brutality. America's imperial foray sparked the creation of the Anti-Imperialist League at home; in response, the occupying authorities increasingly had to make liberalism a real component of its imperial policy to alleviate critics' concerns. "The commitment to democratize the Philippines was . . . a way of governing this possession on which both imperialists and anti-imperialists could agree [and] came to be the principal reason the Americans were there," according to Tony Smith.[28] Unlike in Cuba, America stayed in the Philippines for almost fifty years and had somewhat more to show for it: While far from perfect, the Philippines has, on balance, enjoyed greater freedom than Cuba over the past century. Vastly greater concentration of power and resources was a prerequisite to even marginal success abroad.

But America's liberal imperialism was not an untempered global crusade for liberty—it was part and parcel of the United States' continued concern with its power and security. The war with Spain was, partly, an application of the Monroe Doctrine, protecting American hegemony and unilateral rights over the Western Hemisphere. America's territorial annexations—Puerto Rico in the Caribbean, Guam in the Pacific—gave America control over strategic resupply-and-refueling stations on the oceanic approaches to and from North America. It was also a war of prestige, a way of illustrating to the world America's arrival on the world stage, much like what the Japanese achieved by defeating Russia seven years later. The problem was not, as it was in the 1790s, to play the Europeans off each other and create space for the continued survival of the young American republic—it was to balance power and make room in the global division of power and influence for new American aspirations. In Hunt's analysis, "the combined appeal of liberty and greatness now easily triumphed over a narrow, cautious, self-limiting conception of national mission."[29]

Similarly, much of American expansion in the Pacific in the late nineteenth century—which predated the war with Spain—was driven by pragmatic concerns, trade foremost among them. The trading history of the United States and Hawaii started as early as the 1840s. The United States signed a trade treaty with China in 1844 and, famously, forced its way into Japan for another trade treaty in 1853–54. The need for resupply and fuel on the long transpacific journey led to the first American presence in Samoa in the 1850s, setting the stage for its annexation in 1899. The Pacific frontier was so important that the United States embarked on constructing a "New Navy" starting in 1883. These moves "had a definite defensive component: the expansion of America's defensive perimeter outward in order to establish political, economic, and military dominance in the Caribbean, Atlantic, and Pacific approaches to the United States."[30]

Another facet of the United States' growing liberalism in the late nineteenth century was its participation in the embryonic movement to create institutions and legal norms of global governance. Such institutions included scientific and technical bodies founded to establish global standards and exchange information, such as the International Meteorological Association (1873), the General Conference on Weights and Measures (1875), the Universal Postal Union (1875), and the International Telegraph Union (1908); treaties on the protection of submarine cables (1888); the exchange of government documents, scientific and literary publications, journals, and legislative chronicles (1889); patents and copyright (1911); and assistance and salvage at sea (1913).

But they also included explicitly liberal causes, such as the 1864 Geneva Convention (which the United States signed in 1882), some of the Hague Conventions of 1899 and 1907, the creation of an Inter-American International Commission of Jurists (1908), a treaty for the suppression of the African slave trade (1890), similar efforts against the "white slave traffic" (i.e., sex trafficking, in 1904 and 1910), and an Agreement for the Suppression of Obscene Publications (1910).[31] American citizens also participated in non-governmental organizations (NGOs), including founding the American Red Cross in 1881. Such institutions were part of the liberal project of bringing the world under rational and legal control but also reflected American intentions to shape their direction to preserve and extend American power. For both reasons, American participation in the founding and maintenance of international institutions has a much earlier provenance than the post–World War II era.

Theodore Roosevelt is a pivotal figure in the emergence of a more ideologically motivated foreign policy, one imbued with "a sense of mission and purpose." His legacy is contested: Nau and Kissinger consider him a realist and contrast him to the liberal internationalism of Wilson and, for Nau, the conservative internationalism of James K. Polk and Ronald Reagan. But "Roosevelt's ideological vision could more accurately be characterized as a sort of liberal quasi-imperialism." In Roosevelt's ideology, he understood "civilization" as a "progressive phenomenon" that civilized nations had a duty to spread for the sake of less advanced peoples. Central was the idea of "self-government as the ideal for all peoples and aiding it as a primary purpose of outside intervention."[32] Roosevelt's interventions were smaller and overshadowed by the events of following decades, but his Corollary to the Monroe Doctrine, receivership of Haiti and the Dominican Republic, reoccupation of Cuba, enforcement of the Open Door Policy in China, and midwifery of Panamanian independence were, for his day, strikingly aggressive attempts to use American hegemony in the service of liberal ideals. Roosevelt placed far less faith in international law and international institutions than Wilson and was more skeptical of when and how other peoples might adopt liberal ideals, but he undoubtedly believed they should, someday, and with American help.

Wilson, then, was not a bolt from the blue. The United States had already spent one century defining itself as a liberal power, followed by two decades positioning itself as the muscular champion of liberalism across the world before Wilson famously argued, before Congress in April 1917, "The world must be made safe for democracy." Wilson's name has come to stand for an entire movement and school of thought, but he did not invent it. The context of Wilson's phrase is less famous but more illuminating. He also said in the same speech:

> A steadfast concert for peace can never be maintained except by a partnership of democratic nations. No autocratic government could be trusted to keep faith within it or observe its covenants. . . . [We] fight thus for the ultimate peace of the world and for the liberation of its peoples, the German peoples included: for the rights of nations great and small and the privilege of men everywhere to choose their way of life and of obedience. The world must be made safe for democracy. Its peace must be planted upon the tested foundations of political liberty.

Wilson articulated the democratic peace theory decades before social scientists would make the same argument. Christopher Layne has persuasively argued that Wilson took the United States to war in 1917 not because he truly feared a German victory or a threat to the Western Hemisphere, but because he wanted to buy a seat at the table for shaping the postwar world along liberal lines.[33] In January 1918, Wilson told Congress that the United States had entered the Great War "that the world be made fit and safe to live in; and particularly that it be made safe for every peace-loving nation which, like our own, wishes to live its own life, determine its own institutions, be assured of justice and fair dealing by the other peoples of the world as against force and selfish aggression." Wilson was especially interested in ensuring that the world would be safe for every state that "wishes to live its own life [and] determine its own institutions"—that is, for democratic countries. Because Wilson believed in the fundamental harmony among democratic countries' interests, he concluded, "All the peoples of the world are in effect partners in this interest."[34]

World War I was only the largest and best-known example of Wilson's commitment to advancing liberalism in the service of American power. Wilson launched lengthy, unilateral military occupations of Haiti (1915–34) and the Dominican Republic (1916–24) in (unsuccessful) efforts to improve their governance and forestall German interference. He bought the Virgin Islands (1917), again to prevent possible German inroads in the Western Hemisphere. And he sent US troops to Russia to combat the Bolshevik Revolution. After the war Wilson tried, and failed, to get the United States to participate in the League of Nations, the world's most ambitious effort up to that time at cooperative security and global governance. Virtually none of Wilson's liberal dreams succeeded. Tony Smith's judgment on Wilson seems apt: "The obvious lesson is that arrogant moralizing and abstract reasoning may easily run afoul of the constraints imposed by social reality."[35] Wilson stands as a testament that championing liberalism cannot be the sole or untempered goal of US foreign policy.

But that failure has overshadowed the extent to which the United States continued to participate in the growth of international institutions and liberal norms and exercise its power in the service of liberal imperialism in its near abroad—even during the supposedly isolationist 1920s and 1930s. The United States (somewhat reluctantly) joined the International Labor Organization in 1934, and signed treaties on consular and diplomatic rights and immunities in 1932 and on extradition in 1935. The United States joined a Pan-American sanitary code in 1924 and a mechanism for arbitration of disputes among American states in 1929. It signed another treaty banning slavery and the slave trade in 1929 and agreed to the creation of an International Wine Office (1927, in Paris, naturally). Perhaps most significant, it hosted talks for a number of naval arms control agreements in the 1920s and, infamously, signed a treaty banning war as an instrument of national policy in 1928—perhaps the crowning result of Wilson's dreams almost a decade after he left office. At the same time, the Calvin Coolidge administration redeployed US Marines to intervene in Nicaragua's civil war (building off an earlier, narrower intervention) to help the Nicaraguan government—ostensibly committed to democracy—fight against rebels led by Augusto Sandino and to oversee its 1928 presidential election. The United States' refusal to involve itself in Europe's security or the League of Nations was not a global doctrine of isolation or noninterference.

To the extent that Wilsonianism included disarmament, trust in international institutions to manage world order, and a repudiation of balance-of-power politics, it was clearly a failure and represents an extreme reaction against realism. Few scholars or policymakers defend Wilsonianism in its original or purest form. But Wilsonianism as the idea of basing world order on cooperative security among free peoples willing to defend themselves has an enduring, living cache. According to McDougall, "as a blueprint for world order, Wilsonianism has always been a chimera, but as an ideological weapon against 'every arbitrary power anywhere,' it has proved mighty indeed."[36]

Superpower: 1939–89

Shorn of its naiveté and utopianism, leavened with a dose of reality, Wilsonianism is a powerful addition to the American foreign policy tool kit. That is why American statesmen continued to use aspects of the Wilsonian vision in the decades since its founder's failure. Even before World War II, President Franklin Roosevelt told Americans that "the United States will never survive as a happy and fertile oasis of liberty surrounded by a cruel desert of dictatorship."[37] He affirmed the defense of democracy was a central aim in the war—a conflict that probably did more to enhance American power than any other episode in history. He described the war as "democracy's fight against world conquest" and argued for the Lend-Lease Program because it would enable the European democracies to fight "for their liberty and our security."[38] The Atlantic Charter proclaimed the Allied leaders' "wish to see sovereign rights and self government restored to those who have been forcibly deprived of them."[39] Months later the joint declaration by the "United Nations" of allied powers declared they were fighting "to defend life, liberty, independence and religious freedom, and to preserve human rights and justice in their own lands as well as in other lands."[40] The United States would go even further, insisting on the democratization of Germany and Japan in addition to the liberated territories. (George Kennan, notably, thought the democratization of Japan a waste of time—a vignette that nicely illustrates how dogmatic realism can impose myopia on even the most penetrating minds.)

The Cold War, which followed, was conventional great power rivalry between the two preeminent powers of the mid-twentieth century. Put another way, in the twentieth century the United States fought two hot wars and a cold one to prevent any power or alliance of powers—Wilhelmine, Austro–Hungarian, Ottoman, Nazi, Italian, Japanese, or Soviet—from achieving hegemony over Europe or Asia, following the classic realist understanding of the main goal of balance-of-power politics. The consistent goal was to prevent the material resources of half the world from falling into the hands of a hostile power. Between World War II and the Cold War, the United States simply swapped certain key enemies and allies, first allying with the Soviets against the Germans and Japanese before allying with the Germans and Japanese (and others) against the Soviets, a classic example of power-balancing.

In that sense, the Cold War did not differ greatly from the multipolar world that preceded it except in the number of contestants. Even the sharp ideological disagreement was not unique to the Cold War: Protestant and Catholic coalitions had faced off in the sixteenth and seventeenth centuries, and the Holy Alliance had sought to uphold monarchy against liberalism in the nineteenth. And the supposedly bipolar competition of the Cold War was strongly influenced by the independent initiatives of other powers. The People's Republic of China was initially aligned with the Soviet Union because of their shared communist ideology, fought against the United States in the Korean War (1950–53), and acquired nuclear weapons in 1964. However, not wanting to be a Soviet satellite and mistrustful following border clashes in 1969, it tilted away from the Soviet Union and toward the United States following President Richard Nixon's visit in 1972. The move altered the global balance of power not only away from the USSR and toward the United States, but also away from Europe and toward Asia as China raised the profile of the region through its defection. Similarly, the Non-Aligned Movement (NAM) represented a significant proportion of states in the international system that resisted pressure to join either side, compelling the superpowers to vie for the developing world's loyalties through aid, investment, and sometimes coercion. The NAM was thus a form of balancing by the Global South against the North.

But the Cold War was also an ideological contest between democracy and communist totalitarianism. In the opening years of the Cold War, policymakers increasingly came to understand that a conflict was opening up between two fundamentally opposed political and economic systems: one devoted to individual liberty and self-government, the other to authoritarian communism. Crucially, the contest for power between the two sides was indistinguishable from the ideological clash. As Smith says, "Wilsonianism was an indispensable weapon in the realist's doctrine of containment."[41] The United States was working to contain the Soviet Union—an expression of classic realpolitik—but also to build liberal order: "By the late 1940s, these two projects became fused. Openness and containment went hand in hand."[42] The fusion of America's realist instincts with its liberal ideals captures exactly why the Cold War strategy was enduring and successful—and why a similar synthesis is called for today.

Perhaps the most explicit statement of this fusion came in 1947 when President Harry Truman told Congress, "At the present moment in world history nearly every nation must choose between alternative ways of life. . . . One way of life is based upon the will of the majority, and is distinguished by free institutions, representative government, free elections, guarantees of individual liberty, freedom of speech and religion, and freedom from political oppression." The other "relies upon terror and oppression, a controlled press and radio, fixed elections, and the suppression of personal freedoms." Truman was unequivocal, and his sweeping language became the Truman Doctrine: "I believe that it must be the policy of the United States to support free peoples who are resisting attempted subjugation by armed minorities or by outside pressures." Truman insisted that the United States support democracy abroad because it was essential to American security: "If we falter in our leadership, we may endanger the peace of the world—and we shall surely endanger the welfare of this Nation."[43] Truman's declaration amounted to a global security guarantee granted to every democratic state in the world—perhaps the most ambitious foreign policy doctrine outlined by a US president in history, yet also one that, by its strategic deployment of liberal ideology, was a plausible extension of 150 years of American foreign policy tradition, an effective tool of US Cold War strategy, and a precedent future policymakers should not ignore.

American support for liberalism was not limited to wartime rhetoric. US Cold War strategy also included championing economic liberalism, cooperative security, and global governance through international institutions.[44] After World War II (and probably well beforehand), the United States was economically strong enough not to need tariff protection and could use economic liberalism as a weapon to spread its influence and power abroad. Free markets, low trade barriers, economic interdependence, and rule-based arbitration for trade disputes led to greater prosperity—and thus greater power—for liberal states. Greater prosperity and power would also make communism less attractive within liberal societies. To that end, the United States helped create the postwar global financial institutions, the World Bank and International Monetary Fund (IMF), to foster worldwide reconstruction and development; launched the first round of the General Agreement on Tariffs and Trade in 1947; financed Europe's recovery through the Marshall Plan; and virtually mandated European economic interdependence by channeling Marshall Aid through a single coordinating agency, the Organization for European Economic Cooperation.

Similarly, the United States served as the anchor for several cooperative security institutions, most successfully in the North Atlantic Treaty Organization (NATO), created in 1949, and the Australia–New Zealand–United States Treaty (1951). It also participated in the Southeast Asia Treaty Organization (1954), the Central Treaty Organization (1954), and the Inter-American Treaty of Reciprocal Assistance (1947) and signed a number of bilateral defense treaties as well. The UN proved no more effective than the League of Nations in security affairs but became a useful coordinator and clearinghouse for intergovernmental institutions and initiatives that had proliferated since the late nineteenth century.

The Cold War has become one of the central points of dispute between rival schools of interpretation of American diplomacy. For example, Christopher Layne, in developing his argument that the United States foolishly sought "extraregional hegemony," cites NSC-68, the Truman administration's basic strategy document, written in 1950, as evidence that the United States was overextending itself for immaterial and inessential goals. The document argued the United States should seek "to foster a world environment in which our free society can survive and flourish," even if there were no Soviet threat. John Ikenberry quotes the exact same passage in NSC-68 to support his argument that the United States wisely and successfully created a benign liberal hegemonic order to secure its interests and the interests of world order.[45] Where revisionists see a morality tale of imperial overstretch, others see grand-strategic acumen.

The war in Vietnam may represent the apex of America's Cold War aspirations to use liberalism as a weapon against Soviet tyranny. It was, more or less, the effort to create a functioning, prosperous democracy where there had not been one, with the express purpose of helping it defend against communist attack and thereby demonstrate the superiority of the American model against the Soviet one. McDougall rightly judges Vietnam "a liberal war."[46] As such, it also serves as a cautionary tale about the limits of promoting liberalism. I reflect further on the difficult task of mixing democratization with stability operations in the next chapter.

Vietnam's corrupt military government is also a reminder that US Cold War strategy was not unadulterated liberal Wilsonianism. It was mixed with a heavy dose of realpolitik. The United States supported, trained, armed, equipped, or otherwise helped autocratic regimes, from Fulgencio Batista's in Cuba, Rafael Trujillo's in the Dominican Republic, Anastasio Somoza's in Nicaragua, and a string of autocrats in South Korea and Pakistan, to the Hosni Mubarak, Saddam Hussein, and Saudi regimes in the Middle East. Cold War strategy was best described as "*selective* liberal democratic internationalism."[47] It is easy to criticize these compromises for their hypocrisy, but the pursuit of liberty has never been, and should never be, a single-minded crusade. The United States accepted help from the absolutist French monarchy to gain its independence from Great Britain and allied with the Soviet Union itself to defeat Nazi Germany. The hedging of liberal ideals with the constraints of political realities is necessary—but, we must admit, easily abused. The United States would have critically weakened itself if it had worked only with stable liberal democracies during the Cold War, but it is doubtful the United States needed to support all the regimes, especially in Africa and Latin America, that it did. Choosing exactly when and where to leaven liberalism with realpolitik is one of the hardest questions of grand strategy, one that can only be answered on a case-by-case basis. (I attempt this difficult assessment in chapters 6 through 9.)

Nonetheless, even the Nixon and Ford administrations—guided by Kissinger, the dean of American realism—participated in the Conference on Security and Cooperation in Europe, and Ford signed the conference's Final Act in Helsinki in 1975, which contains expansive language pledging the signatories to individual freedoms and self-government: "The participating States will respect human rights and fundamental freedoms, including the freedom of thought, conscience, religion or belief, for all without distinction as to race, sex, language or religion." Notably, the statement draws a direct connection between freedom and security: "The participating States recognize the universal significance of human rights and fundamental freedoms, respect for which is an essential factor for the peace, justice and well-being necessary to ensure the development of friendly relations and co-operation among themselves as among all States."[48]

Jimmy Carter tried to put human rights at the center of his foreign policy, but Reagan probably had a more lasting impact because of his greater attention to power. In announcing the creation of what would become the National Endowment for Democracy, he told the British Parliament that "freedom is not the sole prerogative of a lucky few, but the inalienable and universal right of all human beings." In his view, that had clear implications for US foreign policy: "The objective I propose is quite simple to state: to foster the infrastructure of democracy, the system of a free press, unions, political parties, universities, which allows a people to choose their own way to develop their own culture, to reconcile their own differences through peaceful means."[49] At the same time, Reagan engaged in the greatest peacetime military buildup in US history. In 1987 and 1988, he published the United States' first public national security strategies under a new congressional requirement. They stated baldly that "we proceed from our fundamental belief that a world composed of free, sovereign democracies will be a safer, more stable world" and that "to ignore the fate of millions around the world who seek freedom betrays our national heritage and over time would endanger our own freedom and that of our allies."[50] The combination of increased US power with even more strident support for liberty abroad contributed to the birth of America's unipolar moment.

Unipole: 1989–Present

The historical record clearly shows a tradition of US support for liberalism abroad long before 1989.[51] As Layne rightly highlights, "the grand strategic equation of world order with US security reflects a historically rooted belief that to be secure, the United States must extend abroad both its power and its political and economic institutions and values."[52] But contrary to Layne's assessment, the strategy of pursuing power and liberty together was effective. The United States became the most powerful nation in history. And to a greater extent than is widely recognized, it also succeeded in fostering liberalism abroad. Its compromises are well known. Some, such as the alliance with the Soviet Union during World War II, were clearly necessary; others, including support for right-wing dictatorships of lesser importance during the Cold War, were probably not. The United States also amassed an impressive record of failure, of which Vietnam is only the best known. But the United States was instrumental in turning the idea of self-government into a global norm. Its power created a favorable environment for the consolidation of liberalism in Western Europe after World War II, for the creation of a liberal trading regime and a system of cooperative security among democratic countries, and for the gradual evolution of liberalism in East Asia during the Cold War.

On this foundation, liberalism was poised to spread globally after the fall of the Soviet Union. The post–Cold War era brought US power and liberal order to new heights of prominence. Scholarship increasingly confirmed what presidents and policymakers had long argued: The growth of democracy makes America and its allies safer because democracies do not fight each other. (All four post–Cold War US presidential administrations have explicitly invoked the democratic peace theory in their national security strategies.) There seemed to be no major competitors to liberalism, which became the default choice of transitioning regimes in Eastern Europe, Latin America, and Africa. The most powerful states in the world, including the United Kingdom, a newly reunited Germany, and an apparently democratizing Russia, embraced liberal ideals. The post–Cold War era became the high point of liberalism in recorded history.

But the era also contained countervailing tendencies that threatened the sustainability of liberal order and American security. The fall of the Soviet Union removed the United States' greatest threat and barrier to action and made it seem (wrongly) that the United States no longer needed to take into consideration the views and concerns of other great powers. Norms of sovereignty eroded as liberal activists called for humanitarian interventions. With greater power and fewer restraints, some US policymakers believed the United States had the capability and permission to act with greater impunity abroad.[53] But in the 1990s the country cut budgets for the military, the State Department, and foreign aid, creating a widening gap between American aspirations and capabilities. The subsequent war in Iraq brought disrepute to American power, competence, and leadership. In the same era, the failure of democracy in Russia, the rise of China, and the nuclearization of North Korea, Pakistan, and (effectively) Iran reintroduced balance-of-power politics from hostile autocratic nuclear powers, while globalization and state failure enabled armed nonstate actors to act with greater force and freedom than before.

The Rhetoric of Liberalism

President George W. Bush gave the most ambitious expression to the democratic peace theory in his second inaugural address: "The survival of liberty in
our land increasingly depends on the success of liberty in other lands. The best
hope for peace in our world is the expansion of freedom in all the world," he
claimed. "It is the policy of the United States to seek and support the growth
of democratic movements and institutions in every nation and culture, with
the ultimate goal of ending tyranny in our world," which ranks alongside the
Truman Doctrine as the boldest and most strident linkage between American power and liberal order in history.[54] His administration embedded these
claims in its 2002 and 2006 national security strategies, which were expansive
in their claims about the ties between democracy and American security. The
2002 strategy stated, "America will encourage the advancement of democracy
and economic openness . . . because these are the best foundations for domestic stability and international order."[55] The 2006 strategy went further and
claimed that "because democracies are the most responsible members of the
international system, promoting democracy is the most effective long-term
measure for strengthening international stability; reducing regional conflicts;
countering terrorism and terror-supporting extremism; and extending peace
and prosperity."[56]

Despite the controversy that attended Bush's foreign policy initiatives,
his "privileging of liberalism and democracy falls squarely within the mainstream of American diplomatic traditions."[57] The same concepts reappeared
in President Barack Obama's 2010 national security strategy: "The United
States supports the expansion of democracy and human rights abroad
because governments that respect these values are more just, peaceful, and
legitimate." It is significant that Obama claimed that democracy makes governments more peaceful. That is what enables him to claim that democracy
abroad serves the United States' national security: "We also do so because
their success abroad fosters an environment that supports America's national
interests. Political systems that protect universal rights are ultimately more
stable, successful, and secure."[58] His 2015 national security strategy similarly argued that "defending democracy and human rights is related to every
enduring national interest."[59]

Obama was not the first Democratic president to emphasize the democratic peace. Bill Clinton's seven national security strategies were remarkable for the consistency with which they invoked it. From 1994 to 1996, his
administration claimed that "democratic states are less likely to threaten
our interests and more likely to cooperate with the United States to meet
security threats and promote free trade and sustainable development." The

1997 and 1998 strategies said that "democratic governments are more likely to cooperate with each other against common threats, encourage free trade, and promote sustainable economic development. They are less likely to wage war or abuse the rights of their people. Hence, the trend toward democracy and free markets throughout the world advances American interests." In 1999, Clinton argued, "The spread of democracy and respect for the rule of law helps to create a world community that is more hospitable to US values and interests." And by 2000, Clinton had become even more clear and explicit: "Our national security is a direct beneficiary of democracy's spread, as democracies are less likely to go to war with one another, more likely to become partners for peace and security, and more likely to pursue peaceful means of internal conflict resolution that promote both intrastate and regional stability."[60]

Clinton's embrace of the democratic peace was perhaps not surprising, because it dovetailed with the liberal internationalism and multilateralism with which he felt comfortable. But, surprisingly, similar language animated the national security strategies of the supposedly more realist administration of President George H. W. Bush. In 1990, he wrote that the United States seeks "a stable and secure world, fostering political freedom, human rights, and democratic institutions." In 1991, he grew more pronounced: "Our interests are best served in a world in which democracy and its ideals are widespread and secure." By 1993, in a national security strategy published as he was leaving office, he was fully in tune with the democratic peace argument. In a foreword to the document, Bush wrote, "Our policy has one overriding goal: real peace—not the illusory and fragile peace maintained by a balance of terror, but an enduring democratic peace based on shared values." He went on: "History teaches that representative governments responsive to their people are least likely to turn to aggression against their neighbors."[61]

The Record of Liberalism

These claims were not simply rhetorical tools designed to legitimize otherwise "realist" policy or to win public support for policies that were less liberal under the surface. Time and again, US presidents faced with foreign policy crises or opportunities have typically turned to promoting democracy as the best long-term solution for safeguarding American interests. Different presidents interpreted and pursued this aspiration in different ways, as should be expected, and their democracy initiatives were not always successful or well founded, but the consistency of their beliefs is striking. During the Cold War, Reagan was confrontational while Nixon pursued détente, but both adhered

to the broader strategic framework of containment. Similarly, in the post–
Cold War world, Clinton worked more through multilateral institutions,
while George W. Bush assembled ad hoc coalitions. Nonetheless, they both
made democracy abroad a key part of US foreign policy.

One of the most significant American foreign policy initiatives since the
end of the Cold War, embraced by both the Clinton and George W. Bush
administrations, was the expansion of NATO, which was motivated in large
part by a desire to spread the democratic peace. Clinton's national security
adviser Anthony Lake was "keenly interested in pushing NATO's expansion
as part of the administration's strategy of enlarging the community of democracies," according to James Goldgeier. "Clinton had stressed the theme that
democracies do not go to war with one another and thus that US foreign policy strategy should focus on promoting democracy."[62] The administration's
argument was that the prospect of membership in NATO incentivized the
states of Eastern Europe to democratize and reform, which in turn spread the
zone of peace. Similarly, former UN ambassador Jeane Kirkpatrick claimed,
"There is . . . only one reliable guarantee against aggression. It is found in the
spread of democracy. It derives from the simple fact that true democracies do
not invade one another and do not engage in aggressive wars. . . . Membership
in NATO will help to achieve those goals." And George W. Bush announced
his support for further NATO enlargement in his first speech to the alliance
in Warsaw in 2001, at which he praised NATO for "protect[ing] democracy
in an ever-widening Europe" and called on aspiring states to "work to become
free-market democracies at peace with themselves and their neighbors" as a
condition of membership.[63]

The most significant military operations during Clinton's administration—operations in Somalia, Haiti, Bosnia, and Kosovo—were democratic
peace-building operations, which I discuss in more detail in chapter 5. George
W. Bush's major foreign policy initiatives, of course, were his responses to
the terrorist attacks of September 11, 2001, the wars in Iraq and Afghanistan. Bush argued that democratization was the best long-term solution to
jihadist terrorism. He told the National Endowment for Democracy in late
2005 that a key "element of our strategy in the war on terror is to deny the
militants future recruits by replacing hatred and resentment with democracy
and hope across the broader Middle East." Democracy undermined terrorism because "if the peoples of that region are permitted to choose their own
destiny, and advance by their own energy and by their participation as free
men and women, then the extremists will be marginalized, and the flow of
violent radicalism to the rest of the world will slow, and eventually end." This,
in turn, would enhance US security: "By standing for the hope and freedom
of others, we make our own freedom more secure."[64]

The wars in Iraq and Afghanistan (more on which below) had other triggering causes, of course—ending safe haven for al-Qaida in Afghanistan and eliminating Iraq's suspected weapons of mass destruction—but Bush argued that democratization was the long-term solution that would ensure both countries remained stable and friendly to US interests after the immediate goals were achieved. Bush backed up his democratic rhetoric with action: Despite ongoing insurgencies, the United States nonetheless successfully pushed the new governments in both Iraq and Afghanistan to hold repeated elections. Iraq held two elections and a constitutional referendum in 2005, and Afghanistan ratified a democratic constitution in 2004 and held elections in 2004 and 2005. Such expensive and risky undertakings in the midst of pressing security concerns suggest the president genuinely believed that democratization would help defeat the insurgencies, expand the democratic peace, and enhance US security.

Bush's emphasis on democracy was evident in other foreign policy programs, such as the Greater Middle East Initiative, a package of diplomatic and aid engagements intended to foster democracy throughout Southwest Asia. Similarly, Bush established the Millennium Challenge Corporation (MCC) to channel foreign aid to countries that demonstrated "good governance," defined partly by their score on civil liberties, political rights, voice and accountability, and other democratic criteria. Bush publicly pressured longstanding US partners such as Egypt and Saudi Arabia to liberalize their governments, and he gave rhetorical support to the "color revolutions" in Ukraine (2004), Lebanon (2005), and Kyrgyzstan (2005) and bolstered military and economic ties to Georgia after its revolution (2003).

Obama was initially less outspoken about democracy and human rights than his two predecessors in reaction to the perceived excesses of the Bush administration and its difficulties in Iraq and Afghanistan.[65] He said in his speech in Cairo in June 2009, "I know there has been controversy about the promotion of democracy in recent years, and much of this controversy is connected to the war in Iraq." Yet he said two sentences later, "That does not lessen my commitment, however, to governments that reflect the will of the people. . . . I do have an unyielding belief that all people yearn for certain things: the ability to speak your mind and have a say in how you are governed." Obama specifically argued that more democracy would lead to peace: "Governments that protect these rights are ultimately more stable, successful and secure." Despite his hesitancy, he remained explicitly committed to the universal applicability of democracy and human rights and the idea that democracy abroad helped expand global stability.[66]

The tension between Obama's desire to pursue a more "realistic" foreign policy and to promote democracy was evident in his response to uprisings in

Iran in 2009 and the Arab world in 2011. Obama planned to engage the Iranian government over its nuclear program, which likely fed his hesitancy to criticize the regime or offer rhetorical support to the mass protests that broke out in Iran immediately after the country's election results were announced in June 2009. But he eventually did both after his reticence was roundly criticized, saying that "the Iranian people have a universal right to assembly and free speech. If the Iranian government seeks the respect of the international community, it must respect those rights and heed the will of its own people. It must govern through consent and not coercion."[67]

Later in Obama's tenure, a series of uprisings rocked the Arab world starting in December 2010, eventually toppling the governments of Egypt, Tunisia, and Libya and sparking civil wars in Yemen and Syria. Again, his administration was initially reluctant to back the protesters but eventually embraced the Arab Spring as an opportunity for democratization in the region that, he believed, would be ultimately beneficial for US national security. For example, White House press secretary Robert Gibbs initially said, on January 27, that "President Mubarak has for several decades been a close and important partner with our country," before adding that "we consistently have advocated for the universal rights of assembly, of free speech, of political reform" in Egypt.[68] Days later, Obama joined the protesters' call for Mubarak to step down, may have helped facilitate his ouster through ties to the Egyptian military (according to some accounts), and embraced the movement as a welcome step toward democracy. Later, in May 2011, Obama went further: "We support a set of universal rights. Those rights include free speech; the freedom of peaceful assembly; freedom of religion; equality for men and women under the rule of law; and the right to choose your own leaders—whether you live in Baghdad or Damascus; Sanaa or Tehran." That is why, Obama said, "it will be the policy of the United States to promote reform across the region, and to support transitions to democracy."[69]

Obama's most striking response to the Arab Spring was to intervene militarily in Libya to defend human rights and advance democracy. In March 2011, he argued in a televised speech that a massacre of civilians in Libya would hurt US national interests. "We knew that if we waited one more day, Benghazi, a city nearly the size of Charlotte, could suffer a massacre that would have reverberated across the region and stained the conscience of the world. It was not in our national interest to let that happen," he said. He called for a transition to democracy in Libya: "We continue to pursue the broader goal of a Libya that belongs not to a dictator, but to its people." He argued that war in Libya was essential to protecting the new democratic movements in the Arab world. If the international community did not stop dictator Muammar Qaddafi, "the democratic impulses that are dawning across the region would be eclipsed by the darkest form of dictatorship, as repressive leaders concluded that violence is the best strategy to cling to power." And finally he argued it was an essential part of the United States' longstanding and global commitment to freedom: "We must stand alongside those who believe in the same core principles that have guided us through many storms: . . . our support for a set of universal rights, including the freedom for people to express themselves and choose their leaders; our support for governments that are ultimately responsive to the aspirations of the people."[70] Like Clinton in the Balkans and Bush in Iraq and Afghanistan, Obama was faced with a foreign crisis to which he responded by defending and encouraging the growth of democracy overseas.

The Overreach of Liberalism?

Every president in the post–Cold War era has sustained the United States' commitment to encouraging liberalism abroad. But the wars in Iraq and Afghanistan raise serious questions about the planning and conduct of US foreign policy, including the role of liberalism in it. The United States achieved suboptimal outcomes in both countries: Iraq looks increasingly like an unmitigated loss since the rise of the so-called Islamic State of Iraq and Syria (ISIS); Afghanistan might avoid the worst of Iraq's chaos, but the ultimate outcome is still in question. Critics have used the wars to call into question the capacity, even competence, of the US national security establishment and called for a rethinking of America's role in the world today— questions that animate much of this book. Some have gone further and indicted the very idea of intervention, claiming that complex operations such as reconstruction, stabilization, counterinsurgency, and democratization are nearly impossible to achieve on any reasonable timetable or at any cost worth paying. In this view, the American effort to foster stability and liberal governments in both countries was doomed to failure, a function of imperial overstretch. The fallout from the wars has given new life to advocates of restraint who believe there is no meaningful connection between American security and liberal order and that efforts to build liberal order are expensive ways of proving its futility.

Any effort that purports to offer a way forward for US grand strategy must offer some sort of response to these criticisms that accounts for the wars' causes, consequences, and failures and describes how a new strategy will avoid repeating their mistakes. I respond to the broader criticisms about democratization and stability operations throughout this book. Here I address the wars in Iraq and Afghanistan in particular. The historical record of the wars suggests structural factors and policy errors contributed to the suboptimal outcomes, but it does not support the broader critique of democratization.

Almost no one will argue that the international community devoted adequate attention or resources to Afghanistan for the first five or six years of the effort there, when it was underresourced and overshadowed by the war in Iraq.[71] According to wide-ranging studies by the RAND Corporation of reconstruction and stabilization operations undertaken by the United States and the UN, the initial military deployment to Afghanistan was one of the smallest of its kind in terms of absolute numbers, the ratio of soldiers to the local population, and the ratio of soldiers to the land mass of the country. Comparable missions in Bosnia or Kosovo had far greater resources. There were only two thousand US troops in Afghanistan by the end of 2001 and fewer than ten thousand by the end of 2003, when the country was regularly wracked by factional clashes between warlords and coming under the sway of criminal gangs and drug traffickers. Adm. Michael Mullen, then the chairman of the Joint Chiefs of Staff, famously told Congress in 2007, "In Afghanistan we do what we can. In Iraq we do what we must."[72] When the top military official in the United States essentially admits that the United States did not devote to Afghanistan the resources required to accomplish the mission, there are no plausible grounds for arguing that the war in Afghanistan—at least as of 2007—disproved the feasibility of stabilization or democratization initiatives. By the end of the Bush administration, the war was going poorly, and the Taliban were resurgent.

Partly in recognition of that fact, Obama accelerated the surge of troops, money, and attention to Afghanistan that Bush started in his last two years in office. But Obama undermined his own surge with three countervailing policies. First was Obama's attempt at compromise, which only led to strategic incoherence. The president faced a basic strategic choice between a lean, pared-down counterterrorism mission focused on al-Qaida and a larger and more ambitious counterinsurgency strategy to beat back the Taliban while improving Afghan governance. The second was by far the better option and had the backing of the two successive high-level strategy reviews because it articulated a clear end state—a legitimate Afghan government capable of denying terrorists safe haven on its own—that would allow the United States to withdraw with its interests intact. But even the first option had some logic to it by limiting America's investment and lowering its aims in South Asia.

Instead, Obama chose neither option, attempted to compromise, and got the worst of both. He achieved neither the economy of the first option nor the ambition of the second. Obama ordered two surges, bringing the total to over a hundred thousand by mid-2010—far more than required for a narrow counterterrorism operation. Afghanistan, the third-largest military operation since Vietnam, had definitively become Obama's war. Yet even as he doubled down, Obama began hedging. The crises of 2009 led Obama to a "reassessment of whether the war was as necessary as he first believed," according to *New York Times* reporter David Sanger. He came to believe that "progress was possible—but not on the kind of timeline that [he] thought economically or politically affordable."[73] He was concerned the war was a drain on the US economy (although it cost less than one half of 1 percent of GDP in 2009). Despite two strategy reviews' recommendations to adopt a counterinsurgency strategy, the new approach "is not fully resourced counterinsurgency or nation building, but a narrower approach tied more tightly to the core goal of disrupting, dismantling, and eventually defeating al Qaeda and preventing al Qaeda's return to safe haven in Afghanistan or Pakistan," according to an internal NSC memo.[74] He deployed far fewer troops than Gen. Stanley McChrystal recommended for a counterinsurgency campaign. In contrast to his campaign rhetoric, Obama spent the rest of his presidency carefully avoiding saying the United States aimed to "defeat" the Taliban or "win" the war. The president escalated the war while simultaneously doubting whether it could be won.

And because he decided against counterinsurgency, he also backed off his commitment to promoting accountable and effective government in Afghanistan, his second major error. While he continued publicly to argue that improved governance was important to the overall mission, privately the same internal NSC memo stated that the United States would only be "selectively building the capacity of the Afghan government with military [sic] focused on the ministries of defense and interior," a move with major long-term consequences. Following the president's guidance, a group of White House staffers began convening in 2010 to search for an "Afghan Good Enough" solution and exit, an obvious effort to move the goalposts and make it easier for the United States to declare victory and leave. Civilian aid to Afghanistan decreased every year after 2010. By eschewing investments in Afghan governance and reducing civilian aid while still deploying a hundred thousand troops, Obama abandoned any vision of a political end state that would allow the United States to disengage with its interests intact. He also ended up with the most expensive, lumbering, and inefficient "CT-only" option imaginable.

And, of course, Obama set a deadline to begin withdrawing troops from Afghanistan, his third major strategic failing and the single most consequential decision of the war. The announced withdrawal was an obvious and unforced strategic error—so much so that Obama eventually reversed himself and halted the withdrawal in late 2015. Unfortunately, the damage had been done. Obama spent nearly his entire presidency talking about withdrawing from Afghanistan. He intended the withdrawal deadline to pressure the corrupt and intransigent Afghan government to reform, but critics argued, rightly, that it would incentivize hedging behavior instead as our local allies, in the face of uncertainty, became preoccupied with securing their personal interests instead of their country's. And, clearly, the deadline emboldened the Taliban and undermined the surge. Six years later, the Taliban is resurgent but the Afghan government has not cleaned up its act. The withdrawal incurred the costs critics feared without accomplishing the goals its advocates intended—and the withdrawal will not end up actually happening, making the entire exercise profoundly futile.

On top of these errors were a host of others—including poor coordination and management of the whole endeavor, European allies' reluctance to employ hard power, and some Afghans' abuse of international aid to line their own pockets. But historians are likely to conclude that the most significant failings were that Bush gave Afghanistan too few troops and not enough money and that Obama gave it too little time and not enough faith. Together, despite the remarkably enduring bipartisan agreement that Afghanistan was important, the effort there was never given the resources, attention, time, and leadership needed for success. This phenomenon is not entirely unique to the war in Afghanistan. It is partly a function of the "limited liability" strain of America's strategic culture, which "encourage[s] the pursuit of foreign policy aims by disproportionality limited means," such that "the United States has generally been unwilling to pay the costs that would be fully commensurate with the goals and policies articulated by US foreign policy officials."[75] The United States did not start a serious effort to train and equip Afghan security forces until 2007, and it did not mount a credible counterinsurgency campaign until 2009.

At the same time, the second US war in Iraq (2003–11) probably weakened the US position in the Middle East. It might have proved otherwise.[76] In 2003, the United States, motivated by a widely shared concern over Iraq's alleged weapons of mass destruction and its record of aggression, launched a war to overthrow the Iraqi regime. That war was essentially over in a matter of weeks. However, the United States failed to plan adequately for postwar reconstruction partly because the United States has underinvested in its own stabilization, reconstruction, and peace-building capabilities for decades—calling into question the wisdom, even the justice, of the initial invasion. Planning for war without planning for a subsequent peace bespeaks strategic and moral myopia: Just war aims at a better peace.

The resulting power vacuum enabled a local al-Qaida franchise to launch a terrorist campaign against US forces and Iraqi civilians. The organization publicly pledged loyalty to Osama bin Laden in 2004, styling itself al-Qaida in Iraq (AQI). The group was responsible for the most damaging attacks in Iraq over the years. It was especially adept at launching attacks that did not simply kill people but also caused major strategic damage to the new Iraqi government. For example, it bombed the headquarters of the UN Assistance Mission in Iraq in August 2003, assassinating the special representative of the secretary general, Sergio Vieira de Mello. Afterward the UN relocated many of its civilian personnel outside the country, a major move because other international organizations and NGOs typically follow the UN's lead. AQI thus deprived Iraq of needed international assistance in the crucial early months just after the fall of the Ba'athist regime. Years later, in an even more damaging attack, AQI destroyed the al-Askari Mosque in Samarra in February 2006, igniting the sectarian civil war of 2006–7.

Both structural conditions and US policy mistakes contributed to the failure of the US occupation.[77] The power vacuum and inept US occupation allowed other groups, including Ba'athists, Sunni tribes, and Shi'a militias, to launch an insurgency against American forces—to which the US Army initially responded incompetently, using conventional tactics to respond to an unconventional enemy, exacerbating the situation. The factions also competed for power against each other, erupting into open civil war in 2006. The war in Iraq thus became a counterinsurgency against nationalist Iraqi forces as well as a major battlefield in the global war against al-Qaida affiliates. The surge of American forces to Iraq in 2007 was a belated and obviously necessary last-ditch attempt to live up to America's responsibilities, give Iraq a chance at stability, and defeat a major arm of the global jihadist movement. It, and an accompanying movement among Sunni tribes to turn against al-Qaida, succeeded in blunting the violence, reversing the insurgency's gains, and setting Iraq on a potential path toward stability.[78]

A status of forces agreement (SOFA) provided for the continuing presence of US forces through the end of 2011. Both Iraqi and American policymakers expressed interest in renewing and extending the SOFA, but their collective failure to agree on details led to a breakdown in talks and the complete withdrawal of all US troops outside of normal embassy operations—an astonishing diplomatic failure by the Obama administration that robbed the United States of leverage over Iraq's trajectory in the near future and deprived Iraq of needed security assistance in a still-fragile environment. Serious nonpartisan scholars warned as early as 2006 that Iraq was an "intervention-prone conflict" that had a high likelihood of evolving into a wider regional war in the aftermath of a US withdrawal without consolidating security first.[79] They were right. Following the US withdrawal and the simultaneous outbreak of civil war in Syria, insurgent and terrorist groups recovered, recouped, and renewed their assault. They made rapid gains because Iraqi security forces were incapable—and, sometimes, unwilling—to stand up to them and because many Sunnis had come to believe (perhaps rightly) that the government in Baghdad would never treat them fairly. Without an American presence to provide combat support or stiffen their resolve, Iraqi forces proved far less reliable than expected.

The US effort to democratize Iraq was ambitious and, if successful, would have been one of the most defining strategic developments in the Middle East in a generation. Instead, the war left two failed states, a resurgent jihadist group, and a comparatively strengthened Iran in its wake. Obama regularly said the United States would work toward a "responsible withdrawal" from Iraq. That it starkly failed to do. A residual US troop presence would not have solved Iraq's political problems but almost certainly would have blunted the growth of ISIS. Assuming the United States will someday find itself undertaking stability operations elsewhere in the world, the war in Iraq is the strongest possible case for improving the United States' reconstruction and stabilization capabilities.

What are the lessons of Iraq and Afghanistan?[80] It may be emotionally satisfying to settle on a single, sweeping lesson that offers a comprehensive explanation for everything that went wrong—thus the attraction of the morality tale of American hubris and overstretch—but it is unlikely a single explanation can account adequately for an array of problems in two different wars across two administrations and more than a decade of warfare. Such sweeping judgments are overbroad. The history of both wars reveals a more complex picture in which the ultimate outcome was the result of specific policy failures and enemy adaptation. And using the two wars to make generalizations about interventionism and American overstretch is unjustified: The wars in Iraq and Afghanistan are not the only two interventions the United States has ever undertaken. Using them to dismiss all future interventions overgeneralizes from too few data points.

Structural factors in the international environment played a role: American policymakers had become acclimated to believing they could act with greater impunity than before because of America's power disparity and eroding norms of sovereignty, beliefs others in the international community did not share, leaving the United States relatively isolated. Globalization and the diffusion of technology enabled a new lethality to unconventional warfare that most military planners had not anticipated.[81]

Specific policy errors and misjudgments by individual policymakers also played a major role. A large part of the problem in Afghanistan early on was simply the lack of adequate resources. "The administration never devised a coherent course of action that squared the resource levels it was willing to commit with the strategic ends it sought to achieve," according to Hal Brands.[82] Defense Secretary Donald Rumsfeld's commitment to military transformation and the Bush administration's early aversion to stability operations dovetailed with the UN's reaction against the manpower-intensive operations in Kosovo and East Timor: Neither the United States nor UN devoted significant numbers of personnel to the reconstruction effort. More money, troops, leadership, and time cannot guarantee victory, but their absence can guarantee defeat. In Iraq, similarly, the US military planned for a swift and successful invasion but persistently rejected plans for a larger force that would have been required for an effective occupation and reconstruction operation.

In addition, poor planning seems to have played a large part in early missteps in Iraq. (In Afghanistan, there simply was no time for planning.) The State Department, Office of the Secretary of Defense, and Central Command developed separate and uncoordinated plans for postwar Iraq, while the Coalition Provisional Authority was not authorized until weeks before the invasion and not established until after the fall of the Ba'athist regime. As a result, the occupation authorities badly mishandled key decisions in Iraq's political reconstruction. Better policy planning—specifically, integrated interagency strategic planning—would help prevent a reprise of the botched early years of occupation in Iraq.

In both countries, reconstruction and stabilization efforts were inadequate, poorly coordinated, and wastefully implemented. Reinvesting in the tools of civilian power and reconstruction capabilities—the US Agency for International Development (USAID), the State Department, and Army Civil Affairs—is essential to prevent similar problems in future interventions. Finally, the irresponsible exits from both countries (and Libya) were foreseeable, avoidable, appalling errors—a function of their being driven more by political than strategic considerations. When the United States undertakes stability operations, it should focus on "transition" rather than "withdrawal" as a more effective goal that allows the United States to slowly reduce its investment while still preserving and consolidating its gains.

Iraq and Afghanistan did not fail because the United States' ambition was too high or because it aimed at the supposedly unrealistic goal of democratization. They failed because the United States did not match its ambitious goals with correspondingly ambitious plans, resources, budgets, expertise, and competence. "After 9/11, the president and his advisors overestimated how much American power could achieve, and they underestimated the costs, risks, and uncertainties that inhered in their endeavors," in Brands's estimation.[83] Matching goals with resources is the heart of strategy: The United States did not develop and implement a strategy of reconstruction and democratization in either country. Iraq and Afghanistan do not disprove the possibility of democratization as a tool of US foreign policy—because the United States never adequately tried.

Conclusion

Democracy promotion does not explain every American foreign policy initiative. But the trend is clear. When faced with a new threat or opportunity to advance US interests, American policymakers consistently believe that the best long-term solution is to promote liberalism. Realists treat ideology as epiphenomenal, but an idea that is so consistent, pervasive, and durable is not an accident or rhetorical window dressing—it is a component of US grand strategy. As Jonathan Monten insightfully argues, "the concept of the United States as agent of historical transformation and liberal change in the international system therefore informs almost the entire history of US foreign policy."[84] The spread of liberalism is part of the United States' long-term grand strategy.

This history also highlights that the United States has persistently defined its security in broader terms than territorial integrity. At least since its emergence as a great power (with some traces visible even earlier), it has viewed the international climate as an integral part of its national security. Finally, this history shows both the successes and failures of the American pursuit of power and liberty. Critics sometimes seem to imply that because the American record is not perfect, it is therefore indefensible. Such a stance is logically flawed—it amounts to the so-called nirvana fallacy, or letting the perfect be the enemy of the good, assuming there is a standard of achievable perfection that is usefully applied to the behavior of states and statesmen. It also ignores the alternatives—not pursuing liberalism at all—or the comparable records of other great powers in history, such as the Roman, British, and Soviet Empires, against which the American record generally stands out. Iraq and Afghanistan were not America's first forays abroad, nor its first failures. Yet, despite occasional failure and hypocrisy, the history of American foreign policy is remarkable for its success and, relatively speaking, its justice. The American pursuit of liberal power has been successful in producing security for the United States and, more often than not, in encouraging liberalism around the world as well. Some scholars and policymakers, in criticizing President George W. Bush for his conduct of the war in Iraq, seemed to include the effort to foster democracy in Iraq in their criticisms and consequently sought to distance themselves from support for global democracy. This is the epitome of shortsightedness, throwing the democratic baby out with the Iraqi bathwater. In doing so, they were overlooking a long history of American presidents, Democrats as well as Republicans, who have forcefully argued that the United States should foster democracy abroad as a means of assuring American security. In no prior era did scholars or policymakers believe previous failures delegitimized future efforts. The challenge, then as now, is to "learn from the mistakes of an earlier generation without discarding the original Wilsonian inspiration of linking the defense of American national security to the expansion of freedom and justice."[85]

Notes

1. For a recent general history of US foreign policy, see Herring, *From Colony to Superpower*. For specific treatments of the role of liberal ideology in US diplomatic history from its critics, see Hunt, *Ideology and U.S. Foreign Policy*, chapters 2 and 5; McDougall, *Promised Land, Crusader State*; Kissinger, *Diplomacy*; Martel, *Grand Strategy*; Layne, *Peace of Illusions* (for coverage since World War II); and Dueck, *Reluctant Crusaders* (for selected case studies). For a more favorable approach to the same topic, see Mead, *Special Providence*; Kagan, *Dangerous Nation*; and Nau, *Conservative Internationalism*.
2. Hunt, *Ideology*, 17.
3. Dueck, *Reluctant Crusaders*, 22, 24.
4. Kissinger, *Diplomacy*, 18.
5. Kagan, *Dangerous Nation*.
6. The font of this school was Williams's *Tragedy of American Diplomacy*. Contemporary examples include Hunt, *Ideology and U.S. Foreign Policy*, Layne, *Peace of Illusions*, and McDougall, *Promised Land*. See Hunt, *Ideology*, 8–11, for a brief synopsis.
7. Gaddis, *Cold War* and *We Now Know*.
8. Nau, *At Home Abroad*, 7.
9. Monten, "Roots of the Bush Doctrine."
10. See Wood, *Empire of Liberty*, for coverage of this era of US history.
11. Smith, *America's Mission*, 7.
12. Monroe, "Seventh Annual Message."
13. Kagan, *Dangerous Nation*, 72.
14. McDougall, *Promised Land*, 83–84.
15. Ibid., 78.
16. Hunt, *Ideology*, 30.
17. Ibid., chap. 3.
18. Niebuhr, *Children of Light*, 184.
19. Mead, *Special Providence*, 54, 81.
20. McDougall, *Promised Land*, 53.
21. Owen, *Liberal Peace*, chap. 4.
22. Hunt, *Ideology*, 133.
23. Mead, *Special Providence*, 164.
24. McDougall, *Promised Land*, 206. If the second century was a "fulfillment," as I agree it was, it is unclear why McDougall has such problems with it.
25. Monten, "Roots of the Bush Doctrine."
26. McKinley, "Second Annual Message."
27. McKinley, "Third Annual Message."

28. Smith, *America's Mission*, 42.

29. Hunt, *Ideology*, 41.

30. Art, "Defensible Defense," 13.

31. Dates reflect when the United States signed or joined, which was often later than when an organization was created or treaty drafted. US Department of State, *Treaties in Force*, contains much of this data, though some organizations, such as the International Meteorological Association, were later superseded by a UN organization whose entry in *Treaties in Force* reflects a much later date of creation. Other data are found on individual agencies' websites.

32. Quinn, "Theodore Roosevelt," 44, 49.

33. Layne, *Peace of Illusions*, 176.

34. Wilson, "Address to a Joint Session of Congress."

35. Smith, *America's Mission*, 79.

36. McDougall, *Promised Land*, 146.

37. Quoted in Smith, *America's Mission*, 124.

38. Roosevelt, "Fireside Chat."

39. Roosevelt, "Statement on the Atlantic Charter."

40. UN, "Declaration by the United Nations."

41. Smith, *America's Mission*, 144.

42. Ikenberry, *Liberal Leviathan*, 207.

43. Truman, "Special Message to Congress."

44. Free trade was novel for the historically protectionist United States. But other principles of economic liberalism were evident as early as the 1776 Model Treaty, which called for free ports and the freedom of neutrals to trade, in the establishment in the nineteenth century of naval squadrons in the Mediterranean and the Pacific to protect American shipping, and in the scores of landings by US Marines, mostly in Central and South America, to protect American lives, property, and interests.

45. Layne, *Peace of Illusions*, 63; Ikenberry, *Liberal Leviathan*, 168.

46. McDougall, *Promised Land*, 195.

47. Smith, *America's Mission*, 181. Emphasis in original.

48. The Helsinki Final Act, 1.(a).VII–VIII.

49. Reagan, "Address to Members of the British Parliament."

50. *National Security Strategy*, 1988, 4, 11; 1987, 5, 13.

51. This section is adapted from Miller, "American Grand Strategy and the Democratic Peace." Used with permission.

52. Layne, "From Preponderance to Offshore Balancing," 88.

53. Ikenberry, *Liberal Leviathan*, chap. 6.

54. Bush, "Second Inaugural Address," repeated in *National Security Strategy*, 2006, 1.

55. *National Security Strategy*, 2002, v (unnumbered).

56. Ibid., 2006, 3.

57. Monten, "Roots of the Bush Doctrine," 113.

58. *National Security Strategy*, 2010, 37.

59. Ibid., 2015, 19.

60. Ibid., 1994, i; 1995, i; 1996, ii; 1997, 6; 1998, 2; 1999, 2; 2000, 6.

61. Ibid., 1991, 4; 1993, ii.

62. Goldgeier, "NATO Expansion."

63. Kirkpatrick, "NATO Enlargement."

64. Bush, "Remarks to the National Endowment for Democracy."

65. Bouchet, "Democracy Tradition."

66. Obama, "Remarks in Cairo, Egypt."

67. Obama, "President's News Conference."

68. Gibbs, "Press Briefing."

69. Obama, "Remarks at the State Department."

70. Obama, "Address to the Nation on the Situation in Libya."

71. There are far fewer attempts to write the history of the Afghan war than the Iraqi one. See Jones, *In the Graveyard of Empires*; Collins, *Understanding the War in Afghanistan*; and Giustozzi, *Koran, Kalashnikov, and Laptop*, for the best attempts at general narrative, though they are already outdated. A forthcoming volume from Coll, author of *Ghost Wars*, will fill in some of the gaps. Fairweather, *Good War*, rushes to judgment about the ultimate outcome of the conflict. Woodward, *Bush at War* and *Obama's Wars*, and Chandrasekaran, *Little America*, cover policymaking in 2001–2 and 2009–11, with no coverage in between. Some newer accounts approach the subject with a journalistic or memoirist approach, including Gall, *Wrong Enemy*, and Bolger, *Why We Lost*. Barfield, *Afghanistan: A Political and Cultural History*, is the best book on Afghanistan in English published in the last fifteen years, but it is almost wholly devoted to the pre-9/11 history. Suhrke, *When More Is Less*, is the first monograph-length attempt at an academic treatment of the subject, one whose thesis is exactly wrong. There is a much larger literature from think tanks and military periodicals assessing the war's progress and recommending ways forward, most of which are outdated. My own reading of the war in Afghanistan can be found in Miller, "Finish the Job," "The US and Afghanistan after 2014," and my forthcoming book, *Misreading Afghanistan* (in press).

72. Julian Barnes, "U.S. Calls Iraq the Priority," *Los Angeles Times*, December 12, 2007.

73. Sanger, *Confront and Conceal*, 29, 56, 128. See chapters 2, 5, and 10 for the broader narrative of Afghan policy. Also David Sanger, "Charting Obama's Journey to a Shift on Afghanistan," *New York Times*, May 19, 2012, http://www.nytimes.com/2012/05/20/us/obamas-journey-to-reshape-afghanistan-war.html.

74. Woodward, *Obama's Wars*, 387.

75. Dueck, *Reluctant Crusaders*, 27.

76. The definitive history of the war in Iraq will not be written for many years. The first draft is available in Ricks, *Fiasco* and *The Gamble*; Woodward, *Plan of Attack*, *State of Denial*, and *The War Within*; Robinson, *Tell Me How This Ends*; and Gordon and Trainor, *Cobra II* and *The Endgame*.

77. Byman, "Autopsy of the Iraq Debacle."

78. Biddle, Friedman, and Shapiro, "Testing the Surge."

79. Biddle, Friedman, and Long, "Civil War Intervention."

80. The military's official effort at learning lessons from the wars was published through the Joint and Coalition Operational Analysis (JCOA) as *Decade of War*, volume 1, *Enduring Lessons from the Past Decade of Operations*. No volume 2 has been published yet. See also Robinson et al., *Improving Strategic Competence*; Brennan, "Withdrawal Symptoms"; Betts, "Pick Your Battles"; Boot, "More Small Wars"; Cordesman, *Afghanistan and Iraq*; Khalilzad, "Lessons from Afghanistan and Iraq"; Johnson, *Wars in Peace*; Brown and Scales, *US Policy in Afghanistan and Iraq*; Hanson, *Between War and Peace*; and Friedman, Sapolsky, and Preble, *Learning the Right Lessons*.

81. Some scholars had anticipated the rise of unconventional warfare, but their views did not guide the Pentagon's policy or doctrine in the 1990s.

82. Brands, *What Good Is Grand Strategy?*, 170.

83. Ibid., 145.

84. Monten, "Roots of the Bush Doctrine," 113.

85. Smith, *America's Mission*, 235.

3

The New World Disorder

In February 2013, Gen. Martin Dempsey, then chairman of the Joint Chiefs of Staff, told Congress that "I will personally attest to the fact that [the world is] more dangerous than it has ever been." Director of National Intelligence James Clapper said the same month, "In almost 50 years in intelligence, I don't remember when we've had a more diverse array of threats and crisis situations around the world to deal with."[1] In his annual threat assessment to Congress, Clapper listed as threats to the United States cyberattacks, terrorism, organized crime, proliferation of weapons of mass destruction, espionage, space-based threats, pandemic disease, mass atrocities, and resource competition—and then gave a *tour d'horizon* of traditional state-centric threats in every geopolitical region of the world.[2]

What is a threat? A widely used definition is that a threat is a combination of power, offensive capabilities, offensive intentions, and geographic proximity.[3] By that definition, the United States faces an alarming array of threats and potential threats in the twenty-first century. The rise of new powers and the dispersion of wealth to nonstate actors has eroded, though not ended, the United States' overwhelming military and economic dominance: More states and actors have significant power at their disposal. The proliferation of a broad range of weaponry, including but not limited to weapons of mass destruction, has given even minor states significant offensive capabilities. The triumph of liberalism over communism did not put an end to other hostile ideologies, such as *juche* and jihadism.[4] Globalization and technology (especially cyberweapons) have shrunk distance and made even geographically distant actors able to harm the United States, especially given the globally dispersed presence of American troops, allies, bases, and interests. The combination of widely dispersed power, easily available weapon technology, the continued popularity of rival ideologies, and the shrinkage of distance have created a witches' brew. That is why high-ranking US officials have sounded increasingly dire warnings in recent years—rightly, in my view.

The very complexity of the security environment and the multiplication of potential threats have made it difficult to even describe the threat picture in an analytically useful way. Some attempts, like Clapper's, are simple lists that fail to shed light on underlying dynamics or global security trends. On the other hand, scholars' tendency to lump threats together under one of two headings—"conventional" or "unconventional"—are too broad and under-specified to be of much use. In an effort to be both simple and specific, I argue it is easiest to understand the diverse array of threats under three headings: nuclear autocracies, armed nonstate actors, and the transnational jihadist insurgency.

The preeminent threat to liberal order and to the United States is the efforts of autocratic states armed with nuclear weapons, including both great and regional powers, to expand their influence through illegitimate means, including coercion, intimidation, and subversion. Unlike during the Cold War, when the United States faced only two nuclear autocracies, it today faces three and may soon be facing five: Russia, China, North Korea, and soon Iran—all of whom are at least uncooperative with, if not outright hostile to, the United States—and possibly Pakistan, depending on the future of democracy and the military's relationship to militant groups there. There is a considerable gap between the great powers of Russia and China, on the one hand, and the three regional powers on the other. The common thread is their ability to use nuclear deterrence as a shield to guard against retaliation for other forms of aggression and coercion. The nuclear autocracies are the traditional, state-centric threats that used to dominate security studies and US foreign policy during the Cold War and earlier.

Second, the United States faces a type of threat that was usually overlooked during the Cold War: the threats from failed states and the armed nonstate actors that operate from them, such as pirates, organized criminals, drug cartels, and terrorists. Since 2001, some scholars have argued that failed states are, themselves, threats. I disagree. A failed state is a threat to the human security of those who live in it, and failed states usually threaten their immediate neighbors as well by exporting refugees, disease, insurgencies, and organized criminal networks—but they rarely threaten whole regions, the world order, or the United States. Rather, the major threat from failed states is the armed nonstate groups that find a permissive operational environment in them because the rule of law is weak or nonexistent and security forces are weak or easily bribed. These are the new, unconventional threats that have become increasingly fashionable in security studies over the last twenty-five years.[5]

The third major threat in the twenty-first century is what counterinsurgency theorist David Kilcullen has called the jihadist insurgency: campaigns by violent jihadist militants and terrorists to eject the "West" from "Muslim lands," overthrow secular governments, replace them with jihadist regimes, and establish the supremacy of their brand of Islam across the world. The transnational jihadist movement is a blend of the first two families of threat, constituted mostly by nonstate actors (terrorists, insurgents, and drug traffickers) but also partially state-sponsored. Various factions are backed by Iran, parts of the Pakistani government, and, indirectly, some Persian Gulf countries (through the "private" donations of wealthy elites). Defending against and confronting jihadists, then, is a highly complex task that requires the United States to implement all the pillars of its grand strategy in close coordination.

Nuclear Autocracies

Traditionally scholars and policymakers argued that the main goal of US (and, before it, British) grand strategy should be to prevent a hostile power from gaining hegemony over Eurasia, especially Europe and East Asia.[6] Variants of this argument animated debates among nineteenth- and twentieth-century strategists such as Alfred Mahan, Halford Mackinder, Nicholas Spykman, and Zbigniew Brzezinski about which parts of Eurasia were most geographically important for controlling the rest of the world. This idea's historical genealogy has given it a status it does not deserve. There is nothing sacred about Europe and East Asia. Those regions simply had the greatest concentrations of wealth, power, and exploitable natural resources in the early modern era. The increasing diffusion of wealth throughout the world through globalization has lessened the overwhelming importance of those geopolitical regions; the spread of nuclear weapons has dramatically altered it. As Robert Art has argued, "nuclear weapons have . . . invalidated traditional geopolitical logic."[7] There are centers of power, wealth, opportunity, and danger in every geopolitical theater now, while nuclear weapons have raised the cost of traditional conquest and annexation among great powers to prohibitive levels. Europe and East Asia still have a preponderance of wealth outside of the United States, but because of diffusion of wealth and nuclear weapons, a single hegemon capable of taking control of half the world's resources by conquest is exceedingly unlikely to arise.

The only plausible scenario in which the resources of Eurasia fall under the control of a united bloc hostile to the United States would involve a Sino–Russian alliance, the prevention of which should remain a central goal of US diplomacy. The two countries have moved to strengthen ties since the end of the Cold War. More recently, the war in Ukraine has isolated Russia from the West and driven it toward China. The two states have shown interest in stronger trade ties, including joint development of energy resources. China is interested in access to energy supplies that do not come from the volatile Middle East, while Russia is keenly interested in finding another market for its energy products not vulnerable to Western sanctions. Putin said in September 2015, during a state visit to China, that "Russian–Chinese ties have now probably reached a peak in their entire history and continue developing."[8] The two states have not, however, moved toward a mutual defense pact or taken any significant steps toward forming a traditional countervailing coalition against the United States—which, despite their supposed "strategic partnership," is a distant prospect.[9]

The preeminent threat to the United States in the contemporary security environment is not a powerful state attempting to conquer Europe or Asia. The main threat is efforts by powerful, autocratic states armed with nuclear weapons to expand their influence through illegitimate means and thereby undermine liberal order: Russia, China, North Korea, soon Iran, and possibly Pakistan. Why these five? First, they are the only autocracies with nuclear weapons (or a near-nuclear capability). Second, aside from their nuclear capabilities, they are the five most militarily capable autocracies in the world: They are the top five nondemocratic states on the Correlates of War National Material Capabilities ranking, which accounts for a state's military expenditures, military personnel, industrial production, population, and other militarily relevant factors.[10] Third, they have all expressed varying levels of opposition or outright hostility toward the United States, its allies, its ideals, or its leadership of the international system. These five have the power, offensive capabilities, and (relatively) offensive intentions required to constitute a threat to the United States. Most autocracies are too weak to be a serious threat to the United States (e.g., Zimbabwe) or do not profess hostility toward it (e.g., Saudi Arabia), while other powerful states with nuclear weapons are either allied (e.g., the United Kingdom) or at least neutral (e.g., India).[11] In the following sections I will review the military capabilities, hostile intentions, and potential flash points with each of the nuclear autocracies.

Some critics may doubt the utility of this exercise. It has been fashionable in security studies to argue that conventional war is dead, great power conflict is over, competition will take place through trade instead of war, the face of war will be "new" war or a "war amongst the people," or that war of all forms is becoming extinct, while nonstate actors will define world politics.[12] As some liberal internationalists claimed, after the Cold War "the threat to international order was no longer great-power war, as it had been for centuries, but violence and instability emerging from weak, failed, and hostile states residing on the periphery of the system."[13] A foreign policy based on power balancing is, in this view, out-of-touch or anachronistic. To some

readers it may seem old-fashioned, and possibly paranoid, to rehearse numbers of guns and bombs and to measure state power by industrial output and
nuclear yield. More, it will strike some as not only anachronistic but possibly dangerous because such paranoia could ignite a "new Cold War." In the
new era of globalization and interconnectedness, some argue, war has been
delegitimized, great power war is "subrationally unthinkable," hard power
is increasingly obsolete, and military bean counting contributes little to the
understanding of world politics.[14] The Kellogg-Briand Pact worked after all.

This view is wrong on two counts. First, it betrays a shallow understanding of what militaries are for and how weapons are used. Even if great power
war is unlikely, military power is still relevant for the conduct of international
diplomacy: It gives states the ability to wage coercive diplomacy, initiate
and win militarized crises, demonstrate resolve, achieve prestige, intimidate
opponents (both domestic and international), and more.[15] Big guns let their
owners throw their weight around—even without having to fire them. Russia
and China, among the most militarily powerful states in the world, have a lot
of weight. Russia's annexation of Crimea was nearly bloodless—not because
its actions were peaceful, but because Ukrainian officials understood that
they had no realistic chance of defeating the Russian army.

But second, the view that great power war is unthinkable almost certainly underappreciates the human capacity for stupidity and wickedness.
Total wars—wars of conquest and annihilation—among great powers may
be unlikely because of nuclear weapons, but they are not impossible. At
the same time, lesser, limited wars have never stopped and are still happening. A similar view about the obsolescence of war was widely held as
received truth in the years before World War I, another era characterized
by rapid technological growth and remarkable international connectedness.
Norman Angell, a British politician, famously argued in his book *The Great
Illusion* that because war did not pay, rational policymakers would never
fight. The book, published in 1909, did not account for the existence of irrational policymakers, who conclusively disproved Angell's theory. Despite
that, variants of his argument are still made today. Reinhold Niebuhr rightly
criticized liberalism for its "fatuous and superficial view of man," excoriated
"statesmen and guides [who] conjured up all sorts of abstract and abortive
plans for the creation of perfect national and international communities,"
and damned "the sentimental softness in a liberal culture [that] reveals its
inability to comprehend the depth of evil to which individuals and communities may sink."[16] Policy built on utopian assumptions about human nature
will prove useful only so long as everyone behaves as expected—which is
to say, not very long. So long as human beings remain prone to ignorance,
fear, malice, greed, hatred, miscalculation, accident, bigotry, and barbarity,

war is likely to recur. As Plato (allegedly) said, "only the dead have seen the end of war."[17]

It is a feature of intellectual life to take seemingly new phenomena, such as the end of the Cold War or the rise of nonstate actors, and overgeneralize them as if they were the dominant feature of the system. This tendency has led commentators to vastly underappreciate the persistence of old-fashioned, conventional, state-centric threats that have defined world politics for centuries: great power rivalry and conventional war.[18] Realists rightly point out that Russia, China, and others have *already* started to balance against the United States.[19] In fact, the multiplicity of actors, increasing complexity of global affairs, and shrinking resource base make conflict, miscalculation, and accident alarmingly possible.[20]

The good news is that today global power is overwhelmingly concentrated in the hands of the democratic great powers. Table 3.1 illustrates the proportion of world GDP, military capabilities, military spending, and global power (as measured by the Pardee Center) held by democratic great powers, the United States and its allies, and the nuclear autocracies. The United States and its allies—almost all democracies—possess somewhere between half and two-thirds of global power. The nuclear autocracies possess between a tenth and a fifth. It is notable, however, that the gap is much closer in terms of raw military capabilities—27 percent versus 40 percent—largely because of the power potential in China's massive population, economic growth, and access to natural resources.

Russia

The collapse of the Soviet Union led some observers to hope that a new era of great power relations had dawned. Russia's disavowal of communist ideology and its apparent embrace of democracy led some, prematurely, to believe that Russia would come to see the world America's way and that, instead of obstructing or opposing the US-led liberal order, Russia would join it. At the same time, some argued that Russia no longer possessed the capacity to mount a serious military threat to the United States because it had lost nearly half of its territory and population, was absorbed in internal affairs during the 1990s, and was in the grip of an ongoing economic and demographic crisis— its weaknesses evidenced by two difficult conflicts in Chechnya. It seemed that Russia no longer possessed the intent or the capability to threaten the United States.

Neither of these assertions proved true. The failure to help consolidate democratic forces in Russia was probably one of the greatest failings of US

Table 3.1. Global Power Distribution

	% World GDP[a]	% Material Capabilities[b]	% Global Military Spending[c]	% Global Power[d]
Democratic Great Powers				
United States	25.9	14.1	38.6	23.6
India	2.6	7.3	2.3	7.5
Japan	8.5	4.2	3.3	4.0
Germany	5.5	2.4	2.8	3.1
United Kingdom	4.4	2.1	3.7	2.8
France	4.0	1.9	3.4	2.5
South Korea	2.2	2.4	2.0	1.6
Total	53.1	34.4	56.1	45.1
All Democracies	66.4	58.3	74.7	72.1
US Allies				
European Union	26.2	—	—	—
NATO (non-US)	19.6	15.6	17.7	19.9
Pacific Allies	9.2	9.6	8.4	8.4
ME Allies	1.6	1.7	1.8	1.9
South Asia Allies	0.1	0.1	0.2	0.2
Latin America Allies	0.6	0.5	0.3	0.5
African Allies	0.2	0.4	0.2	0.3
All Allies	31.3	27.9	28.6	31.1
United States plus Its Allies	57.2	42.0	67.2	54.7
Nuclear Autocracies				
Russia	3.5	3.9	4.4	3.7
China	8.7	19.7	7.2	13.3
Pakistan	0.3	1.4	0.4	1.0
Iran	0.4	1.3	1.1	0.8
North Korea	—	1.3	—	0.2
Total	12.9	27.6	13.1	19.0

[a] World Bank, *Data*.
[b] Singer, "Reconstructing the Correlates of War Dataset," Correlates of War v. 4.0.
[c] International Institute for Strategic Studies, *Military Balance*, chap. 10.
[d] Pardee Center for International Futures, *Data*.

foreign policy in the 1990s.[21] Russia's abortive transition to democracy left it, instead, a corrupt, oligarchic dictatorship. President Boris Yeltsin's incompetent effort at economic liberalization set the stage for his successor, Vladimir Putin, to end Russia's brief experiment with democracy through a crackdown on domestic dissidents, opposition parties, independent media, and wealthy businessmen capable of challenging his rule, including the imprisonment of tycoon Mikhail Khodorkovsky in 2005 and (probably) the assassinations of former Russian intelligence official Alexander Litvinenko in 2006 and opposition leader Boris Nemtsov in 2015. Freedom House downgraded Russia from "partly free" to "unfree" in 2005, where it has stayed. Putin has even indulged in small symbolic acts to demonstrate his affection for the Soviet Union—such as adopting as Russia's national anthem the tune of the old Soviet anthem, in 2000.

Internationally, Russia no longer purports to be leading a global revolution to overthrow all capitalist states—certainly a change for the better—but Russia's contemporary ideology is not consistent with US interests, a whole and free Europe, or liberal order.[22] Putin's ideology, and that of his philosophical influences and inner circle, is not merely nationalist—it is aggressively chauvinist, wistfully imperialist, and quasi-messianic.[23] Niebuhrian self-criticism and humility is, to put it mildly, lacking in Russian officialdom under Putin. This argument is likely to find a more receptive audience today, after Russia's invasion of Ukraine, than when I first made it in 2012, but, in truth, the invasion of Ukraine was only the culmination of a long-gathering trend of greater Russian assertiveness. Putin famously lamented the collapse of the Soviet Union as "a major geopolitical disaster" in 2005 and has regularly cast Russia as the defender of a stable and fair multipolar international system against alleged US unipolarity and, more recently, of global traditionalism against Western multiculturalism.[24] In a 2007 speech, Putin bluntly outlined an agenda for opposing the United States' supposed hegemony:

> I consider that the unipolar model is not only unacceptable but also impossible in today's world. . . . The model itself is flawed because at its basis there is and can be no moral foundations for modern civilization. . . . Unilateral and frequently illegitimate actions have not resolved any problems. . . . Today we are witnessing an almost uncontained hyper use of force—military force—in international relations, force that is plunging the world into an abyss of permanent conflicts. . . . We are seeing a greater and greater disdain for the basic principles of international law. One country, the United States, has overstepped its national borders in every way. This is visible in the economic, political, cultural and educational policies it imposes on other

nations. . . . And of course this is extremely dangerous. It results in the fact that no one feels safe. I want to emphasize this—no one feels safe! . . . I am convinced that we have reached that decisive moment when we must seriously think about the architecture of global security.[25]

Putin backed his rhetoric with action. A major aspect of Russian foreign policy has been its reassertion of influence over its "near abroad" through (unsuccessful) opposition to NATO's expansion, the creation of the Collective Security Treaty Organization, a Eurasian customs union, and the Shanghai Cooperation Organization, and through the use of its gas supplies as leverage over Europe, especially Ukraine. Russia opposed the US war in Iraq (2003), the Rose Revolution in Georgia (2003), the Orange Revolution in Ukraine (2005), and the Tulip Revolution in Kyrgyzstan (2005); was probably involved in the cyberattack on Estonia (2007); suspended its participation in the Treaty on Conventional Armed Forces in Europe (2007) and subsequently withdrew from the treaty altogether (2015); invaded Georgia (2008); opposed NATO's action in Libya (2011); completed Iran's first nuclear reactor (Bushehr I, in 2011); sold arms to the Syrian government; effectively stopped US action against Syria for its use of chemical weapons (2013); and intervened militarily to shore up the Bashar al-Assad regime in Syria (2015). Considering Russia's foreign policy since 2000, the most surprising aspect of Russia's invasion of Ukraine and annexation of Crimea in 2014 was not Putin's boldness, but Western analysts' naiveté.[26] The annexation of Crimea and intervention in Syria were not major shifts but only the most extreme examples of growing Russian assertiveness in the age of Putin.

It is worth stressing this point because it is one that advocates of restraint badly misjudged. Gholz, Press, and Sapolsky wrote in 1997, "In an extreme scenario, if Russia were to elect a hyper-nationalist leader, he could not magically restore the power of the Warsaw Pact." They point out that Germany alone is richer than Russia and that "it is hard to believe that prosperous, technologically sophisticated Germany—let alone the combined European force that would likely evolve if there were a serious threat of Russian hegemony—would be unable to stop a resurgent Russian invasion."[27] Three years later, Russia got its hypernationalist leader, and he is making a concerted effort to revive Russian arms and glory. The biggest reason Putin is unlikely to revive the Warsaw Pact is that most of its members joined NATO and are thus protected by the United States' nuclear umbrella—the very policies Gholz, Press, and Sapolsky opposed. Europe, meanwhile, has largely failed to live up to Gholz's expectations. After Russian invasions of Georgia and Ukraine, the only combined European force that exists is held together by the United States in NATO, which Gholz called for dismantling. Europe is richer and more technologically advanced than Russia but appears unable to muster the political will to oppose Russia on its own, something Gholz did not anticipate.

There are several flashpoints that could trigger further deterioration in US–Russian relations. The US Air Force flew Georgian army units from Iraq to fight Russian troops in Georgia in 2008, which could plausibly have been interpreted as American participation in hostilities—probably the closest the United States and Russia have come to war since the Cuban Missile Crisis. The US and Russian air forces are flying sorties over Syria on separate, unco-ordinated missions in dangerous proximity to one another. Turkey's downing of a Russian jet in November 2015 is a clear illustration of how the situation could turn hostile. US and Russian interests clash most clearly in Eastern Europe—especially the Baltics and Ukraine. At the time of this writing, Rus-sia has sponsored pro-Russian rebels in eastern Ukraine, and some Ameri-can policymakers have called for giving weapons to the embattled Ukrainian government. Further crisis is likely if Kiev tilts further toward the West, for example, by pushing for membership in NATO. If Putin's popularity at home erodes, it is not hard to imagine him allowing a foreign crisis to spiral danger-ously to win nationalist plaudits.

Russia is not the only state to match autocracy at home with opposition to the US abroad, but its opposition is more worrisome because of its military capability. In fact, Russia's army and nuclear forces remain among the larg-est and most formidable in the world. Russia has embarked on several waves of defense reform since 1997, which collectively have reduced Russia's reli-ance on conscripted personnel, improved training and professionalization, upgraded equipment, started toward the creation of a professional noncom-missioned officer corps, increased pay, streamlined its command structure, and improved the army's mobility. "Russia remains a significant military power," according to *The Military Balance*, "with a sizeable nuclear arsenal."[28] It has an active-duty military force of 845,000 personnel, some 8,500 nuclear warheads (the world's largest inventory), four tank brigades with one of the largest modern tank fleets in the world (including the T-90, one of the few tanks capable of challenging the M1 Abrams), over five dozen submarines (some capable of launching nuclear missiles), and it is one of only ten coun-tries in the world to maintain an active-duty aircraft carrier. In 2007, Rus-sia resumed its Cold War policy of conducting regular flights by strategic bombers on long-range patrols.[29] It also has invested in cyber capabilities (or in nonstate cyber proxies), as illustrated by its probable role in the cyber intrusions against Estonia and Georgia in 2007 and 2008. Russian forces are not impressive compared to total US forces worldwide—but the United States would not be able to mobilize and bring to bear all American forces worldwide in a militarized crisis with Russia. Russian forces, concentrated in Eurasia, would present a formidable challenge to US and allied forces in that theater.

Finally, Russia is a declining power—which may make it even more dangerous in the short term. Putin's rule has not fixed Russia's economic problems or slow-motion demographic suicide, and Russia is surrounded by more dynamic neighbors.[30] Each year that passes further erodes the foundations of Russia's remaining strength and widens the gap between Russia and the rich Western democracies. Putin and his advisers surely know this, which means they understand that their best moment for seizing as much of Russia's former glory as possible is now: Their chances of success diminish with time. That may explain in part Putin's gambles over Ukraine and Syria. The closer Russia's elite feel to a tipping point, after which they will no longer be taken seriously as a great power but for their nuclear weapons, the more desperately they will search for ways to extend their grip on power.

China

At the end of the Cold War, China replaced Russia as the great power of most concern among some scholars and policymakers. China's inexorable economic growth, its program of military modernization, and its more obvious and brutal forms of repression made it easier to fear. Trends in scholarship and publishing also helped: Because Russia had been intensely studied and written about for decades, publishers and professors were eager to find a new topic to focus on.

There is enough truth to these concerns to count China as a top-tier concern for the United States. China clearly poses a greater danger today than it did during the Cold War. From 1950 to 1972, the United States and China were declared enemies and fought to a bloody stalemate in the Korean War, but China was crippled by economic weakness and was not a nuclear power until 1964. From 1972 to 1989, the United States and China reached a rapprochement while still officially disagreeing over the status of Taiwan, but China's power also began to grow quickly as it liberalized its economy and modernized its armed forces. Today, for the first time, the United States may soon face a China that is both powerful and increasingly hostile.

That China's power is rising is indisputable, most visibly seen in its rapid economic growth. The Chinese economy is, by most accounts, the second or third largest in the world and could surpass America's as early as 2019—if it hasn't already.[31] But China's military modernization has also brought it into the ranks of the world's preeminent military powers. China's defense spending is growing so fast it may draw even with that of the United States within ten years. Years of steady investment have given China all the accoutrements of a great military power, including five dozen submarines, a constellation of satellites, an aircraft carrier (commissioned in 2012), and some 250 nuclear warheads (enough for a second-strike capability). It continues to expand its inventory of ballistic and cruise missiles and may have test-fired in 2012 a new intercontinental ballistic missile capable of hitting the entire continental United States. It has focused in recent years on creating a power-projection capability and has explored opening or leasing its first extraterritorial military facilities in Gwadar, Pakistan, or the Seychelles.[32] Much of its large army is unsuited to contemporary military operations, but ongoing reforms are slowly making China's land forces more flexible and capable of combined-arms operations. China has an increasingly self-sufficient manufacturing and design base for its land forces, though it remains heavily reliant on Russia for more complex air and naval systems.[33] Like Russia, China has also developed significant cyber capabilities. US cybersecurity firms have identified specific units of the People's Liberation Army devoted to espionage that have been engaged in a wide-ranging, multiyear campaign to steal data from corporations and governments.[34] The Chinese air force may soon benefit from the most sophisticated and technologically advanced aerospace research in the world: A new Chinese jet, the J-21, may be derived from stolen designs for the US military's F-35.

China's increasing strength has emboldened it to aim at denying US influence in East Asia and globally. Chinese policymakers, like their Russian counterparts, continue to talk openly about their intent to oppose American unipolarity, revise the global order, and command a greater share of global prestige and influence. President Xi Jinping expressed his hope that China and Russia would lead the "establishment of a multi-polar world and [the] democratization of international relations" during a visit to Moscow in 2010, when he was serving as vice president. The phrase "democratization of international relations" is China's way of calling for an end to US leadership in international affairs, and it has been found in official Chinese policy documents and speeches by Xi and other Chinese officials in recent years.[35] Like Russia, China has generally led opposition to major US diplomatic and security initiatives. Some observers have interpreted its sponsorship of the new Asian Infrastructure Investment Bank as an effort to construct alternate institutions of world order.

The several flashpoints where Chinese revisionist aims might lead to a militarized conflict with the United States or its allies include Taiwan, the Korean Peninsula, and disputed islands in the East and South China Seas. According to the US Department of Defense, "Beijing is developing capabilities intended to deter, delay, or deny possible US support for the island"—Taiwan—"in the event of conflict. The balance of cross-Strait military forces and capabilities continues to shift in the mainland's favor."[36] US relations with China are prone to regular downward spikes, including during the Tiananmen Square massacre in 1989 and subsequent sanctions against China, the 1996 Taiwan Strait Crisis, the United States' accidental bombing of the Chinese embassy in Belgrade in 1999, the crash landing of an American EP-3 reconnaissance aircraft in China in 2001 after its collision with an aggressive Chinese fighter aircraft, China's antisatellite missile test in 2007, ongoing trade and currency disputes, and annual US weapon sales to Taiwan. Changing power dynamics in a bilateral relationship fraught with regular crises and several flashpoints makes a militarized crisis with China more likely today than at any point since the Vietnam War.

However, some perspective is in order. China's power is still mostly latent, and the threat it poses to the United States is potential and hypothetical rather than present and imminent. According to the Correlates of War National Material Capabilities index, China is already more powerful than the United States—but that is because the index includes China's massive urban population, which could be drafted into service in time of war, a measure of potential rather than mobilized power. Raw size is a poor measure of the overall strength of the Chinese economy, which continues to lag because of the inefficiency of China's state-owned enterprises, corruption, inadequately developed higher education, and looming demographic problems. China is still mostly a regional power, not a global one (though its heavy investment in Africa may change that). Most of the ruling Communist Party's energies are taken up with the challenges of maintaining stability in a massive country wracked by hugely disruptive social and economic changes, fighting corruption, alleviating rural poverty, and sustaining its own legitimacy. One scholar has claimed that, by some measures, the United States is even more powerful relative to China today than it was in 1989.[37]

There is a psychological element to the US–Chinese relationship: The Chinese feel the confidence that comes from believing tomorrow will be even better for them than today, and Americans feel a corresponding insecurity. That confidence can fuel more stridency among Chinese policymakers than their actual power might merit—fueling, for example, their "Go Out" policy since the late 1990s and accounting for China's more aggressive regional policy since 2008 and its construction of new islands and airstrips in the South China Sea. At the same time, American insecurity can foster fears that China has become a "revolutionary power" that will fundamentally alter global norms, institutions, and relationships.[38] Chinese policymakers' expectations that their strength will continue to grow may

make them relatively less prone to risky behavior or confrontational policies toward the United States in the short term: They can always delay confrontation until tomorrow, when they will be in a stronger position to win.
That could change quickly if a downward economic spike or severe bout of
internal turmoil causes a "negative shift in bargaining power,"[39] convinces
the Chinese elite that they have reached a generational apex of their power,
and pressures them to capitalize on it before it passed. A Chinese-led future
depends on China continuing to rise for several decades to come, which is
not a sure thing. China's currency devaluation and stock market turmoil in
2015 may herald an economic slowdown in the near future.

Iran, North Korea, and Pakistan

In addition to Russia and China, three more states are or could quickly become
nuclear autocracies hostile to the United States. North Korea and Iran are
avowed enemies of the United States; Pakistan has teetered on the brink since
2001. Pakistan and North Korea tested nuclear weapons in 1998 and 2006,
respectively, and Iran is a near-nuclear power. All three states have invested in
medium-range ballistic missiles that could hit US allies and bases abroad. And
the United States must take seriously the possibility that any of the three will
soon be able to produce missiles that could hit the US homeland—Admiral William Gortney testified to the US Senate in March 2016 that North Korea likely
already possesses ICBMs capable of hitting the continental United States.[40]

Readers may question my inclusion of Pakistan on a list of "autocracies." North Korea, a totalitarian communist dictatorship, is obviously one
of the most repressive and barbaric governments in the world. Iran is relatively more open—it has an elected legislature—but the theocratic Council
of Guardians holds veto power over virtually all public policy and candidates
for elective office, and the country is clearly "not free" according to Freedom
House. But Pakistan's form of government is more complex. It has been ruled
by a military dictatorship for almost half of its independent existence, but
even during periods of civilian rule—including during its so-called decade
of democracy from 1988 to 1999 and from 2008 to the present—the army
appeared to retain more influence over public policy than is normal in democratic countries, probably including veto power over foreign and defense
policy and over the defense budget. Pakistan today has a vibrant independent
media and elected provincial and national legislatures, and Freedom House
characterizes it is "partly free." It is best to understand Pakistan's government as a hybrid between an illiberal civilian oligarchy and a military autocracy, with rival centers of power within the government struggling to retain

control of their access to spoils and sources of patronage. The situation, however, could change quickly.[41]

Similarly, readers may question my inclusion of Iran on a list of nuclear-weapon states. Pakistan has the world's fastest-growing nuclear arsenal, currently thought to number 100 to 120 weapons and increasing by ten per year. North Korea's nuclear weapons are low-yield, its arsenal is very small, and its delivery systems are still embryonic—but they continue to improve. Iran, by contrast, has not tested nuclear weapons and does not have a publicly acknowledged nuclear weapon capability at the time of this writing. However, its steady progress mastering the nuclear fuel cycle and enriching uranium has made it a "near-nuclear" power, and, as Barry Posen has argued, "'near nuclear status' might be deterrent enough under some conditions."[42] More than a decade of efforts by the United States, the other permanent members of the UN Security Council, Germany, the UN, and the International Atomic Energy Agency to dissuade, deter, or coerce Iran into halting its nuclear activities through negotiations, sanctions, reports, and "naming and shaming," culminated in an agreement in 2015 that essentially codified Iran's nuclear break-out capability. An alleged attempt by Israel to assassinate Iranian nuclear scientists,[43] and another reported attempt by Israel and the United States to sabotage Iranian nuclear facilities with a computer virus,[44] may have slowed but not halted Iran's progress toward completing the nuclear fuel cycle. The last resort—military action against Iran—has so little support in the United States or internationally as to be politically infeasible. Israel alone does not have the ability to completely wipe out Iran's nuclear facilities. Even an implausible coalition of the United States, Israel, and Saudi Arabia might only set back Iran's nuclear program by a few years.[45] Because everyone is aware of these facts, they have probably already factored them into their calculation of the security dynamic in the Middle East. The United States and other powers are treating Iran *as if* it already possesses a nuclear deterrent because policymakers seem to believe there is little they can do to stop it from acquiring one—which explains Iran's successful bargaining toward an agreement in 2015 that left in place much of its nuclear infrastructure and expertise, had poor inspection and enforcement mechanisms, and expires after a decade. For all intents and purposes, Iran has achieved a nuclear deterrent without the cost of having actually built nuclear weapons.

Even if Iran's near-nuclear status is granted, some scholars dismiss nuclear proliferation as a security concern at all. "The further spread of nuclear weapons presents no additional threats to America's security" because both states and terrorists can be deterred from using them, according to the school of structural realism.[46] This view manages to combine the liberal naiveté about human nature with the realists' blind spot for culture and ideology. It presumes all policymakers in all states, regardless of their belief systems or political structures, are equally rational and trustworthy with nuclear weapons, a view that cannot be taken seriously. Even if it is true nine times out of ten, 90 percent is still not good enough when it comes to nuclear weapons. Further, as with every weapon system, the effect of nuclear weapons is not limited to their military application. Even if nuclear weapons make conventional war less likely, they also embolden their owners (if the owners are ideologically predisposed toward aggression), give them more clout, and enable them to engage in coercive diplomacy and aggressive posturing below the threshold of conventional war—the "stability–instability paradox." As for terrorists with nuclear weapons, some claim terrorists can be deterred because the United States can threaten to eradicate the entire religious or ethnic groups whose cause they champion.[47] Such a threat might be credible from a barbaric regime known for cruelty and repression; it would obviously not be credible from the United States. The argument that nuclear proliferation does not threaten American security is the sort of academic theory so obviously at odds with common sense that it widens the gap between scholarship and policymaking.

None of the three smaller nuclear autocracies pose the same level of conventional threat as Russia or China. North Korea has the fourth-largest standing army in the world and thousands of pieces of long-range heavy artillery that could devastate Seoul. But its air and naval forces are much smaller, most of its military equipment is old, and the nation suffers from shortages of food and fuel. Iran's armed forces are similarly struggling with aging equipment and supply shortages because of UN sanctions and economic problems, though it will be able to reinvest in its military strength following the lifting of sanctions. Pakistan's armed forces are more formidable, having been equipped by both US and Chinese arms sales. For example, its tank fleet includes several hundred T-80s and a Chinese variant of the T-90, and its air force includes American F-16s.

However, because of their technological inferiority and relative conventional weakness, the Iranians, North Koreans, and Pakistanis have worked to level the playing field by investing in unconventional and terrorist capabilities. The Islamic Revolutionary Guard Corps (IRGC) and its client Hezbollah are among the most sophisticated terrorist organizations in history—the latter having fought the Israeli army to a standstill in 2006. Pakistan has long fostered and tolerated a wide range of militant groups that have acted against India and Afghanistan (including Lashkar-e-Taiba and the Taliban), some of which fought against US troops in Afghanistan or directly targeted the US homeland. North Korea has "the world's largest special-operations forces" and has an established track record of terrorist attacks against its southern neighbor, a US ally.[48] North Korea has also invested heavily in cyber capabilities. It was almost certainly behind the theft of a huge trove of files and movies from Sony Pictures Entertainment in 2014 in retaliation for that company's production of a film satirizing the country—a disturbing precedent of a state hiding behind its nuclear deterrent while conducting a cyberattack and threatening blackmail against American citizens.

While the United States could surely defeat any state's conventional forces if war broke out, it is unclear if it could effectively manage the aftermath. Assuming the IRGC and the North Korean State Security Department have studied the insurgencies in Iraq and Afghanistan, they could be even more effective than Iraq's Ba'athists, the Afghan Taliban, or al-Qaida in Iraq were in denying the United States and its allies the ability to foster peace and stability in the aftermath of a conventional war. As a result, it is not at all clear that the United States is currently capable of defeating Iran or North Korea *and* following up with a successful stabilization and reconstruction campaign. The Obama administration made clear in its 2012 defense strategy guidance and 2014 quadrennial defense review that US forces "will no longer be sized to conduct large-scale, prolonged stability operations," which echoes a larger problem: Instead of preserving hard-won capabilities in reconstruction and stabilization, the United States is simply hoping such operations will be unnecessary in the future. (I take up these questions in greater detail in chapter 5.) That means that if war with North Korea or Iran comes, the United States might win the war but lose the peace—much as it did in 1919, and possibly with similar results.

The security challenges from Iran, North Korea, and Pakistan are different from those of Russia and China because of the countries' smaller size, weaker conventional capabilities, less robust delivery mechanisms, and varying levels of official hostility. For all three, unless and until they build intercontinental ballistic missiles or nuclear-capable submarines and bombers, the deterrence dynamic will not mirror that of the Cold War.[49] War with Iran or North Korea is probably more likely than war with the Soviet Union or China was because Iran and especially North Korea appear to be less rational, less predictable, and less responsive to deterrence. Short of war, their relationships with the United States may instead take the form of frozen conflicts, perpetual coercive bargaining, or a nuclear standoff providing cover for the sponsorship of unconventional proxies. Iran might quietly benefit from a reordering of the Middle East to account for its implicit nuclear capabilities or, if less cool heads prevail, could risk a crisis if it publicly tests a nuclear weapon. In Pakistan, much depends on whether the civilian government is able to consolidate its control over the military, whether the state continues to support some jihadist groups, whether it is successful in its counterinsurgency campaign, and whether militant groups provoke a war with India. The future of the Korean Peninsula is, to an alarming degree, in China's hands because of its relationship with North Korea. The existence of multiple simultaneous cold wars with unstable nuclear powers is a major reason why the contemporary security environment is highly risky, why scholars who argue the United States enjoys unprecedented safety are wrong, and why the advocates of restraint are misguided.

Barbarians

In addition to the traditional state-centric threats from hostile nuclear powers, the United States faces a different type of threat. Scholars call them "armed non-state groups."[50] They include a menagerie of thugs, including terrorists, pirates, organized criminal groups, drug lords, slavers, and war criminals. While "armed non-state group" is accurate, it is also clumsy. An older term for enemies of civilization is still accurate: barbarians.

The barbarian threat is not new, has often been overblown, and, individually, such groups rarely pose a large threat to US national security. But their access to the technology, weapons, transportation, communications, and failed states of the globalized era have made them more dangerous than previously, as al-Qaida dramatically demonstrated in 2001. Travel and communication is easier, weapons are more lethal, and state failure is more widespread (giving them more space to operate with impunity), while US and allied border, port, and infrastructure security has not kept up. Osama bin Laden did massive harm to the United States in ways inconceivable for a nonstate actor during the Cold War; the same may soon be true of the drug gangs in Mexico.

But even barring another 9/11 or a crippling cyberattack, the aggregate effect of an increasing number of hostile nonstate actors throughout the world is to raise the cost of sustaining liberal order, slows the gears of normal diplomatic and economic exchange, heightens risk and uncertainty, and gives rival great powers an additional tool, in the form of nonstate proxies, to extend their influence and disrupt the agenda of the United States and its allies. A broader understanding of "security" suggests that threats to liberal order are threats to the United States because barbarism attacks the foundations of liberal civilization. Armed nonstate groups undermine law, erode borders, corrupt police and security forces, kill and maim, kidnap, extort, addict, hijack, and enslave. Individually, they rarely cause enough harm to justify treating them as a national security threat. But in aggregate they close off access to liberal civilization, they expand a zone of lawlessness and anarchy, and they blunt human development. In fact, armed nonstate groups attack the foundations of liberal order more directly than nuclear autocracies do. Russia and China usually operate more subtly (excepting Russia's invasion of Ukraine), happy to benefit from world order as much as possible while exploiting its weaknesses through coercion, intimidation, or subversion when opportunity presents itself. Barbarism, by contrast, is more overtly violent and criminal. If nuclear autocracies are like cancer to liberal order, barbarians threaten death by a thousand cuts.

These kinds of threats have loomed large in discussions of US national security since 2001. Many discussions of the subject have emphasized terrorism to the exclusion of other nonstate actors; some have emphasized the unconventional threat to the exclusion of traditional, state-centric threats altogether. Because the specific terrorist group responsible for the 2001 attacks was itself a part of a broader ideological movement, scholars and policymakers have sometimes been too focused on its particular characteristics and thus failed to come to terms with the broader phenomenon of armed nonstate groups. And some policymakers seem especially eager not to recognize the linkage between such groups and the blight of state failure, which enables nonstate groups to organize, train, recruit, and operate with impunity. All told, the United States has yet to incorporate a mature understanding of modern barbarism into its grand strategy.

For clarity's sake, armed nonstate groups can be classified by the motive that drives them. Broadly, there are two: profit or politics, greed or grievance. Pirates, drug traffickers, organized criminal networks, and slavers are in it for the money. Terrorists and war criminals do it for a chance at power. I treat jihadist groups separately, below.

Domestic Terrorists and War Criminals

Nonjihadist terrorism is at least as old as the French Revolution. An anarchist assassinated President William McKinley in 1901, and Confederate and (probably) communist sympathizers assassinated two other presidents in 1865 and 1963, respectively. Assassins felled two US senators and eight representatives over the years, including a Republican congressman from Arkansas assassinated by the Ku Klux Klan in 1868 for his support for Reconstruction. Anarchists attempted dozens of bombings across the country in 1919, targeting two governors, four US senators, a Supreme Court justice, and the attorney general. From the 1960s onward, a variety of domestic terrorist groups and individuals have launched occasional attacks, including the Weather Underground, the Symbionese Liberation Army, the Animal Liberation Front, the Earth Liberation Front, the Black Liberation Army, the Aryan

Nation, the Ku Klux Klan, Timothy McVeigh, Eric Rudolph, and Theodore Kaczynski, among others.

A new and potentially worrying development is the intersection of domestic terrorism with the transnational jihadist movement (more on which below). A few American citizens and permanent residents, including Nidal Hasan, Tamerlan and Dzhokhar Tsarnaev, Faisal Shahzad, Syed Farook, and Tashfeen Malik have committed or attempted to commit acts of terrorism on American soil motivated by some variant of jihadist ideology. (Shahzad had some links to the Pakistani Taliban.) Similar attacks in Britain, France, the Netherlands, Australia, and Spain suggest they are not aberrations but part of a broader phenomenon that Western governments have yet to understand. These cases have been rare, but their incidence could become far more damaging than other types of terrorism. Jihadism is more indiscriminate in choosing its targets than, for example, the Earth and Animal Liberation Fronts. A pattern of successful attacks could attract the attention and support of international donors and recruits eager to spur jihad in America. And the damage of terrorist violence is not only the immediate death and destruction they cause, but also the damage they do to the culture of democracy. Terrorist attacks subvert democratic norms, advancing political claims and grievances through violence rather than debate. Because jihadist-inspired terrorists purport to act in the name of a specific, identifiable minority group (Muslims), their violence could erode the fabric of trust among Americans and prompt some to view American Muslims with suspicion or malice. Americans largely resisted the temptation to turn on American Muslims in the aftermath of 9/11 (George W. Bush far outshone Franklin Roosevelt in this respect), but their magnanimity and level-headedness may not survive if homegrown jihadist attacks become more regular or public figures exploit Americans' fears for political gain. The popularity of calls for a halt to Muslim immigration to the United States after terrorist attacks in Paris and San Bernardino in late 2015 suggests this is not an implausible scenario. A continuation of this trend would be a significant blow to American values and the American way of life.

Terrorists are a species of war criminal—but there are others. Other types—perpetrators of genocide, ethnic cleansing, and massive human rights violations—are rarely a direct threat to US national security, but they are a threat to liberal order. The United States should view them in the same light that it views efforts by the nuclear autocracies to expand their influence through illegitimate means. Sometimes the particular issue at stake (disputed islands in the South Pacific or a massacre in central Africa) is peripheral to American concerns, but the principle (nonaggression, respect for civilian immunity) is so important as to merit an international response. The question is, again, what sort of world do we want to live in? Is it better to live in a world in which war criminals believe they can massacre people with impunity, fearing no accountability or reprisals from the international community, or a world in which dictators believe there are certain lines even they cannot cross?

Pirates, Traffickers, Slavers

Like terrorism, piracy is quite old. Pompey the Great led a war on piracy in 67 BC across the Mediterranean, and a golden age of piracy dawned over the Caribbean in the seventeenth and early eighteenth centuries before the East India Company and Royal Navy began to enforce freedom of the seas. The United States fought small wars against the Barbary pirates of North Africa in 1801–5 and 1815 because of their threat to US shipping in the Mediterranean—but the plague has never been definitively wiped out. Pirates remain active around the world, especially near strategic waterways such as the Straits of Malacca and off the coast of Somalia. In 2011, pirates attacked 439 ships and took over 800 hostages, though their operations have been significantly reduced in recent years.[51] Pirates regularly launch hundreds of attacks on ships each year to steal cargo or kidnap and ransom the crew, costing the world economy billions in military operations, higher security costs and insurance premiums, and more. Somali piracy alone cost the world economy nearly $7 billion in 2011.[52] Piracy, like terrorism, is a direct threat against life, property, and US command of the commons, but it is also an attack on liberal principles—in this case, the principle of the freedom of the seas, a prerequisite of open markets and a liberal trading regime.

Organized crime typically centers on buying and selling illegal goods on a black market, including drugs, weapons, people, organs, endangered animals, and archeological artifacts. Criminal enterprises are a national security threat because of their violent control of a lucrative black market, not their product (except arms smugglers). Most of today's illegal drugs were legal—some were trafficked by the British East India Company in the eighteenth and nineteenth centuries—until the early twentieth century. The prohibition of several major narcotic and hallucinogenic substances, evolving into the "war on drugs" by 1971, fostered a massive black market, in turn generating the violent crime and armed gangs that surround illegal money. The global market in cocaine and opiates was worth some $153 billion in 2010. The major transnational drug-trafficking groups are located in South and Central America, smuggling Colombian, Bolivian, and Peruvian cocaine northward into the United States and Europe, and in South and Central Asia, smuggling Afghan and Pakistani heroin into the Middle East, Russia, and Europe.[53]

Organized criminals are businessmen; they tend to avoid needless violence. The smugglers' destructive wake is subtler than the wanton bloodlust of the terrorist: Drug lords spread corruption, undermine the rule of law, and fuel state failure. Buying off policemen, border control officials, judges, and investigators is the cost of doing business, easily done with $153 billion to spend in poor countries. Transparency International's Corruption Perceptions Index, which ranks countries from least to most corrupt, ranks Colombia and Mexico as highly corrupt, at 94th and 103rd on the list, respectively; Pakistan and Afghanistan are even worse, at 126th and 172nd.[54] "The global illicit opiate and cocaine markets represent two of the biggest transnational drugs and crime threats of our time," according to the UN.[55] By contrast, the organized criminal networks that smuggle diamonds or ivory out of Africa are relatively less of a concern to the United States. They are a threat to liberal order but a minor one.

Transnational trafficking is a national security threat to the United States largely because of where it occurs. The blight of corruption and drug-related violence in America's immediate southern neighbor could easily spill over the border, causing crime and violence to spike and the quality of governance to erode in America's border states. The same bribery and corruption that enables drug trafficking weakens the border and makes it easier for other nonstate actors, including terrorists, to cross. The collapse of the Mexican state, while unlikely, would be a major threat to American security. In South and Central Asia, the intersection of the drug trade with jihadist groups has funded the Taliban insurgency and, probably, the terrorist campaign against Pakistan. Militants' deeply entrenched presence has turned the Afghanistan–Pakistan border into a veritable jihadist narco-state, virtually unreachable by the security forces of either neighbor and creating a haven safe from anything but America's alleged drone program. The cocaine and heroin kingpins are fabulously wealthy and powerful, they oppose US interests, undermine US allies, enrich America's enemies, and they are headquartered in some of the most strategically important areas of the world.

Finally, if the United States were to take action against any trafficking group unrelated to its own immediate national security interests, it should surely be human traffickers. Despite the legal abolition of slavery in every country in the world—largely accomplished in the eighteenth and nineteenth centuries—the global slave trade was worth about $32 billion in 2010, according to the UN.[56] The persistence of the global slave trade is an affront to liberal values so heinous that the United States could do worse than to follow in the footsteps of the Royal Navy and make abolition an explicit goal of US foreign policy.

Failed States

Armed nonstate actors have an important relationship with failed states.[57] Understanding the relationship is important for formulating an effective response. Failed states are not *direct* threats to US national security in themselves, but, by providing a permissive operating environment for nonstate actors, they *indirectly* threaten US interests and, more frequently, liberal order. It quickly became received wisdom after the terrorist attacks of September 11, 2001, that failed states are dangers to the world because they incubate global terrorist groups. In truth, few failed states have generated the kind of global menace that al-Qaida was, and some scholars have since argued that state failure is not a significant cause of transnational terrorist threats.[58] There is some truth to their corrective analysis. But even if al-Qaida and Afghanistan were highly unusual, it is nonetheless true that weak and collapsed states pose other dangers to their neighbors, whole regions, and occasionally the world.

For example, some twenty million people, including six hundred thousand Americans, died in 1918–20 of Spanish influenza, a disease that surely spread faster and lasted longer in part because of Europe's weakness and poverty following World War I. The disease killed more people worldwide than the war itself. Today, epidemics such as HIV/AIDS, Ebola, or bird flu could kill millions, cripple poor states' health care systems, and destabilize regions as armies and governments lose human capital. Keeping such diseases in check is as much a governance problem as a scientific and medical one.

Some threats are more direct than disease. The Mafia arose in the lawless regions of Sicily in the late nineteenth century and became a blight of organized crime and gang warfare in twentieth-century Italy and America. The illegal opium trade flourished in the weak and ungoverned Golden Triangle border area between Laos, Myanmar, and Vietnam in the twentieth century—until Afghanistan's collapse created an even more inviting environment for global narcotic traffickers in Central Asia in the 1990s. The collapse of the Soviet Union and rise of nonstate armed groups in weak postcommunist states led to civil unrest, violence, and regional instability from the Balkans to the Caucasus and Central Asia, killing hundreds of thousands of people in the Balkans, reigniting nationalist chauvinism in Russia, and creating a clutch of frozen-conflict zones that serve as safe havens for criminals and smugglers. Parts of West Africa collapsed in the 1990s as Sierra Leone, Liberia, and Côte d'Ivoire exported lawlessness and insurgent movements to each other. Central Africa saw one of the most lethal wars in the continent's history from 1997 to 2003 in part because the Democratic Republic of the Congo was unable to uphold basic law and order or protect its borders. And piracy along the eastern coast of Africa has increased over the last two decades since Somalia's collapse into anarchy.

These threats collectively take a massive human toll in the states directly affected. States grow poorer: "During civil war countries tend to grow around 2.2 percentage points more slowly than during peace," according to Paul Collier. Per capita incomes fall and production, including of food, declines. Instability causes capital flight: Citizens with means shift up to 10 percent of their private wealth abroad. It also causes the flight of human capital: The most educated and skilled citizens emigrate, leaving the country bereft of the talent it needs for reconstruction. And, of course, people who live in postconflict failed states are less healthy and educated, have fewer opportunities, and die younger. Infant mortality rises by an average of 13 percent during a civil war, an effect that lingers long after it ends.[59]

But failed states also pass costs on to their neighbors, the region, and even the entire world. Civil war and state failure typically cause neighboring states to increase spending on defense as a precaution, which can trigger a regional arms race while decreasing resources available for social welfare and investment. War itself is infectious: Instability in one country is an ideal condition for marginalized groups from a neighboring country to take refuge and launch their own insurgency. Refugees from failed states are a considerable economic cost on neighbors, more so if they are carrying infectious diseases such as HIV/AIDS, as they often are. State failure disrupts cross-border trade in the region, which can be a major economic burden because most countries' largest trading partners are their immediate neighbors. Citizens of failed states buy fewer goods, produce less for the world economy, create no businesses, and invent no products, but they have more opportunities to contribute to crime and political violence that crosses borders.[60]

Failed states are sinkholes in the world. They contribute nothing good and actively detract value from the region, much as a condemned building used by criminals spreads blight and drags down home values throughout a neighborhood. Multiplied several times over in all the states now failing from one cause or another in nearly every region, failed states present a systemic risk to liberal order, of which the United States was the principle architect and beneficiary. That is why state failure is a national security problem to be taken seriously in Washington. The threats emanating from failed states are likely to spill over international boundaries more frequently because globalization has reduced states' insularity from each other. The twenty-first century is likely to see a steady increase in cross-border low-intensity conflict, transnational drug and human trafficking, piracy, international refugee flows, pandemic disease, environmental disaster, and terrorism.

The Transnational Jihadist Insurgency

The third major threat to the United States in the twenty-first century is what David Kilcullen has called the jihadist insurgency: an effort to eject the "West" from "Muslim lands," overthrow secular governments, replace them with jihadist regimes, and eventually establish the supremacy of their brand of Islam across the world. Jihadist groups are distinct from armed nonstate actors. They are a transnational network, tied together by a visionary ideology and backed by some state and quasi-state actors, and thus they are a fundamentally different kind of threat than pirates or drug traffickers.

Jihadist Ideology

The war against jihadist groups is not a war against Islam. It is tiresome to say so because that statement is so obviously true, but it is also so often misunderstood. Scholars and policymakers who hasten to distance Islam from terrorism often wind up making the opposite mistake and by arguing that Islam has *nothing to do* with jihadist terrorism. That is obviously nonsense.[61]

Jihadists use Islamic rhetoric, symbols, and concepts in the construction of their ideology. They endlessly debate fine intricacies of Islamic theology. They direct their arguments at Muslim audiences and seek new recruits from among Muslims. They invoke the Koran, quote the hadiths of Muhammad, and find bases for their beliefs in the jurisprudence of Islamic law. They themselves claim to be Muslims—indeed, the only true Muslims—and they explicitly claim that their religion motivates, inspires, and even commands them to commit their horrific acts of violence. *They* believe that Islam has a great deal to do with their behavior. Some scholars have argued that the clash between rival interpretations of Islam should be seen as a civil war within the Islamic world—jihadists, Islamists, traditionalists, and reformers all attempting to pull Islam in different directions—in which case jihadism has a strong, complicated, and important relationship to Islam and its future.

Scholars and policymakers sometimes evade these awkward facts by arguing that jihadists' religious claims are either false or irrelevant. The first evasion is irrelevant; the second is false. The falsity of jihadist theology has absolutely no bearing on its existence as a hostile ideology fervently believed in by thousands of well-armed people who wish to harm the United States and its allies. Its theological status does not change the threat it poses or, necessarily, its ability to find more recruits from within the Islamic world. And jihadist religious claims are certainly relevant. Success in war depends on knowing your enemy. Social scientists who dismiss the religious claims of jihadists, treating religion as epiphenomenal to some other, deeper cause, betray a materialist, secularist bias and do not help us understand our enemy. The secularist view—that jihadism is the product of frustrated rational actors lashing out at their disempowerment in corrupt, poor, repressive societies left behind by globalizing modernity[62]—is true but incomplete, the shallow understanding of secular modernity unable to come to grips with the enduring power of religious identities.

Religion powerfully intermixes with politics in all societies in the world, including the United States—whether it is the religion of Christianity or the religion of Enlightenment secularism. That Islam has become entwined with the politics of countries in which it predominates is unsurprising and, naturally, has given rise to attempts to construct a coherent political ideology along Islamic lines—what is broadly called "Islamism." The term is best understood as the transmutation of Islam into a political ideology. Bassam Tibi has argued that "Islamism grows out of a specific interpretation of Islam, but it is not Islam: it is a political ideology that is distinct from the teaching of Islam."[63] Much as the American founders claimed that civic republicanism was a natural consequence of Protestantism, similarly many Muslims are grappling with the question of what politics flows most naturally from their faith. As such, Islamism is not necessarily violent or, always, opposed to majoritarian rule, representative institutions, or elections (though Tibi believes it is). Probably the best example of a peaceful Islamist movement is Tunisia's Ennhada Party, which briefly held power after the Arab Spring and peacefully conceded defeat in elections in October 2014. Turkey's Justice and Development Party is a slighter version of a peaceful Islamist movement, though its commitment to political liberalism has been cast in doubt the longer it has held power. Egypt was briefly ruled by the Muslim Brotherhood before the 2013 military coup. Islamist governments are illiberal—they tend to be hostile to religious freedom and women's rights—and thus cannot be included in the ranks of reliable democratic partners in a global liberal order. But neither are they necessarily threats to US national security.

Jihadism is a variant of Islamism. It is the effort to impose Islamist goals—however defined—by force. Jihadists have invented theological justifications to attack their enemies, mostly fellow Muslims, for their impiety or disloyalty to the jihadist cause, leading to the rise of jihadist terrorist and insurgent groups and, occasionally, jihadist governments (including the Taliban in the 1990s and the Iranian regime) and state-like entities (such as ISIS and some organizations within Pakistan). Jihadist movements are threats to the national security of states they seek to overthrow, many of which are US allies; they are also threats to their neighbors because of the expansionist drive inherent in jihadist ideology. Jihadist ideology ultimately seeks the dominance of its brand of Islam over the world (a goal shared by some of the more expansionist versions of Islamism).[64] While individual jihadist groups typically are not focused primarily on *global* jihadist revolution—working rather for local revolutions—the global vision inherent in their ideology means that local jihadist groups naturally see affinities with related groups around the world and understand them to be working for the same broad goal, even when they may disagree on priorities, targets, and tactics. Further, local jihadist groups will often trade information, successful tactics and techniques (the insurgencies in Iraq and Afghanistan learned from one another), and rhetorical support and will offer safe haven and training to each other. In Pakistan, where multiple jihadist groups overlap and conjoin, they sometimes cooperate on specific tactical operations. That is why it is coherent to speak of one "transnational jihadist insurgency" made up of disparate, fragmented groups.

Jihadist Organization

Jihadist movements are threats to US national security because of their open hostility to the United States and its allies, totalitarian and illiberal beliefs, commitment to violent revolution, and global ambition. A few have attempted to attack the United States directly, including al-Qaida and the Pakistani Taliban; many more have targeted US soldiers deployed abroad and US allies and partners around the world. All are threats to liberal order. They cause instability, political violence, state failure, organized crime, and economic backsliding across the Middle East, South Asia, and parts of Africa. Contrary to the claims of some scholars, they are much more than a mere terrorist threat.[65] Recognizing the threat from jihadist movements comes with important caveats. They are not monolithic: There are myriad internal divisions, including between Sunni and Shi'ite; Arab, Iranian, and South Asian variants; and groups with global versus local focus. In addition, I do not mean to equate jihadist movements with al-Qaida or ISIS. Jihadist movements were born at least as far back as Egypt's Muslim Brotherhood in 1928, slowly gathered steam with the failure of Arab nationalism and socialism from the 1950s through the 1970s, and came to international attention through the Islamic revolution in Iran and the Soviet–Afghan War. America's War on Terror is a brief chapter in that longer story; jihadist movements will long outlast al-Qaida and ISIS, and they will continue to pose a threat to America and, probably more so, to its allies for the foreseeable future.

Many analysts only note the threat from the original core of al-Qaida and repeat the Obama administration's disingenuous claim that the organization is near defeat. The claim is wrong, but even if it were true, it would be irrelevant. A global network of jihadist movements, of which al-Qaida was only the most famous, share a deeply rooted religiously inspired ideology that is hostile to the United States, its ideals, and its way of life. Their victory anywhere would give fellow jihadists safe haven, while their victory in Pakistan, with its nuclear weapons, or in Saudi Arabia, with its oil wealth, would be a major threat to US national security and world order. And some jihadist movements have, of course, directly targeted the United States and its allies in dozens of attacks and attempted attacks over the last decade.

The jihadist movements are not made up of a single institution or group with formal membership. Rather, they are a menagerie of terrorist groups, insurgencies, and state institutions motivated by a broadly common ideology and shared vision. The movement also includes Pakistani groups such as Lashkar-e-Taiba, Jaish-e-Mohammad, and Tehrik-e-Taliban Pakistan; Afghan groups such as the Taliban and the Haqqani Network; Middle Eastern groups such as ISIS, al-Qaida in the Arabian Peninsula (AQAP), and Hamas; African groups such as al-Qaida in the Islamic Maghreb (AQIM), Boko Haram, and al-Shabaab; and Iran's proxy, Hezbollah. Jihadism appears to be growing. The number of jihadist groups, the number of jihadist fighters, and the number of jihadist attacks all increased substantially in recent years, according to a RAND Corporation report. The number of jihadist groups increased by 58 percent since 2010, the number of fighters more than doubled in the same time frame, and attacks increased nearly tenfold since 2008.[66] As of this writing, jihadist groups appear to be stronger and more widely spread than at any point since before 2001.

In addition to these nonstate actors, the jihadist movement also includes the IRGC—especially its Quds Force—and probably some portions of Pakistan's agency Inter-Services Intelligence (ISI), powerful nodes in the jihadist network. Many groups get funding from wealthy Middle Eastern elites who occupy a quasi-official role as deniable funnels of cash from the oil sheikdoms to jihadist groups. These disparate groups sometimes coordinate at the tactical level for individual operations but do not take orders from a single, unified hierarchy. Bin Laden was not the Lenin of a proto-jihadist superstate; he was more akin to Che Guevara, a popular icon who inspired more movements in his wake.[67]

The only thing comparable during the Cold War to the global proliferation of jihadist groups was the Soviet Union's sponsorship of communist insurgencies around the world. But the jihadist movements are likely to be more resilient, harder to defeat, and more dangerous because they are decentralized; because their ideology is not linked to the fate of one particular regime; because they believe death will only bring them greater reward; because much of their funding comes indirectly from oil wealth, demand for which will probably prove more durable than the Soviet Union; because globalization has made it easier for them to operate on a global scale; and because of the higher risk that jihadists will acquire and use weapons of mass destruction since they are not accountable to a deterrable sponsoring power.

Conclusion

Tyrants with nukes and barbarians and jihadists at the gates: The world remains a dangerous place. In the next chapters, I outline the courses of action the United States has followed and should continue to follow to address great powers and armed nonstate groups. Chapter 4 reviews two key concepts— the balance of power and the democratic peace—as complementary courses of action against great powers. Chapter 5 reviews the relationship between kinetic operations against armed nonstate groups and stability operations to redress the conditions of state failure in which such groups grow and operate.

Notes

1. "Defense Secretary Panetta Warns Automatic Spending Cuts Could Mean Furlough," PBS Newshour, February 20, 2013; Jack Moore, "Clapper: Sequestration 'Quite Damaging' to National Intelligence," Federal News Radio, February 15, 2013.
2. Office of the Director of National Intelligence, *Worldwide Threat Assessment*.
3. Walt, *Origins of Alliances*, chap. 2.
4. *Juche* is North Korea's official ideology of "self-reliance," which blends Korean nationalism with elements of Marxism-Leninism.
5. Smith, *Utility of Force*; Van Creveld, *Transformation of War*; Kaldor, *New and Old Wars*; Thompson, *Armed Groups*; Odierno, "U.S. Army in Time of Transition"; McKinney, Elfendahl, and McMaster, "Why the U.S. Army Needs Armor."
6. The most recent formulation is in Posen, *Restraint*.
7. Art, "Defensible Defense," 9.
8. Daniel Wiser, "Putin Touts 'Peak' for Russia–China Relations as Two Countries Develop Military, Economic Ties," *Washington Free Beacon*, September 2, 2015, http://freebeacon.com/national-security/putin-touts-peak-for-russia-china -relations-as-two-countries-develop-military-economic-ties/.
9. Menon, "Limits of Chinese-Russian Partnership."
10. Correlates of War v 4.0. See Singer, "Reconstructing the Correlates of War Dataset," for background on the project.
11. I do not argue that all autocratic governments are inevitably hostile to the United States. I reject the notion that liberalism must "extirpate hostile ideologies abroad" to be safe, as Layne claims (*Peace of Illusions*, 120).

12. Smith, *Utility of Force*; Van Creveld, *Transformation of War*; Kaldor, *New and Old Wars*.

13. Ikenberry, *Liberal Leviathan*, 222.

14. Mueller, *Retreat from Doomsday*. See also Forsberg, "Toward the End of War."

15. Art and Waltz, *Use of Force*.

16. Niebuhr, *Children of Light*, 11, 18, and *Irony of American History*, 173. Niebuhr's Christian Realism, as a species of *human nature realism*, has better and more profound resources to criticize the naiveté of liberalism than the structural and neostructural realism dominant in the academy today.

17. Plato didn't say anything of the sort. This is one of those famous apocryphal quotations invented by contemporaries and put into the mouths of ancients to borrow their intellectual authority.

18. See Kupchan, *End of the American Era*, and Mearsheimer, *Tragedy of Great Power Politics*, for longer treatments of this argument, though both err in different ways. Kupchan rightly argues that great power rivalry will resume but then oddly argues that it would be "healthy for America to lighten its load and step back from at least some of the onerous international responsibilities of the last six decades" (p. 33). It is unclear why, if the former is true, America can afford to do the latter. Mearsheimer attributes to *all* states at *all* times the same offensive realist drive to maximize power that is almost certainly true only of some states under certain conditions.

19. Both Posen and Layne argue that Russia's and China's behavior should be understood as balancing.

20. MacMillan, *Rhyme of History*, and Ferguson, "Sinking Globalization," explore ways today's world could rapidly unravel as it did a century ago.

21. On Russia's partial and ultimately failed transition to democracy, see Mendelson, "Democracy Assistance and Political Transition" and "Russians' Rights Imperiled."

22. Rumer and Stent, "Russia and the West."

23. Galeotti and Bowen, "Putin's Empire of the Mind"; Barbashin and Thoburn, "Putin's Brain." Russian messianic pretension predates Putin. Kissinger wrote in 1994 that "analysts frequently explain Russian expansionism as stemming from a sense of insecurity. But Russian writers have far more often justified Russia's outward thrust as a messianic vocation." See *Diplomacy*, 25.

24. Vladimir Isachenkov and Nataliya Vasilyeva, "Putin Defends Russian Conservative Values," Associated Press, December 12, 2013.

25. Putin, "Prepared Remarks at 43rd Munich Conference."

26. It was a naiveté I did not share. See Miller, "I Predicted Russia's Invasion of Ukraine," *Shadow Government* (blog), *ForeignPolicy.com*, March 7, 2014, http://foreignpolicy.com/2014/03/07/i-predicted-russias-invasion-of-ukraine/, and "Crimea Proves That Great Power Rivalry Never Left Us," *Shadow Government* (blog), *ForeignPolicy.com*, March 21, 2014, http://foreignpolicy.com/2014/03/21/crimea-proves-that-great-power-rivalry-never-left-us/. Nor was I the only one; see also Gray, "21st Century Security Environment," 21.

27. Gholz, Press, and Sapolsky, "Come Home, America," 18–19.
28. International Institute for Strategic Studies, *Military Balance*, chap. 5, esp. 225; Federation of American Scientists, "Status of World Nuclear Forces."
29. "Russia Restarts Cold War Patrols," BBC, August 17, 2007.
30. Graham, "Sources of Russia's Insecurity."
31. "Catching the Eagle," *Economist*, November 20, 2013.
32. "China to Open Its First Military Base Abroad in Indian Ocean," NDTV, December 12, 2011.
33. International Institute for Strategic Studies, *Military Balance*, chap. 6, esp. 252–58 and 286ff.
34. Mandiant Intelligence Center, "APT1"; "Second Chinese Military Unit Linked to Hacking," *CNN.com*, June 10, 2014.
35. "Beijing and Moscow Make the Case for Multi-Polar Global Solutions," *RT.com*, March 24, 2010; Teddy Ng, "China, France Stress a Multipolar World as Hollande visits Beijing," *South China Morning Post*, April 25, 2013; "Chinese President Calls for Multipolar World, Democratization of Int'l Relations," *Xinhua*, November 3, 2010; Yun Sen, "BRICS and China's Aspiration for the New 'International Order,'" *Brookings.edu*, March 25, 2013, http://www.brookings.edu/blogs/up-front/posts/2013/03/25-xi-jinping-china-brics-sun.
36. Office of the Secretary of Defense, *Military and Security Developments*, I.
37. Beckley, "China's Century?"
38. Economy, "Game Changer."
39. Fravel, "Power Shifts and Escalation."
40. International Institute for Strategic Studies, *Military Balance*, 216. North Korea has developed but not tested the KN-08 ICBM. A US general told the Senate Armed Services Committee in 2015 that he believed North Korea could hit the US homeland with a nuclear-armed ICBM, an assessment that does not seem to be widely shared by most defense analysts.
41. See, for example, Haqqani, *Pakistan*, and Abbass, *Pakistan's Drift*.
42. Posen, *Restraint*, 79.
43. Raviv and Melman, *Spies against Armageddon*.
44. Farwell and Rohozinski, "Stuxnet and Future of Cyber War."
45. See Kroenig, "Time to Attack Iran," for a discussion of possible scenarios.
46. Art, "Defensible Defense," 25. See also Waltz and Sagan, "Spread of Nuclear Weapons."
47. Art, "Defensible Defense," 27.
48. International Institute for Strategic Studies, *Military Balance*, 216.
49. Ochmanek and Schwartz, *Challenge of Nuclear-Armed Regional Adversaries*.
50. Ulrich Schneckener, "Fragile Statehood, Armed Non-State Actors and Security Governance" in Bryden and Caparini, *Private Actors and Security Governance*; Mandel, *Global Security Upheaval*; Mulaj, *Violent Non-State Actors*; Thompson, *Armed Groups*; Shultz and Dew, *Insurgents, Terrorists, and Militias*.
51. Frederick W. Smullen, "New Threats, New Thinking," in Franke and Dorff, *Conflict Management and Peacebuilding*.

52. Oceans beyond Piracy, "Economic Cost of Somali Piracy 2011."

53. UN Office on Drugs and Crime, *World Drug Report 2010*, 16, 35. Most marijuana and amphetamines are produced and consumed locally, which requires fewer resources for smuggling and thus smaller and less militarized criminal gangs.

54. Transparency International, *Corruption Perceptions Index, 2014*.

55. UN Office on Drugs and Crime, *World Drug Report 2010*, 16.

56. Ibid., 35; UN Office on Drugs and Crime, *Global Report on Trafficking in Persons*.

57. This section is adapted from Miller, "Case for Nation-Building." Used with permission.

58. Simons and Tucker, "Misleading Problem of Failed States"; Hehir, "Myth of the Failed State."

59. Collier, *Breaking the Conflict Trap*.

60. Ibid., chap. 2.

61. For overviews of jihadism, Islamism, and Islam, see Tibi, *Islamism and Islam*; Habeck, *Knowing the Enemy*; and Benjamin and Simon, *Age of Sacred Terror*.

62. Pape, *Dying to Win*.

63. Tibi, *Islamism and Islam*, 1.

64. For example, Abul A'la Maududi, a Pakistani intellectual and founder of its Jamaat-i Islami political party, wrote, "The objective of Islamic jihad is to eliminate the rule of a non-Islamic system and establish in its stead an Islamic system of state rule. Islam does not intend to confine this revolution to a single State or a few countries; the aim of Islam is to bring about a universal revolution. . . . The goal of such an all-embracing doctrine is naturally bound to be world revolution." See Laqueur, *Voices of Terror*, 398. Maududi's writings are widely influential in Islamist and jihadist circles.

65. Robert Art dismisses the rise of "Islamic fundamentalism" as an important feature of the security environment, independent of its impact on terrorism. See *A Grand Strategy for America*, 38.

66. Jones, *Persistent Threat*, x, 35.

67. In this analogy, thinkers such as Sayed Qutb and Hassan al-Banna played Karl Marx's role in developing Islamist ideology. Ayatollah Khomeini aspired to be the Lenin of the Shia world, while the "caliph" of ISIS is auditioning for the same role among Sunnis.

PART II

STRATEGIC COURSES OF ACTION

4

The Balance of Power and the Democratic Peace

American policymakers have consistently used liberalism as a tool against the great powers. They believed it helped distinguish rivals from allies, spread the democratic peace, and altered the balance of power in America's favor. But are they right? A critic may question why the United States should balance only against the autocratic great powers, such as Russia and China, and not emerging democratic ones, including India and Brazil; why economic liberalism is relevant; or why the United States should invest in international institutions such as the UN and NATO.

Why is liberalism the feature that defines who "we" are and whom we balance *against*? The United States does not have an established alliance with the emerging democratic great powers and, in the case of India, had nearer the opposite. US–Indian relations during the Cold War were cold and aloof, bordering on outright rivalry. In the structural realist's view, domestic politics and ideology do not affect state behavior, and alliances are formed on the basis of interest, not belief. If that is true, India's rise to power could be seen as a potential threat equal to China's, and a grand strategy premised on partnering with democracies against autocracies is dangerously naive and moralistic. In this chapter, I argue that while realists are right to highlight the irreducibly important role of power in international affairs, liberal internationalists are right to highlight how norms, especially liberal norms, shape the environment in which power is exercised. The United States must balance power *and* champion liberalism as mutually reinforcing components of its grand strategy.

The Insights of Realism

After the Cold War, realists such as Kenneth Waltz and John Mearsheimer argued that the collapse of the Soviet Union would usher in great power

rivalry—including among democratic powers—the end of NATO, and instability in Europe. They argued that economic integration would not halt great
power rivalry: It had not prevented World War I despite the European economies being *more* integrated then than the world economy is today. They
argued that nationalism was far more important than democracy in shaping
international behavior. And they discounted the importance of international
institutions, claiming that the underlying distribution of power was the only
relevant variable and that whatever effect institutions appeared to have in
moderating state behavior was better explained as a function of the power
dynamics working through institutions.[1]

Their predictions have proven partly true. Russia's and China's consistent
diplomatic opposition to the United States and their military modernization are forms of balancing, as was North Korea's and Pakistan's development
of nuclear weapons (and Iran's attempt to do the same). Nor should this be
surprising: Realists' predictions were partly right because their underlying
theories about states and human nature are partly true. States jealous of their
sovereignty with no recourse to higher authority must rely on their own
efforts to check others' power and ensure their own safety.[2] Realists rightly see
"no possibility of a genuine unity of the nations," as Niebuhr put it, and therefore seek "to construct the most adequate possible mechanism for equilibrat-
ing power on a world scale." This balance of power "can undoubtedly mitigate
anarchy."[3] In a world of angels, realism would be wicked for its cynicism. In a
world of human beings, it is simply prudent.

The realist scholars were right that the Cold War was simply another
phase in the perennial contest for power and influence among great powers.
The end of the Cold War marked the end of one state (the Soviet Union),
not the system of rivalry itself. States are still states, and they are, and always
have been, primarily driven by their pursuit of "interest defined in terms of
power,"[4] because it is the best guarantee of survival in an anarchical system.
That is why the post–Cold War era shows some remarkable continuity not
only with its predecessor, but also with eras even further removed. Now an
era of multipolarity seems to be dawning in which possessing nuclear weapons buys automatic entrance into the club of great powers.

The basic insight of realism means that if American statesmen want to
get anything done, they must use the means prescribed by realists. As Henry
Kissinger put it, "the pretensions of the most aggressive member of the international community are kept in check by a combination of the others; in
other words, by the operation of the balance of power."[5] If in war there is no
substitute for victory, in grand strategy there is no substitute for power. Power
is the lifeblood of politics, and much of it (though not all) does indeed flow
from the barrel of a gun. The United States should certainly remain engaged

in international institutions and diplomatic negotiations. But it will find itself more successful the more powerful it is.

The Weaknesses of Realism

But the realist vision had clear flaws. Some of its predictions were simply wrong. NATO did not collapse; it expanded. Instability did not return to Europe—at least, not among the democratic powers. The incident most likely to trigger instability among Europe's democratic powers—German reunification—came and went. Japan and India did not emerge as threats or security rivals to the West. States' continued devotion to international institutions— NATO expanded from sixteen to twenty-eight members, the EU from twelve to twenty-eight; the World Trade Organization (WTO) was formed in 1995, the Organization for the Prohibition of Chemical Weapons in 1997, the International Criminal Court in 2002—suggested they valued such institutions more than realists expected them to. Even China's rise could be read as confirming liberal expectations because China has, so far, worked to gain influence in the existing regime of institutions (it joined the WTO in 2001) rather than to replace them, and its rise has so far not been the occasion for war. In this interpretation, the allure of wealth afforded by economic liberalism has, so far, blunted any aggressive or militaristic aspects of China's rise. These developments suggest that realists overstate their argument (e.g., by arguing that "*the* defining element of the global system is the distribution of power, not democracy, culture, globalization, or anything else"[6]) and seems to validate at least part of the liberal internationalist vision. Realists generally avoid attaching timelines to their predictions, which make their claims inherently nonfalsifiable. They can always claim that the breakdown of the democratic peace is just around the corner. But a quarter-century after the end of the Cold War, the statute of limitations has run out. Structural realists' insistence that they will be proven right, someday, is simply unpersuasive.

Second, realism attempts to offer a dispassionate, amoral view of the world and shrugs off ethical thinking as an irrelevant, dispensable luxury— or, worse, dangerous foolishness. This is one of the reasons that pure realism is typically confined to the academy and rarely has influence, in its most dogmatic forms, among policymakers.[7] Policymakers are human beings who have convictions, or at least instincts, about right and wrong. Charles Hill rightly argued, "A purely rational or technocratic approach" to grand strategy "is likely to lead one astray"; one needs "literary insight," or, in other words, a grasp of the "inchoate aspects of affairs within and between states."[8] One scholar tentatively suggested that policymakers "may actually share" the beliefs and "cultural preferences" of their constituents and that "to a greater extent than is generally recognized by international relations theorists, the cultural assumptions voiced by elite foreign policy officials may be internalized and genuine."[9] That this rather obvious insight is at all contested speaks volumes about the gap that still separates most scholars from the White House Situation Room. While policymakers may prove flexible in how they adapt their moral compass to the needs of the moment, they rarely practice the art of completely severing their moral instincts from public acts. The most senior policymakers are politicians who understand that the American public expects some sort of moral foundation to public policy, even if inarticulately expressed. Realism is strikingly unrealistic in its expectation of amoral policymakers; this is one aspect of human nature they badly misjudge. Scholars who wish to bridge the divide that so often exists between the academy and the policymaker must be comfortable articulating the moral instincts of actual human beings. As Niebuhr rightly said, "men and nations must use their power with the purpose of making it an instrument of justice and a servant of interests broader than their own."[10] The intuitive moral appeal of liberal internationalism may explain why US policymakers seem to have been drawn to variants of it more than to realism.

Even in balancing power, the United States should still strive for some kind of fairness in world order. "A stable order is not possible without introducing instruments of justice into the agreements which are to provide for order," Niebuhr argued, because "an unjust order quickly invites the resentment and rebellion which lead to its undoing," which is why "mere equilibrium between [the great powers] will not suffice to preserve the peace." Niebuhr's concern for justice is what sets Niebuhr apart from conventional realists and why he called himself a Christian Realist. Many realists are fond of borrowing Niebuhr's moral credibility for their policies, but Niebuhr also cautioned, "A purely realistic approach to the problem of world community offers as little hope of escape from anarchy as a purely idealistic one."[11]

The same point can be put more pragmatically. Realists are shortsighted because they neglect the importance of liberal order—the dominance of liberal norms in the "milieu," or international social order—to American security. As Tony Smith argued, "realism has absolved itself of the need to investigate the historically constructed definition of national security, growing out of a country's cultural, economic, social, and political interests."[12] Realists believe that building a fair and just world order and serving "interests broader than their own" is a waste of resources. But working toward fairness has practical benefits: It upkeeps the health and viability of world order, maintains buy-in from states who consent to that order, and, perhaps, could even mollify states who might otherwise feel the order is unjust or marginalizes them. Realists may not care about morality, but states do, and reaching an accommodation with other great powers means, in part, compromising with their perceptions of what is just. Niebuhr, again, warns against the self-defeating "'realism' of those who are myopically realistic by seeing only their own interests and failing thereby to do justice to their interests where they are involved with the interests of others." Such realists "counsel the nation to consult only its own interests." But, he warns, "a consistent self-interest on the part of a nation will work against its interests, because it will fail to do justice to the broader and longer interests, which are involved with the interests of other nations. A narrow national loyalty on our part, for instance, will obscure our long range interests where they are involved with those of a whole alliance of free nations."[13] The best understanding of the "national interest" takes into account the broader world in which the nation is situated.

Third, the structural realist case is obtuse for ignoring the role of ideology in constructing threat perceptions, to the point that many realists have abandoned the idea altogether.[14] Stephen Walt, a prominent international relations scholar and self-proclaimed realist, rightly noted decades ago that states do not balance against raw power, but against power that they perceive to be threatening. Threat, in turn, is composed in part of a state's perceived intentions: States that the United States believes have an intention to harm it are threats; those that lack hostile intent are not.[15] This is a classic case of scholarship confirming common sense. As John Owen has explained, "people perceive their material environment through 'lenses,' formed by the ideas they hold, that give that environment meaning. The lenses, and thus the meaning assigned to the material environment, vary according to the ideas held by the subject."[16] The United Kingdom is one of the most powerful states in the world today, with one of the richest economies and most sophisticated technological industrial bases, a blue-water navy, nuclear weapons, and an expeditionary military capability. Yet US policymakers have not seen a need to balance against it since the Treaty of Washington (1871) because Americans rightly believe the United Kingdom does not have hostile intentions toward the United States.

Policymakers understand ideological solidarity to be a signal for friendly intent and thus common interests. "Liberals view foreign states with prejudice," according to Owen. They believe "liberal states are safe and illiberal states potentially dangerous."[17] Policymakers believe power is threatening or nonthreatening depending on whether they believe it is rightly or wrongly wielded—that is, according to the ideology that governs its exercise. Illegitimate power is threatening, while legitimate power is safe. Policymakers' definition of what counts as an "interest" or what constitutes a "threat" is itself partly shaped by ideology. Even Layne, who thinks policymakers are foolish for doing so, agrees: "Liberal ideology shapes both the way policymakers define US interests and their perception of threats to those interests."[18] He argues that liberals' prejudices are mistaken, but he overlooks that the prejudices help create the reality on which they are based. "Liberals believe them to be true, and therefore they act as though they were true," according to Owen.[19] Democracies do not fight each other in part because they see the world in similar ways, define their interests similarly, and apply their domestic norms of peaceful dispute resolution to international relations between democracies.[20] (Nor is this a sleight of hand. I discuss below other reasons why the democratic peace works.)

American policymakers thus believe, with good reason, that Indian power is in the safe, legitimate, just hands of the democratically elected Indian government, while Chinese power is in the untrustworthy hands of an unaccountable dictatorship. That is why American policymakers understand Indian power to be safer than Chinese and why they should seek to partner with India but balance against China—and also why US policymakers respond differently to India's nuclear program than to Iran's.[21] Nor is this a uniquely American or democratic inclination: Many regime types tend to promote their own system of government and ideology to increase their influence in other states. Catholic and Protestant powers did so during the Wars of Religion, as did France during the Napoleonic Wars, the Soviet Union in Eastern Europe after World War II, and as Iran has attempted to do so in its neighborhood since 1979—long before the United States and UN undertook democratic peace-building in the post–Cold War era to spread global liberalism.[22]

The Insights of Liberal Internationalism

In response to the weaknesses of realism, liberal internationalists, led by G. John Ikenberry, argued that liberal order would be sustained by the growth of international institutions, global norms, and the spread of democracy.[23] In this view, the liberal international order would prove too alluring for up-and-comers such as China to challenge. Instead of working against the system, outside powers would be co-opted by it and gradually modify their behavior to conform to norms of international conduct. Liberal internationalism argued that norms and institutions would thus end the era of power politics permanently, make power-balancing irrelevant, and replace it with an increasingly dense network of interconnectedness. They are apt to see the post–Cold War world as remarkably consistent with their expectations: "Coercive domination and realpolitik behavior have their limits and liabilities in a world of democracies."[24]

Political liberalism is clearly relevant to US national security. Established liberal free-market democracies rarely, if ever, fight one another. They instigate fewer militarized crises against fellow democracies and are more prone to resolve them through peaceful adjudication when they do. The more democratic states there are, the fewer there are that could become enemies of the United States. In addition, democracies are less likely to use violence against their own people and therefore are less likely to draw in outside intervention. They rarely, if ever, sponsor international terrorism. Free-market regimes have better long-run economic prospects, rarely experience famine, and produce fewer refugees than nondemocracies, which means they require less international aid, are more likely to trade with and invest in the United States, and are more likely to become centers of innovation and productivity.[25] They are more prone to accede to international agreements and stick to them—they have "contracting advantages"—because of domestic political norms that they transplant to relations among each other.[26]

Scholars have offered a range of reasons why democracies behave differently, which collectively suggest the benefits of democracy are not ephemeral accidents but permanent features of this form of government. Citizens of democracies believe they share values with other democracies and thus are slower to see other democracies as potential enemies or combatants. Democracy enforces peaceful dispute resolution domestically, a norm that democratic leaders simply apply to the international arena, especially in disputes with other democracies. Institutional considerations are also relevant. Democracies typically constrain the government's war powers through civilian control and checks and balances, making it harder to launch a war. The public, which pays the cost of war, is likely to be more selective about the wars it chooses to fight when given the choice. And democracies are unable to control information about themselves because of the freedoms of speech and press, which decreases misperceptions that could lead to war and, in a militarized dispute, improves the credibility of a democracy's military threats and decreases opponents' willingness to gamble on war.[27]

Economic liberalism is also relevant to US national security, although for a different reason than traditionally advanced. The traditional case is similar to the democratic peace theory: Some have called it the capitalist peace or the commercial peace. States enriched by open trade and globalizing economic forces will be unwilling to risk war, isolation, and impoverishment. Some thinkers have argued that liberal economic arrangements will help gradually liberalize autocratic regimes by growing a middle class that will push for greater freedom,[28] although China's rise seems to undermine that theory.[29] At least as far back as Alexis de Tocqueville, thinkers have speculated that entrepreneurship tames aggression by redirecting people's ambitions into trade instead of war. This, I think, is wrong: Realists are right to point out that economic interdependence did not stop the slide to war in 1914.

But the spread of economic liberalism is useful for US national security for two other reasons. First, it enriches liberal democracies, increasing the proportion of global wealth under democratic control. While illiberal regimes also grow richer, there is good reason to believe that over the long run, growth in liberal regimes—with their commitments to the rule of law, transparency, and free-market competition—will be more deeply rooted, sustainable, and ultimately greater than, for example, the highly corrupt and inefficient state-directed crony corporatism of China. China's breakneck economic growth cannot be sustained and is almost certain to slow, or even reverse, in coming years.[30]

Second, economic liberalism is effectively history's greatest act of sabotage. Economic liberalism does not cause a gradual evolution toward democracy, as a previous generation of thinkers assumed. It causes massive social and cultural disruptions that can lead to civil unrest, rioting, strikes, polarization between newly empowered groups and threatened traditionalists—and, possibly, democracy at the far end of a very difficult process. There is nothing evolutionary about liberalism's effect on illiberal regimes.[31] By exporting economic liberalism to autocratic states, the United States is smuggling a time bomb into those societies that will cause domestic turmoil there for decades. China has so successfully unleashed the entrepreneurial talents of its people that it is now more preoccupied with keeping its grip on power over a society grappling with massive social dislocation than with plotting to overthrow American hegemony. There are risks to this approach—a government threatened by domestic turmoil might deliberately provoke international conflict to stoke nationalist loyalty—that highlights the need for cautious power-balancing and the promotion of *political* liberalism alongside its economic counterpart.

A final strength of liberal internationalism is its grasp of the importance of the international milieu to American security. It does a much better job explaining how and why the United States should invest in liberal order. "A milieu-oriented grand strategy is one in which a great power seeks to make the international environment congenial to its long-term security and interests through building the infrastructure of international cooperation, promoting trade and democracy in various regions of the world, and establishing partnerships," according to Ikenberry.[32] Liberal internationalists have over-emphasized the importance of international institutions to world order. All else equal, it is useful to have an array of institutions, such as the UN, the World Bank, the International Monetary Fund, and the World Health Organization, to host global discussions on issues of common concern, establish common technical standards, establish expectations and norms, increase the transparency over and the predictability of international conduct, enable international cooperation, and generate and exchange information.[33] Because realists are right that the United States is not omnipotent and must recognize its limits, there is every reason for the United States to participate in international institutions, benefit from others' cooperation, and gain the marginal benefit they afford. But liberal order is more than institutions and is most deeply rooted in the norms and ideologies that undergird them.

Liberal internationalists are strong where realists are weak—they understand the importance of democracy, free markets, and international institutions, and they are right to retain some sense of moral purpose to US foreign policy. As an ideology, liberalism is more universal than ideologies based on race, class, religious sect, language, or any other particular characteristic, making it uniquely suited to a world order of sovereign and equal states. It is also less prone to provoke resentment or backlash than explicitly imperialistic ideologies, resting as it does on the notion of equality before law, making American leadership more acceptable and durable than, for example, Soviet, Nazi, or British imperialist leadership. It is more easily mediated by rule-based, impartial institutions, making a liberal regime more predictable and consistent. It has proven capable of reforming itself and inspiring later generations of liberals to improve on and correct the abuses and hypocrisies of their forbearers. A grand strategy that includes promoting the liberal democratic peace has much to say for it.

The Weaknesses of Liberal Internationalism

Nonetheless, liberal internationalism has some clear weaknesses. As noted above, the end of the Cold War did not end great power rivalry. Liberal internationalists wrongly claimed, "It is now generally understood that the current grand strategy of deep engagement runs no risk of generating 'hard' counterbalancing."[34] The evidence says otherwise: Russia, China, and others *are* working to balance against the United States, having adopted "countervailing strategies" against US power that include the "soft balancing" of diplomatic resistance, hard balancing of military modernization and buildup, internal balancing of economic reform, and nuclear proliferation.[35] Ikenberry's repeated claim that states "have not responded to unipolarity with clear and determined efforts to balance against the United States" is false.

Some of the more strident liberal pronouncements—that war was obsolete or that history had ended, that "war-driven change is removed as a historical process"[36]—seemed naive even before Russia's invasion of Ukraine. Liberal internationalists overstated their argument when they claimed the rules of the game had changed for *everyone*, not just for democratic powers—probably because they overemphasized the importance of institutions and trade and underemphasized the importance of democratic norms, which are far less universally accepted. Contrary to their expectations, the "inside order" of liberal hegemony did *not* become the "outside order" for the international system as a whole,[37] but only for an expanded community of newly democratized states. Liberal internationalists were thus also wrong that the fundamental dynamic among great powers had changed. International institutions are weaker than liberals hoped; the realities of power are more enduring than they wished.[38] Fostering trade and participating in international institutions is not enough to change the behavior of powerful autocracies hostile to liberal values. They may blunt the most overt forms of aggression, but they do not halt the pursuit of power. The United States can look forward to a world of deepening norms and institutions with Europe and Japan (and hopefully India); with Russia and China, it is business as usual—which means balance-of-power politics.[39] Liberal internationalism has insights to offer but clearly fails as a comprehensive paradigm.

Liberal internationalists also, at least initially, did not recognize the threat to liberal order that might arise from the United States itself. Because US policymakers believed in the immediate aftermath of the Cold War that the United States was a unipolar power unrivaled by any other state in any dimension of national power, they had fewer incentives to accept the limitations and restraints that came with participation in liberal institutions at the same time they believed they could pursue a greatly expanded set of interests.[40] As I argued above, these beliefs were unjustified, but to the extent US policymakers took action based on these beliefs, they harmed liberal order.

There are difficulties with economic liberalism as well. As noted above, the "capitalist peace" argument is almost certainly false. Beyond that, economic liberalization creates losers as well as winners—it spreads risk as well as wealth. Some have raised concerns that the ruthless and rapid moves of global markets could work against the United States and undermine its global economic leadership in hard times, but the United States' relative resilience in the aftermath of the 2008 financial crisis and the dollar's continued status as the world's reserve currency seems to provide grounds for confidence.[41] But there are other potential problems with economic liberalism. Rising income inequality and the enduring "digital divide" have fostered antagonism between the rich and poor. Globalization is not equal; it is clearly driven by the United States, Europe, and Japan, which gives other states reason to complain of being second-class citizens of the global order, even if they are growing richer. "Economic interdependence does promote shared interests, but it also creates shared vulnerabilities," as Charles Kupchan argues. "Whether interdependence breeds trust or instills resentment depends entirely upon the political context in which economic integration takes place." Globalization might provoke a backlash and "produce populist and statist regimes running on the fuel of economic nationalism and strategic rivalry."[42]

Some scholars have argued that there are related problems with political liberalism. While individual states might be democratic, the international system remains anarchic and ruled by power. The international community's undemocratic nature gives people and nations reason to continue to aspire for recognition, even if they live in democratic countries: "In the absence of a democratic international system that accords all nations the rights and status they seek, nationalism impels them to continue the struggle for recognition, thus serving as an endemic source of competition." That is why, in the view of some realists, "nationalism could counter, if not overwhelm, a democratic peace."[43] I find this unpersuasive. The notion of a united and democratic Europe, or a democratic Japan or India, declaring war on the United States over a trade dispute or, worse, a matter of nationalistic honor, is too fanciful to be relevant for US grand strategy. A more cogent critique is that the process of democratization is itself highly destabilizing and may even make regimes more warlike in the short run.[44] This does not challenge the *relevance* of liberalism to US national security but the possibility of its peaceful spread—which I address below.

Conservative Internationalism

The growth of democracy, free markets, and international institutions abroad alters the balance of power in the United States' favor. Tony Smith judges that "liberal democratic internationalism has been the American way of practicing balance-of-power politics in world affairs."[45] This is the key point that links US support for liberalism to vital US security interests and harmonizes the realist and liberal schools of thought in international relations scholarship. Liberalism is a weapon that advances US national security. When Gholz, Press, and Sapolsky argue that the United States has only "two tools with which to achieve" its goals—namely, "economic and military power"—they betray a shallow understanding of the tools of statecraft. Ideology is another highly potent tool of statecraft.[46] Liberalism creates a global milieu, a culture of world order favorable to US interests. Specifically, the spread of democracy grows new democratic allies for the United States. The first wave of democratization—in Western Europe in the late nineteenth century—converted the United States' original great power rivals, the United Kingdom and France, into allies during World War I. The democratization of postwar Germany and Japan during the Cold War achieved the same thing in the twentieth century. And the spread of democracy in Eastern Europe since the Cold War has again expanded the list of American allies, many of whom contributed to the multinational coalition against al-Qaida after 9/11. The spread of economic liberalism increases the world's wealth, especially the wealth available to liberal regimes. And the spread of liberal international institutions entrenches liberal norms and routinizes state behavior along liberal patterns. Robert Art is exactly right when he argues, "Morality aside, considerations of simple realpolitik dictate the spread of democracy."[47]

That is why scholar Henry Nau recommends what he calls *conservative internationalism*. Conservative internationalism, which he associates with the foreign policy of Harry Truman and Ronald Reagan, among others, attempts to blend the strengths of realism and liberal internationalism while avoiding their weaknesses. Like liberal internationalists, conservative internationalists see value in the spread of democracy around the world because it is an effective tool for changing the balance of power in America's favor. Like realists, conservative internationalists appreciate the enduring realities of power. They seek only incremental increases in liberalism in strategically important regions, do not put an excess of faith in international institutions, and believe military power is a vital component of successful diplomacy.[48] Tony Smith, in advocating a similar idea of "selective liberal internationalism," argues that its virtue lies in how "policymakers hold it to be in the United States' security interest for democracy to expand abroad, yet are aware that this country's power is too limited for it to promote such reforms imprudently."[49]

Nau identifies eleven tenets that collectively distinguish conservative internationalism from both realism and liberal internationalism.[50] First, akin to its liberal counterpart, "the main goal of conservative internationalist foreign policy is to expand freedom and ultimately increase the number of democratic, constitutional, and republican governments in the world." But, second, akin to realism, conservative internationalism focuses on material, not ideological, threats. Nau argues events abroad have to have (or threaten) a material effect on the United States to trigger an intervention. Third, tacking back toward liberalism, conservative internationalism does not merely seek a static balance of power; it seeks "incremental opportunities to expand freedom" or a "balance of power tilted toward freedom." Fourth, leavening such aspirations with a dose of realism, it seeks such opportunities "primarily on the periphery or borders of existing free societies."

Fifth, conservative internationalism is more comfortable with the threat and use of force because it works in tandem with the other instruments of national power: "Force is not a 'last' resort that kicks in after diplomacy and economic sanctions fail; it is a 'parallel' resort that accompanies diplomacy at every turn." But, sixth, this school of thought will "give equal weight to force and diplomacy" because the latter is as important to winning the peace as the former is to winning a war. Seventh, conservative internationalism does not equate diplomacy with international and multilateral institutions, such as the UN.

Eighth, while conservative internationalism champions democracy, it also recognizes that "culture constrains democracy," and thus its growth is difficult and uncertain. That means, ninth, that the most effective tools for promoting its growth is "economic engagement or the free movement of goods, capital, and people" or, to put it another way, trade, not aid. But, tenth, that does not mean economic liberalization automatically yields political liberty: "Ideologies shape human behavior more deeply than material forces, and cultures do not disappear with prosperity." Finally, this school of thought accepts the primacy of American public opinion in determining the course of US foreign policy. This means conservative internationalists are mindful of public support for difficult and time-consuming efforts to spread freedom abroad.

Nau's construction of a school of thought that attempts to combine the strengths of liberalism and realism while avoiding their weaknesses is powerful and persuasive. I depart from Nau's framework in some areas. His first principle focuses on increasing the number of democratic states in the world. I suggest a slightly different formulation: The United States should seek to increase the proportion of global power under democratic control. The raw number of democratic states in the world does not matter, because some states matter more than others.

Nau is most concerned to foster democracy on the borders of existing free states because he believes that is where the spread of democracy is most important and most realistic, which leads to his view that the United States should be most concerned with shoring up democracy in Eastern Europe and East Asia and should not have invested its resources in trying to democratize Iraq or Afghanistan. Nau is being too geographically literal and arbitrary—even quixotic—to look for democratization only in areas that share land borders with existing democracies. Location is not (solely) what makes a state a strategically important partner: Size, resources, intellectual and human capital, relationship to its region, and other factors go into making up a state's potential usefulness to the United States. I use different criteria than Nau in determining where democratization is feasible and would most benefit the United States, and thus I am more willing than Nau to recommend US investment in democracy outside Europe and East Asia.

Nau is right that ideological factors are usually more deeply rooted than material ones, which makes his insistence that the United States wait until events abroad threaten a material harm to the United States until intervening is, in my view, unwarranted. Precisely because ideology is so important, I am readier to use it as a marker for potential future threats and am not as hesitant to recommend an intervention abroad. Winston Churchill recognized the threat of national socialism as early as he did precisely because he understood its ideology; he did *not* wait until Germany threatened material harm to the United Kingdom to warn of the dangers.

In addition, Nau's ninth and tenth points are contradictory. He is right that economic liberalization does not guarantee political liberty abroad; I doubt, then, that it is *the best* tool the United States has for championing liberalism. In fact, some foreign aid, such as the sort delivered through the Millennium Challenge Corporation (MCC, which gives aid to poor but democratic or democratizing countries that have designed their own economic development programs) or the National Endowment for Democracy (which seeks to build the "infrastructure of democracy," such as political parties and independent media), may be exactly the sort of aid that helps grow bureaucratic competence, civil society, and democratic habits but that cannot be supplied by trade agreements. And Nau's concerns that foreign aid could lead to welfare-state dependency is irrelevant. Much US foreign aid is not food aid or even economic aid—which perhaps could be better supplied through trade and private partnerships—but military aid, as the United States provides weapons and training to countries fighting terrorists, drug traffickers, and insurgents. Nau's argument is most apt when applied to *economic* assistance. Foreign aid is probably a more effective tool for both *governance* and *security* assistance than he gives it credit for.

Liberal internationalism is essentially a true description of the world that exists *among democratic states*. The democratic peace theory—that established democracies rarely, if ever, fight each other—is true, or true enough, to inform policymaking. Nau has gone beyond the democratic peace theory to talk of the "convergence" of democratic identities. In his view, the behavior of states is not determined solely by the distribution of power, but also the distribution of identity. The convergence of democratic identity across the world means that democratic states tend to see the world in similar terms and act on broadly similar agendas.[51] Another scholar has pointed out that because of "the limited time and information available to policymakers," they are forced "to rely not only upon broad cultural assumptions but also upon specific mental shortcuts or preconceived beliefs."[52] Liberalism is the best intellectual shortcut, an efficient "operational code," a mental map of world affairs that is simple but accurate enough to guide policymaking. Given scarce resources and time, it is an invaluable insight for policymakers to know that they do not have to worry about a potential war with India so long as it sustains its democratic heritage. Realists' disregard for states' forms of government led them to ignore the revolution wrought by the expansion of democracy around the world. They proved misguided in their analysis of NATO and sounded downright blinkered when they counseled caution toward democracies and autocracies alike: One characterized Japan as a "rival" to the United States equal to China,[53] while another warned of a rising and united Europe as a "counterweight" to the United States alongside Russia and China.[54] Yet another warned of the dangers of a rising India.[55] The realist map is distorted and a poor guide to navigating world politics. It is ironic that many realists who espouse variants of "restraint" or "retrenchment" are the very ones who have an unnecessarily expansive view of threats to the United States, needlessly warning about dangers from democratic great powers.

Promoting liberalism fits naturally with the need to balance against the nuclear autocracies. US grand strategy has long sought to prevent the rise of a hostile hegemon in strategically important areas of the world—especially Europe and East Asia—by maintaining a favorable balance of power through military strength and a network of allies. A commitment to liberalism is, in a sense, the corollary to resistance to hegemony. Liberalism is, at root, the diffusion of power among many actors, thus limiting the chances for tyranny. The same holds internationally: The United States should work to keep power diffused among many sovereign states and international organizations to prevent the rise of a hostile, coercive hegemon. Regimes committed to those ideals at home are more likely to apply them abroad, while autocracies are more likely to seek to expand their power at others' expense, both domestically and internationally.

Realists and liberal internationalists were both wrong to see their views as mutually exclusive. Power-balancing is not the opposite of liberalism but the constraints in which the latter operates. Liberalism is not the opposite of power politics but the ideological lens policymakers use to interpret which powers are threatening and which are friendly, which are potentially hostile and should be balanced against, and which are allies. Spreading liberalism, investing in good governance, and allying with fellow democracies are key ways of creating a more favorable balance for the United States—a point missed by structural realists and one reason why NATO has endured beyond realists' expectations. "Realism and liberal democratic internationalism could work in tandem, the former identifying America's natural allies in balance-of-power terms, while the latter built up the strength of these allies," in Smith's view.[56] That is why American grand strategy is both broader and more consistent than either realists or liberals have recognized and why the post–Cold War era shares so many continuities with its predecessors.

Objections

The spread of democracy, free-market capitalism, and international institutions have positive implications for American security, suggesting the United States should continue to make their spread a goal of its foreign policy. Critics have raised three questions. First, is spreading liberalism possible? Second, is it cost-effective? Third, is it just?

Critics have sometimes doubted the feasibility of liberalism in other cultural settings, a reasonable query given the complex ties between culture, history, and habits of governance. America's efforts to foster liberalism abroad have famously sunk in the quagmire of the Mekong Delta and the sands of Mesopotamia. Just because democratization is good does not mean it is possible. US efforts to promote it sometimes create partial democracies, which can be unstable and dangerous.[57]

This is the weakest objection. It seems that many Americans—and some scholars—have overreacted in the collective eagerness to avoid "another Iraq" and have come to believe that the growth of democracy abroad faces insurmountable challenges. But democracy and free-market capitalism have a much stronger track record outside the West than is often recognized. Recent doubts about their feasibility in non–Western states typically stem from overgeneralizing from a few, well-known examples of failure, while overlooking the larger number of lesser-known cases of success.

In 2013, thirty-five countries outside of Europe and its cultural offshoots were rated "free" by Freedom House or were rated with a score of 7 or higher on the Polity IV data set (which measures a country's level of democracy), or both. They include giants such as India, Japan, and South Africa and microsovereignties such as Tuvalu, Vanuatu, and the Federated States of Micronesia. They include African states such as Benin, Botswana, and Ghana; East Asian states such as South Korea, Taiwan, and Mongolia; South Asian states such as Pakistan and Kyrgyzstan; and predominantly Islamic states such as Turkey and the Comoros. All told, roughly one-third of all "non–Western" countries worldwide are free societies.[58] Niebuhr himself wrote of his doubts of the possibility of democracy in the "Orient."[59] He was wrong. As was Samuel Huntington; a "clash of civilizations" is not inevitable.[60] Democracy appears to be more transferable than Huntington believed it to be. It is also the best tool for taming nationalism. There are democratic states on every settled continent and in every major cultural bloc.[61] Democracy remains more common in the West (nearly all states in Europe and some 85 percent in the Western Hemisphere are free), but it is, without doubt, possible elsewhere.

This is, in fact, an odd time to doubt the feasibility of democracy's spread. The past few decades of democratic growth have made such doubts increasingly difficult to sustain. The contemporary era is the high tide of liberalism in all of recorded human history. In the post–Cold war era, a higher proportion of states are liberal, and a larger percentage of the human population is living under liberal governance, than ever before. Pessimism about its spread stemming from the wars in Iraq and Afghanistan is a classic case of overinterpreting the recent past and extrapolating a trend based on too-few data points. In the long run, the rise of democracy is one of the most remarkable phenomena of the past century—and statesmen at the time knew it. Secretary of State Elihu Root told a Conference of the American Republics in 1906 that

> capacity for self-government does not come to man by nature. It is an art to be learned. . . . Yet no student of our times can fail to see that not America alone but the whole civilized world is swinging away from its old governmental moorings and intrusting the fate of its civilization to the capacity of the popular mass to govern. By this pathway mankind is to travel, whithersoever it leads. Upon the success of this our great undertaking the hope of humanity depends. Nor can we fail to see that the world makes substantial progress toward more perfect popular self-government.[62]

Critics who dismiss democratization in the name of "realism" are turning realism into a dogma, inflexible and heedless of evidence as all fundamentalist dogmas are. There is a useful debate about how best to foster liberalism around the world, which I address in chapter 11. But the realist complaint that fostering liberalism is impossible is false. The term "realism," like "restraint," operates as a rhetorical device, implying that its opponents are somehow disconnected from the way the world really is and that their theories run counter to the facts. When it comes to liberalism, it is realists who are disconnected. True realism, based on facts, would recognize from evidence that ideas matter, liberalism is an asset for American security, and its spread is empirically possible. Rejecting the encouragement of liberalism as a tool of US foreign policy is a unilateral disarmament of one of the most powerful tools available for protecting the United States while promoting a just and lasting peace in the world. Spreading democracy is a pragmatic exercise of power to alter the balance of power in the United States' favor.

The second objection is similar to the first but more nuanced: Fostering liberalism abroad may be possible, but it may not be cost-effective. Do the benefits of upholding liberal order outweigh the costs? Are the net benefits of sustaining liberal order greater than the net benefits of alternative grand strategies, such as restraint?[63] Or is the United States at risk of "imperial overstretch" and "strategic overextension," the point at which the resources required to maintain its position exceed the benefit of doing so?[64]

These questions can be approached in several different ways, none of which persuasively show that a grand strategy of building liberal order is economically unsustainable. Scholars have computed the direct cost of different military deployment patterns and found, unsurprisingly, that the cost of a globally deployed US military presence is higher than the cost of "restraint"— but, importantly, the cost of either is easily sustainable given the United States' massive economic foundation. The direct cost of a globally deployed military posture—probably between 4 and 6 percent of GDP—is nowhere near "imperial overstretch."[65] Since 1940, the United States spent an average of 7.4 percent of its GDP on defense. The figure drops to 6.9 percent if we exclude defense spending during the years the United States was at war between 1940 and 1990 and to 6.2 percent for all years of peace since 1940. Since the end of the Cold War, the average has dropped dramatically to 3.7 percent, is currently 3.3 percent, and is scheduled to drop to 2.7 percent by 2020. This will be the smallest level of defense spending as a percentage of GDP since 1940. The United States sustained more than twice that level of defense spending for four decades during the Cold War. The greatest barrier to a modestly larger defense posture is political will, not economic sustainability.[66]

The real argument is over the opportunity cost of investing US resources, energy, attention, and prestige in upholding liberal order versus not doing so. Advocates of restraint argue that the United States pays an opportunity cost by investing in military and diplomatic tools rather than domestic economic and social programs, such that it is undermining its own economic health by overextending itself abroad. Paul Kennedy, for example, contends that investments in defense crowd out investments in the civilian sector to the extent that the United States' "growth rates will be slower than in those countries dedicated to the marketplace and less eager to channel resources into defense."[67] One problem with this approach is that the economic models that purport to show the economic impact of military spending versus domestic spending are uncertain and contested; some scholars contend that military spending actually contributes to economic growth.[68] Kennedy's classic argument about the relationship of economic strength to military power is that great powers have a tendency to expand until the economic costs of expansion outweigh its benefits, thus undermining the economic foundation of the state and prompting decline.[69] This argument, however, was drawn from cases of imperialism and mercantilism; its logic does not apply to the novel case of liberal order-building. The United States rarely conquers and administers territory, so it neither incurs the costs nor takes the direct benefit of imperial rule, limiting the usefulness of analogizing to past great powers. In fact, liberal order is an economic *asset* to the United States because it includes an open trading regime.

Another problem with the argument about relative opportunity costs is that the United States would pay an enormous opportunity cost by *not* investing in liberal order, a point advocates of restraint rarely consider. Liberal order already exists and provides benefits to the United States. The opportunity to sustain the already-existing liberal order—by staying in NATO, for example—is a major asset for the United States. Divesting from liberal order forgoes those benefits. And even if policymakers are uncertain about the benefits of liberal order, prudence counsels continued investment. Sustaining an existing liberal order is cheaper than building a new one from scratch; sustaining liberal order at low cost today makes more sense than divesting from it only to rebuild it at high cost later.

The debate is intractable because liberal order has no price tag: Liberal order is either priceless or worthless. Advocates of restraint believe that liberal order has zero value because they do not believe the culture of world order matters for American security. Advocates of internationalism argue that liberal order brings concrete benefits and its absence would incur costs, but not ones that can be quantified. If the culture of world order matters at all, it matters a great deal; policymakers should certainly take great care with the kind of culture they help create. Social scientists might take counsel from Aristotle: "Our discussion will be adequate if it has as much clearness as the subject-matter admits of, for precision is not to be sought for alike in all discussions. . . . It is the mark of an educated man to look for precision in each class of things just so far as the nature of the subject admits."[70] The question is not "how much does liberal order cost?" but rather "what kind of world do we live in?" If the world is as described by advocates of restraint, then no conceivable level of costs associated with upholding liberal order would be justified. But if the world is as described here, then, similarly, no level of benefits associated with restraint are very attractive.

Instead of focusing on the relative costs and benefits of engagement versus restraint, some critics have leveled a third, and probably the strongest, objection to a liberal grand strategy: It is unjust. Many voices have warned against what they see as the self-righteousness, hubris, and hypocrisy of America's democracy promotion abroad.[71] As one scholar put it, "spreading democracy by forceful means can too easily become a blank check for unbridled military interventionism."[72] More, the attempt smacks of utopianism. Promoting democracy, according to this view, has a proven track record of failure and thus is not merely impractical—it is hubristic and morally wrong. Niebuhr quite clearly warned against the "deep layer of Messianic consciousness in the mind of America" and the utopian projects it leads to, and he counseled that policymakers in powerful states must cultivate a suspicion of their own motives and an awareness of how the best-intentioned endeavors go awry.[73] He specifically warned against the "covert religion" of progress, which leads to a false sense of "redemptive history" or a belief that "the end of life is the creation of a democratic society," and rightly reminds us that "no society, not even a democratic one, is great enough or good enough to make itself the final end of human existence."[74] Colin Dueck argued US foreign policy betrayed a "tendency towards moralistic crusading; a conception of war as atavistic and unnatural; the disconnection between the use of force and the use of diplomacy; a reluctance to consider limited aims in wartime."[75] Turning American foreign policy into a crusade to convert the world to democracy and usher in a millennial reign of liberty and peace would be a frightening new form of imperial tyranny, the more so because it would come disguised with angels of light to the sounds of harps and trumpets.

I agree. I wholeheartedly reject the notion that the United States has a special mission to spread democracy, that spreading democracy should trump all other national security considerations, and that the United States should impose democracy by force on peoples who do not want it. That is one reason why it is helpful to review the history of American support for liberalism: to learn from McKinley's failures and Wilson's naiveté and Lyndon Johnson's arrogance, which long predate the Bush and Obama administrations' mismanagement of their wars. I argue simply that both theory and evidence supports the notion that the spread of liberalism has positive implications for US national security and that, therefore, the United States should take advantage of opportunities, when they arise, of encouraging its further spread—much as it has done for the last century and more. Doing so is a pragmatic pursuit of security, not an idealistic quest for global justice.

There are four major differences between the pragmatic encouragement of liberalism and the crusade Niebuhr and others rightly warn about (and that also distinguish this approach from the liberal imperialism of the Progressive Era). First, in the pragmatic model, the motivation comes from within, not without. It begins with a selfish calculation about how to produce security for the United States, not a sense of divine mission or a providentially given task. Second, as a consequence, the spread of liberalism is a means as well as an end. The United States should foster liberalism because it is a convenient tool to buy security for itself, not solely because it is good in itself (although it is valuable that it is also good in itself because harmonizing self-interest with justice undergirds our defense with international legitimacy, removing grounds for grievance and reducing the likelihood that discontented revisionist powers will arise). Third, the United States should not try to force democracy on peoples who do not want it. (I find it odd that this even has to be said, because it refutes an argument no one makes.) Fourth, because fostering liberalism is part of strategy, not mission, the United States should take advantage only of the cheapest, easiest, or most strategically relevant opportunities to spread liberalism. It should avoid investing large amounts of time and resources in cases that are only peripheral to US national security, especially cases that are both hard and irrelevant (although the United States *should* attempt cases that are hard when they are strategically vital, as I argue was the case in Afghanistan). This approach attempts to combine the grounding of the earlier realist Puritanism with a recognition of the United States' power, role, and responsibilities in the twenty-first century. I illustrate how to apply these principles in chapters 6 through 9.

I belabor these points because championing liberalism is the strain of America's foreign policy tradition that is out of favor at the moment. Americans are at risk of willfully neglecting the importance of liberalism to US security. The setbacks in Iraq and Afghanistan were tragic for those countries, but if they were used to justify a reversal of over a century of American support for liberalism abroad, the tragedy would reverberate far beyond the Middle East and South Asia. The call by some scholars and policymakers to return to the earlier era of restraint and realism before World War II or before the War of 1898 ignores the reality of America's role in the world today: America cannot unmake its power, nor should it ignore the responsibilities that come with such power.

Finally, the record of US foreign policy is starkly at odds with the picture painted by critics who advance the normative critique against it. I am unimpressed with accusations that the United States has been overly zealous, hubristic, or imperialist—a "crusader state"—for democracy, pursuing a grand strategy of "primacy" or "predominance" blessed by liberalism.[76] The evidence in favor of such a view is well rehearsed—a few references to Vietnam and Iraq are sufficient for most[77]—but the evidence against it is rarely considered. A liberal hegemon worth the name trying to enforce liberalism and entrench American primacy globally would have acted differently than the United States has since 1989. In fact, "the United States often plays less of a role in world affairs than one would expect given America's considerable material power," in part because of the strain of "limited liability" in its strategic culture.[78]

For example, the United States did not insist on the liberalization of Kuwait in 1991. It famously failed to intervene to stop the genocide in Rwanda. It was dragged into the Balkans after three years and watched as hundreds of thousands were killed. It gave only token support to UN peace-building operations in Central America and Africa. It did not intervene to stop the decades-long blight of state failure and humanitarian atrocities in Somalia,

the Democratic Republic of the Congo, or Afghanistan. When it did intervene in Afghanistan, after 2001, it did so in response to a direct attack and
made only desultory and unimpressive efforts to liberalize and rebuild the
country. The United States did not go to war against North Korea or Iran to
enforce the nonproliferation regime. It did not intervene in the war between
Ethiopia and Eritrea or the Great African War of the 1990s; did not halt Hugo
Chávez's rise to power in Venezuela; did not halt or reverse coups against
democratically elected governments in Turkey, Mali, Pakistan, Thailand, or
Egypt; did not find opportunities to use the Arab Spring to advance liberalism in the Middle East; and did not invest in the reconstruction of Libya
after overthrowing its government. It did not join a host of beloved liberal
institutions and treaties, such as the International Criminal Court, the Kyoto
Protocol, the Law of the Sea Treaty, or the Convention on the Rights of the
Child. Perhaps most damningly, it put out only a paltry and ineffective effort
to push for the full democratization of Russia after the fall of the Soviet Union
and did nothing to stop Putin's reestablishment of autocracy there.

At the height of its power, in 1989, the United States withdrew a quarter of its troops from East Asia and 80 percent of its military forces from
Europe, cut its active-duty military personnel and its defense budget by a
third, destroyed its own chemical weapons stockpile, and demobilized three-
quarters of its nuclear warheads. This is not the strategy of a crusading liberal
hegemon bent on global domination.

The single point of documentary evidence suggesting the United States
was pursuing a strategy of hegemony was a draft defense planning guidance
(DPG) paper written and leaked in 1992 that said the United States aimed
to "prevent the re-emergence of a new rival." Critics universally cite the
draft and have wildly, almost comically, exaggerated its importance. The key
phrase was eliminated in the final draft. Hegemony was never endorsed as
official US policy, was hardly characteristic of the administration of George
H. W. Bush (who is usually characterized as a moderate realist), and was
not implemented by subsequent budgetary or deployment decisions carried
out by an entirely different administration throughout the remainder of the
decade. This 1992 draft is not the secret master plan for world domination
that its critics make it out to be. It was overheated rhetoric by a mid-ranking
official, quickly corrected, and never implemented.[79]

Some of these departures from the playbook of liberal hegemony were
missed opportunities. Some were wise choices based on a prudent recognition of America's limited resources and national security priorities. I am not
arguing that the United States should have played the liberal crusader. Rather,
I am highlighting the difference between what the United States has actually done and what a truly hegemonic, crusading liberal power would have

attempted. Christopher Layne, critical of what he believed was the United States' drive for predominance, argued, "First—and fundamentally—hegemony is about raw, hard *power*." If so, then the United States' willing surrender of hard power in the form of cuts to its defense budgets, reduction in the size of its military, and demobilization of its nuclear arsenal in the 1990s empirically falsifies Layne's claim that the United States was pursuing hegemony. He also argued, "When it comes to grand strategy, hegemons practice the adage 'If you've got it, flaunt it.'"[80] Compared to its almost unlimited opportunities to flaunt since the end of the Cold War, the United States has been sparing in its choice of where and how to employ its power abroad. It has been more fitful than hubristic, more fickle than fundamentalist. The moral critique of the United States as a crusading hegemon does not hold water.

Today

Today the United States faces up to five hostile autocracies armed with nuclear weapons. America's goal is not to "contain" the nuclear autocracies, which would be a simplistic attempt to replicate the Cold War paradigm in new and different conditions—and which would also be impossible and self-defeating. The United States should welcome Russia's, China's, and the other autocracies' legitimate engagements with the rest of the world, including their trade and diplomatic relations. There are no grounds for attempting to isolate or embargo trade with the nuclear autocracies.

Rather, the United States and its allies should prevent the nuclear autocracies from expanding their influence through illegitimate means, including invasion, conquest, annexation, coercion, subversion, blackmail, extortion, and terrorism. The nuclear autocracies have long records of pursuing such policies, including Russia's annexation of Crimea in 2014 and invasion of Georgia in 2008, its use of gas supplies to bully Ukraine, China's regular threats against Taiwan and North Korea's against South Korea, and Iran and Pakistan's continued support for jihadist militants and proxies across the Middle East and South Asia. Allowing these policies to succeed would reward aggression, thereby constructing an international system in which aggressors accrue power and eventually dominate nonaggressors.

The solution is to construct a different kind of system, one in which aggression is met with collective resistance.[81] Rhetoric and repeated action are how norms, expectations, institutions, and behavior are shaped. To use a common metaphor, if you want a peaceful schoolyard, you have to set the precedent that bullies are not tolerated, often by saying so loudly and by facing down a bully at the first sign of trouble. If you don't want the sole responsibility for facing down bullies, you have to be diligent about cajoling others to join you every time, so that it becomes part of the schoolyard culture. If you don't, the bully will, and a different schoolyard culture will grow, one dominated by his will to power. This is why the United States is right to treat issues far from its shores as national security concerns.[82] While the United States does not have an immediate interest at stake in what happens to Ukraine or the Senkaku/Diaoyu Islands, it has an interest in the sort of world we live in—a world in which coercion, intimidation, blackmail, and subversion are allowed with impunity or a world in which free states band together in collective defense. This rather obvious point is why policymakers routinely use (and sometimes overuse) Britain's appeasement of Adolf Hitler at Munich in 1938 as a cautionary tale.

How can the United States create a better "schoolyard culture" in international politics? Investing in liberal order requires, first, sustaining a global US defense posture. It requires creating, sustaining—and, selectively, expanding—a network of alliances. It means prioritizing alliances with rich, powerful democracies willing and able to work against the nuclear autocracies. It means investing in democratic prosperity by prioritizing trade relationships with and the distribution of foreign aid to poor democracies and partial democracies in regions that are strategically important to the United States. It means reexamining current ties to autocratic regimes, evaluating if the benefits from such ties outweigh the cost they exact on broader US foreign policy goals. It means investing and retaining leadership in the institutions of liberal order and an open trading regime. And it means—selectively, carefully, and humbly—working for the democratization of partial democracies.

The United States should not "disengage from its current alliance commitments in East Asia and Europe," as advocates of restraint recommend.[83] It is odd this argument comes from those who warn of the costs of America's "preponderance." Alliance is the cheapest means of sustaining American security abroad because it relies on allies to provide means and resources instead of providing it all ourselves. The United States' alliances are not a constraint on American freedom of action; they are, rather, "extensions of the American System to the opposite shores of America's two oceans."[84] That is why "the United States should work to sustain the military predominance of liberal democracies and encourage the development of military capabilities by like-minded democracies in a way that is consistent with their security interests."[85] And sustaining alliances means sustaining an overseas military presence. Alliances are little more than legal fictions until given heft by joint exercises, combined command structures, military sales, and shoulder-to-shoulder interaction by soldiers training alongside one another.[86]

The United States has consistently seen democracy—either its defense or expansion—to be a central part of its foreign policy, both as a goal in itself and as a tool for keeping America safe. It has not always succeeded, nor has it always been consistent or honest. And democracy promotion has always been appropriately coupled with pragmatic concerns, such as defending the homeland, and pursued within the constraints of what is achievable. But as a general framework in which to understand America's role in the world—a grand narrative that explains who we are and what we aim at—there is no credible alternative.

Notes

1. Mearsheimer, "Back to the Future" and *Tragedy of Great Power Politics*; Waltz, "Emerging Structure of International Politics" and "Structural Realism after the Cold War"; Kupchan, *End of the American Era*.
2. Waltz, *Theory of International Politics*, chap. 6.
3. Niebuhr, *Children of Light*, 174.
4. Morgenthau, *Politics among Nations*, 5.
5. Kissinger, *Diplomacy*, 20.
6. Kupchan, *End of the American Era*, 28.
7. Hunt is correct that realism is a distinct ideology; see *Ideology and U.S. Foreign Policy*, 8. Layne's contention that realism is "nonideological" is false.
8. Hill, *Grand Strategies*, 7.
9. Dueck, *Reluctant Crusaders*, 19. One is reminded of how shocked—shocked!—Captain Renault was upon discovering gambling at Rick's Café.
10. Niebuhr, *Irony*, 40.
11. Niebuhr, *Children of Light*, 175, 176, 181.
12. Smith, *America's Mission*, 31.
13. Niebuhr, "Augustine's Political Realism," 134. Ikenberry makes a similar point in different ways through his emphasis on America's participation in the institutions it creates for others and its provision of public goods and "voice opportunities" for other states.
14. For example, "motivational realists" claim to incorporate the role of ideology, human intention, and beliefs. Kydd, "Sheep in Sheep's Clothing."
15. Walt, *Origins of Alliances*. That does not mean any ideologically defined bloc will enjoy perfect harmony among all its members, as if there was an Islamic peace or a communist peace analogous to the democratic peace. Walt found weak support for ideological solidarity among Muslim states in his original study. And the democratic peace, after all, holds not simply because of feelings of camaraderie among policymakers of democratic countries, but because of institutional features unique to democracy, such as the separation of powers and a free press, that constrain war-making powers. But ideological solidarity does mean that conflict between ideologically similar states might require added justification while alliances among them might be easier and more enduring. Witness, for

example, the routine solidarity among Muslim-majority states on issues thought to threaten Islamic identity, such as Palestine or Kashmir. See also Ray, "War on Democratic Peace."

16. Owen, *Liberal Peace*, 18.

17. Ibid., 38.

18. Layne, *Peace of Illusions*, 118.

19. Owen, *Liberal Peace*, 38.

20. Ibid., and Schultz, *Democracy and Coercive Diplomacy*.

21. Hayes, "Identity and Securitization in the Democratic Peace."

22. Owen, "Foreign Imposition of Domestic Institutions" and *Clash of Ideas in World Politics*. But see note 15 above for why there is not parallel "Islamic peace" or "autocracy peace" or "Confucian peace."

23. Ikenberry, *After Victory* and *Liberal Leviathan*; Ikenberry and Slaughter, *Forging a World of Liberty under Law*.

24. Ikenberry, *Liberal Leviathan*, 252.

25. Lynn-Jones, "Why the United States Should Spread Democracy"; Owen, *Liberal Peace, Liberal War*; Smith, *America's Mission*, 326ff; Art, *Grand Strategy for America*, 71–73; Doyle, "Kant, Liberal Legacies, and Foreign Affairs." For the contrary view, see Layne, "Kant or Cant," and Spiro, "Insignificance of the Liberal Peace." For responses to these critiques, see Oneal and Russett, "Assessing the Liberal Peace" and "Classical Liberals Were Right," as well as Russett, "And Yet It Moves." Cox, Ikenberry, and Inoguchi, *American Democracy Promotion*, also covers the debate. In dismissing the democratic peace, Layne cites four militarized crises between democracies that did *not* result in war, which therefore do not falsify the democratic peace theory (see *Peace of Illusions*, p. 257, footnote 22). He also cites World War I, claiming Germany was a democracy. Germany was not a democracy: Its Polity2 score for 1914 is 2, well short of democracy. It is striking how rarely structural realists and advocates of restraint even address the democratic peace argument: Posen, Kupchan, Gholz, and Layne offer only brief, dismissive, and unsatisfactory responses.

26. Lipson, *Reliable Partners*; Deutsch, *Political Community and the North Atlantic Area*.

27. Owen, *Liberal Peace*; Schultz, *Democracy and Coercive Diplomacy*; Brown, Lynn-Jones, and Miller, *Debating the Democratic Peace*.

28. Bearce and Omori, "How Do Commercial Institutions Promote Peace?"; Gartzke, "Capitalist Peace."

29. Gallagher, "'Reform and Openness.'"

30. This is a contested claim among international relations scholars bound to deterministic theories about the rise and fall of great powers. Among comparative political scientists and historians familiar with the record of rapid economic growth in transitioning societies, it probably sounds obvious.

31. Huntington, *Political Order in Changing Societies*.

32. Ikenberry, *Liberal Leviathan*, 164.

33. Keohane, *After Hegemony*; Oye, *Cooperation under Anarchy*.

34. Brooks, Ikenberry, and Wohlforth, "Don't Come Home, America," 20.

35. On "soft balancing," see Pape, "Soft Balancing against the United States"; Paul, "Soft Balancing in the Age of US Primacy"; and He and Feng, "If Not Soft Balancing, Then What?" Ikenberry has persistently claimed balancing is not happening (for example, see *Liberal Leviathan*, 37), but even he acknowledges that other states have started to resist US leadership as it has grown more unilateral and detached from institutional constraints (272–73).

36. Ikenberry, *Liberal Leviathan*, 130.

37. Ibid., 223.

38. Mearsheimer, "False Promise of International Institutions," develops this argument further—probably too far.

39. Kagan, *Of Paradise and Power*.

40. Ikenberry, *Liberal Leviathan*, chap. 4.

41. Stokes, "Goodbye America?"

42. Kupchan, *End of the American Era*, 102, 104, 110.

43. Ibid., 115, 118. Kupchan does not explain why he believes nationalism might break apart the democratic peace but is not strong enough to break apart the EU, which he sees as destined to become a rival pole to the United States. Kupchan also engages in some strategic ambiguity about what his argument actually is. If he is predicting that the United States and Europe may engage in nonviolent "rivalry" over trade and influence, his prediction is underspecified, entirely consistent with the democratic peace theory, and not particularly interesting. If he is predicting that the United States and Europe will fight a war with each other, his prediction is novel, provocative, and wrong.

44. Mansfield and Snyder, *Electing to Fight*.

45. Smith, *America's Mission*, 144.

46. Gholz, Press, and Sapolsky, "Come Home, America," 7.

47. Art, *Grand Strategy for America*, 71.

48. Nau, *Conservative Internationalism*.

49. Smith, *America's Mission*, 322.

50. Quotes in this section are from Nau, "Conservative Internationalism," 6–11.

51. Nau, *At Home Abroad*.

52. Dueck, *Reluctant Crusaders*, 37.

53. Layne, "From Preponderance to Offshore Balancing," 119.

54. Kupchan, *End of the American Era*.

55. Posen, *Restraint*, 71.

56. Smith, *America's Mission*, 144.

57. Goldsmith, "Making the World Safe for Partial Democracy?"

58. I obviously disagree with their characterization of Pakistan. I am deliberately counting the "West" as widely as possible: The tally of thirty-five non-Western democracies does not include any country in Europe or the Western Hemisphere, nor Australia, New Zealand, São Tomé and Príncipe, or Cape Verde.

59. Niebuhr, *Irony*, 123–26.

60. Huntington, *Clash of Civilizations*. A clash among civilizations remains a high possibility *outside* democratic states (among nondemocratic states) or *within* democratic states (by illiberal terrorists and insurgents) but not *between* them.

61. Diamond, *Spirit of Democracy*. There appears to be some backsliding since 2005; it is unclear if it is a long-term trend or a temporary blip.

62. Elihu Root, "Speech of Elihu Root," address at the Third Conference of American Republics, in US Department of State, *Papers Relating to the Foreign Relations of the United States, 1906*, 128.

63. This is the main point of contention between Gholz, Press, and Sapolsky, "Come Home, America," and Brooks, Ikenberry, and Wohlforth, "Don't Come Home, America."

64. Kennedy, *Rise and Fall*, 514ff.

65. Art, *Grand Strategy for America*, 161–63.

66. Office of Management and Budget, *Historical Tables*.

67. Kennedy, *Rise and Fall*, 532.

68. Brooks, Ikenberry, and Wohlforth, "Don't Come Home, America," 20ff.

69. Gilpin, *War and Change*; Kennedy, *Rise and Fall*.

70. Aristotle, *Nichomachean Ethics*, book I, chap. 3.

71. Lieven and Hulsman, *Ethical Realism*.

72. Art, "Defensible Defense," 9.

73. Niebuhr, *Irony*, 69.

74. Niebuhr, *Children of Light*, 131, 132, 133.

75. Dueck, *Reluctant Crusaders*, 26.

76. McDougall, *Promised Land, Crusader State*; Dueck, *Reluctant Crusaders*.

77. In Layne's argument that the United States is overextending itself, he cites just three examples: Vietnam, Iraq, and, oddly, Bosnia. *Peace of Illusions*, chap. 6.

78. Dueck, *Reluctant Crusaders*, 26–27. Dueck argues that US policymakers betray a consistent tendency to search for grand strategy on the cheap and minimize US investment abroad where possible.

79. The draft version of the 1992 DPG is cited by Posen, Ikenberry, Dueck, Layne, Art, and others. See Eric Edelman, "The Strange Career of the 1992 Defense Planning Guidance," in Leffler and Legro, *In Uncertain Times*.

80. Layne, *Peace of Illusions*, 4.

81. I am drawing here on the idea that actors help create the sort of world they inhabit with their choices and behavior. On the social construction of the international polity, see, for example, Ruggie, *Constructing the World Polity*.

82. This is also why Posen is wrong to distrust hypothetical causal chains.

83. Layne, "From Preponderance to Offshore Balancing," 87.

84. McDougall, *Promised Land*, 212.

85. Ikenberry and Slaughter, *Forging a World of Liberty*, 29.

86. In other words, F. G. Hoffman's recommendation of forward partnership "*without* extensive forward-stationed forces" ("Forward Partnership," 35) relying heavily on naval power and Special Operations Forces is bound to prove ineffective. Rotational forces are unlikely to create the sort of sustained relationships that forward partnerships require.

5

Barbarians, Failed States, and Stability Operations

Great power rivalry and nuclear autocracies are not the only threats to American interests in the contemporary security environment. Unconventional threats from hostile nonstate actors operating in weak and failed states—pirates, terrorists, drug traffickers, organized criminal networks, war criminals, and slavers—also pose a threat to the United States and liberal order. These kinds of threats have often been overblown. However, their ability to threaten the United States has been magnified through technology, globalization, and state failure. Travel and communication are easier, weapons are more lethal, and state failure is more widespread (giving them more space to operate with impunity). Even if the claims of globalization have been exaggerated, as some scholars claim,[1] and the United States is at low risk of another 9/11 or a crippling cyberattack, the aggregate effect of an increasing number of hostile nonstate actors throughout the world raises the cost of sustaining liberal order and slows the gears of normal diplomacy and trade.

Similar to its response to the threat from nuclear autocracies, the United States has a two-pronged approach to nonstate actors. First, it takes the fight directly to them, killing, capturing, or prosecuting as many as possible. But second, and more controversially, it invests in good governance abroad, helping fix the failed states that provide a permissive operating environment in which nonstate actors grow and thrive. The particular means by which the United States invests in good governance can and should vary depending on the circumstances of state failure, the importance of the state, and the nature of the threats emanating from it. In cases of low or nonviolent threat when state failure results from incompetent governance or endemic poverty (such as in West Africa or Haiti), the United States can give foreign aid and technical assistance and use its diplomatic weight to rally similar support from allies, partners, and international organizations. In cases of higher, more direct, and violent threat when state failure results from civil war, insurgency, terrorism, criminal gangs, or drug smugglers, it may be necessary for the United States to participate in international peace-building or stability operations. These options—foreign aid and stability operations—are often dissociated from each other, as if the first was a matter of charity and the second a matter of war, which explains why they often seem poorly implemented and peripheral to national security interests. In fact, both are tools for responding to a common problem: weak states and the barbarians who hide in them.

Kinetic Operations

Properly responding to armed nonstate actors is, first, a simple matter of killing, capturing, or prosecuting as many as possible—what the military calls "kinetic operations." Some critics may be wary of the call to combat armed nonstate groups around the world. John Quincy Adams famously counseled that the United States "goes not abroad, in search of monsters to destroy" because "she would involve herself beyond the power of extrication, in all the wars of interest and intrigue." Adams worried that the United States would be bogged down in endless and unwinnable conflicts but also that the amount of power the United States would have to marshal for such a global contest would itself become a threat to liberty at home. "She might become the dictatress of the world. She would be no longer the ruler of her own spirit," Adams warned.[2]

Advocates of restraint are fond of quoting Adams, but he was speaking in 1821 when the United States was focused on building its internal energies and engaged in sectional conflict. To the extent that Americans went abroad, they went west toward the Great Plains, the Rockies, and Texas and east to trade in Europe. The situation in which the United States finds itself in 2016 is dramatically different. The United States *is* abroad. It did not go abroad in search of monsters but in search of trade—and found monsters waiting, as, in fact, it did in Adams's time when it confronted pirates in the Mediterranean. The United States faces a simple choice: Come home, which would be economically ruinous and impractical, or combat the monsters it has found, to sustain its access to the world. Fighting pirates and terrorists is the cost of doing business in a globalized world.

The United States has a long history of undertaking targeted military and law enforcement action against hostile nonstate actors, both domestically and internationally. Military operations against the Barbary pirates were only the earliest precursors. The United States established a permanent naval squadron in the Mediterranean in 1815 to counter piracy there. During the nineteenth century, aside from the Mexican and Civil Wars, the US Army was almost entirely focused on countering Native American tribes, including in the Seminole Wars (1816–18, 1835–42, and 1855–58), the Black Hawk War (1832), the Creek War (1836), the Ghost Dance War (1890–91), and many others.

US Marines put down the Cacos rebellion in Haiti during the US occupation there and fought a six-year war against the insurgent forces of Nicaraguan revolutionary Augusto Sandino from 1927 to 1933. The Federal Bureau of Investigation (FBI) fought a decades-long war against the Mafia, a transnational organized criminal outfit, from bootlegging during Prohibition to drug smuggling, gambling, and other activities during the later twentieth century. The FBI and Drug Enforcement Administration—and, occasionally, the US military—have waged a "war on drugs" since 1971. Even manhunts for individual terrorists and militants have a long history. In 1916, President Woodrow Wilson ordered a punitive expedition against Pancho Villa, a Mexican insurgent who had attacked American towns along the US–Mexican border. American forces reportedly aided in the capture of Ernesto "Che" Guevara, a transnational Marxist insurgent and terrorist, in 1965, and Pablo Escobar, a Colombian drug lord, in 1993, long before the raid on Osama bin Laden's compound in 2011.[3] And the United States assisted counterinsurgencies against communist guerrilla movements around the world during the Cold War.

Over the last decade, the United States has spearheaded several multilateral initiatives to coordinate global action against hostile nonstate actors. It championed UN Security Council Resolution 1373 in September 2001 to galvanize unprecedented worldwide action against terrorist groups. The resolution obligated all states to crack down on terrorist financing (coordinated from the US side through the Department of Treasury's Office of Terrorism and Financial Intelligence), deny safe haven to terrorist groups, and share information about terrorist groups with other states.[4]

Similarly, the United States unraveled Pakistani nuclear scientist A. Q. Khan's private nuclear technology smuggling ring in 2004 and established the Proliferation Security Initiative in 2003, a voluntary coalition of states that work "to stop trafficking of weapons of mass destruction (WMD), their delivery systems, and related materials," according to the US State Department.[5] The US-led Joint Interagency Task Force–South (JIATF-S) is a similar multilateral organization dedicated to countering transnational drug trafficking in South and Central America. Combined Task Force 151, organized under US Central Command's Combined Maritime Forces in 2009, is a UN-authorized multilateral counterpiracy coalition in the Gulf of Aden,[6] and Interpol helps coordinate international cooperation against transnational organized crime.

These initiatives are worthwhile, if sometimes unwieldy because of their multilateral nature. The United States would be wise to retain the capability to operate unilaterally when necessary, as, for example, it does in some counterterrorism efforts under the Department of Defense's Special Operations Command (SOCOM). In addition, the United States and the international community may want to expand the list of rogue actors at which it targets such efforts. For example, at the 2005 World Summit, the international community signed up to enforce the "Responsibility to Protect," a norm legitimizing international intervention to stop genocide, ethnic cleansing, war crimes, and crimes against humanity, but has yet to establish an implementing task force to target those who commit such acts. The UN's special adviser on the prevention of genocide or the US undersecretary of state for civilian security, democracy, and human rights should be charged with the responsibility to initiate a "genocide watch" to warn of impending crimes and a "war criminal watch list" akin to the terrorist watch list to facilitate the global pursuit and capture of wanted international criminals. In addition, the continued existence of the transnational human trafficking trade—slaving, to use its older and still-accurate label—is a blot on the international community, hardly alleviated by the existence of the UN Global Initiative to Fight Human Trafficking. The issue is ripe for a US-led multinational and interagency military and law enforcement antislaving task force.

There are two strategic questions about how best to pursue kinetic operations. First, should the United States use the military or law enforcement? Whose rules of engagement should apply? Second, should the United States take action itself or work through allies and partners? Traditionally, the United States has treated virtually all nonstate actors as criminals, except Native Americans and communist insurgents. The military has gradually become more involved in counterdrug and counterpiracy operations but only in a supporting role: The rules of engagement are those of law enforcement, seeking to apprehend and prosecute, rather than kill. This is a change from the days of the war against the Barbary pirates and perhaps not for the better. In older formulations of just war, certain crimes, including piracy, were understood to be acts of war against civilization, in response to which the forces of *any* nation were justified in undertaking military operations against them. That norm has been inconsistently applied to terrorists after 2001. The international community might consider switching to the military's rules of engagement and authorizing offensive kinetic operations against pirates, drug traffickers, and slavers. (It would be unwise for the United States to do so unilaterally unless in exceptional circumstances.) For example, authorizing the multinational JIATF-S coalition not only to detect, monitor, and track traffickers and report their locations to law enforcement but also to destroy their vehicles and labs would impose dramatically higher costs on them.

The second question—should the United States or its allies assume primary responsibility?—is a very old debate. The Nixon Doctrine is a useful formulation: "We shall furnish military and economic assistance when requested in accordance with our treaty commitments. But we shall look to the nation directly threatened to assume the primary responsibility of providing the manpower for its defense."[7] Sometimes, the nation most directly threatened is the United States, and the United States rightly takes the lead and pays the highest costs to organize a coalition and undertake operations against threats, as it does against al-Qaida and, more or less, against the South American drug trade (Colombia and Mexico are more directly threatened). In other cases, the United States is less directly threatened and can afford to give low-cost support through logistics, intelligence sharing, and staff support to efforts led by the UN, the EU, or another ally. Even then, US policymakers should recognize that the United States is usually the best candidate to play a coordinating role anyway because it has the experience, expertise, and infrastructure already established for coalition management. The United States has played a leading role in the international system for seventy years, and there is considerable path-dependence in favor of continued American leadership of coalitions against common threats.

The Problems with "Counterterrorism Only"

An ounce of prevention, however, is worth a pound of cure, and here is where the United States and the international community have much more work to do. The underlying conditions that enable hostile nonstate actors to operate are poor, weak, and failed states.[8] State failure incubates serious threats to regional and international order, such as transnational insurgent movements (Liberia, Uganda), organized crime and drug-trafficking networks (Southeast Europe, Central Asia), piracy (Somalia, Southeast Asia), the occasional global terrorist organization (Afghanistan, Pakistan, Iraq, Syria, and Yemen), and even pandemic disease (AIDS, Ebola). State failure, when left unaddressed, causes demonstrable harm to neighbors, whole regions, and occasionally the international order itself.

In response to state failure, the international community has few good options. The international community could resurrect a trusteeship or mandate system under which regional powers take over failed states semipermanently and assume responsibility for keeping order in their respective neighborhoods. Despite some scholarly attempts to flesh out this option,[9] it remains unrealistic because there is no political will for renewed imperialism, by whatever name, among either the great powers or the developing world.

On the other end of the spectrum, the United States and its allies could ignore the problems, allow anarchy to consume failed states, and pay ever-higher costs to isolate themselves and launch targeted stand-off strikes against ever more powerful rogue actors. Under this option, the United States would make no attempt to solve the underlying problems of state failure, only to keep the threats they incubate small enough not to reach too far beyond their borders. This seems to be the emerging preference of US policymakers in the aftermath of Iraq and Afghanistan—and, in some cases, this is probably the least bad option. The United States cannot stabilize every region and fix every failed state; it must prioritize which failed states are strategically relevant—and which irrelevant. Some failed states, such as Somalia, Yemen, and the Democratic Republic of the Congo, are doomed to stay failed.

However, there are serious problems with applying this approach dogmatically and relinquishing the tools of stability operations. First, kinetic operations isolated from other instruments of national power will not solve underlying problems: They are Band-Aids, not cures; the disease goes untreated. To use another metaphor, kinetic operations are akin to mowing the grass rather than treating the lawn; the grass grows back. Direct operations against armed nonstate groups are necessary but, usually, insufficient by themselves. That leads to the second problem: When the United States is faced with a national security threat and has the resources and capability to address the root problems—to perform surgery or treat the lawn—but refuses, it is shortsighted, strategically myopic, and unjust.

It is unjust toward Americans and a dereliction of government's duty to protect its citizens. Relying exclusively on kinetic operations to keep a threat at bay while refusing to address the root problems leaves Americans exposed to persistent danger. By taking only minimal action to stave off immediate threats, policymakers give such groups time to adapt, train, recruit, and operate. If the United States has the opportunity to address underlying problems but simply chooses not to act, it is paying a substantial opportunity cost for a small short-term gain, neglecting the opportunity to spread stability and liberal order.

But it is also unjust toward the people who live in failed states that harbor nonstate threats. Deliberately leaving states in conditions of anarchy because they are inconvenient to fix while arrogating the right to intervene periodically, at one's own discretion, to kill or arrest a few bad actors or blow up a few facilities is tantamount to an indefinite state of war in which violence is occasional but peace is never achieved. Critics sometimes accuse the United States or UN of imperialist bullying when they intervene with stability operations.[10] But they rarely consider how imperialist, bullying, and cynical is the alternative: The rich world damning the poor to endless cycles of failed governance and perpetual violence, stopping in now and then to target a few thugs whose violence happens to be inconvenient for the rich. Just war aims at peace; a war plan that does not explain how it will produce victory and peace is not just.

The United States does not have a moral obligation to fix every failed state. Nau rightly "counsels intervention only when US military and moral interests are equally engaged and when US values overlap with those of developing nations or great-power stakes are high."[11] In other words, interventions must meet two criteria. First, the United States should undertake a stability operation only when a failed state threatens American national security—such as when it offers safe haven to terrorists or threatens to destabilize a geopolitically important region. Second, the United States should undertake stability operations only when it has a reasonable chance of success—that is, when it might plausibly result in the failed state becoming a valued partner with the United States. This criterion can easily be abused by critics who argue that stability operations and foreign aid are *in principle* unlikely to succeed and the United States should rarely or never try them. Such critics betray a shallow understanding of stability operations, as I argue below. Nonetheless, these criteria eliminate most failed states in the world. Somalia and Yemen meet the first criterion but not the second. The Democratic Republic of the Congo fails both. Iraq and Syria probably fail the second criterion until the parties reach a political settlement that addresses the grievances that underlie the perennial political violence there. Contrary to conventional wisdom, I argue that Afghanistan meets both criteria.

The debate over the proper approach to combating al-Qaida and the Taliban in Afghanistan is a specific example of the broader problem with the "counterterrorism-only" school of thought. During the debate about how to respond to worsening conditions in Afghanistan from 2008 to 2011, some policymakers and scholars, including Vice President Joe Biden, Col. Gian Gentile, and Douglas Porch, argued the United States should give up on counterinsurgency, reconstruction, stabilization, and democratization in Afghanistan. Such endeavors, they argued, had failed in previous efforts in other countries, were failing in Afghanistan, and were almost inevitably doomed to failure because of problems inherent in the project itself. Trying to stabilize, much less democratize, Afghanistan (or other failed states) was too hard, too costly, and naive, considering the realities of Afghan culture and history and the deeply rooted causes of violence and state failure there. The effort was, anyway, irrelevant to US national security: What really mattered was killing al-Qaida, not paving roads in Kandahar. Finally, the effort to make Americans the architects of Afghanistan's future was downright hubristic and imperialist. Instead of nation-building in Afghanistan, the United States should simply sustain an indefinite worldwide assassination campaign against al-Qaida's senior leaders.[12]

There are a number of problems with this view. First, these critics rarely demonstrated a nuanced appreciation for the realities of Afghan culture and history; to the extent that their argument that state-building was too hard rested on their understanding of Afghan history, it was fatally flawed.[13] More important, such critics tended to exaggerate the failures of counterinsurgency and overlook examples of success.[14] Critics' assertions that Iraq and Afghanistan demonstrated the futility of counterinsurgency and stability operations ignored the varying outcomes—including the successes—that have resulted from US operations. If counterinsurgency was futile, the past fifteen years would be a consistent record of failure; because the United States has achieved some success in some areas, counterinsurgency and stability operations are demonstrably *possible*, though certainly hard. Stephen Biddle rightly argued that "the Iraq surge did suggest that COIN [counterinsurgency] was not impossible" and that "the Afghan experience shows that current US methods *can* return threatened districts to government control, when conducted with the necessary time and resources."[15] Biddle separately concluded that the surge in Iraq played a key role creating a "synergistic reaction" with the Anbar Awakening that "created something new that neither could have achieved alone"—an example of how counterinsurgency interacts with the unique political circumstances of the country in which it takes place.[16] Other scholars have made similar arguments about counterinsurgency operations in Vietnam.[17]

Furthermore, these critics failed to offer a convincing explanation for how their alternative—counterterrorism operations without accompanying efforts at reconstruction and stabilization—would result in lasting security for the United States, let alone stability in the region. Political order is the essential condition for the successful termination of military operations. "Central to strategic victory in all wars fought by the United States has been the creation of a favorable political order," according to Nadia Schadlow, which requires a strategy for, and use of, nonmilitary tools of power. "The Iraq situation"— and, clearly, the Afghan one as well—"is only the most recent example of the reluctance of civilian and military leaders, as well as most outside experts, to consider the establishment of political and economic order as *a part of war itself*" or, in other words, that "combat operations and governance operations are both integral to war and occur in tandem."[18] Foreign aid, stability operations, and democratization are weapons of war to be used against enemies who breed on state failure, tyranny, and chaos. This is a straightforward gloss on Clausewitz: "War springs from some political purpose . . . [therefore] the political aim remains the first consideration. Policy, then, will permeate all military operations." Military operations that do not achieve their overriding policy goal—such as counterterrorism operations that do not create an alternative political order—are ineffective and little different from random violence. "War is not merely an act of policy, but a true political instrument, a continuation of political intercourse, carried on with other means."[19]

An assassination campaign against al-Qaida in Afghanistan and Pakistan might keep the immediate threat at bay but would enable the group to reform elsewhere in the world—as it quickly did in Yemen, Iraq, and Syria. Nor is it clear that the campaign against al-Qaida in Afghanistan and Pakistan is even sustainable without broader efforts at stabilization there. Even the rumored drone program almost certainly would require safe airfields, cooperative sources for targeting intelligence, and overflight rights. Chaos or Taliban conquest would endanger all three. That is why Gen. David Petraeus, then serving as commander of the International Security Assistance Force in Afghanistan, told Congress in 2011, "I am concerned that funding for our State Department and USAID partners will not sufficiently enable them to build on the hard-fought security achievements of our men and women in uniform. Inadequate resourcing of our civilian partners could, in fact, *jeopardize accomplishment of the overall mission.*"[20] The drawdown of US forces from Afghanistan will almost certainly allow the Taliban and, thus, al-Qaida to return because the new political order there is not yet strong enough.

Finally, relying solely on drones and raids by Special Operations Forces to take down al-Qaida would do nothing to address America's broader interests at stake in South Asia, all of which are affected by the outcome of the war in Afghanistan, including Pakistan's stability and the security of its nuclear arsenal, the global heroin trade (headquartered in Afghanistan), NATO's future and credibility, American relations with Iran and Russia, the development of Central Asian energy resources, and the future of liberalism in the Islamic world. Kinetic operations, isolated from other instruments of national power, are not a strategy. They are a tactic—a highly effective and necessary one, insufficient by themselves. "Tactics without strategy are the noise before defeat."[21]

The view of war reflected by the counterterrorism-only school of thought is myopic, narrow, and troubling. It amounts to a declaration that the United States reserves the right to kill anyone it deems to be a terrorist, anywhere in the world, forever. Niebuhr would, one imagines, caution against the unchecked and self-justifying power reflected in that policy. "Great disproportions of power" he cautioned, "tempt the strong to wield their power without too much consideration of the interests and views of those upon whom it impinges."[22] States should not maintain a state of war indefinitely just because it is inconvenient to settle the political conditions that led to the war in the first place. Violence should be the last resort, not the first.

If the United States cannot fix every failed state, neither can it afford to fix none of them. The United States cannot make a principle out of not intervening. Some have called for just such a principle in reaction to the failures in Iraq and Afghanistan. Barry Posen, for example, argues that "the counterinsurgency operations of the last decade were largely misdirected and ought not be repeated" and that the United States should simply "avoid certain missions altogether, especially coercive state and nation building."[23] While superficially appealing for its apparent simplicity and realism, this prescription presumes the United States has the ability to choose which crises it will face and determine in advance which tools of national power it will need, a presumption that is supported by nothing in the history of diplomacy or warfare. If it is true that "you may not be interested in war, but war may be interested in you," then today we might observe that the United States may not be interested in counterinsurgency and stability operations, but insurgents, terrorists, and failed states may have an interest in the United States. Ignoring them is shortsighted, ignores the realities of globalization, misunderstands the nature of armed nonstate actors, and is sure to cost more in the long run than is necessary. It amounts to a national resignation to play global whack-a-mole with the crisis *de jour*, sniping pirates one day, drone-bombing terrorists the next, and fencing drug cartels into narco-statelets. Such policy is reactive, defensive, and event-driven, the opposite of what strategy is supposed to be. Should the United States find its interests threatened by insurgents, terrorists, pirates, or drug traffickers and the stakes are sufficiently high to justify the costs, it will need to retain the ability to mount stability operations and peace-building efforts.

The debate over Afghanistan illustrates a broader principle. When faced with any armed nonstate groups that threaten US national security, its allies, or liberal order, the United States faces a basic strategic choice between containment and rollback.[24] It can choose to tolerate the problem as an endemic and permanent feature of life and rely on kinetic operations alone to mitigate risk, with the clear understanding that the problem will not go away and may get worse, with all the morally questionable implications that entails, or it can choose to use all the instruments of national power at its disposal, including foreign aid and stability operations, to address the root causes of disorder and instability.

Foreign Aid

When faced with state failure that incubates threats to liberal order, the least-bad alternative for the international community is to address the root causes of barbarism by fostering the growth of responsible and accountable governance in the places where it is most sorely lacking. In the easiest scenarios, such interventions take the form of civilian aid and development assistance for states that are merely poor. This is the work done by such intergovernmental organizations as the World Bank, the Asia Development Bank, and the International Monetary Fund, and such US agencies as the MCC and the Agency for International Development (USAID). Collectively, these organizations have undertaken decades of civilian development and aid to poor states.

The most famous and still one of the most successful examples of the use of foreign aid to advance US national security is the Marshall Plan.[25] The United States gave about $118 billion in today's dollars to help Europe recover after World War II. Secretary of State George Marshall, in the speech announcing the plan, described the poverty of Europe and explained why the United States had to act:

> Aside from the demoralizing effect on the world at large and the possibilities of disturbances arising as a result of the desperation of the people concerned, the consequences to the economy of the United States should be apparent to all. It is logical that the United States should do whatever it is able to do to assist in the return of normal economic health in the world, without which there can be no political stability and no assured peace. Our policy is directed not against any country or doctrine but against hunger, poverty, desperation and chaos.[26]

The logic was threefold. It was partly humanitarianism, helping relieve human suffering and combating "hunger, poverty, desperation and chaos" after the greatest war in history; it was partly economic selfishness, helping the US economy by putting money in the pockets of some of the United States' most important trading partners; and it was partly strategic, bolstering the newly liberated but fragile democratic governments of Europe against possible communist agitation. Although Marshall said the plan was not aimed "against any country or doctrine," his reference to the "possibilities of disturbances arising as a result of the desperation of the people" was an unmistakable reference to communist agitation in Italy, Greece, and even France after the war. "The United States used the Marshall Plan to forge a political consensus in Western Europe in support of liberal values,"[27] as one scholar said, or another, "By providing the seed money for the recovery of Western Europe, the Marshall Plan transformed its beneficiaries from poverty cases into partners."[28] Finding a policy that hit the overlap between US self-interest, liberal order, and humanitarian concern strikes me as a perfect model of strategic thinking.

The scale of US postwar assistance was awesome. Marshall aid is often isolated from its context, as if it were a bolt from the blue. In fact, the United States gave an enormous amount of foreign aid around the world, starting immediately after World War II, years before the Marshall Plan. Marshall Aid cost about 1 percent of GDP from 1949 to 1952, but this was only part of the

outpouring of American aid. It counts only the aid given through one program—the European Recovery Program—in one region, in four years. All
told, the United States spent something closer to an average of 2.25 percent of
its GDP in foreign aid on all programs and all countries from 1946 through
1952.[29] Today the United States has almost completely disarmed itself of this
tool of national power: Foreign aid fell to less than a tenth of one percent of
GDP by 2001, rising only slightly thereafter during the efforts in Iraq and
Afghanistan.

The Marshall Plan was effective. Its implementers hailed the program as a
success and cited rising economic indicators across Europe as proof: Europe's
economy grew by a third, agriculture by a tenth, and industrial output by 40
percent compared with prewar levels.[30] At least one later historian has cast
doubt on just how large a role Marshall aid played in Europe's recovery, point-
ing to indigenous investment, preexisting social and human capital, and the
relatively small percentage of national income the Marshall aid amounted to
in recipient nations.[31] Another pointed out that the Marshall Plan actually
failed to meet some of its own goals.[32] But most historians have been willing to grant the Marshall Plan more credit for Europe's recovery. One argued
that the Marshall Plan provided at least a "crucial margin of help" to Europe,
because it "not only had a multiplier effect on the European economy as a
whole but on the European mood and initiative."[33] Europeans certainly contributed to their own recovery, but Marshall aid empowered their efforts to
greater effect. Still another has gone further. While also stressing the psychological element to Marshall aid, he argued, "The Plan's contribution, even in
strictly economic terms, must be considered more than 'marginal' or even a
'vital margin.' The Marshall Plan provided essential goods and capital that
helped to power Europe's economy, its industrial modernization and helped
to launch the boom to come."[34] More: The Marshall Plan indisputably played
a role in fostering European integration, a major contribution to stability on
the continent, Western solidarity in the Cold War, and liberal order. "The real
significance of the Marshall Plan lies not so much in its immediate accom-
plishments as in its long-term impact" by laying the foundations on which
future growth and integration could occur.[35]

The Marshall Plan was a success from which today's policymakers can
learn. But they need to learn discerningly, not replicate slavishly. Invoking the
Marshall Plan to justify today's foreign aid programs carries a danger: "The
success of the Marshall Plan has generated false hopes that the application of
capital and technology could do for Third World countries, inner cities, and
post-communist Eastern Europe what was achieved in Western Europe in the
wake of World War II."[36] The situation of Western Europe in 1945 was unique;
no policy template from one era should be slapped down onto other problems

in dissimilar circumstances. Much foreign aid given since the end of the Marshall Plan has not been as effective because it operated on faulty assumptions about how aid works. The Marshall Plan analogy is useful because it illustrates that aid can be an effective instrument of strategic investment that advances America's national security interests. That leaves many unanswered questions. What sort of investments to make, through what kind of programs, in which countries will vary according to what US interests are at stake, what needs must be met, and what preexisting conditions are in target states.

Foreign aid since the Marshall Plan has had a mixed record.[37] The challenges facing newly independent former colonies were different and, in some ways, more deeply embedded than the postwar destruction in Europe, leading to slower and more fragile gains. In the 1960s, donors built programs on the tenets of "modernization theory," a now-discredited school of thought that posited a specific sequence of social, economic, and political steps required for democratization and development, leading to large and wasteful programs that had little effect on recipient countries.[38] Aid was enlisted as a weapon in the Vietnam War and thus suffered from the same crisis of legitimacy the military faced after its defeat there. In the 1970s, the Nixon administration refocused aid on basic human needs, such as food and medicine, in the belief that aid could not affect a country's political structure—but ignored that the quality of governance was often the biggest factor influencing a country's level of human development. Jimmy Carter then shifted focus again to human rights, with much the same problem: The best protection for human rights is an effective, accountable, liberal government dedicated to the rule of law.

Democracy assistance changed fundamentally in the early 1980s, when Reagan founded the National Endowment for Democracy to funnel money toward the construction of the "infrastructure of democracy," including not only electoral bodies, political parties, and legislatures but also independent media and labor unions.[39] The effort to promote institutional reform and civil society gathered steam in the 1990s with the end of the Cold War, the cresting of the "third wave" of democratization, and the conversion of even intergovernmental institutions such as the World Bank to the cause of what they called governance reform (they continued to avoid the rhetoric of "democracy").[40] While problems remained, some scholars began to see signs that US democracy aid was growing more effective. The difference was significant. In the 1970s, "aid providers from the United States and elsewhere conceived of development largely in social and economic terms," but by the 1990s, "the donor community accepted the idea that a country's political development could have major impact on its socioeconomic development."[41] Foreign aid has come full circle and is again an effective tool for fostering accountable and liberal governance.

Stability Operations

Foreign aid is generally unpopular with the American public, but it at least escapes the infamy that attaches to another vital instrument of national power: stability operations. For failed states in the midst of conflict or recently recovering therefrom, intervention takes the form of what the military calls stability operations (the term I use in this book), what the UN calls peace operations, what the State Department calls reconstruction and stabilization operations, what some scholars call "international state building," and what critics deride as "nation-building."[42] At the extreme end, stability operations can include an international transitional administration (as in Kosovo or East Timor) or a military occupation for states that have been overthrown or destroyed (as in Germany, Japan, and Iraq). Broadly, stability operations involve deploying military force, restoring order, rebuilding governments, and sometimes kinetic operations. Elsewhere I have described this as "armed state building" and defined it as the attempt by liberal states to use military, political, and economic power to compel weak, failed, or collapsed states to govern more effectively and accountably, as understood by Westphalian and liberal norms.[43]

Critics sometimes argue that stability operations are not a military mission—that soldiers are not trained for them and lack a doctrine for how to perform them, and therefore the United States should not undertake them. This criticism tries to reverse-engineer strategy, defining ends in terms of what means are available—arguing that because the tools are imperfect, policymakers should design a plan that does not require them—instead of vice versa. Strategic thinking should flow both ways, from ends to means as much as means to ends. If national security requires a stability operation, then it is a military mission; consequently, a key strategic initiative is to create the tools required for their success. I address this challenge in chapters 11 and 12.

The United States more or less invented this form of intervention when it midwifed Cuban independence following the War of 1898. Instead of annexing the island, as it did other territories seized in the war, the United States rebuilt infrastructure, set up a new government, oversaw four elections, and left. It undertook similar efforts in Haiti (1915–34), the Dominican Republic (1916–24), and Nicaragua (1927–33) to prevent state failure from inviting in European influence that might threaten the Panama Canal.

Better-known (and more successful) were the US occupations and reconstructions of Germany and Japan to prevent the growth of communist influence in postwar Europe and Asia. Scholars have done a poor job, to date, extrapolating lessons from those occupations. A simplistic approach suggests that "total war, total defeat, and extensive occupation" are required for "coerced conversion" of failed states to stability and democracy.[44] But there is no reason to believe that what was required to rebuild Germany and Japan can or should be applied indiscriminately to other failed states. Different states fail in different ways and thus require different strategies of stabilization and reconstruction. The United States undoubtedly can learn valuable lessons about the conduct of stability operations from studying its record in Germany and Japan but should do so in the context of studies of all other stability operations as well.[45]

More recently, under the aegis of the UN and sometimes NATO, the international community embraced the reconstruction and stabilization mission after the Cold War, overseeing relatively successful interventions in Namibia, Nicaragua, Mozambique, El Salvador, Guatemala, Bosnia, Kosovo, East Timor, Sierra Leone, and elsewhere. Appropriately, the United States took only a supporting role in most of these operations, leading only in the cases of Bosnia and Kosovo, reflecting its interests in European stability.

The Bill Clinton administration's largest military deployments were stability operations. As Clinton took office, he continued and expanded the US mission to relieve famine and humanitarian suffering in Somalia. Following the model that the international community pursued elsewhere, the intervention gradually evolved from a humanitarian mission to a democratic peace-building operation because policymakers believed stability and democracy were the best long-term solutions to Somalia's many problems. The second UN Operation in Somalia (UNOSOM II), backed by seventeen thousand US troops, was mandated to "assist the people of Somalia to promote and advance political reconciliation, through broad participation by all sectors of Somali society, and the re-establishment of national and regional institutions and civil administration in the entire country."[46]

The next year, Clinton deployed some seventeen thousand US troops to reinstate Jean-Bertrand Aristide as the democratically elected president of Haiti, a post he had been ousted from by the Haitian military three years previously.[47] As in Somalia, after the initial goal was achieved the international community undertook a longer democratic peace-building operation. The United States endorsed and contributed personnel to the follow-on UN Mission in Haiti and its partner international civilian mission, mandated to facilitate the restoration of democratic rule and monitor human rights violations, especially of the freedoms of expression and association in the lead-up to elections.

The major foreign policy crisis Clinton faced was instability and war in the Balkans, in response to which he deployed two major stability operations. The initial interventions in Bosnia (1995) and Kosovo (1999) had a variety of causes and goals—including stopping genocide and ethnic cleansing and preventing instability from spilling over into neighboring NATO-member states. But once the initial campaigns were over, the United States and the international community began lengthy and expensive stability operations because policymakers believed that democracy was the long-term solution to the instability and violence that had plagued the region. The Dayton Accords aimed "to promote free, fair, and democratic elections and to lay the foundation for representative government and ensure the progressive achievement of democratic goals throughout Bosnia and Herzegovina."[48] After the war in Kosovo, the UN, with US backing, established an interim administration there to foster "the development of provisional democratic self-governing institutions to ensure conditions for a peaceful and normal life for all inhabitants of Kosovo," according to the UN Security Council resolution authorizing the mission.[49]

Clinton and, later, George W. Bush gave $2.4 billion in economic and military assistance to Bosnia from 1995 to 2009 and $1.1 billion to Kosovo from 1999 to 2009, among the larger disbursements of US aid outside of the Middle East and Afghanistan.[50] Clinton also deployed 15,000 troops to Bosnia and some 6,400 to Kosovo, along with Somalia and Haiti the largest US military deployments between the Gulf War and Operation Enduring Freedom. Bosnia has held a half dozen national elections since 1995, and Kosovo has held four since 1999. Both were ranked "partly free" by Freedom House in 2015.

Are Stability Operations Feasible?

Doubts persist about the feasibility of stability operations. Any mention of stability operations necessarily invokes Vietnam, Iraq, and Afghanistan. As with the debates about counterinsurgency and democratization, critics are fond of claiming that stability operations are too hard, too costly, and peripheral to US national security. Even Henry Nau, whose "conservative internationalism" informs much of this book, is skeptical that they can be both successful and cost-effective. The effort to impose order and freedom on another society comes perilously close to the sin of trying to "manage history," about which Niebuhr warned, "The illusions about the possibility of managing historical destiny from any particular standpoint in history, always involve, as already noted, miscalculations about both the power and the wisdom of the managers and of the weakness and the manageability of the historical 'stuff' which is to be managed."[51] Stability operations rarely go as planned.

Stability operations are hard. The United States and the international community grew gun-shy after the famously bungled operations in Angola, Liberia, and Somalia in the 1990s. The second UN Angola Verification Mission oversaw a presidential election in 1992, the unfavorable outcome of which was seized upon by Jonas Savimbi's rebel group to renew its decades-long civil war, suggesting that rapid elections in a postconflict environment can exacerbate problems. The UN Observer Mission in Liberia drove the country's peace process toward an election in 1997 but failed to disarm factions first. Charles Taylor, the most ruthless and well-armed warlord in Liberia, simply terrified the citizenry into electing him. In Somalia, the UN and United States failed to deploy anything that country needed to impose order over fractious warlords and restart the nonfunctioning government. In all three cases, the states in question ended up worse off because of outside meddling. That is why some scholars have argued that "the United States has neither the skills nor the resources needed" for stability operations, because "the US military is designed for fighting, not for peacekeeping or police work. . . . It has virtually no organized capacity for nation building."[52]

The experience in Somalia was especially influential in shaping scholars' and policymakers' attitudes toward stability operations. In the two decades since the failure of UNOSOM II, it is routinely cited as evidence that some states are so far gone that outsiders cannot foster stability and democracy in them. Fareed Zakaria, for example, wrote, "The trouble with trying to fix failed states is that it implicates the United States in a vast nation building effort in countries where the odds of success are low and the risk of unintended consequences is very high. Consider Somalia. [That operation] highlights the complexity of almost every approach to failed states."[53]

But it does not. We might call this the Somalia Fallacy. Despite its dramatic public impact, the mission in Somalia is not a useful historical analogy to generalize about failed states and stability operations. To make a useful generalization, we should start with a typical failed state, or, better yet, several of them. Somalia was not a typical failed state—it was an extreme outlier. It has been nearly the most completely failed state in the world for almost two decades. Even more, UNOSOM II was not a typical UN intervention: It was a singularly, uniquely inept one marred by an inadequate mandate, poor resources, unclear command and control, and no political will. Stability operations in Somalia saw the deployment of the most inept UN mission to the world's most failed state. It is unsurprising that what resulted was a famous catastrophe, but observers should not treat it as a blueprint for how all interventions are doomed to play out.

Stability operations have proven to be a viable and successful option in the past because most interventions do not have to contend with Somalian levels of anarchy, and the United States and UN have also learned to operate with a measure of greater sophistication. The failures have been big, public, and humiliating, but in the last two decades, the United States and UN have racked up better outcomes in Namibia, Mozambique, Nicaragua, El Salvador,

Guatemala, Bosnia, Croatia, Kosovo, Timor-Leste, Liberia (the second time), and Sierra Leone (which came back from the brink of failure). Few of those countries are fully rebuilt, modern, stable liberal democracies. Civil unrest still occasionally flares up. But the international interventions changed their trajectories and put them on a path of sustainable political and economic progress. None have reverted to large-scale political violence. Their peace agreements have held. They have all held relatively open and competitive elections. Most have seen positive postwar economic growth. A few have shown improvements in the quality and accountability of their governance, according to the World Bank's governance indicators—probably the hardest task of postconflict reconstruction.[54]

The bottom line is that these countries are better off now than they were at the nadir of their respective wars and failures, and they are generally improving, not backsliding. This is a realistic, achievable, and useful standard of success that policymakers can use to determine if an intervention is worth the cost and effort—something that Nau and other skeptics overlook. Using a sliding scale also enables us to distinguish between utter failures (e.g., resumed war in Angola), middling outcomes (e.g., Cambodia, which has settled on an undemocratic peace), shallow successes (e.g., Nicaragua, which enjoys peace and political freedom but economic stagnation), and outright victory (e.g., Sierra Leone, Germany). That makes a real difference in human lives and is typically good enough to secure whatever regional or global interests led to the intervention in the first place.

Stability operations are often unpopular with the American public because of how they are framed. Michael Lekson and Nathaniel L. Wilson point out that "with the possible exception of Bosnia, popular support for serious and sustained efforts in this regard has come about only when they have been seen as an element of the active conduct of a specific kind of armed conflict"—namely, Vietnam, Iraq, or Afghanistan.[55] Other stability operations—those unconnected with a concurrent shooting war—are, mistakenly, viewed as less vital or relevant for US national security. In fact, they are the opposite. Stability operations that take place *before* the outbreak of war are probably *more* effective at securing US national security interests at lower cost because they take place in a more permissive operating environment with fewer active opponents. The persistent failure of US policymakers to frame stability operations as essential preventative exercises of hard power against defined threats has seriously undermined their prospects.

Seen in proper perspective, stability operations are not international charity. They are not a superfluous, dispensable exercise in appeasing Western guilt, an expensive tribute to humanitarianism, or an act of unvarnished selflessness. Stability operations are a necessary response to the danger of failed states that threaten regional stability. They are a strategic investment in weak states to increase their capacities. They are an effort to target countries whose weakness threatens international order to improve specific abilities, such as their ability to provide public security, defend borders, produce and sell goods, and suppress illicit activities (including terrorism and organized crime). They are a pragmatic exercise of hard power to protect vital national interests.

Toward a Doctrine of Stability Operations

One of the greatest improvements the United States should make in this aspect of its grand strategy is to formulate a coherent doctrine of stability operations. Stability operations are one of the most complex undertakings a state can attempt. There is no silver bullet or single variable that explains all cases of success and failure—not the rule of law, availability of health care, amount of paved roads, timing of elections, GDP growth rate, and not even the security environment. The UN Mission in Haiti in 1994, for example, ultimately failed to restore political stability not because of violence, insurgency, or civil war but because of endemic political gridlock and institutional weakness that the UN failed to address.

Successful stability operations require close attention and responsiveness to local conditions. This will require a reorientation in how we think about state failure. Scholars and policymakers tended in the past to view state failure as an easily defined condition. State failure, in this view, is a singular, monolithic phenomenon; states all fail the same way but to varying degrees. Thus, organizations such as the Fund for Peace measure a range of variables associated with state failure, including demographics, refugee populations, economic decline, security incidents, and so forth, aggregate them into a single score of failure, and rank all countries in the world, most failed to least, in their Fragile States Index.[56] In 2014, South Sudan and Somalia topped the list, followed by the Central African Republic, the Democratic Republic of the Congo, Sudan, Chad, Afghanistan, Yemen, and Haiti.

The Fragile States Index illustrates the problems with this approach to state failure. Somalia and Sudan present polar-opposite problems. Somalia's failure is one of too little government; it is literally anarchic. Sudan's failure is one of too much government of the wrong kind; it is tyrannical and genocidal. Afghanistan, meanwhile, is waging a counterinsurgency, while Yemen is collapsing from civil war and terrorism. Putting these diverse states together on a single list of "failures" does little to illuminate the vast differences between them or suggest ways of resolving their problems. Instead, it encourages a cookie-cutter approach to stability operations that overlooks the different problems each state faces and therefore the different solutions required.

Different states fail in different ways. It is helpful to think of statehood as comprising five complementary aspects: security, legitimacy, capacity, prosperity, and humanity. States must be able to exercise coercion, articulate a theory of justice, operate institutions to provide governance, exchange and use goods and services, and orient their activities toward human flourishing. They are mediators of violence, justice, the social contract, economic exchange, and human community.

State failure can be understood under the same headings. States fail in any of these five aspects of statehood, suggesting a typology of failed states: anarchic, illegitimate, incompetent, unproductive, and barbaric. Anarchic states lack security, as, for example, Iraq did in 2006. Illegitimate states cannot command the loyalty or consent of the population because of some perceived injustice—perhaps including Tunisia and Egypt in early 2011. Incompetent states lack functioning institutions and simply cannot deliver goods and services, such as Haiti. Unproductive states are not simply poor; they have malformed economies because of war, looting, smuggling, and black markets, such as parts of West Africa in the 1990s. Barbaric states murder their own citizens on a large scale, such as Sudan.

These different types of failure imply different strategies of state-building. What Iraq needed in 2006 was different from what Haiti needs today. The international community must be able to study the situation on the ground, understand the type and degree of state failure, and tailor a stability operations strategy accordingly. Such a strategy requires a culture of institutional learning, a bottom-up approach in which missions in the field design themselves as much as headquarters in New York or Washington design them, and more rapid decision making.[57]

Conclusion

A century of experience suggests that development assistance and reconstruction and stabilization missions are a necessary response to the threat of failed states and the armed nonstate groups that operate within them. Foreign aid and stability operations are strategic investments in weak states to increase their capacities, like their ability to provide public security, defend their borders, produce and sell goods, and suppress illicit activities. They are a pragmatic exercise of power to protect vital national interests. While such interventions are difficult and costly, they are far from impossible, and the international community appears to be improving its track record and internalizing lessons learned from hard experience.

The United States and its partners do not have the ability or interest to intervene and fix every failed state, nor do they have enough money to bring prosperity to every developing country. American policymakers must take a hard look at where weak states most clearly threaten American interests and where underdevelopment most damages American opportunities. Near the top of the list must be Mexico, whose war with the drug cartels threatens to spill over into American territory and deplete the resources of one of America's top trading partners, and Afghanistan and Pakistan, whose lawless regions offer safe haven to terrorists of global reach. US aid, equipment, and training to Mexican and Afghan law enforcement and security forces should thus be a top priority for American foreign policy. (It is unclear if opportunities exist for the United States to give meaningful help to Pakistan or Yemen.) Also near the top of the list must be India's perennial struggle against rural poverty. As a fellow democratic great power and a rising economic superpower, India might anchor stability in South and East Asia and form a lasting and prosperous trade relationship with the United States, but its seeming inability to improve its infrastructure, aid poor farmers, and rid itself of corruption is holding it, and the world, back. US civilian aid to India could be among the most strategic uses of US aid in the world.

The United States can and should respond to the rising tide of state failure across the world with foreign aid and stability operations to support competent democratic government. The aggregate consequences of state failure and anarchy across much of the world—such as the rise of terrorist groups, organized crime, drug cartels, human traffickers, and piracy—collectively erode global stability and liberalism and raise the cost of US leadership. Effective foreign aid programs and stability operations—that is, programs that are well funded, well planned, and, when necessary, well armed—are the answer to this challenge. Foreign aid and stability operations, when successful, hold out the promise not just of treating these various symptoms but also addressing the disease.

Notes

1. Porter, *Global Village Myth*.
2. Quoted in McDougall, *Promised Land*, 36.
3. Runkle, *Wanted Dead or Alive*; Bowden, *Killing Pablo*.
4. UNSCR 1373, September 28, 2001.

5. US Department of State, "Proliferation Security Initiative."

6. Combined Maritime Forces, "CTF-151: Counter-Piracy."

7. Nixon, "Address to the Nation on the War in Vietnam."

8. The following is drawn from Miller, "Case for Nation-Building."

9. Fearon and Laitin, "Neotrusteeship and the Problem of Weak States"; Krasner, "Case for Shared Sovereignty."

10. Chandler, *Empire in Denial*.

11. Nau, *At Home Abroad*, 190.

12. Gentile, *Wrong Turn*; Porch, *Counterinsurgency*.

13. Miller, "Graveyard of Analogies."

14. Ucko, "Critics Gone Wild"; Gventer, "Counterinsurgency and Its Critics."

15. Biddle, "Afghanistan's Legacy," 75–76. See also Byman, "Friends like These."

16. Biddle, Friedman, and Shapiro, "Testing the Surge," 10–11.

17. Krepinevich, *Army and Vietnam*; Sorley, *Better War*; Moyar, *Triumph Forsaken*.

18. Schadlow, "War and the Art of Governance," 85–86. Emphasis in original.

19. Clausewitz, *On War*, 87.

20. Petraeus, "Statement before the Senate Armed Services Committee." Emphasis added.

21. Another apocryphal quote, this one wrongly attributed to Sun Tzu. Gentile uses this phrase to criticize advocates of counterinsurgency, claiming that it is a mere tactic absent guiding strategic logic. But his preferred alternative—the "counterterrorism-only" approach I critique here—is the paradigmatic case of tactics without strategy. See Gentile, "Strategy of Tactics." Gentile cites Sun Tzu in a footnote but the aphorism is not found in Sun Tzu's book.

22. Niebuhr, *Irony*, 135.

23. Posen, *Restraint*, 145, xiv.

24. Biddle, *American Grand Strategy after 9/11*.

25. Mills, *Winning the Peace*; Schain, *Marshall Plan*; Kunz, "Marshall Plan Reconsidered"; Behrman, *Most Noble Adventure*; Hogan, *Marshall Plan*. See Milward, *Reconstruction of Western Europe* and "Was the Marshall Plan Necessary?," and Esposito, *America's Feeble Weapon*, for more skeptical takes.

26. Marshall, "Speech at Harvard University."

27. Layne, *Peace of Illusions*, 78.

28. Kunz, "Marshall Plan Reconsidered."

29. Calculations from data derived from the US Agency for International Development, *U.S. Overseas Loans and Grants* (also known as "the Green Book"), and from the Bureau of Economic Analysis.

30. Hogan, cited in Kunz, "Marshall Plan Reconsidered," 12.

31. Milward, *Reconstruction of Western Europe* and "Was the Marshall Plan Necessary?"

32. Imanuel Wexler, "The Marshall Plan in Economic Perspective," in Schain, *Marshall Plan*, 150.

33. Mills, *Winning the Peace*, xi, xii.

34. Behrman, *Most Noble Adventure*, 334.

35. Wexler, "Marshall Plan," 151, in Schain, *Marshall Plan*.

36. Rostow, "Lessons of the Plan."

37. Carothers, *Aiding Democracy Abroad*, chap. 2, offers a brief history of US foreign aid.

38. Gilman, *Mandarins of the Future*. The seminal texts of modernization theory included Lipset, *Political Man*, and Rostow, "Stages of Economic Growth." Huntington, *Political Order in Changing Societies*, is the definitive rebuttal. See also Carothers, "End of the Transition Paradigm."

39. Muravchik, *Exporting Democracy*, chap. 13.

40. Huntington, *Third Wave*.

41. Carothers, *Aiding Democracy Abroad*, 46.

42. No one calls it "nation-building" except critics who want to imply it is overly ambitious and outside the military's core competence. For simplicity's sake, I use the military's term.

43. Miller, *Armed State Building*, 7.

44. Art, "Defensible Defense," 42.

45. A satisfactory study of the occupations of Germany and Japan has, astonishingly, not been done. See Miller, "Bibliographic Essay." My own effort to study the broader universe of cases is in *Armed State Building*.

46. UNSCR 814, March 26, 1993.

47. All figures for US troop deployments are drawn from Kane, "Global U.S. Troop Deployment, 1950–2005," online dataset available through the Heritage Foundation, Center for Data Analysis Report #04–11.

48. Dayton Peace Accords, annex 3, available as UNSCR 999, November 30, 1995.

49. UNSCR 1244, June 10, 1999.

50. Figures for US foreign assistance are drawn from US Agency for International Development, *U.S. Overseas Loans and Grants*.

51. Niebuhr, *Irony*, 72.

52. Schwenninger, "Revamping American Grand Strategy," 30–31.

53. Fareed Zakari, "The Failed-State Conundrum," *Washington Post*, July 19, 2010, http://www.washingtonpost.com/wp-dyn/content/article/2010/07/18/AR20100 71802734.html, accessed April 17, 2015.

54. Kaufman, Kraay, and Mastruzzi, "Worldwide Governance Indicators."

55. Michael Lekson and Nathaniel L. Wilson, "A Future U.S. Grand Strategy," in Franke and Dorff, *Conflict Management and Peacebuilding*, 123.

56. The Fund for Peace, *Fragile States Index 2014*.

57. Howard, *UN Peacekeeping in Civil Wars*.

PART III

REGIONAL APPLICATION

6

The Frontline

Europe and East Asia

The previous chapters outlined the history and theory of America's grand strategic objectives and courses of action. The United States provides security for itself by balancing power, championing liberalism, fighting barbarism, and building states. This is the theoretical architecture of American grand strategy. What does it look like in practice? This involves several related questions. How is liberal order constructed and sustained? How should the United States prioritize when and where it acts? What tools and resources should it employ, under what circumstances?

These questions are important because the United States cannot do everything, everywhere, all the time, and not every region is equally important. The United States should seek to increase the proportion of global power under democratic control—but where and how? It should rebuild failed states that harbor threats to liberal order—but which ones? Democratizing Fiji would increase democratic power in the world—but only by a tiny percentage and in a strategically unimportant country. The Democratic Republic of the Congo is probably the second most failed state in the world after Somalia, but fixing it—the most spacious country in sub-Saharan Africa, the fourth most populous on the continent, one of the poorest states in the world, in a state of continuous failure, civil war, or tyranny for almost its entire independent existence—would be a gargantuan, multigenerational, multitrillion-dollar effort that would dwarf any intervention in history for no commensurate strategic purpose. If Pakistan, by contrast, consolidates and deepens its transition to democracy, it would be a game changer for the twenty-first century and beyond.

Recognizing which states, regions, and issues are most important to US national security helps identify which threats and opportunities to US interests are most important and therefore where the United States should devote its time, money, military power, diplomatic efforts, and more. This is what turns theory into strategy. Works that only describe a master concept of a proposed grand strategy leave themselves open to endless interpretation and offer little practical guidance and no sense of priorities.

In other words, we need more than an argument that liberal order is important. We need to know how it is built. Ikenberry defines liberal order primarily as a *political* order among states and emphasizes the construction of intergovernmental institutions to create and mediate it. But liberal order is better understood as a *culture* of world politics. Culture is "socially established structures of meaning," or the "webs of significance" that human beings spin for themselves, the analysis of which is "not an experimental science in search of law but an interpretive one in search of meaning."[1] As a culture, liberal order depends on beliefs, ideas, and ideology—and on the action that flows from them, including habits, practices, and what Tocqueville called "mores," whether or not they are formally captured in intergovernmental agreements and institutions.

This suggests a very different view of how to implement grand strategy. For realists, grand strategy is a comparatively simple matter of assessing states' relative material power and recommending ways to enhance and use it. For liberal internationalists, grand strategy is a matter of building liberal institutions. In the approach outlined here, grand strategy includes both of the previous notions but also works to establish one particular set of ideas— liberal ideas—as the "socially established structures of meaning" for world order. This does *not* reduce grand strategy to public diplomacy. Liberal culture cannot be declared by fiat, manufactured according to predetermined blueprint, or orchestrated by a single maestro. Simply proselytizing for liberal principles, as Wilson attempted, does not produce liberal order. Culture emerges from the complex interplay among actors and between actors and the system they inhabit.[2] The culture of liberal order is akin to an emergent property of specific practices—such as self-government, civil liberties, and open trade—when they are widely shared by powerful actors in a system. If liberal order is a sort of "constitution" of world order, it is an unwritten one—with all the advantages and disadvantages that come with its ambiguity and flexibility.

The creation of culture is even less a science than its interpretation. Reduced to a simplistic but useable formulation, liberal order emerges from a world dominated by powerful liberal states. Liberal order exists today because almost all of the world's richest and most militarily powerful states are democracies. As Robert Art argues, "the solidity of democracy within the great powers is important because that makes its advance elsewhere more likely."[3] That is why US grand strategy should aim at increasing the proportion of power under democratic control. This can be accomplished by increasing existing democracies' share of economic or military power, by increasing the number of democracies in the world, or both. Nau recommends the United States work to increase the number of democratic states in the world—but he fails to note that not all states are made equal. Some matter more than others. He prioritizes states that are on the borders of existing democracies, which seems an arbitrary criterion by which to identify states that matter. Instead, the United States can prioritize where to invest in the growth of liberal order in largely realist terms: Powerful states, potentially powerful states, and strategically situated states should get the most attention. Grand strategy seeks to identify and invest in states that offer the greatest return on investment: those that are powerful enough to make a difference in world order and that are already friendly to the United States or open to liberal ideas (such as India). By contrast, turning illiberal or hostile states into liberal states and supporters of liberal order requires a vastly greater and riskier effort for an uncertain return. The United States should undertake such efforts only when compelled by necessity, as in Germany and Japan after World War II.

The following chapters are my attempt to translate these concepts into specific policy proposals. I review the geopolitical theaters in order of their importance to US national security: Europe, East Asia, South Asia, the Middle East, Latin America, and Africa. This ranking reflects the relative power, wealth, and threat in each region (see table 6.1). Europe and East Asia still have a disproportionate share of the world's wealth and power, and there are major conventional threats in both regions. South Asia is, contrary to received wisdom, the third most important region in the world, is growing in importance as India grows more wealthy and powerful, and is home to both state and nonstate threats. The importance of the Middle East is on a long-term decline, although there are major state and nonstate threats there. Latin America is important chiefly because of trade, drug trafficking, and its proximity to the US border. The absence of either major centers of power or major state-based threats in either Africa or Latin America makes both regions of lesser importance to the United States.

Europe and East Asia are the most important regions, but they are also the regions in which the architecture of US grand strategy is most well developed. Sustaining the entrenched alliance relationships with democratic great powers and institutions already present in both regions is a low-cost way of sustaining American security and liberal order in the most important regions in the world. Because of the democratic peace and the convergence of national identities among democratic great powers, "the United States can avoid costly arms races with the world's richest nations and sustain a role in the world that would not be bearable if America had to rely on its own resources alone."[4] These alliances anchor regional stability, uphold liberal order, and threaten unacceptable cost to Russia, China, and North Korea for aggression. Both sets

Table 6.1. Distribution of Power across Regions

Region	% World GDP[a]	% US Trade[b]	% National Material Capabilities[c]	% Global Military Spending[d]	No. of Nuclear Powers	% Global Power[e]
Europe[f]	25.2	37.4	22.4	23.9	3	23.1
East Asia	28.8	32.0	31.8	17.1	2	20.6
South Asia	8.9	2.2	10.6	3.5	2	9.0
Middle East[g]	5.9	4.7	7.1	9.5	1	4.3
Latin America	7.6	21.9	6.8	4.6	0	5.8
Africa[h]	4.5	1.7	6.4	2.6	0	5.0
United States	16.5	—	14.1	38.8	1	21.0

[a] World Bank, *Data*. Data computed with international dollars on a purchasing power parity basis.
[b] US Census Bureau, "U.S. International Trade Data."
[c] Correlates of War v. 4.0. See Singer, "Reconstructing the Correlates of War Dataset."
[d] International Institute for Strategic Studies, *Military Balance*, chap. 10.
[e] Pardee Center for International Futures, *Data*.
[f] Includes Canada.
[g] Does not include North Africa except Egypt.
[h] Does not include Egypt.

of alliances are deep and long-lasting, and maintaining and deepening them rightly has been, and should continue to be, everyday business for the US national security establishment. Maintaining NATO and the network of alliances in East Asia is thus the top priority for US foreign policy. It is unoriginal to point this out, which makes it important to do so: Scholars' natural desire to say something novel sometimes leaves important commonplaces unstated.

The United States has a less well-developed military posture in South Asia and the Middle East and virtually nothing established in Latin America and Africa, somewhat justified by their lesser importance to American security and the smaller role they play either supporting or opposing liberal order. However, as I argue below, the United States should make greater investments in some of these regions. If it were to systematically realign its global aid and alliance posture, it would involve bolstering ties to full or partial democracies with whom it does not currently have an established relationship. Tony Smith, in advocating for what he calls "selective liberal democratic internationalism," argued that "important stakes must be involved or that the likelihood of success is high before the United States commits itself."[5] In order to avoid overstretch or utopian aspirations, the United States should seek stronger ties only with states that meet three criteria. First, they should be either full or partial democracies. Second, there should be an opportunity for partnership with the United States to consolidate or advance liberal, accountable governance. And third, the state should be able to offer the United States some strategic benefits, such as a platform of access to the region, cooperation against a terrorist group or drug-trafficking organization, or cooperation against a nuclear autocracy. (That does not limit the United States to partnering only with large, rich, or powerful states. Smaller states might still play an important role regionally or by virtue of their geography.) In other words, the United States should prioritize its investment in new relationships abroad by looking at how powerful or potentially powerful a state is, where it is located, and its commitment to liberalism or its prospects for liberalization. The purpose is twofold: US aid, investment, and security cooperation will help democracies—especially new, transitioning, or weak ones—consolidate self-government and strengthen institutions of good governance. In return, those countries can join the existing network of US partners that act as a stabilizing presence in key regions against the nuclear autocracies or failed states.

The greatest opportunity to enhance US security and liberal order in the twenty-first century is to partner with democratic great powers not already in the alliance system in strategically important regions—which is the long way of saying "India." The US–Indian relationship is the single greatest unrealized opportunity for US security and liberal order in the twenty-first century. Investing in the Indian economy would increase the proportion of global wealth in democratic hands, and working more closely with India on issues of global concern would add resilience and strength to liberal order, especially if US relative power declines. Enhancing US–Indian ties through aid, trade, technical assistance, joint military exercises, weapon sales, strategic talks, and cultural exchange should be the top new initiative for US foreign policy in coming decades.

The next priority for US engagement should be quietly supporting liberalism among its allies in strategically important regions whose historical track record on liberalism is shaky: Turkey, Thailand, the Philippines, and, possibly, Pakistan, depending on the fate of its civilian government. The United States has close ties to all four, meaning it has the opportunity and the relationship capital (except in Pakistan) to speak quietly to policymakers in those countries about the importance of civilian rule, the peaceful transfer of power, the rule of law, and civil liberties. In terms of resources, this means the United States should deploy more diplomats trained in local languages for longer tours of duty, hold more joint exercises to foster relationships among mid- and senior-ranking military officers, and sponsor more training opportunities in the United States for diplomats and soldiers from those countries. Growing relationships among mid-ranking civilian and military personnel is the sort of unglamorous but long-term investment that pays strategic benefits in unquantifiable ways. This should be a high priority for US policymakers but need be neither public nor resource-intensive. (It is also an illustration of how the less-versus-more nature of the grand strategy debate is shallow. Some situations are highly important and need consistent time and attention but not money and troops.)

The next priority should be weak states and failing states in strategically important regions or weak states in any area that are sources of armed nonstate actors—but that also have the potential to become partners with the United States if given time and investment. This category includes Iraq, Afghanistan, Colombia, and Mexico and would include North Korea if it collapsed but would exclude Somalia, Yemen, and the Democratic Republic of the Congo. The first five are in important regions or harbor nonstate threats and are or have the potential to become strategically important states in their respective regions. Despite the safe haven the latter states provide for pirates and jihadists, there are few prospects that either state will recover from failure or becoming useful partners for the United States and meaningful supporters of liberal order. I recognize many scholars and policymakers believe Afghanistan should be put in the second category. I argue in the next chapter why they are wrong.

The next priority should be to work for liberalization and improved ties among potentially powerful democracies and partial democracies not in the alliance system in strategically important regions: Ukraine, Bangladesh, Indonesia, and Malaysia. These states are free or partly free, suggesting they are not hostile to liberalism and may be willing to receive US aid, trade, and technical assistance. They are poor and weak, but they have the population, landmass, and location to become strategically important players in their regions if they improve their governance and economic performance, suggesting they are worth investing in.

Finally, the United States has an opportunity to bolster ties with powerful and potentially powerful democracies and partial democracies not in the alliance system in regions of lesser importance: Brazil, Nigeria, and South Africa. Improving ties with these countries is not a *priority*, but it is an *opportunity* to strengthen the liberal order and America's position in it. If the United States is able to devote more diplomatic attention and foreign aid to these countries without pulling resources away from the previous categories, it should do so.

Who does this leave out? It omits scores and scores of microsovereignties and minor states that offer little and threaten less to US national security or world order. It omits most states in Africa, Latin America, and even the Middle East because those regions are not as important to US security. It omits autocracies in strategically important regions that are not allies of the

United States, such as Vietnam and Belarus. And it omits even the autocratic allies in strategically peripheral regions. The United States stands to gain little by pushing its autocratic Middle Eastern allies—Egypt, Jordan, Morocco, and Bahrain—to democratize. Except Egypt, these countries are poor, weak, and not influential. Their liberalization would add little to global freedom or liberal order. The Middle East is a theater of lesser importance, and the United States would be foolish to expend the necessary resources to liberalize hard cases such as the Middle Eastern autocracies. Nor do they need to democratize to help counter the threat from Iran. I emphasize these points because proposed grand strategies often fail to specify what that United States should *not* do and thus lead to unclear boundaries and mission creep. A clear and strong sense of priorities keeps grand strategy from becoming utopian.

Europe

Europe is the most important geopolitical theater for the United States because of the concentration of wealth, power, and democratic countries there and because of Russia, still the preeminent nuclear autocracy in the world. Counting Russia, Europe accounts for about a quarter of global power, more than a third of US trade, and three of the world's nine nuclear weapon states. Europe is the largest concentration of liberal democracies in the world, the headquarters for many of the world's most important international institutions, and collectively constitutes a primary pillar of support for liberal order. A crisis in Europe would threaten the United States' most important allies, interests, and values and involve a confrontation with its most dangerous rival. Fortunately, US objectives in Europe were mostly achieved by the end of the Cold War, though the failure of democratization in Russia in the 1990s was a major missed opportunity. Today US strategy should be, mostly, to stay the course: Stay in NATO, maintain the alliance, resist Russia's attempts to expand its influence through illegitimate means, and keep the peace.

NATO

NATO is the most important international institution in the world for the United States, and its upkeep should be a major concern of US policymakers.[6] Scholars often observe that NATO is built on the Franco–German relationship. That is true but not exclusively so. NATO is also built on the Anglo–American "special relationship," rumors of the death of which are routinely exaggerated. The special relationship rests on shared values and culture; was created during a century of mutual hostility, suspicion, competition, and admiration; was put into practice in the joint management of global finance, trade arrangements, and sea supremacy before the world wars; was cemented by the wartime coalitions; and today consists in deep and abiding institutional networks and ties between American and British public officials, entrepreneurs, and businessmen at all levels.[7] To take just one example, the scope and extent of reported intelligence sharing between the United States and the United Kingdom is far beyond that with other US allies and would probably challenge most realist theories of state behavior and sovereignty. Sustaining the special US–UK relationship is a vital interest of American national security.

The expansion of NATO after the Cold War was a pragmatic expansion of US influence in its most important region and helped create an important limitation to Russia's future imperial revanchism. The argument against NATO's expansion—that it "expanded US obligations in ways that did little for US security and needlessly antagonized Russia"[8]—is exactly wrong. Expanding NATO brought Eastern Europe under the umbrella of liberal order, limited Russian influence, solidified European unity, and deepened US influence.[9] While Russia has indulged in aggression against non-NATO states, it is unlikely to attempt overt hostility against a NATO member state because of the risk of escalation and general war. In addition, expanding NATO added allies who contributed Special Operations Forces to the hunt for al-Qaida after 2001. NATO expansion clearly enhanced US national security in US efforts against both Russia and al-Qaida. Its continued expansion is likely. It is already slated to welcome Montenegro into the alliance in mid-2016. Macedonia's entry is probable within a few years, Sweden's accession (where public support for NATO membership has been rising) is possible, and Bosnia's more distant. The inclusion of Georgia is problematic unless it resolves its disputes with Russia, while moves to include Kosovo, Austria (because of its postwar pledge of neutrality), Serbia, or Ukraine would likely trigger a crisis with Russia and are not worth the risk. Mexico's inclusion, as I discuss in chapter 9, is also possible. Expanding NATO globally, as some have suggested,[10] is an appealing concept on paper but would detract from mission focus and alliance cohesion and should not be pursued.[11]

NATO faces some internal challenges. Its purpose has been watered down by taking on ever more missions, including cyberdefense, counterpiracy, and peacekeeping, and weakened by uneven burden sharing in out-of-area operations in Afghanistan and Libya.[12] The allies' threat perceptions have diverged—the United States' from Europe's, Eastern Europe's from Western Europe's, and Turkey's from everyone else's—because of the fall of the Soviet Union, the rise of Iran, and the increasing power disparities within the alliance. Tactical cohesion has suffered as the United States and a few others have developed high-tech weaponry and communications that are not interoperable with other allies' less advanced systems. The allies fear being dragged into war by an overactive United States but also fear being abandoned by an isolationist one.[13] The alliance risks drifting into all-purpose debating society whose chief effect will be to bestow the positive glow of multilateralism on American initiatives. Refocusing it on its main mission—European defense—should help alleviate some of these concerns by focusing on a common threat and defining and limiting the US role. The United States should increase the size and frequency of joint military exercises in Europe and consider reconfiguring the deployment of its troops, still heavily concentrated in Germany, while avoiding using NATO for peacekeeping or other operations outside of Europe.

NATO and the US position in Europe could be threatened by the erosion of democracy in Central and Eastern Europe and Turkey, some of the youngest democracies in the world. NATO has included autocracies in the past (Greece, from 1952 to 1973; Portugal, from 1949 to 1975; and Turkey, during a few interruptions of military rule since 1952). But since 1989, NATO has functioned as a cooperative security community of European liberal democracies. The prospect of NATO and EU membership was a key incentive for Eastern European countries to democratize and liberalize in the first place.[14] The 2008 financial crisis and ensuing Great Recession have exacerbated a growing sense of disillusionment some Europeans felt toward the European project. Concomitantly, Europe has seen the rise of illiberal parties, including Golden Dawn in Greece, Fidesz and Jobbik in Hungary, and the Freedom Party in Austria, fueled in part by the refugee crisis in 2015. For different reasons, the strength of Turkish democracy is also uncertain. US foreign aid to Eastern Europe and Turkey—specifically, humanitarian relief for refugees, aid and training to independent media, civil society, election-monitoring teams, countercorruption bureaucracies, prosecutors and judges, and other parts of the infrastructure of a free society—should be the top priority for foreign aid globally. (That does not mean it should be the largest dollar expenditure; security assistance is far more expensive than the civilian assistance needed in Eastern Europe and Turkey. But aid to Eastern Europe and Turkey should be the last to be cut.)

Ukraine

The biggest crisis in Europe is the war in Ukraine. The Ukrainian government pressed for closer ties to the West after the 2005 Orange Revolution ousted the pro-Russian administration of Viktor Yanukovych, including by formally applying for a NATO membership action plan in 2008. Russian government officials made clear in repeated public and private statements since the Cold War that Ukraine's accession to NATO would be unacceptable to Russia because of Russia's naval facility in Crimea and cultural ties to Kiev. Following civil unrest in Ukraine in 2013 and 2014, Russia invaded Ukraine under the pretext of protecting ethnic Russians and annexed Crimea after overseeing a referendum—widely recognized as fraudulent—in March 2014. At the time of this writing there is sporadic fighting between Ukraine and pro-Russian rebels—almost certainly supported by Russian soldiers, weapons, and equipment—in eastern Ukraine.[15]

The current crisis in Ukraine is the place where the long-brewing confrontation between NATO's expansion and Russia's revival has finally taken place and is probably the most dangerous moment in Europe since the Prague Spring. Some realists have interpreted Russia's move as an expression of understandable defensive concerns against Western expansionism.[16] There is no moral logic to this criticism. Putin and his circle define Russia's security interests to include its sway over its near abroad, including the former Soviet republics and Eastern Europe, and thus believed NATO's expansion was a form of "aggression"—but that does not mean Russian security perceptions are legitimate or that the West is obliged to accommodate them. John Owen and William Inboden rightly argue that "Russia feels threatened by the eastward expansion of the EU and NATO not because of some immutable law of international relations but because Russia is ruled by an authoritarian, antidemocratic regime."[17] Or, as Kissinger claimed well before the age of Putin, Russia is "torn between obsessive insecurity and proselytizing zeal" such that "the requirements of conquest and of security became merged in the minds of Russian leaders."[18] Accommodating Russia's expansionist security perceptions would legitimize them and encourage more of the same from Russia and other states. Nor is there a moral equivalence between Russia's expansionist view of its security requirements and the nesting of American security in liberal order. Superficially both states define their security in extraterritorial terms, but Russia's depends on the unilateral dominance of other states, while liberal order helps secure the independent aspirations of those uninterested in belonging to Russia's sphere of influence. The United States and its allies have clear title to the moral high ground in Ukraine.

The United States and its allies probably missed an opportunity in late 2013 by failing to take Putin up on his call for a Ukrainian plebiscite. Crimeans and eastern Ukrainians might have willingly voted to accede to Russia, and an internationally sanctioned referendum before the Russian invasion, with observers from the UN or the Organization for Security and Cooperation in Europe to effect the formal, peaceful partition of Ukraine—akin to Czechoslovakia's "Velvet Divorce" in 1993—could have resolved the crisis for all sides, enabling western Ukraine to move closer to the West and Russia to retain its access to the Crimean coast without rewarding aggression, a good example of balancing liberalism with realpolitik. Since Russia's invasion, the United States and its allies have been virtually locked into opposing Russia and working (probably fruitlessly) to reverse the annexation. The United States is limited to applying sanctions and sending weapons to Ukraine's military. Because of the importance of the European theater and because the conflict in Ukraine will play a role in constructing Russian policymakers' views of what they can get away with in the future, the United States and NATO should do everything short of war to make Russia's aggression costly, including leveraging the global financial system against Russia and arming the Ukrainian government.

The conflict in Ukraine appears to be on a glide path toward a frozen conflict in which Ukraine will not join NATO but will resist Russian interference to the extent possible, while Russia will exercise unrecognized, de facto sovereignty over Crimea and possibly eastern Ukraine. Other zones locked in frozen conflicts and legal ambiguity have become safe havens for organized crime, drug trafficking, and sex slaving, an unwelcome development on Europe's doorstep. Some additional aid to Ukrainian law enforcement might mitigate the fallout of eastern Ukraine's descent into state failure after the shooting stops.

Europe's Periphery

Lesser priorities in Europe include the successful conclusion of the long-running stability operations in the Balkans. The stability operations in Bosnia and Kosovo have been broadly successful in that there has been no return to political violence in either country. Consolidating that success, learning from it, and transitioning to normalcy are important final steps. The incorporation of the Balkan states into the regional political and security architecture—Croatia and Slovenia have already joined NATO and the EU—is possible. Similarly, the United States should be prepared to support Europe in mounting stability operations or lending reconstruction assistance to Moldova, Transnistria, Abkhazia, or South Ossetia if the opportunity arises. Those regions, caught between state failure and frozen conflicts, function as way stations for organized crime, drug smuggling, and sex slaving into Europe. They are not high priorities for the United States, but a low-cost operation in which the United States provides logistics, staffing, intelligence, and other support for a European-led mission would be a wise investment in stability in Europe's last remaining fringes.

The formation of an independent EU military force is not something US officials need to worry much about. It is likely to be limited to regional peacekeeping, which only helps to spread the burden for such operations to allies whom US officials routinely berate for doing too little. The rise of a truly significant unified continental military power is a very distant prospect. In addition, while European unity is in America's interest, the United States has little to no role in sorting out the EU's internal troubles. The United States should be prepared to lend quiet economic assistance to troubled members as a last resort to prevent the union's breakup. And if the EU does begin to fragment, the United States should take an active role to preserve some institutions of European unity, even if less robust than the union. But until that eventuality, the United States is properly a spectator of domestic European events.

East Asia

East Asia is the second most important geopolitical theater for US interests, accounting for a third of US trade and a slightly smaller proportion of world GDP, two nuclear-weapon states (and perhaps two more near-nuclear states), though only a fifth of global power. Even as US allies such as Japan and South Korea have continued to rise in economic importance and clout, China's economic expansion and military modernization and North Korea's acquisition of nuclear weapons have made the region far more unstable and dangerous. The United States' strategy in East Asia should aim at containing North Korea (or managing the aftermath if it collapses) while working to entice and compel China into peaceful coexistence with liberal order. As in Europe, these goals can be pursued through a network of alliances with East Asian liberal democracies backed by American power.

China

It is tempting to believe that US strategy toward China depends on China's strategy toward the world. If China is a revisionist power that aims to fundamentally alter world order, exclude the United States from the western Pacific, and dominate its neighborhood, the United States should be prepared for major and repeated crises, even war. But if China's aims are more modest—developing enough power-projection capability to ensure the continued flow of energy and raw materials to sustain economic growth and, thus, political stability—they do not necessarily conflict with US security or liberal order.[19]

Some scholars and policymakers are convinced that the United States and China are on course for a clash. American observers have interpreted China's rising power, military modernization, and diplomatic ambitions as evidence that it seeks to exclude the United States from the western Pacific and turn the region into a Chinese sphere of influence. Realist scholar John Mearsheimer has argued that "China's rise is unlikely to be tranquil" because in the long run "it will attempt to dominate Asia the way the United States dominates the Western Hemisphere," which the United States and Asian neighbors will naturally resist. "The result will be an intense security competition with considerable potential for war," fueled by Chinese nationalism and historical grievances.[20] Some policymakers have taken time to publicly war-game what a war with China might look like.[21] Scholars have warned that changes in power often lead to conflict between rising and declining states. Some argue that established hegemons inevitably decline because the costs of sustaining leadership outweigh the benefits, while rising powers initiate wars to win the recognition and spoils they believe they deserve.[22] Others have warned that if and when American policymakers believe that the decline in America's relative power compared with China's becomes deep and irreversible, they will gravitate toward a harder-line stance in the hopes of staving off further decline or, worse, might provoke a war while they are still confident the United States can win.[23]

Others have developed the opposite view: China's rise has been and will continue to be peaceful because of the resilience and appeal of liberal order. China's main interests, in this view, include continuing economic growth and political stability. China does not aim to overthrow liberal order but join it; it is more vested in the status quo than widely appreciated.[24] Moves to accommodate China's growing power are, in this view, welcome: China joined the WTO in 2001 and gained an increase in its voting power at both the IMF and the World Bank since 2008. Despite its official communist ideology, China is actually interested in relatively free and open markets because they are the cheapest way for China to secure access to energy and raw materials. In this view, China's development of its "String of Pearls" bases and naval facilities in the Pacific and Indian Oceans is an acceptable part of its trade strategy, not military preparations for future great power war.[25]

There are problems with both views. It is likely that there are advocates for both sets of goals among Chinese policymakers, the United States has limited insight into their deliberations, Chinese intentions can change quickly in the future, and it is unlikely that the Chinese have a single master plan that they are following and will follow consistently for the foreseeable future.[26] In addition, the theories that underlie both views tend to be deterministic. War with China is not inevitable, and neither is peace, largely because nothing in history is inevitable.[27] Policymakers in both countries have real choices, and history may (and probably will) take unexpected turns in coming decades. China may not continue rising.[28] It may collapse or liberalize.[29] The United States may preemptively withdraw military forces from the Pacific region. If war comes, it may be primarily between China and Japan, or China and India, rather than with the United States. The security dynamic may not mirror the Cold War or fall easily into the conventional categories of analysis, such as hegemony, competition, or cooperation, but evolve into something distinctive.[30] A simplistic effort to replicate containment is bound to fail.[31] For any of these reasons, premising US strategy on a future inevitably—inevitable war or inevitable peace—places far too much confidence in our ability to predict the future. The United States cannot afford to formulate its strategy toward China on the basis of either scenario but should rather prepare for both. To the extent possible, it should entice China to join the liberal order through trade and by making reasonable adjustments to international organizations. When necessary, it should compel China in the same direction through alliance diplomacy and coercive bargaining.[32]

China is not an enemy of the United States, but neither is it a partner. Its consistent diplomatic opposition to US initiatives, its conflicted stance toward liberal order, and its aggressive posturing toward US allies in East Asia suggest that China is best understood as a strategic rival. If bilateral relations warm, the United States and China might cooperate in containing North Korea, preventing war on the peninsula, reconstructing the North after a collapse, and resolving Taiwan's status. Alternatively, if tensions rise, China might use the threat of an untethered North Korea or hostile maneuvers toward Taiwan as coercive bargaining tactics against the United States and its allies. China regularly resorts to coercive diplomacy, and the United States is regularly compelled to decide how to respond. It still has a number of territorial disputes with neighbors—over Taiwan; Arunachal Pradesh, with India; the Senkaku/Diaoyu Islands in the East China Sea, with Japan; and the Spratly Islands, with a number of other states. Because China is clearly more powerful than most of its neighbors, "the best way for China to settle them on favorable terms is probably via coercion."[33] The United States will be faced with the decision about how to respond when it does.

One case study is illustrative. In 2014, China announced the establishment of an "air defense identification zone" around the disputed Senkaku/Diaoyu Islands. On first glance, the United States has no intrinsic interest in who owns a few islands half a world away. Some things simply do not matter to the United States. Learning how to stay uninvolved is an important virtue of international diplomacy. If the islands are irrelevant to the United States, it does not show wise leadership to spend time and resources worrying about them. But there are concrete things at stake in the disputes over the Spratlys and the Senkaku/Diaoyu Islands—not the physical territory, which is negligible, or the perceptions and opinions about US resolve that might be formed by US policy or nonpolicy toward them, but the balance of power in East Asia and its impact on US allies. The rise of China is the largest shift in the distribution of world power since the fall of the Soviet Union. Historians often chide the Eisenhower administration, rightly, for its rash threat to use nuclear weapons to defend Taiwan's claim to the disputed islands of Quemoy and Matsu in 1958. The difference is that China was weak and the outcome of its dispute over Quemoy and Matsu was irrelevant. By contrast, today China's efforts to expand its power anywhere in the world, especially by coercion, intimidation, or subversion, threaten the balance of power and America's allies in the region.

These considerations elevate the otherwise unimportant disputes over a few minor islands on the other side of the world into a matter of great power diplomacy and alliance cohesion. The islands do not matter to the United States, but how China throws its weight around, how it relates to its neighbors, and what it thinks it can get away with do. When China unilaterally attempts to impose an air defense identification zone over a disputed area, US policymakers should understand that China is attempting to rewrite the balance of power in East Asia and the rules of international diplomacy in its favor at the expense of the United States and its allies. That is a threat to liberal order.

The disputed islands thus provided an excellent opportunity for the United States to force the issue with China. The Obama administration's decision to fly B-52s through the air defense identification zone in defiance of China's announcement was a good start, as were its public criticism, efforts to rally a regional response, and declaration that the Senkaku/Diaoyu Islands are covered by the US–Japan alliance. The United States should respond with similar forcefulness to China's construction of new islands in the South China Sea, which amount to a blatant landgrab that threatens to destabilize East Asia in China's favor and undermine the principle of the peaceful resolution of territorial disputes. Such a confrontation need not be belligerent, but it should be firm. The goal is not to start a war or to humiliate the People's Republic but to counter China's coercive diplomacy in kind and forcibly socialize China into responsible great power behavior. Crucially, these steps must be embedded in a broader regional strategy to engage and balance China, or, isolated, they will lose their impact.

Taiwan

These are the principles that should govern US policy toward Taiwan: It is the Ukraine of East Asia—the point at which conflicting aspirations and expectations of rival great powers could come to a head. It is far more important than the Spratlys because it is populated, prosperous, and wealthy; more important than Ukraine because it is (by congressional mandate) treated as a major non-NATO ally; and more important than virtually any other disputed territory in the world because of the unique history of American involvement and its commitment to liberal democracy and capitalism.

The governing authorities of Taiwan were allied combatants in World War II, ejected from the mainland after the war by the Chinese communists. The United States recognized the government of the Republic of China as the sole legitimate government of all China and signed a mutual defense treaty with it in 1955. The Taiwan Relations Act of 1979, which replaced and abrogated the treaty when the United States recognized the People's Republic, falls short of a mutual defense guarantee but commits the United States to helping Taiwan provide for its own defense through weapon transfers and proclaims that the use of force or intimidation against Taiwan would be of "grave concern" to the United States. This history makes a US security commitment to Taiwan impossible to walk away from.[34]

The United States' current policy of strategic ambiguity, weapon sales, and discouraging Taiwanese independence is an example of a muddled, incoherent jumble that succeeds insofar as it takes few risks because everyone has been habituated to expect it. Path dependency is a powerful force because bureaucratic inertia is cheap. But if it creates few crises, policy drift also solves no problems. Unresolved disputes are dry powder to which future tensions are the spark. The United States should look for opportunities for strategic shift: if China liberalizes, to gradually loosen its commitment to Taiwan and allow peaceful reunification, or, if China turns aggressive, to increase arms sales and use Taiwan's threat of independence as leverage against Chinese ambitions.

North Korea

North Korea is a perennial candidate for America's next war. In the decades since the end of the Korean War, the communist dictatorship has amassed an impressive record of criminality and barbarism, including sponsoring terrorism, proliferating nuclear technology, becoming one of the largest currency counterfeiters in the world, starving much of its own population, and propagating a cruel and dehumanizing ideology. North Korea regularly provokes and harasses its neighbors. It withdrew from the Nuclear Non-Proliferation Treaty in 2003, tested nuclear weapons in 2006, 2009, and 2013, and claimed to have tested a hydrogen bomb in early 2016. It regularly tests ballistic missiles capable of reaching South Korea and Japan. It probably sank a South Korean warship in 2010. North Korea is both a failed state and a nuclear power; it threatens the United States with both its strength and its weakness.[35] A war with North Korea would almost certainly kill more Americans than in any war since Vietnam, if not World War II (and vast numbers of Koreans). But a collapsed North Korea might be just as bad, as loose nuclear material could be released onto the world's black markets. If the world were to take the "responsibility to protect" seriously, it might invade and overthrow the North Korean government and try its leaders for crimes against humanity. That, needless to say, will never happen.

The United States' strategic goals toward North Korea are the simple goals of crisis diplomacy with dangerous rivals: face them down, avoid war if possible, win one if necessary. Denuclearization is not a realistic goal of US policy. There is no prospect that North Korea will peacefully give up its nuclear weapons. Posen's suggestion that "it may be possible to convince the North to forgo its nuclear weapons" if the United States withdraws its military forces from the peninsula is nearly Wilsonian in its naiveté.[36] The six-party talks, suspended in 2009, officially aim at the denuclearization of the Korean Peninsula and will never succeed. They are useful as a channel of multilateral dialogue with China, communicating to China the regional costs it pays for supporting North Korea, but not for any direct effect they will have on the North Korean situation.

Should the United States aim at regime change in North Korea? Regime change by invasion and overthrow is an impossible and foolish goal to pursue against a nuclear power: The cost in human lives is too high to justify. But the United States can and should (and mostly already does) pursue all means short of war to destabilize the regime and prompt its internal collapse. The regime is already isolated economically; there are few sanctions left that the international community could meaningfully impose. The United States could do much more (in partnership with South Korea) to spread propaganda against the regime, advertise its crimes, rally diplomatic support in the region, and encourage and welcome defectors. It could also air-drop newspapers and hand-crank radios across the border and broadcast news, anti-regime messaging, and reports about the regimes' human rights abuses. Such moves risk provoking even more aggressive posturing by the North, but at least they might sow distrust among a population beaten and brainwashed into submission, give it a taste for what freedom of information might feel like, and plant seeds that could grow following a regime collapse.[37]

And North Korea's regime is likely to collapse at some point over the next thirty or forty years. Under its current leadership, there is no prospect of gradual liberalization. But it is too incompetent, poor, and reliant on a deranged personality cult to survive indefinitely. As the regime decays, it may become even more aggressive and unpredictable. That means the United States should prepare for one of the largest and most difficult stability operations in history. If the United States is forced into war with North Korea or if North Korea collapses from within, the international community, led by South Korea, must be prepared to feed the population, handle massive refugee flows, administer the country, and chart a course for its political future while securing its nuclear weapons and material and defending against unconventional attacks by North Korean intelligence and military personnel.[38] South Korea has, rightly, developed plans for such an eventuality and should lead international efforts to stabilize a postcollapse North Korea,[39] but the United States will have to be involved at some level because of its commitments to South Korea and its equities with China. It is impossible to say what the political dispensation could look like because that will depend on how North Korea collapses. If it collapses from military defeat in a war that China supports, China's security interests are unlikely to count much in a postwar settlement. But if North Korea collapses like the Soviet Union, perhaps following a cutoff of Chinese aid, a more collaborative effort by the United States and China to decide the status of US troops, North Korea's nuclear weapons, and Korean reunification becomes possible.

Alliances

As in Europe, the United States' best course of action in East Asia is to sustain and selectively expand a network of allied liberal democracies whose cooperative security upholds liberal order in the region. The Pacific patchwork of bilateral and trilateral treaties and ally designations with Japan, South Korea, Australia, New Zealand, Thailand, the Philippines, and Taiwan is uncoordinated, lacks a unified command like NATO's, and suffers from disunity, a potential weak point to the American position in that theater—a function of the United States' strategy of "rule by relationships" in East Asia in contrast to the "rule by rules" it uses in Europe.[40] The hub-and-spokes series of bilateral and trilateral relationships flowed from the fact that the United States was "more dominant and wanted less out of East Asia" than Europe.[41] It was also a practical necessity because of poor relations among the United States' East Asian allies.

But that is no longer true. East Asia's rise in importance to US security interests, the rise of democracy in the region, and the decline of America's relative power there suggest the incentives and opportunities for creating a dense network of institutions and commitments have changed. Now that the United States wants more from its East Asian partners—more diplomatic coordination, more training exercises, more help ensuring freedom of the seas, more guarantees for the peaceful settlement of territorial disputes with China—and is less able to simply dictate solutions, it has greater reason to invest in regional institutions of cooperation. The Obama administration's "pivot" or "rebalance" to Asia was a sound concept, though it is unclear what practical steps it took or what lasting effect it had.

American policymakers should explore the possibility of a Pacific Treaty Organization to mirror the North Atlantic one, bringing together its East Asian allies (not including Taiwan) into a system of collective security. That would require overcoming understandable historical grievances between the South Koreans and Japanese—which, as the example of postwar Franco–German rapprochement illustrates, would be difficult but not impossible as their democratic identities converge.[42] Consolidating and deepening the Pacific alliances would reassure America's partners of US staying power and dissuade them from accommodating China.[43] Alternatively, or simultaneously, Japanese rearmament is another, more dramatic option to bolster the Pacific liberal order—like Britain in Europe, Japan is America's most important partner in the Pacific.[44] China would oppose either move and perceive them to be threatening; such steps might therefore be usefully held in reserve to counteract any potential Chinese aggression or future increase in hostility.

Thailand and the Philippines present both problems and opportunities. As original members of the long-defunct Southeast Asia Treaty Organization and, since 2003, designated major non-NATO allies, Thailand and the Philippines have long counted themselves allies of the United States—important ones, considering their strategically located naval and port facilities. The Philippines has an even longer relationship with the United States, having been on the receiving end of the United States' longest and most overtly imperialistic venture abroad. The legacy of American imperialism in the Philippines has not hurt its soft power there: Filipinos have a more favorable impression of the United States than do any other people in the world.[45] Both states have had problems with corruption, the rule of law, and the peaceful transfer of power, which limits how deep the bilateral relationship with the United States can be. More proactive involvement by US diplomats to solidify their governance capacity and their commitment to democracy could help create a tipping point for the region. As with Eastern Europe and Turkey, foreign aid targeting the infrastructure of democracy in these countries would be a wise strategic investment.

In addition to its established allies, the United States could bolster ties with newer or partial democracies such as Indonesia and smaller states such as Malaysia and Papua New Guinea to expand its established network of democratic allies. Indonesia, one of the most populous countries in the world and a relatively stable democracy since 1999, has the potential to become a major regional power, especially if political liberalization helps peacefully settle its internal sectarian conflicts. Selling advanced naval systems and conducting joint training exercises with Indonesia could help it become a reliable US partner in the effort to safeguard freedom of the seas in a region vital to ocean-going trade and could help reinforce each other's resistance to China's coercive diplomacy. Doing so could also give US policymakers credibility and leverage to push, quietly, for continued reform and democratization.

A major tool for advancing many of these goals is the Trans-Pacific Partnership (TPP) for free trade. In the words of one scholar, "the TPP is designed to promote a free-market, US-led alternative to China's version of 'state capitalism' in Asia, and to tie states in the region into US-led institutional frameworks."[46] A multilateral economic framework would accelerate US investment and economic ties to strategic countries in the region and could become the foundation on which greater defense ties could be formed. And more frequent interaction between the United States and its Pacific partners could generate the trust and credibility for US officials to quietly encourage the deepening of democratic norms across the region.

Notes

1. Geertz, *Interpretation of Cultures*, 5.
2. Wendt, "Agent-Structure Problem."
3. Art, *Grand Strategy for America*, 29.
4. Nau, *At Home Abroad*, 86.
5. Smith, *America's Mission*, 322.
6. Glaser, "Why NATO Is Still Best."
7. Dumbrell, *Special Relationship*; Louis and Bull, *"Special Relationship"*; Bartlett, *"Special Relationship."*
8. Posen, *Restraint*, xi.
9. Sarotte, "Perpetuating U.S. Preeminence." See also Zelikow and Rice, *Germany Reunified and Europe Transformed*.
10. Daalder and Goldgeier, "Global NATO."
11. Sjursen, "On the Identity of NATO."

12. Hallams and Schreer, "Towards a 'Post-American' Alliance?" See also Yost, "NATO's Evolving Purposes."

13. Press-Barnathan, "Managing the Hegemon."

14. On the relationship of NATO and democracy, see Reiter, "Why NATO Enlargement Does Not Spread Democracy"; Waterman, Zagorcheva, and Reiter, "NATO and Democracy"; Epstein, "NATO Enlargement and Spread of Democracy"; and Schimmelfennig, "NATO Enlargement."

15. For background on the war in Ukraine, see Charap and Darden, "Russia and Ukraine"; Charap, "Ukraine Impasse"; Yurgens, "Positive Stalemate for Ukraine"; and Freedman, "Ukraine and the Art of Limited War."

16. Mearsheimer, "Why the Ukraine Crisis Is the West's Fault."

17. Owen and Inboden, "Putin, Ukraine, and the Question of Realism."

18. Kissinger, *Diplomacy*, 24.

19. See Etzioni, "Is China a Responsible Stakeholder?"; Jisi, "China's Search for a Grand Strategy"; Kissinger, "Future of U.S.–Chinese Relations" and *On China*; Kaplan, "Geography of Chinese Power"; Subramanian, "Inevitable Superpower"; and Friedberg, "Future of U.S.–China Relations."

20. Mearsheimer, *Tragedy of Great Power Politics*, 362. See also Roy, "Hegemon on the Horizon?"

21. Dobbins, "War with China."

22. Gilpin, *War and Change in World Politics*.

23. Copeland, *Origins of Major War*, 242–43.

24. Johnston, "Is China a Status Quo Power?"

25. Kang, "Why China's Rise Will Be Peaceful." See also Xiang, "Washington's Misguided China Policy."

26. Schweller and Pu, "After Unipolarity"; Breslin, "China and the Global Order."

27. Glaser, "Will China's Rise Lead to War?"; Kissinger, "Future of US–Chinese Relations."

28. Babones, "Middling Kingdom."

29. Shambaugh, "Coming Chinese Crackup"; Lind, "Democratization and Stability in East Asia."

30. Acharya, "Power Shift or Paradigm Shift?"

31. Shambaugh, "Containment or Engagement of China?"

32. See Friedberg, "Future of U.S.–China Relations," for a discussion of the range of views and possibilities. See Christensen, "Fostering Stability or Creating a Monster?" for a discussion of the indeterminacy of theories of China policy.

33. Mearsheimer, *Tragedy*, 376.

34. Tucker, "China–Taiwan"; Lee and Schreer, "Taiwan Strait."

35. Miles, "Waiting Out North Korea"; Levin, "What if North Korea Survives?"

36. Posen, *Restraint*, 105.

37. Fitzpatrick, "North Korea."

38. Gompert, "North Korea."

39. Kwanwoo Jun, "South Korea Sets Plan to Rebuild North's Economy after a Possible Reunification," *Wall Street Journal*, September 11, 2014.

40. Ikenberry, *Liberal Leviathan*, chap. 3.
41. Ibid., 100.
42. Nau, *At Home Abroad*, chap. 6. But see Taylor, "Japan and South Korea," for a more pessimistic view.
43. Ross, "Balance of Power Politics."
44. Hughes and Krauss, "Japan's New Security Agenda"; Menon, "Reorienting Japan"; Adelman, "Japan's Security Dilemma."
45. Pew Research Center, *America's Global Image*.
46. Stokes, "Goodbye America?," 75.

7

The Opportunity
South Asia

South Asia is home to two nuclear-weapons states, a third of the planet's population, the densest network of jihadist groups, the epicenter of global terrorism, the world's largest democracy, and one of the rising economic superpowers of the century. It is also part of neither the Middle East nor East Asia. It actually accounts for a greater share of global GDP, national military capabilities, and overall global power than the Middle East.[1] Unheralded by most scholars or journalists—or the organization of the US bureaucracy—the region is a distinct geopolitical theater and has quickly become a top-tier region of concern for the United States, almost certainly more important to national security in the twenty-first century than the Middle East. It is also a region that US policymakers have a history of misunderstanding and mishandling. One of the easiest improvements to US grand strategy would be for policymakers to redraw the lines on their mental map.

South Asia is the headquarters of the transnational jihadist movements, not the Middle East. Policymakers familiar with Hezbollah, Hamas, and ISIS may be forgiven for thinking that jihadist terrorism is primarily a phenomenon of the Arab world and that therefore US counterterrorism efforts need to focus on Middle Eastern states. But while much of the motivation and thinking for contemporary jihadism has come from the Arab world, the actual operational execution has been impressively global—and has its densest network in Pakistan.[2]

US objectives in South Asia are complex. The most important is to strengthen ties with India, invest in its economy, improve counterterrorism cooperation, and encourage it to become a pillar of support for liberal order—the single most important opportunity in any region in the twenty-first century. The second is to find a workable solution to the various intertwined problems in Afghanistan and Pakistan, including denying safe haven for al-Qaida, preventing the Taliban from returning to power in Afghanistan, halting Pakistan's support for some jihadist groups while supporting Pakistan's fight against others, helping Pakistan secure its nuclear arsenal, preventing further proliferation of nuclear technology, preventing war with India, achieving a peace settlement in Afghanistan, and supporting the nascent and fragile democracies in both countries.

This is a difficult and ambitious agenda, especially since some of these goals work at cross purposes with others. While Europe and East Asia are more important, South Asia is more difficult—and thus merits a central focus in American diplomacy for the foreseeable future.

India

The most obvious opportunity for the United States in the twenty-first century is India.[3] US–Indian ties offer a host of strategic opportunities for the United States. The two countries share common concerns over China and Islamist terrorism. By itself, India holds 7.5 percent of "global power," according to the Pardee Center's Power Index—the third most powerful state in the world and more than any single European ally. Much of its power is latent and potential and has yet to be translated into real influence—it only produces 2.6 percent of global GDP, does not compete with China militarily, and has an underdeveloped diplomatic corps.[4] It is underperforming because of decades of socialist economic planning and persistent problems with corruption and poor infrastructure, but that means it has tremendous room for growth. Thanks to its economic liberalization since 1991, India is one of the two great rising economic superpowers of the twenty-first century and, with a large talent pool of educated, English-speaking youth, a valuable US trading partner. Unlike China, its rise is likely to be more sustainable. Its population is and will remain younger, thanks to its lack of a repressive one-child policy. India's growth has benefited from more innovation in high-end information technology industries, compared with China's heavily state-directed infrastructure investment. And, of course, India is the great democratic miracle of the world. Indians with grievances are free to express them legally in speech and print and at the ballot box and can hold protests and rallies without as much fear of a violent crackdown from the government. The most remarkable aspect of Indira Gandhi's brief suspension of democracy in 1975–77 was that she ended it voluntarily, held elections, was voted out of office, and accepted the result. India's continued fidelity to democracy disproves almost every trope about how democracy cannot work in a poor country, a pluralistic country, a non-Western culture, or a country with a sizeable Muslim population. (It has the third largest population of Muslims in the world, with Muslim majorities in several states.) India's commitment to liberalism has limits. Indian women do not always enjoy the equal protections that their law promises them. And while India has a long history of religious pluralism, both Hindus and Muslims have evinced such hostility to proselytism and conversion that Indians effectively cannot choose their own faith. Yet India remains one of the freest and most liberal non-Western states in the world.

Bolstering ties with India presents an almost irresistible wealth of benefits for the United States in both South and East Asia. The strategic calculus has been so clear that three successive US presidential administrations have moved to improve the bilateral relationship. Clinton's initial efforts to bolster ties with India in 1997 and again in 2000 paved the way for Bush's Civil Nuclear Cooperation Initiative,[5] and Obama rightly expressed support for India's bid for a permanent seat on the UN Security Council in 2010.

Today India receives very little economic aid from the United States. This is an unfortunate legacy of the 1960s and 1970s. The United States and other rich countries made India the great test case of foreign aid, dumping an awesome amount of money on the country in the early, optimistic years of postcolonial nation-building. Historically India still ranks as one of the top recipients of US aid in the world, having received some $66 billion over the last seventy years. Much of it was squandered, and the United States essentially halted foreign aid to India after India's 1974 nuclear test. But allowing these previous failures to obstruct present opportunities would be folly. India's economic liberalization means it is far more capable of making efficient use of economic assistance. And the United States has changed the way it delivers aid, no longer handing out money for massive and wasteful infrastructure projects designed by Western "experts." The United States' Millennium Challenge Corporation (MCC), for example, prioritizes aid to countries that demonstrate fidelity to transparency and accountable governance and that design and implement their own aid programs (similar in some respects to how the original Marshall Plan was administered)—a perfect match for India, a capable but underperforming democratic great power. There is no limit to how much assistance the United States can and should give to India through this mechanism. The MCC should become, essentially, the India Investment Corporation.

More important than aid is trade. Unlike other poor countries that the United States should target for economic assistance, India can become a major trading partner, and trade with the United States should be one of the engines that drives Indian growth and development—perhaps the fastest and cheapest way to increase the proportion of global power under democratic control in the world. India is the United States' eleventh largest trading partner in goods[6]—but is still dwarfed by Europe and Mexico. US tools such as the Overseas Private Investment Corporation and the Export–Import Bank should make encouraging US trade with India their top priority, and the

United States should make the US–India Trade Policy Forum, started in 2005, a major and continuing channel for strengthening bilateral ties.

The United States gives India no military assistance. Except for a brief span between the Sino–Indian War of 1962, when India appeared to be an ally against the communist Chinese, and the Indo–Pakistani War of 1965, when the United States sanctioned both combatants, the United States has never given military aid to India and has surprisingly few ties to the Indian military. That has changed in recent years—India conducts more exercises with the United States than with any other foreign military[7]—but too slowly. The Indian military is an obvious candidate for strategic investment, including counter-terrorism training, joint naval exercises, and weapon sales. The US military's hard-won expertise in counterinsurgency operations might be welcomed by Indian forces still grappling with several Maoist and separatist movements. The Indian market for weapons by itself could become a major component of the US–Indian trade relationship.[8] The United States should also explore a deeper and broader intelligence liaison relationship with India's Research and Analysis Wing and Intelligence Bureau, although Indian sensitivities have limited how much the United States has been able to strengthen bilateral military ties and may preclude intelligence cooperation for the present. American officials should persistently look for opportunities to demonstrate good faith and overcome Indian suspicions—something that would be easier with more diplomats who speak local languages living in India for longer tours of duty.

Pakistan

Pakistan is the hardest problem in US foreign policy.[9] It is not (quite) the most important—sustaining NATO, managing China's rise, and improving ties with India are more so—but the range of problems and difficulties surrounding Pakistan is more complex. The biggest threats to US interests in South Asia come from Pakistan—but the United States' supposed ally in South Asia is Pakistan itself. The United States can and does derive some strategic benefits from its on-again, off-again alliance with Pakistan—but it also pays steep costs. The alliance is neither completely useless and counter-productive nor unproblematic, as its troubled history shows.[10] If the United States sees opportunities to deepen the positive aspects of its relationship with Pakistan—which seems difficult, at best—it should certainly seize them, but it should also lay contingency plans for a strategic shift away from Pakistan altogether.

Pakistan has been a useful ally against both the Soviet Union and al-Qaida. Pakistan was a formal treaty ally of the United States from 1954 to 1979, a signatory to two treaties—those of SEATO and the Central Treaty Organi-zation—that both contained mutual defense guarantees. Pakistan withdrew from those treaties in 1972 and 1979, respectively, and the United States does not currently have a formal treaty obligation to Pakistan. However, Pakistan's cooperation was crucial in defeating the Soviet Union in Afghanistan in the 1980s and has lent some assistance to US counterterrorism efforts since 2001. In 2004, Bush designated Pakistan a major non-NATO ally (MNNA)—almost certainly a mistake.

Washington and Islamabad have had a long intelligence liaison relation-ship that goes back to the early days of the Cold War. According to Bruce Riedel, Pakistan allowed the United States to use its territory for intelligence collection in the 1960s, including an air base for aerial reconnaissance of the Soviet Union and technical facilities to intercept communications.[11] US–Pakistani intelligence cooperation, like all aspects of the US–Pakistani rela-tionship, cooled following the 1965 war but revived in the 1980s during the Soviet–Afghan War. The United States and Pakistan, among others, cooper-ated closely, including with their respective intelligence assets, to fund and arm the Afghan mujahedin in their war against the Soviet Union. Following the withdrawal of the Soviet Union and the imposition of sanctions on Paki-stan for its nuclear weapons development, ties cooled again.

A similar relationship almost certainly started again after 2001, although details are unavailable or unreliable. Pakistan has cooperated with the United States against al-Qaida and other militants, principally through its law enforce-ment agencies and Directorate C of the ISI, its counterterrorism branch.[12] Pak-istan probably shares selected bits of intelligence it gleans about al-Qaida with American military forces and intelligence agencies, and it is rumored to have given its private consent to the alleged US drone campaign. Pakistan is one of the largest recipients of US military and economic assistance in the world, including more than $8.3 billion since 2001, and Freedom House upgraded it to "partly free" since the ouster of President Pervez Musharraf in 2008.

But that is not the full story. For sixty years Pakistan has defined its national interest as the ability to compete with India, retain its hold on part of Kash-mir, and advance its standing in the Muslim world. To that end it fought four wars with India, sought hegemony over Afghanistan as "strategic depth," devel-oped nuclear weapons, and supported a range of militants as proxies against Afghanistan and India. None of this is in America's interest. And it is increas-ingly clear that, despite US pressure, Pakistan has not played a helpful role in the war against the Afghan Taliban. Elements within Pakistan continue to support militant and terrorist groups. In addition, despite Pakistan's return to civilian rule, the military retains an outsized role in Pakistani governance: It is unclear who is actually in charge in Islamabad, as the civilian government may not have full control over Pakistan's foreign and defense policy. US–Pakistani relations deteriorated sharply in 2011 following the American raid on Osama bin Laden's compound in Abbottabad in May and the deaths of twenty-four Pakistani soldiers in a NATO airstrike on a border outpost in November.[13] Pakistani national security adviser Sartaj Aziz publicly said in November 2014 that Pakistan should not target militants who do not attack Pakistan: "Why should America's enemies become our enemies? When the United States attacked Afghanistan, all those that were trained and armed were pushed towards us. Some of them were dangerous for us and some are not. Why must we make enemies out of them all?"[14] These are not the sentiments of a reliable ally.

At heart, what US policy toward Pakistan should be depends on whether Pakistan is genuinely interested in cooperating with the United States but is held back by incapacity and weakness or whether it is willfully deceptive—only pretending to cooperate with the United States to the minimum extent necessary to keep US aid money flowing. If Pakistan's problem is capacity, the United States should give more aid. If Pakistan's problem is will, the United States should *stop* giving aid and start imposing sanctions. Paradoxically, both are true. There is no single Pakistani policy toward the United States. The government itself is schizophrenic, divided between illiberal civilian oligarchs, some of whom genuinely desire to stop Pakistan's support for militants and develop closer ties with the United States, and military officers, who retain far more influence over Pakistan's foreign and defense policy than is usual for a democracy—and some of whom have continued supporting selected jihadist groups.

How can the United States have a coherent policy toward an incoherent government? Probably the least bad approach is to increase both carrots and sticks simultaneously to encourage the parts of government that favor ties with the United States while weakening the parts that favor supporting militants. The main carrot the United States can offer is economic and governance assistance. Since 2001, it provided $7.4 billion in civilian assistance to Pakistan.[15] Continued investment in the infrastructure of civilian governance and civil society would help strengthen and entrench Pakistan's transition to democracy. Because of the massive strategic implications of the success or failure of democracy in Pakistan, civilian aid to Pakistan—especially aid directed to organizations that foster accountability within government, such as independent media, secular schools and universities, the judiciary, and public prosecutors—should be the top priority for US economic and governance assistance worldwide next to Eastern Europe, Turkey, and India, unless another military coup ends Pakistani civilian rule once again.

At the same time, the United States has more leverage to compel Pakistan to stop supporting militants than is widely appreciated and should not hesitate to use it. There are at least four options: rescind Pakistan's status as an

MNNA; end intelligence cooperation; designate individuals, organizations, or the Pakistani state as sponsors of terrorism; and initiate or expand unilateral US operations in Pakistan. These options could be imposed as a series of escalating punitive measures until the Pakistani military shows a demonstrable commitment to ending support for militants.

The United States could formally rescind Pakistan's designation as an MNNA. The designation is a public symbol of the United States' continuing belief in Pakistan's fidelity as an ally. And the alliance has paid some benefits for the United States. As Pakistani officials are the first to point out, Pakistan has been a generally reliable and helpful ally in the hunt for members of al-Qaida. Pakistani security forces have been a part of operations against many of the senior al-Qaida leaders found in Pakistan, including Khalid Shaikh Mohammed.[16] The Pakistani government is also reported to have privately allowed the United States to carry out the rumored drone strikes against militants in Pakistan, despite its public denunciation of them.[17] And thousands of Pakistani soldiers have been killed fighting against the Pakistani Taliban.

But Pakistan's cooperation against al-Qaida and the Pakistani Taliban is, of course, in its own interest, as both groups have targeted the Pakistani state. Allies are valuable to the extent that they share mutual interests and pursue similar goals. Aside from pursuing al-Qaida, US and Pakistani interests diverge. The war in Afghanistan put Pakistan in a difficult position, forcing it to choose between the United States and the Taliban clients it had fostered and encouraged since 1994, and many Pakistani officials understandably believe they have an interest in maintaining both relationships. But if American policymakers conclude, rightly, that Pakistan has failed to behave as an ally in the war against the Afghan Taliban, the United States should rescind the MNNA designation. So long as Pakistan prioritizes the Taliban over the United States, the United States has little reason to treat the former as an ally. This will still be the case even after the US withdrawal from Afghanistan because it will always be in America's interest to deny safe haven to jihadists.

The move would trigger some diplomatic consequences. Stripping Pakistan of its status as an MNNA would be a public and humiliating breach between the United States and Pakistan. By ending what Pakistanis (falsely) consider to be a sixty-year-old alliance, it would compel Islamabad to rethink its grand strategy and probably increase its ties with China. But dissolving the alliance is unlikely to threaten Pakistan's continued operations against al-Qaida or the Pakistani Taliban. With or without the US alliance, those groups have already given Pakistan ample reason to go after them because of their domestic terrorism against Islamabad.

Another option available to US policymakers is to draw down or end the United States' long-standing intelligence cooperation with Pakistan. Pakistan probably shares selected bits of intelligence it gleans about al-Qaida with American military forces and intelligence agencies, and, as noted above, it reportedly has given its private consent to the alleged US drone campaign, possibly including air strips inside Pakistan for drone operations. Pakistan benefits from this relationship. The United States probably shares some of its intelligence with Pakistan in exchange for the information Pakistan offers to the United States. And the United States has reportedly directly targeted Pakistan's enemies in the course of its alleged drone campaign, including a successful strike against Pakistani Taliban leader Baitullah Mehsud in August 2009 and an apparently unsuccessful one against his successor, Hakimullah Mehsud, in January 2012.[18]

Reducing or eliminating intelligence cooperation with Pakistan would deprive Pakistan of these benefits but would also, of course, hurt the United States' own intelligence operations in the region. However, none of the losses stemming from ending the intelligence relationship would be irreplaceable. Washington's close relationship with Kabul and its growing ties with New Delhi suggest that the United States has alternatives for basing key facilities and sharing intelligence in South Asia. In addition, since whatever information Pakistan shares with the United States comes at Pakistan's discretion, it is unclear how useful the information is: Surely no information is shared that Pakistani officials believe could be used to hurt their own interests or, presumably, their militant proxies. Finally, refocusing counterterrorism operations to focus exclusively on groups that target the United States rather than those who are fighting Pakistan is simply a more economical use of resources. Helping Pakistan fight the Pakistani Taliban might be good diplomacy, but it did not help win the war against the Afghan Taliban—and it might have the unintended consequence of breeding complacency in the Pakistani army about the strength and resilience of homegrown militants.

A more serious step the United States could take would be to designate Pakistan, or specific Pakistani actors, as sponsors of terrorism. Sanctioning retired and active Pakistani army officers complicit with jihadist groups would communicate to Pakistani officials that employment by the Pakistani state does not give them immunity for links to terrorists. It would impose a cost on Pakistan for its use of proxies and refuse to grant the thin cover of deniability such proxies supposedly give them. In addition, the secretary of state could designate Directorate S of Pakistan's ISI as a foreign terrorist organization (FTO). Directorate S, in charge of external operations, plays a role similar to that of Iran's IRGC Quds Force.[19] If the Haqqani Network is a "veritable arm of the ISI," as Adm. Michael Mullen claimed, Directorate S is its shoulder. An FTO designation makes it a federal crime to provide material support to the group, bars members from entering or staying in the United States, and obligates US financial institutions to freeze any of the group's funds it holds. It also "stigmatizes and isolates" the group in the eyes of the international community.[20] This step would end any remaining US ties with Pakistani intelligence.

Designating Directorate S as an FTO would only be possible if the United States argued that it was a rogue organization outside the control of the Pakistani state. US policymakers may feel compelled to argue (or pretend) that Directorate S is rogue because if it is not the necessary and logical next step is to designate Pakistan a state sponsor of terrorism. This final tier of terrorist designation would end all forms of US assistance to Pakistan and trigger a wide range of sanctions and export controls. This step would go beyond merely dissolving the US–Pakistani alliance and would instead begin to treat Pakistan as a hostile power.

Finally, as a last resort, the United States could initiate unilateral operations in Pakistan, including drone strikes and raids by Special Operations Forces beyond the Federally Administered Tribal Areas (FATA). If drones are, as President Obama publicly claimed in 2012, a useful means of launching pinpoint strikes against America's enemies while minimizing the violation of another country's sovereignty,[21] then the United States should consider expanding the scope and scale of the program. Specifically, it might expand the geographic range of its counterterrorism operations. Several top al-Qaida leaders, including bin Laden and Khaled Sheikh Mohammad, were found hiding in major urban centers well outside the FATA. The Afghan Taliban senior leadership is widely believed to be headquartered in Quetta, Baluchistan Province, well beyond reported current US counterterrorism operations capabilities. Precise targeting in a compact urban environment rather than the more wide-open rural environment of the FATA would clearly be difficult, but the potential payoff should at least prompt US officials to explore the option seriously.

A critic may respond that these policy options make no strategic sense because maintaining friendly ties with Islamabad is more important than defeating jihadist groups. Cracking down on Pakistan for the sake of defeating the Afghan Taliban may win the battle of Kabul but lose the war for South Asia by driving Pakistan into open hostility. According to this view, Pakistan is vastly more important than Afghanistan by dint of its sheer size, its nuclear weapons, its role in the Muslim world, and its much bigger and more viable economy. The United States should continue to engage Pakistan, give it more economic assistance, and encourage the growth of civilian rule—essentially the Obama administration's strategy. In this view, if the United States has to take a loss in Afghanistan to preserve good ties with Pakistan, that is an acceptable price to pay.

The obvious rejoinder is, what good ties are left to preserve? During the war in Afghanistan, Pakistan has been virtually in open hostility to the United

States. The United States received few irreplaceable benefits for its aid, alliance, and complicity with Pakistan. Pakistan is, indeed, more important and powerful than Afghanistan, but that simply means it is all the more important to have a coherent, credible policy toward it, not that the United States should never offend it. The United States has paid a steep cost for its strategy toward Pakistan. Terrorists planning attacks against the United States and its allies operate in Pakistan almost unbothered by the Pakistani government. Pakistan's rivalry with India could trigger nuclear war with global radiological fallout. Pretending Pakistan is an ally and giving it money has prevented none of these developments.

The outcome of the conflict in Afghanistan is not immaterial to US–Pakistani relations; the United States cannot simply walk away from Kabul as a gesture of goodwill to Islamabad. Losing in Afghanistan would hurt US interests in Pakistan, not help. Taking a loss there would mean civil war or a Taliban victory in Kabul, which in turn would empower Pakistani militants, give them a safe haven, and put even more pressure on Islamabad to co-opt or appease them. Winning in Afghanistan, by contrast, would put further pressure on militants in Pakistan and demonstrate the United States' commitment to building a lasting stability in South Asia in which militancy has no part. Pakistan may be the horse drawing the Afghan cart, but one does not spend time grooming the horse if the cart is on fire.

Any one of these policy options carries with it risks and downsides for the United States. But the list of possible reprisals—sponsor terrorism, proliferate weapons of mass destruction, meddle unhelpfully in Afghanistan, threaten India—is simply the recent history of Pakistani foreign policy. Furthermore, some US options, such as cutting off aid to Pakistan, would actually benefit the United States by saving it money in a time of fiscal austerity. Some options may push Pakistan closer to China or reduce a small amount of US trade overseas, but those are small consequences compared to the ongoing harm inflicted on the United States by militant groups that Pakistan supports or tolerates. Others, such as cutting off intelligence cooperation or expanding unilateral operations, carry more serious consequences and should be held in reserve against a more serious deterioration in the US–Pakistani relationship in the future.

American policymakers should not initiate every one of these policies simultaneously and hopefully will never need to impose most of them. Rather, the United States should recognize that its current policy toward Pakistan—free cash, a formal alliance, and a blind eye toward Islamabad's failings and betrayals—has failed to secure American interests in South Asia. In light of these enduring features of Pakistani foreign policy, a reappraisal of US policy toward Pakistan is long overdue. In the long term, US policymakers need to start war-gaming alternatives for the US–Pakistani relationship. The Pakistani military, by all accounts, has pursued a decades-long policy of supporting militants, destabilizing its neighborhood, undermining democracy at home, and proliferating technology related to weapons of mass destruction. So long as it remains committed to those policies, the US–Pakistani alliance does not have a future. Washington should seek to diversify its position in South Asia by cultivating and strengthening ties with other states in the region.

Afghanistan

Afghanistan is, contrary to widespread perception, strategically important to the United States. First, it is still the front line in the war against jihadist groups worldwide. It is a vital national security interest of the United States to prevent any jihadist group from enjoying safe haven or seizing power any-where in the world, especially in strategic regions. That is why the United States should increase its military presence in Afghanistan, consistent with the two nations' 2012 strategic partnership agreement, for the next decade or longer. Afghanistan is vital to American national security because it provides a platform from which to directly target al-Qaida and other militant groups in South Asia. Indeed, Afghanistan's value to the United States increased as US–Pakistani relations deteriorated in 2011 and 2012. After Pakistani law-makers called for the end of the alleged US drone program in their territory, Afghanistan may be the only territory from which US forces and a drone program can operate in South Asia.

The war is not only against al-Qaida. There is a wide range of jihadist groups operating in South Asia, possibly including ISIS. The most powerful in Afghan-istan is the Taliban. It is vital to prevent the Taliban from retaking power, just as it is to prevent any jihadist group from taking state power worldwide. A Taliban-controlled Afghanistan would become safe haven for al-Qaida and other jihadist groups. Presidents Bush and Obama both called on the Taliban to denounce al-Qaida and sever ties with it. In fifteen years since 9/11, the Tali-ban have never done so. The groups still retain some level of mutual support. Al-Qaida, the Taliban, and their many affiliates and allies in the region have not been defeated and, as illustrated by recent developments in Iraq, are likely to grow stronger in the power vacuum left in the wake of a US withdrawal.

But Afghanistan's importance is not limited to its role in the war against jihadist groups. The success or failure of Afghanistan will affect all of Amer-ica's interests across South Asia: Pakistan's stability, the security of its nuclear weapons, the US–Indian relationship, NATO's credibility, relations with Iran and Russia, transnational drug-trafficking networks, worldwide democracy, and humanitarian considerations. These real and enduring interests require a substantial and lasting commitment to the region, and they explain why the mission in Afghanistan is not simply to deny safe haven to al-Qaida but also to foster lasting stability in Afghanistan. If Afghanistan falls into chaos again, al-Qaida or similar groups would reestablish a base there—and would in turn increase their attacks on Pakistan. Pakistan—and its nuclear weapons—would be less safe. Russia and Iran, two of America's rivals, would expand their influence. Russia might believe that NATO's record in Afghanistan casts doubt on the alliance's fighting abilities. India would doubt the United States' reliability as a partner, with lasting damage to the potential for US–Indian partnership in the twenty-first century. Transnational organized crime and drug trafficking would find a safe headquarters for business. The experiment of democracy in the Muslim world would be tarnished. And a humanitarian catastrophe would unfold in South Asia.

Unfortunately, the Obama administration plans to reduce the level of American forces in Afghanistan to 5,500 by the end of 2016, almost certainly too low. Taliban militants briefly seized control of Kunduz, Afghanistan's fifth-largest city, in late 2015, suggesting the Afghan army needs more support. Iraq could hardly be a clearer cautionary tale. If the United States withdraws from Afghanistan before Afghan security forces are fully prepared to lead the fight against the Taliban and deny safe haven to al-Qaida, militants are almost certain to regain some degree of safe haven there, much as ISIS gained ground since the withdrawal of US troops from Iraq in 2011—especially since the withdrawal of US troops almost certainly would mean the end of the alleged drone program in South Asia.

The United States has the diplomatic tools in place to sustain a long-term presence. In addition to the strategic partnership agreement, the two governments signed, in 2014, an accompanying bilateral security agreement. The two accords were framed as a decade-long arrangement. The long time frame made sense. Afghan security forces in 2014 did not have the logistics, air support, intelligence, and transportation capabilities they needed to sustain their fight against the Taliban, defend their borders, or deny safe haven to al-Qaida.

Obama's determination to pull out all but a token force changed the outlook for Afghanistan and makes it possible that something like a replay of events in Iraq will take place. If US forces draw down to a minimal presence, as under the current plan, Afghan forces will be as unprepared as their Iraqi counterparts to face a renewed insurgent offensive alone. While they are unlikely to collapse immediately, as some pessimistic observers have predicted, they may withdraw from some districts and provinces in the south and east to minimize casualties and focus on securing major cities and roadways. Such redeployments would be efficient and make military sense, but they would also amount to a tacit cease-fire with local Taliban forces and enable the Taliban (and, thus, al-Qaida) to control some Afghan territory—as ISIS has done in Iraq and Syria. The Taliban would then gain further strength and momentum through their control of the drug trade, as ISIS benefits from the oil industry. Their operational freedom would be further strengthened by the end of the alleged US drone program in South Asia—which requires at least some personnel on the ground for airfield security, logistics, and maintenance. Militants' control of territory would lend them an air of legitimacy and strength with locals and even win some degree of support—whether through loyalty or fear—again just as in Iraq and Syria. Finally, if political wrangling in the capital convinces Afghans that their government cannot meet their needs or protect them, as Sunnis seem to have concluded about Baghdad, they are likely to be more receptive to local solutions, even if they come with the Taliban's imprimatur.

The United States can avoid these scenarios in Afghanistan by retaining a larger stay-behind force. A robust deployment of US troops could continue to train Afghan security forces and conduct counterterrorism raids but also support the Afghan forces' rural counterinsurgency efforts, such as the Village Stability Operations and Afghan Local Police programs that have shown significant promise in recent years. David Barno, former commander of US and coalition forces in Afghanistan, estimated that the United States could achieve these goals with as few as twenty-five thousand troops.[22] The United States might reap even greater benefit in the long run: If the United States succeeds in stabilizing the security situation, it would also have an opportunity to invest in improving Afghan governance and democracy. That, in turn, would help foster an example of democracy in the Muslim world and craft a long-term partnership with a democratic state that borders both Iran and Pakistan. That scenario would be difficult to achieve given the current state of Afghan governance but not impossible.

The essential condition for victory is, and has always been, the construction of a government capable of maintaining order in Afghanistan. This is the simple requirement of counterinsurgency, the primary objective of which is to "foster the development of effective governance by a legitimate government," according to the US Army counterinsurgency manual. Counterinsurgency is competitive state-building: Kabul must outgovern the Taliban to demonstrate to the population why it deserves its support. Only when the international community can be confident that an effective government will enforce its writ throughout Afghanistan can it safely withdraw the props of support it has provided to Kabul.

Which makes all the more alarming the lack of progress on governance in Afghanistan. The Afghan government has ranked almost dead last on Transparency International's Corruptions Perceptions Index every year since 2007.

Its scores on political rights and civil liberties by Freedom House have actually declined since 2008. The World Bank, which rates all states in the world according to six indicators of governance—voice and accountability, political stability, governance effectiveness, regulatory quality, control of corruption, and the rule of law—continues to rank Afghanistan among the very worst in the world in all categories, reflecting the Obama administration's conscious decision not to invest in Afghan governance. The Defense Department reported, "Setbacks in governance and development continue to slow the reinforcement of security gains and threaten the legitimacy and long-term viability of the Afghan Government." After fifteen years, the Afghan government is still one of the weakest and least capable on the planet.[23]

The international community bears part of the blame for its failure to invest greater resources in governance assistance. While the United States has committed $107 billion in aid to Afghanistan since 2001, almost two-thirds has gone toward training the Afghan army and police, according to the Special Inspector General for Afghanistan Reconstruction.[24] What little money has been available for governance assistance has been consumed by expensive elections and voter registration efforts. Despite the widespread acknowledgment that Afghanistan needed massive help and despite the massive sums of money that flowed into the country over the last decade, the Afghan state—its ministries, courts, and regulatory agencies—has received an astonishingly tiny amount of help.

Gen. David Petraeus told Congress in March 2011, when he was commander of the International Security Assistance Force, "I am concerned that funding for our State Department and USAID partners will not sufficiently enable them to build on the hard-fought security achievements of our men and women in uniform. Inadequate resourcing of our civilian partners could, in fact, jeopardize accomplishment of the overall mission."[25] Petraeus's remarkable statement—that the United States could lose the war in Afghanistan without greater funding for civilian reconstruction and governance assistance—fell on deaf ears. US aid for governance and development declined by almost $1.5 billion—one-third of the total—from 2010 to 2011 and continued to decline every year since.[26] This is especially worrisome considering that the World Bank and the Afghan Central Bank recently judged Afghanistan will require $4 billion in assistance per year for ongoing reconstruction efforts.[27]

The good news is that the withdrawal of tens of thousands of combat troops has generated more than enough cost savings to pay for increased civilian aid. Even reversing course and sending twenty thousand or more US troops back to Afghanistan would still leave the US presence there far smaller and more affordable than it was at its peak in 2010–11. A surge of foreign aid to Afghanistan would not appreciably increase the financial burden on the United States—but it could change the trajectory of Afghan governance and mean the difference between state failure and stability.

In addition, investing in face-to-face ties with Afghan officials at all levels of government might finally earn the international community the relationship capital to persuade the Afghans to adopt a series of political reforms that observers have long argued are necessary for the long-term health of Afghanistan's political system. These reforms include devolving more power to provinces and localities, making governors and district chiefs elected rather than appointed, harmonizing the electoral calendar, and reforming the electoral law to abolish the single nontransferable vote system, all of which would make the Afghan state more flexible, responsive, and accountable.

Notes

1. Robert Art, for example, wrongly claims the Persian Gulf is one of three regions vital to the United States because of the concentration of wealth, trade ties, military power, and alliances there. In fact, South Asia ranks more highly than the Persian Gulf on most measures.
2. Robert Kagan, "A Case for Staying the Course," in Rothstein and Arquilla, *Afghan Endgames*.
3. Burns, "Passage to India"; Blackwill, Chandra, and Clary, *United States and India*. It is noteworthy that even Art, who argues the United States should focus on Europe, East Asia, and the Middle East, nonetheless ranks India as one of the top future trading partners with one of the largest military budgets and standing armies and in possession of nuclear weapons. His data does not support his low ranking of South Asia's importance.
4. Miller, "India's Feeble Foreign Policy"; Mehta, "How India Stumbled."
5. Paul and Shankar, "Why the U.S.–India Nuclear Accord Is a Good Deal."
6. Office of the US Trade Representative, "U.S.–India Bilateral Trade and Investment."
7. Flournoy and Davidson, "Obama's New Global Posture," 59.
8. Dasgupta and Cohen, "Arms Sales for India."
9. This section is adapted from Miller, "How to Exercise US Leverage." Used with permission.
10. Cohen, *Idea of Pakistan*; Markey, *No Exit from Pakistan*; Riedel, *Deadly Embrace*; Schmidt, *Unraveling*.
11. Riedel, *Deadly Embrace*, 13.
12. Matthew Cole, "Killing Ourselves in Afghanistan," *Salon*, March 10, 2008.
13. Krasner, "Talking Tough to Pakistan."
14. "Militants Not Dangerous to Pakistan Should Not Be Targeted: Sartaj," *Dawn*, November 18, 2014.

15. Congressional Research Service, "Direct Overt U.S. Aid Appropriations."

16. "Mohammad's Capture Was Months in the Making," *CNN.com*, March 3, 2003.

17. Jane Perlez, "Drones Batter al-Qaida and Its Allies within Pakistan," *New York Times*, April 4, 2010.

18. Syed Saleem Shahzad, "Baitullah: Dead or Alive, His Battle Rages," *Asia Times Online*, August 8, 2009; Amir Mir, "Hakimullah Mehsud Evades US Drones Again," *Asia Times Online*, January 27, 2012.

19. Coll, *Ghost Wars*, and Rashid, *Descent into Chaos*, both document these and other charges in detail.

20. US Department of State, "Foreign Terrorist Organizations."

21. Dan Lothian and Reza Sayah, "Obama's Drone Comment Was No Slip-up, Officials Say," *CNN.com*, January 31, 2012.

22. Barno, *Responsible Transition*.

23. US Department of Defense, *Report on Progress*, 6.

24. Special Inspector General for Afghanistan Reconstruction, "Quarterly Report to the US Congress."

25. Petraeus, "Statement before the Senate Armed Services Committee."

26. Special Inspector General for Afghanistan Reconstruction, "Quarterly Report to the US Congress."

27. Freya Peterson, "Hillary Clinton Announces Major Non-NATO Ally Status for Afghanistan," *Globalpost.com*, July 7, 2012.

8

The Quagmire

The Middle East

Perhaps the most exasperating region for US security interests is the Middle East. To start with, it is unclear where the "Middle East" even begins or ends. Some analysts talk of the "Greater Middle East," which ostensibly stretches from North Africa through the Khyber Pass to the Indus. Such an unwieldy conglomeration ignores the distinctiveness of South Asia, offers nothing useful as a unit of analysis or a region for diplomatic engagement, and proves that Edward Said's "Orientalism" is alive and well in some corners of American thinking. Similarly, some policymakers talk of US strategy in the "Muslim world"—an equally problematic and artificial designation. If the term "Middle East" is to be useful, it should refer to the heartland of the Arab world—Egypt, the Arabian Peninsula, the Levant, and Mesopotamia, not to North Africa or Central Asia—and to its immediate neighbors: Iran, Israel, and perhaps Turkey. The US bureaucracies should reflect these geographic and political realities: The State Department should shed North Africa (except Egypt) from its Bureau of Near Eastern Affairs. The military wisely did as much when it activated Africa Command (AFRICOM) in 2008, but its Central Command (CENTCOM) still covers Afghanistan and Central Asia, which should have been hived off to a South Asia Command long ago.

Prior to World War II, the Middle East was considered strategically peripheral to Westerners. Traders sailed around the impoverished Arabian Peninsula to the fabled wealth of Persia and India. The region was simply an expanse to be crossed on the Silk Road between Europe and China in the Middle Ages. The great empires of modern Europe turned to every other region in the world, including Africa, before colonizing the Middle East very late in the age of empire because the vast desert appeared to be of little use to them. In the nineteenth century, Europe felt more threatened by the Ottoman Empire's weakness than its strength. The Suez Canal was built not to facilitate trade with the Arabian Peninsula but because it shortened the trip to India.

Since the dawn of the modern mechanized age, the Middle East has taken place among the first rank of geopolitical regions chiefly because of its influence in the world oil market. Most scholars and policymakers continue to define access to Middle Eastern oil as a vital national security interest of the United States.[1] There are few other reasons to count the Middle East as important. It produces a smaller proportion of world GDP than either Latin America or South Asia, constitutes less than 5 percent of US trade, and has a smaller proportion of global power than Africa. Much of the political violence in the region is irrelevant to the United States and matters only insofar as it might threaten global oil supplies.

And the importance of oil supplies is, in fact, declining. The United States should work to preserve an open market for global energy supplies for the next decade or so—but not much longer. Almost wholly unnoticed to most observers, the pervasive influence of Middle Eastern oil has been in terminal decline for a generation. Rising production costs, declining reserves, and the availability of alternative fuels and unconventional sources of oil will combine in coming years to decisively undermine the defining role that the Middle East has played in the global energy market in the modern era, which should prompt US policymakers to engage in a wholesale reconsideration of US strategy in the region.

Aside from its fading oil influence, the Middle East is mostly populated by poor, small, corrupt, incompetent autocracies unimportant to US national security and unable (and unwilling) to contribute meaningfully to liberal order. Even if they converted to liberal democracy, they would not significantly add to the proportion of global power under democratic control. If the war in Iraq had been successful and Iraq was now a stable democracy, the war would have added less than two-tenths of 1 percent of global power to the free world. The United States' longer-lasting strategic goals for the region include helping bolster Israel's security, containing the influence of a nuclear Iran, and supporting local allies' efforts to defeat ISIS and other jihadist groups. It can pursue most of these goals through relatively low-cost means, though the deployment of more ground forces to Iraq is probably necessary. While the spread of democracy to the region would be an ideal long-term solution to some of the region's perennial problems, there is no prospect for such an outcome in the foreseeable future. The declining importance of the Middle East also means the United States does not need to sustain its commitment to the defense of its autocratic allies in the region for much longer, the usefulness of whom to US national security is increasingly questionable. This is one region in which the advocates of restraint have it right.

Oil

Conventional wisdom holds that the Middle East is the most important player in the world oil market, which is why stability in the region is a vital national security interest for the United States. For example, Kenneth Pollack, a scholar and former intelligence analyst and National Security Council (NSC) staffer, recently argued that the Middle East contributes the largest share to world oil production and has almost all of the world's spare production capacity. Combined, these factors enable Middle Eastern oil producers to exercise influence over oil prices and, thus, the world economy.[2]

The problem with this view is that it does not take into account *why* the Middle East dominates oil production and does not recognize profound changes afoot in the world energy market. The Middle East dominates oil production not because of the sheer volume of oil it possesses—Canada, the United States, and Venezuela have more ultimately recoverable reserves—but because the region enjoys a *comparative advantage* in the industry: Middle Eastern oil is cheap and easy to get out of the ground. So long as cheap Middle Eastern oil is available, other producers are at a disadvantage. It is economically unprofitable for North American producers of oil from shale, tar sands, or offshore wells to compete against the Middle Eastern producers, and potential producers have a disincentive to invest in production capacity or new production techniques. That is why, by and large, other producers have not stepped up to displace the Middle East even though the United States has long recognized its economic dependency on Middle Eastern oil. The Middle East's dominance of current production and spare production capacity is a function of simple market realities.

Those market realities are changing in ways Pollack and others have overlooked; their picture of the oil market is a static snapshot in time that misses its changing dynamics.[3] The Middle East's comparative advantage is based on four factors. First, Middle Eastern oil is the cheapest oil in the world to produce because of simple geology. Middle Eastern oil lies under flat desert, not under an ocean or in the Amazonian river basin. In 2008, a barrel of oil cost between $6 and $28 to produce in the Middle East and North Africa, compared with a price of up to $39 per barrel elsewhere in the world and up to $113 per barrel for shale oil.[4] Second, most Middle Eastern oil is a superior product. The chemical properties of Middle Eastern "light sweet" crude oil make it easier and cheaper to refine than the "heavy" crude of Venezuela, for example. Third, Middle Eastern oil developers benefited from economies of scale because the cheap oil there has been so plentiful. Even today the region is still home to more than half the world's proven, commercially viable, conventional oil reserves and a third of world oil production. Fourth, the Middle East's dominance of oil production and reserves makes it "too big to fail," which effectively lowers producers' risks. Buyers believe, with justification, that neither the governments in the region nor the developed world would allow a significant disruption to oil production (especially after the embargoes in the 1970s backfired).

The Middle East would not be as strategically important if it lost its comparative advantage or if oil were not so central to the world economy. In fact, both peaked around 1974 and have been in long-term decline ever since. In reaction to the oil embargoes and disruptions of 1974 and 1979, the Western world embarked on a generational and largely successful effort at energy conservation and domestic energy production. The world's energy needs are being met by an ever-expanding menu of inputs, including nuclear power and renewable sources. US oil exports are at an all-time high for the post–World War II era, while oil imports are the lowest in about twenty years. Passenger motor vehicles' fuel efficiency has almost doubled since 1970. The United States' energy intensity—a measure of how much energy is used per dollar of GDP—has more than halved since 1970, falling from 14,370 BTUs per dollar to 6,190 in 2013, according to the US Energy Information Administration. The fall in petroleum and natural gas usage per dollar of GDP was even faster, dropping by roughly two-thirds in the same period.[5] In 2010, petroleum's share of America's energy sources was the lowest it had been since 1951.[6] The world economy's oil intensity, or "the amount of oil needed to produce one dollar of GDP," in the words of the International Energy Agency, "has fallen steadily over the last three decades." That is not the whole story: "The decline has accelerated since 2004, mainly as a result of higher oil prices, which have encouraged conservation, more efficient oil use and switching to other fuels."[7] The introduction of electric and hybrid cars in recent years, while still in its infancy, promises to accelerate, perhaps dramatically, the decline in demand for petroleum-based fuels in the advanced economies. This unheralded success means that because of advances in efficiency and conservation practices and domestic production, the world economy is less sensitive to disruptions in the supply of all forms of energy, imported oil included, than previously.

The Middle East's comparative advantage in oil production is also eroding. Oil production costs in the Middle East are certain to rise. As the world uses up the cheapest and most easily developed oil, oil in the Middle East will become more costly to produce. Some fields in the Middle East have been producing continuously for eighty years and are rapidly maturing (i.e., past their peak production). Saudi Arabia in particular has a high percentage of mature or maturing oil fiends. Thirteen of the twenty largest oil fields in the world are located in the Middle East, and they all entered production between 1928 and 1968.[8] As a field passes its peak, it becomes more technically difficult and costly to continue to extract oil from it. This is especially true once a developer switches to secondary, tertiary, and unconventional methods to extract remaining oil. Production costs in the Middle East will inevitably rise in coming years—that is as certain as the laws of geology and economics. The oil market will be increasingly characterized by harder-to-develop and relatively more expensive oil.

This trend will only accelerate as world demand for oil increases and prices rise. After the oil price spikes of the 1970s, the rest of the world invested in oil production; the Middle East's share of production fell to less than 19 percent by 1985, its lowest point since 1953.[9] Demand for oil is rising relentlessly: Global liquid fuel consumption is likely to run at 111 million barrels per day by 2035—up from 85 million barrels per day today[10]—which is likely to spur worldwide investment in capacity, further eroding the Middle East's market share (and its dominance of production capacity) over the next decade. Rising prices are a powerful incentive for producers to develop new production capacity in other regions and using unconventional methods. Oil recovered from secondary and tertiary drilling technology or recovered from shale, sand, or deepwater rigs will become more commercially viable as prices rise. The fracking boom in the United States is only the most dramatic example of the changes overtaking the global energy market and undermining the geopolitical clout of the Middle East.

The picture here is stark: When unconventional methods of oil development are taken into account, including development of heavy oil, shale oil, and oil sands, the Middle East suddenly becomes a minor player. There may be as many as 7.9 trillion barrels of potentially recoverable oil left in the world from all sources, according to the International Energy Agency, more than 90 percent of it outside of the Middle East.[11] The Middle East dominates the currently proven, conventional, commercially viable reserves, but they account for less than 10 percent of the total oil in the world. Once prices rise and technology improves enough to make unconventional methods commercially competitive, the Middle East will be dwarfed by Canada, the United States, and Venezuela.

The United States can accelerate this process in two ways. When oil prices are high, it should fund and subsidize research and development into alternative energies. Layne rightly calls for "a 'Manhattan Project' to develop new energy sources that ultimately will render the Persian Gulf strategically and economically irrelevant."[12] When prices are low, the Department of Energy should go on a buying binge to stock its Strategic Petroleum Reserve with cheap oil (there is no reason for the reserve to be capped at one billion barrels, as current law stipulates), which will accelerate the transfer of power from the Middle East to the United States and put upward pressure on the price of oil, further incentivizing research and development.

Finally, as the massive unconventional oil deposits become commercially viable, the Middle Eastern oil industry will no longer be too big to fail. Middle Eastern oil producers will lose the implicit discount on risk they gain from dominating the current world oil market and being indispensable. They will, in fact, be dispensable, making it much harder for them to free-ride on the implicit guarantees and subsidies they currently enjoy from their host governments. As they devolve from global politicians to businessmen, governments will rightly ask if they make good business sense anymore.

In 1980, President Jimmy Carter announced what became known as the Carter Doctrine: "An attempt by any outside force to gain control of the Persian Gulf region will be regarded as an assault on the vital interests of the United States of America, and such an assault will be repelled by any means necessary, including military force."[13] As soon as the inevitable shifts in the energy markets take place, the United States should repudiate the Carter Doctrine. The Middle East's geopolitical influence flowing from its competitive advantage in the global oil market is a wasting asset. The United States does not have a vital national security interest in the security of the Middle East for much longer.

The changing realities of the world energy market do not mean the United States can or should ignore the Middle East. Iran's proliferation and Israel's security will rightly keep the region a focus for policymakers' attention. But in global perspective, the United States has more or deeper interests at stake in other regions of the world—Europe and South and East Asia—than the Middle East. US policymakers should recognize the emerging realities in the Middle East. The United States' role in guaranteeing the region's stability in exchange for cheap oil is an obsolescing bargain that is quickly becoming more trouble than it is worth. This is another example of why grand strategic labels such as "engagement" and "restraint" are useless: Either policy, followed globally, would be folly. The United States can and should adopt some form of restraint or retrenchment in the Middle East, even as it increases its engagement in other parts of the world.

Iran

The primary goal of US strategy in the Middle East, then, is no longer to assure access to low-cost oil (at least, not for much longer) or, since the withdrawal of US troops from Iraq in 2011, to contain, defeat, or stabilize Iraq. But the rise of a hostile government in Iran since 1979, its pursuit of nuclear weapons, and its linkage to the global Islamist insurgency have introduced a new security challenge to the United States. Fortunately, Iran is a lesser threat than Russia or China, which are global or near-global powers, and even less than North

Korea: North Korea inhabits an economically important neighborhood, has a close relationship with China, and is near several democratic US allies. North Korea is poorer and weaker than Iran, but it is closer to more things the United States cares about. Iran's neighborhood, by contrast, is less important, which makes its hostility and nuclear capabilities less relevant.

Iran is a threat to US national security interests because it may seek to monopolize regional oil supplies—which I acknowledge would be a challenge, though less serious than most scholars and policymakers believe—and because it threatens Israel, an important US ally. Iran's threat to other allies and partners in the region, including Saudi Arabia, is not a concern in and of itself, independent of their oil production. US alliances with other Middle Eastern states are a means, not an end: They help the United States secure regional stability and a continued flow of energy supplies to the world market. Once oil supplies no longer create geopolitical influence, the alliances are dispensable. The alliance with Israel is different because Israel is a democracy—democratic alliances are ends as well as means, and the Truman Doctrine commits the United States to Israel's defense if nothing else—and Israel is an important symbol of liberal order in an illiberal region.

The US goal is not to prevent Iran from acquiring nuclear weapons; Iran is already a "near-nuclear" power. Its acquisition of nuclear weapons is virtually assured, and crossing the threshold will not change the regional security dynamic, which has already adjusted to treat Iran as a nuclear power. Much of the security literature on Iran focuses on the negotiating dynamic between Iran and the United States and recommending specific bargaining tactics to prevent Iran from acquiring a nuclear weapon. Such literature places unwarranted faith in the ability of negotiations to achieve a denuclearized Iran and will almost certainly be overtaken by events within a few years. The 2015 nuclear deal left key nuclear facilities in place, conceded crucial details of the inspections and enforcement regime to Iranian preferences, and expires after a decade. It is essentially the formal codification of Iran's nuclear breakout capability, with a decent interval to preserve face for American diplomats. The deal is one consequence of the United States' defeat in the Iraq War. That war became, in part, a proxy contest for regional hegemony between the United States and Iran; the nuclear deal was the fruit of Iran's victory.

There is no consensus about the implications of Iran's nuclear status. Some scholars, led by realist Kenneth Waltz, have gone so far as to argue that Iran's development of nuclear weapons will promote stability in the Middle East—a view that, by taking structural realism to its logical extreme, helpfully illustrates its underlying flaws through a *reductio ad absurdum*.[14] Waltz's view that it does not matter who possesses nuclear weapons has all the problems of realism's disregard for ideology and culture in world politics, combined

with liberalism's surprisingly optimistic view of human rationality and decision making. Realists are typically keen to highlight their pragmatism, but on
this issue one is reminded of Niebuhr's critique of liberalism's naiveté. Even if
Waltz's sanguine view of nuclear proliferation and policymakers' rationality is
correct most of the time, few would argue that there can never be exceptions.
Iran and North Korea are the test cases *par excellence*.

But the opposite view is also problematic. Some analysts have warned that
Iranian ideology is alarmingly irrational, motivated by apocalyptic and messianic theology, and that its possession of nuclear weapons thus constitutes
an existential threat not only to Israel but also to world order and civilization itself. If true, the United States should immediately bomb Iran's nuclear
facilities, as some have suggested, and seek regime change by all means possible.[15] No doubt, some Iranian policymakers are true believers in their own
propaganda and would risk all to trigger Armageddon. But the pattern of
Iranian behavior suggests that they are not the only faction within the circle
of Iranian decision makers; other, more pragmatic voices are also present.
Iran is not wholly committed to an ideology of national martyrdom.[16] As with
China, there are competing voices within the Iranian government, the United
States does not always have clear insight into their deliberations, and Iranian
intentions can change over time.

That does not mean a near-nuclear Iran is a responsible member of the
international system. It has been emboldened to play a more active, even
aggressive role in the region in the belief that the international community
is unable to stop its nuclear programs, that the United States has withdrawn
from the region, and that other actions are deterred by Iran's nuclear capabilities. It has already successfully exploited the Syrian Civil War and the rise of
ISIS to increase its influence among weaker states in the region, including
Syria, Iraq, Yemen, and Lebanon. An Iranian-backed Shi'a revolution in Bahrain (where a Sunni monarchy rules over a majority-Shi'a population) would
eject the US Fifth Fleet from the country's naval facilities. Iran's nuclear
capabilities are likely to provoke others, especially Saudi Arabia and perhaps
Turkey, to develop their own nuclear weapon capabilities. Even without apoc-
alyptic motivations, a militarized crisis with Israel is possible and even likely.
A nuclear Iran is both dangerous and destabilizing and constitutes a threat to
Israeli, US, and global security.[17]

The Arab World

Scholars and policymakers have debated the relative merits of different policy
responses to Iran's nuclear capabilities.[18] Various options have been suggested,

including extending the United States' nuclear umbrella over Israel or even the entire region, adopting a full-scale policy of "containment" against Iran, and attempting to strike a grand strategic bargain with it. Formalizing the US–Israeli alliance with a mutual defense treaty and a nuclear guarantee is probably wise, though the alliance faces difficulties (see below). The United States has already unsuccessfully pursued a policy of containment against Iran, including support to Iraq in the 1980s, massive weapon sales to Saudi Arabia, decades of sanctions, and diplomatic efforts to halt Iran's nuclear programs. The first and fourth components of the strategy failed, and the United States is lifting sanctions as part of its nuclear deal with Iran, leaving little of a viable containment strategy left. For lack of alternatives, the United States may have to sponsor a Saudi-led effort to roll back Iranian influence.

The problem is that in Europe, East Asia, and South Asia the United States can partner with powerful liberal democracies to anchor regional stability, counter nuclear autocracies, and foster liberal order. In the Middle East, the United States has far fewer useful allies. The obvious candidate for a counterweight to Iran is, of course, Iraq—the role it played during its 1980–88 war with Iran. But consumed with its own descent into state failure, engaged in a life-or-death struggle with ISIS, and increasingly drawn into Iran's orbit because of its sectarian and autocratic Shi'a-led government, Iraq is unable to act as an effective counterweight to Iran. Israel is a rich, powerful, liberal, democratic MNNA in the Middle East widely believed to have nuclear weapons and implacably opposed to Iran, but the US–Israeli alliance has less regional influence because of Israel's poor relations with the Arab world—the main reason Israel did not join the 1991 or 2003 wars with Iraq. In addition, despite Israel's technological superiority, it may be simply too small to contribute meaningfully to a major war with Iran. And the US–Israeli alliance has some difficulties of its own.

The United States' most important relationship in the Arab world is with Saudi Arabia. The United States has no formal alliance with Saudi Arabia and gives it no foreign aid, but in February 1943 Roosevelt designated the defense of Saudi Arabia "vital to the defense of the United States"[19] and extended it lend-lease aid, roughly analogous to the designation of a country as an MNNA, and the Carter Doctrine further committed the United States to the defense of Saudi Arabia. The kingdom is one of the largest buyers of US military technology, accounting for about a fifth of all US weapon sales since 1950, and the United States has stood ready to defend the kingdom (from the Soviet Union, Iraq, al-Qaida, and now Iran) in return for the Saudis' pledge to maintain a secure flow of energy supplies to the world market. Saudi Arabia led small military operations with Egypt against Iranian-backed rebels in Yemen in early 2015, a template that, on a broader scale, may be the United States' best path forward in the Middle East. A Saudi-enforced security order with participation from other Arab states would not be liberal, but it would be reliably anti-Iranian.

But the kingdom is an unreliable partner because its refusal to liberalize at home risks political instability, while its inability to diversify its economy guarantees its eventual economic stagnation. In addition, the relationship with Saudi Arabia risks pulling the United States into an unnecessary war to defend a wasting asset. The implicit American security guarantee to the kingdom was a reasonable trade-off when the United States was highly dependent on oil for its energy needs. However, as I argue above, that is decreasingly the case. It remains important, but a loss of Saudi Arabian supplies would not harm the US economy nearly as badly as it did in the 1970s. Saudi Arabia's relevance to the world oil market itself is in terminal decline—and in a few decades the United States will be virtually immune from supply disruptions in the Gulf. Some evidence in 2014 suggested the Saudis were deliberately overproducing oil to drive the price down, maintain market share, hurt US producers, and undermine the commercial viability of new, unconventional production techniques.[20] If true, the Saudis are demonstrating that they are aware of the threat of looming changes in the world oil market and, ironically, hastening the day those realities will take hold by selling their cheap oil even more quickly than before. Few things are inevitable in world politics, but the end of cheap Saudi oil is one of them. Continued investment in a relationship with Saudi Arabia is an investment in the past, not the future. Partnering with Saudi Arabia to contain Iran may be the best short-term solution in the immediate crisis, after which the United States should pass the cost of Saudi security and Iranian containment on to the Saudis themselves.

Five other states in the region—Jordan, Morocco, Egypt, Kuwait, and Bahrain—are designated MNNAs but unlikely to be willing or able to anchor a regional strategy or lead efforts to contain Iran. Indeed, the usefulness of any of the Arab states as allies is increasingly questionable considering their general refusal to side openly with the United States on any major issue because they fear their own populations. The Arab Spring—it increasingly looks more like Europe's failed revolutions of 1848, not those of 1989—was thus a lost strategic opportunity. It might have been the hoped-for dawn of liberalism in the Middle East if outsiders, including the United States, had supported its momentum more aggressively.[21] Democracy in the Arab world would have made the region more important to the United States and given it more natural allies against Iran and more reason to remain engaged.

Instead, the US response to the Arab Spring was ineffectual. President Obama was right to tell the Arab world, "We support a set of universal rights. Those rights include free speech; the freedom of peaceful assembly; freedom of religion; equality for men and women under the rule of law; and the right to choose your own leaders—whether you live in Baghdad or Damascus; Sanaa or Tehran." That is why, Obama said, "it will be the policy of the United States to promote reform across the region, and to support transitions to democracy."[22] Unfortunately, the president, gun shy after Iraq, waited five months to give that speech and express support for the Arab Spring, and his administration undertook a superfluous intervention in Libya, strategically peripheral to the Middle East, while refraining from Syria, much closer to the heart of the region—and then failed to mount any sort of reconstruction or stabilization operation in Libya at all, allowing that country to descend into civil war.[23] The administration's approach to the Arab Spring thus achieved the remarkable feat of simultaneously demonstrating the weaknesses of realism, by failing to support the democratic movements early; pure humanitarianism, as the United States wasted resources and political capital on a strategically unimportant country; and restraint, as the United States allowed Libya to descend into chaos by failing to support its reconstruction. Today it is unclear what tools the United States has to affect the course of Arab politics.

US ties to the Egyptian military appear to have played a helpful role in preventing violence during Egypt's revolution and facilitating Mubarak's retirement in 2011, but Egypt subsequently failed to take the next steps toward democracy. The United States' failure to stop, or at least discourage, the military's coup against the government of Mohamed Morsi in 2013 was probably an error. The Morsi government was losing popularity quickly; if the military had allowed it to remain in power, it would have been voted out of power at the next election while Egyptians would have gained more familiarity with the importance of process and precedent for democracy. If the Morsi government made moves to delay or cancel elections, the military would have been on much stronger ground to intervene. Instead, by allowing the coup in 2013, the United States missed an opportunity to push for deeper democratization in Egypt and thus the opportunity to transform the US–Egyptian relationship from alliances of convenience into something more substantial. The current situation has simply reverted to the status quo pre-2011, in which the alliance may not have much to offer the United States. That does not mean the United States should treat these states like enemies or pariahs—Egypt remains influential in the Arab world—but there may no longer be justification to subsidize its defense or give it access to US military technology.

Iraq, Syria, and ISIS

The situation in the Middle East and US options to counter Iran became more complicated because of developments in Iraq and Syria.[24] The eruption of civil war in Syria and the power vacuum created by the withdrawal of US troops from Iraq in 2011 were the perfect conditions for the rise of ISIS—a jihadist army that has seized and held territory in both countries, tapped into Iraq's oil wealth, and become a magnet for aspiring jihadists around the world. Fortuitously for the United States, Iran and ISIS are sworn enemies—but the anarchy in the region has given cover for Iran to expand its influence even further.

The United States has no good options. Some policymakers called for the United States to intervene early in the Syrian Civil War in the hopes of ending Bashar al-Assad's regime—which the Obama administration publicly called for—and depriving Iran of its only significant ally. However, it was probably right not to intervene, for the wrong reasons. The Obama administration demonstrated in Libya that it was unwilling to devote the energy and resources required for stabilization and reconstruction operations, and that country descended into anarchy after the United States helped overthrow its government in 2011 (another war of questionable justice, heedless as it was of *jus post bellum*). A similar strategy in Syria—intervening to overthrow Assad but leaving the "postconflict" operations for others to manage—would have been disastrous. By staying aloof, the United States at least avoided that outcome. This is not a compliment to the United States' strategic acumen. Intervening in the war is exactly the sort of operation the United States should have done and should be capable of doing because it would have served the United States' national security and humanitarian ideals. That the best option was *not* intervening because the United States lacked the political will and operational competence to do so is one of the more damning observations that can be made about US strategy in the post-Iraq era. So long as US officials remain wary of the cost and risk of stability operations, they should avoid launching them: At least by not doing them, they will learn the cost of *not* intervening, which seems to be a lesson they need to learn.

The strategic and moral calculus of intervening in Syria did not change after Syria's use of chemical weapons against rebels and civilians in 2013. The Obama administration's declaration that the use of chemical weapons was a "red line" that would cause the United States to reevaluate its stance toward the war was arbitrary. It communicated that the United States cared more deeply about how civilians are slaughtered than that they were being slaughtered in the first place—a message that only served to highlight the strategic and moral whimsy of US engagement. If the United States is going to intervene on humanitarian grounds, it should at least use meaningful moral criteria.

The situation changed, and became more urgent, with the rise of ISIS. Americans have been justly horrified by ISIS's barbarity, but the group is not more brutal than other jihadists—it is simply more media-savvy. It understands the benefits it gains—in recruiting, fund-raising, and reputation—by advertising its crimes. Nor is the group's barbarity sufficient cause to justify the United States' bombing campaign. Rather, the Obama administration was right to reengage in Iraq in 2014 for the same reason that it should have stayed in Iraq and Afghanistan in the first place: *all* jihadist groups are a threat to US national security, and the United States should either equip local security forces to combat them or deploy US military personnel when local forces are at risk of being overrun. ISIS is particularly dangerous because of its access to oil wealth. That the administration was forced by events to reengage in Iraq is sharp proof of its earlier failures in the region.

But some perspective is in order. Between ISIS and Iran, the latter is plainly the greater threat. ISIS is not more ideologically hostile: The ayatollahs of Iran are merely the Shi'a version of ISIS. The two groups are ideological kin, the Sunni and Shi'a variants of jihadism. But Iran has the resources of a sovereign state and the ability to tax more than sixty million citizens—resources it has used to build a near-nuclear capability. Iran has a permanence ISIS lacks. ISIS has made enemies of every other major actor in the region. Iran, by contrast, has played its cards more effectively, has allies among Shi'a factions across the region, and enjoys Russian support for its Syrian client.

The United States is now trapped in a situation in which lethally danger-ous and depraved jihadists are waging war against two states that are more or less autocratic, under Iran's influence, and teetering on state failure. Because of the United States' passivity, Russia stepped into the power vacuum. While Russian interests partly align with American goals, they also partly diverge—and meanwhile, the United States has made itself beholden to Russia for the achievement of stability in the Middle East, a diplomatic coup for Russia that is likely to have repercussions globally. The ideal outcome—the defeat of ISIS *and* Iran's proxies, the reestablishment of American influence and the estab-lishment of two stable, moderate democracies—will not happen, and it would be utopian and unrealistic for the United States to try to bring it about. War between Iran and its proxies on the one hand and Sunni jihadists on the other, with Russia trying to police a quagmire, has a silver lining to it—America's enemies killing each other and sending the bill to the Russian taxpayer—but not one that any morally serious person should celebrate. Continued war will only deepen the radicalism and fanaticism of both sides, risk drawing in the entire region, perpetuate the worst humanitarian atrocity of the twenty-first century, and eventually export its chaos to the world beyond. Staying aloof and letting all sides bleed is not a strategy.

The Obama administration seems to have tacitly adopted a strategy of détente with Iran, implicitly enabling Iran and Assad to defeat ISIS with back-ing from US and Russian airpower. This approach is wrongheaded. Again, Iran is a greater threat than ISIS. Détente with Iran—of which the 2015 nuclear deal was a major part—guarantees Syria and Iraq will be locked into Iran's sphere of influence, recognizes Iran's de facto nuclear capabilities, and involves the United States in a moral compromise that even realists should find uncomfortable. Passing the buck to Russia achieves all the disadvantages of détente with Iran, with the added folly of boosting Russia's standing in the region.

A mildly better option would be to encourage a Saudi-led coalition to fight both ISIS and Iranian proxies, as it did in Yemen. The disadvantages of this approach are significant: Regional hegemony by Saudi Arabia would extinguish the last sparks of liberalism in the Arab world. Worse, it might risk sparking a Saudi–Iranian war with US and Russian sponsorship on opposite sides. Such a war would hurt the global economy and could escalate into a great power confrontation. But because it could become the culminating battle of decades of Middle Eastern tensions, a postwar settlement (assuming a Saudi victory) could yield deeper stability.

The alternative to a Saudi-led rollback campaign is the least politically popular in the United States: redeploying ground forces to Iraq to resume training and combat support with the Iraqi army and Kurdish forces, picking up the fight where they left off in 2011. A major difference between a new deployment and the 2003 invasion is a narrower mission: US forces cannot occupy, administer, or democratize Iraq but only seek to defeat ISIS and return the region to a basic level of stability. Obama rightly, if belatedly, redeployed some three thousand US troops to Iraq, though they are almost certainly too few compared with how many would be needed to make a serious difference on the ground. In the longer term, once ISIS has been destroyed and Assad removed from power, the United States can begin thinking about fostering conditions for a more lasting peace. To avoid excessive American involvement, the United States should work with the UN and the Arab League (and Russia, if possible) to convene an international conference to consider broader regional issues, such as the government of postwar Syria and the Iraq–Syria border. In that context, and not before, US diplomats can look for opportunities for targeted reconstruction and democracy assistance for Iraq and Syria at a level consistent with the region's relative importance.

A US ground presence would be helpful both for the immediate threat and for future contingencies. If Assad's regime falls, the United States cannot remain aloof. The United States and the international community must be prepared to mount a large and wide-ranging intervention to facilitate post-conflict political reconstruction, meet the humanitarian needs of the population, secure its remaining chemical weapons, and guard against attacks by Ba'athists or Iranian proxies. A hands-off approach in either Syria or Iraq like that used in post-Qaddafi Libya is certain to empower Iran and Sunni extremists and likely lead to endless war in the region. Unfortunately, the United

States is hamstrung from engaging with serious force because of its earlier missteps. That the most strategically sound option is the most unthinkable for US officials speaks volumes about the state of American grand strategy in the twenty-first century.

Israel

Israel is the only truly stable democracy between Gibraltar and the Khyber Pass.[25] (Lebanon, Tunisia, and Pakistan may, or may not, take advantage of their opportunities to build on new democratic institutions in coming years.) Israel is thus a uniquely valuable partner for American efforts to support global democracy. In addition, Israel's value as a trading partner is disproportionate to the relatively small size of its economy. Although its GDP is only around $250 billion, it has a rich-world GDP per capita, a highly educated workforce, and a sophisticated, knowledge-based economy that specializes in industries such as aviation and medical electronics. Israel is the United States' third-largest customer for weapon sales, accounting for $36 billion of purchases since 1950.[26] Finally, Israel is a natural ally in the United States' efforts to contain Iran or respond to Iranian aggression (though it cannot lead a regional coalition or a wider rollback campaign). Israel is more directly endangered by Iran's bellicosity than is the United States and perceives a much higher degree of threat from Tehran's growing regional power. US, British, and Israeli intelligence reportedly collaborated on efforts to sabotage Iranian nuclear facilities through cyberattacks in recent years—which seems to have been an economical and low-risk means of slowing (albeit temporarily) Iran's uranium enrichment.[27]

None of these benefits suggest that the United States should overlook the disadvantages of its current policy toward Israel. In particular, the United States does not need to sustain its high levels of foreign aid to Israel, tolerate the Mossad's long history of espionage against American targets, play a direct role in brokering agreements between the Israelis and their neighbors, or even care very deeply about the Israel–Palestine dispute.

The level of US aid to Israel is out of proportion to Israel's importance to US strategic interests. Since 1951, the United States has given Israel $193 billion in economic and military aid—the vast bulk of it since the Camp David Accords in 1978.[28] That is not simply more than any other country—it is more by a very wide margin. The second-highest recipient, Egypt, has received $118 billion over the same time frame, just 61 percent of Israel's total. Israel has received more money than Iraq, Afghanistan, and Pakistan combined; more than Vietnam during the decade-long US reconstruction and counterinsurgency effort there; and even, astonishingly, more than all of Europe under the Marshall

Plan.[29] Most American aid to Israel—an average of 70 percent since Camp David but rising to 98 percent in 2011—is military aid, specifically the waiving of payments for foreign military financing contracts. This rightly helps Israel maintain its qualitative military edge over regional rivals and, in recent years, build the Iron Dome missile defense system.[30] The United States should simply stop issuing waivers and accept payment, converting aid into trade. Israel is the richest country in the world to which the United States gives foreign aid, and as the third-largest buyer of American weapons, Israel has demonstrated that it can afford to pay. The United States should reserve foreign aid for poor states.

In addition, Israel has a long record of spying on the United States. American officials do not openly discuss this uncomfortable aspect of the US–Israeli relationship, and official documents rarely cite Israel as a counterintelligence threat. Nonetheless, reports occasionally surface (as they did in 2011) of American officials' private frustrations with Israel's alarmingly aggressive espionage in the United States and abroad against American targets.[31] That it is fairly normal for states to spy on one another is true but beside the point: Israel is one of the worst offenders, ranking after China and Russia, in stealing American secrets. Nor is Israeli espionage excusable because Israel means no harm to the United States: Israeli intelligence may be penetrated by Iranian or Chinese agents who know they can get American secrets without the hassle of hacking the Central Intelligence Agency. And the United States should insist, on grounds of principle, that the largest recipient of its foreign aid not steal its secrets.

Finally, American policymakers' time and attention seems disproportionately taken up worrying about the Israeli–Palestinian dispute that is, in truth, unimportant to American interests. Some critics argue that US policy toward Israel is wrong because it is unfair to the Palestinians. Whether or not that is true is beside the point: Many political relationships are characterized by unfairness, but not all of them are relevant to US national security. The question is not whether the Israeli–Palestinian situation is fair—the United States is not the global umpire of fairness—but whether the United States needs to care about it at all. Niebuhr's counsel to work for fairness in world politics was tempered by his caution against overestimating one's own capabilities and his skepticism of grand ideals. This is one area where policymakers would be wise to take counsel more from Niebuhr's skepticism than from his sense of justice.

Some foreign policy analysts have concocted a convoluted and implausible explanation that the Israeli–Palestinian conflict poisons relations with the rest of the Arab world, which in turn takes out its frustration against America. Peace between Israel and Palestine is the master key to unlocking regional stability across the Middle East, they argue, and the United States must become directly involved as an honest broker. This view is so pervasive that even advocates of restraint believe it. Barry Posen claims to distrust hypothetical causal chains that tie distant crises to American security and goes out of his way to disclaim "'domino theories' that string together a chain of individually imaginable, but collectively implausible, major events, to generate an ultimate threat to the United States." Nonetheless, he argues the United States has a vital national security interest in persuading Israel to stop building settlements in the West Bank because of their supposed effect on the broader region and, thence, US relations with the Arab world.[32] This is implausible. As Aaron David Miller argued in a piece recanting a lifetime of trying to be that honest broker in high-ranking positions in the State Department, "in a broken, angry region with so many problems—from stagnant, inequitable economies to extractive and authoritarian governments that abuse human rights and deny rule of law, to a popular culture mired in conspiracy and denial—it stretches the bounds of credulity to the breaking point to argue that settling the Arab–Israeli conflict is the most critical issue, or that its resolution would somehow guarantee Middle East stability."[33]

The Israeli–Palestinian dispute poses no threat to US national security, and its resolution would present no benefits. It seems baffling that the president of the United States must get personally involved in the minutiae of Israeli settlements in the West Bank. President Clinton's intensive effort to broker peace in the final months of his presidency was noble but also, perhaps, unpresidential. Americans tend to read something unique, portentous, and epic into the Israeli–Palestinian conflict. It is nothing of the kind. US strategy toward the Israeli–Palestinian dispute should be to ignore it.

Notes

1. For example, see Art, "Defensible Defense."
2. Pollack, *Path Out of the Desert*, chap. 1. See also Art, *Grand Strategy*, 58–64, for a statement of the conventional wisdom.
3. The following is adapted and selected from Miller, "Fading Arab Oil Empire." Used with permission.
4. International Energy Agency, *World Energy Outlook 2008*, 218.
5. US Energy Information Administration, "Monthly Energy Review," January 2015.
6. US Energy Information Administration, *Annual Energy Review: 2010*, 9.
7. International Energy Agency, *World Energy Outlook 2008*, 92.
8. Ibid., 225.
9. Figures derived from American Petroleum Institute, *Basic Petroleum Data Book*; British Petroleum, *Statistical Review of the World Oil Industry*; US Energy Information Administration, *International Energy Statistics*.

10. US Energy Information Administration, *Annual Energy Outlook: 2011*, 155.

11. International Energy Agency, *World Energy Outlook 2008*, chap. 9.

12. Layne, *Peace of Illusions*, 189.

13. Carter, "State of the Union."

14. Waltz and Sagan, *Spread of Nuclear Weapons*; Waltz, "Why Iran Should Get the Bomb"; Sagan, Waltz, and Betts, "Nuclear Iran."

15. Kroenig, "Time to Attack Iran."

16. Grotto, "Is Iran a Martyr State?"

17. Edelman, Krepinevich, and Montgomery, "Dangers of a Nuclear Iran."

18. Lindsay and Takeyh, "After Iran Gets the Bomb."

19. Franklin Roosevelt, "To the Lend-Lease Administrator," in US Department of State, *Papers Relating to the Foreign Relations of the United States, 1943*, 859.

20. Jay Solomon and Summer Said, "Why Saudis Decided Not to Prop Up Oil," *Wall Street Journal*, December 21, 2014. Alternatively, the US government may be collaborating with the Saudis to drive down the price to hurt Russia.

21. On the Arab Spring, see Bellin, "Reconsidering the Robustness"; Ajami, "Arab Spring at One"; Jones, "Mirage of the Arab Spring"; Berman, "Promise of the Arab Spring"; Anderson, "Demystifying the Arab Spring."

22. Obama, "Remarks at the State Department."

23. Kuperman, "Obama's Libya Debacle."

24. For background on the Syrian Civil War, see Phillips, "Syria's Torment"; Lister, "Assessing Syria's Jihad"; Jones, "Syria's Growing Jihad"; Stevenson, "Syrian Tragedy and Precedent"; and Miller, *Getting to Negotiations in Syria*.

25. The following is selected and adapted from Miller, "Evangelicals, Israel, and U.S. Foreign Policy." Copyright by the International Institute for Strategic Studies. Used with permission.

26. Figures drawn from US Defense Security Cooperation Agency, *Historical Facts Book as of September 30, 2013*.

27. Ellen Nakashima and Joby Warrick, "Stuxnet Was Work of US and Israeli Experts, Officials Say," *Washington Post*, June 2, 2012.

28. US Agency for International Development, *U.S. Overseas Loans and Grants*.

29. The Marshall Plan disbursed $13.3 billion between 1948 and 1952, according to the Marshall Foundation. That is equivalent to about $130 billion today, according to the Department of Labor inflation adjuster.

30. William J. Broad, "Weapons Experts Raise Doubts about Israel's Antimissile System," *New York Times*, March 20, 2013.

31. Adam Goldman and Matt Apuzzo, "US Sees Israel, Tight Mideast Ally, as Spy Threat," Associated Press, July 28, 2012.

32. Posen, *Restraint*, 3, 117. In this case, I counsel more restraint than Posen does insofar as I argue the United States can simply ignore the whole situation.

33. Miller, "False Religion of Mideast Peace."

9

The Periphery

Latin America and Africa

Africa and Latin America are traditionally the least important regions for US security interests—a rare example of conventional wisdom that is still sound. Latin America actually accounts for more than a fifth of US trade, largely because of Mexico—and the potential exists for US trade in the region to expand significantly—but otherwise ranks poorly on measures of wealth, power, and importance to the United States. It comprises less than 8 percent of world GDP (slightly higher than the Middle East), less than 5 percent of global military spending, and less than 6 percent of global power. More telling than the numbers is its neighborhood. Latin America is removed from the Eurasian theater and the world's most important strategic geography. It is not a party to the dynamic among the world's most powerful states. That might have changed: Brazil and Argentina pursued nuclear weapon technology until the 1991 Quadripartite Agreement denuclearized the continent. American interests in Latin America would look very different if it faced two nuclear powers with histories of military dictatorships and populist anti-Americanism in the Western Hemisphere. Preserving the nuclear status quo in Latin America should be a top priority for the United States.

In lieu of nuclear rivalry, the main threat to American security and liberal order in Latin America is the global cocaine trade. The region is home to cartels and traffickers who both cause and flourish in conditions of state failure, and the United States is an irresistible $37 billion market for their product. The creeping legalization of marijuana could introduce some difficulties for the cartels. Marijuana is the most-trafficked illegal drug by far; its legalization would free up Drug Enforcement Administration and border control agents to focus on cocaine at the same time that it would shift some of the traffickers' market from the illicit economy to licit competitors. But the cocaine traffic is unlikely to disappear any time soon.

The threat of the cocaine trade is most dramatic in Mexico, both one of the greatest opportunities and potential dangers in the twenty-first century.

Mexico, one of the few examples of gradual and relatively peaceful liberalization in the world, evolved over the course of the twentieth century from a soft autocracy to a full democracy in 2001. But Mexican democracy is fragile and under threat from drug traffickers, organized crime, and the state's response. Just a decade after Freedom House declared Mexico "free," it downgraded the country to "partly free" in 2011 "due to the targeting of local officials by organized crime groups and the government's inability to protect citizens' rights in the face of criminal violence."[1] The level of violence in some Mexican cities and provinces suggests that the "war" on drugs is not an exaggeration. Mexico is not on the verge of collapse or state failure—but may be on a trajectory to be so if current trends continue or worsen. The stakes are high: Mexico has the size, population, and human capital to be a regional power and an important component of liberal order. After Brazil and Chile, it is probably the best-positioned state in Latin America to take advantage of globalization. But if it continues to lose ground to corrupt officials and violent drug gangs, its recent gains could be undone, and the United States could face gang violence, refugee flows, and a humanitarian crisis creeping across its border.

For that reason, the United States should rank foreign aid to Mexico alongside that to India, Eastern Europe, Turkey, and Pakistan as a high priority—in line with Mexican sensitivities. Americans blessed by historical amnesia may be surprised that Mexicans sometimes display raw feelings for their loss in 1848, but it is Americans' tendency to forget, not foreigners' to remember, that is unusual. Mexican authorities have persistently refused any form of security assistance that involves uniformed American military personnel publicly deployed on Mexican soil. Within that constraint, the United States should pursue all available options to assist Mexican security forces, such as offering training courses in the United States, sharing intelligence, providing equipment, and more. In the future, should US–Mexican relations warm and Mexico consolidate its emergence as a stable and prosperous power, Mexico might join Canada as the last member of NATO on this side of the Atlantic (or, alternatively, the United States might designate it an MNNA).

The best model of bilateral counternarcotics cooperation—in fact, one of the best models of effective US foreign aid—is Colombia, the United States' strongest partner in Latin America. With brief periods of democratic and semidemocratic rule in the 1870s and 1930s, Colombian democracy has been remarkably well rooted since 1958, especially considering its internal challenges. Colombia has been waging a counterinsurgency and counternarcotics campaign against the Revolutionary Armed Forces of Colombia (FARC), a Marxist insurgent and drug-trafficking organization, since 1966—the world's longest-running armed conflict. The FARC traffics drugs to finance its insurgency, while the lawlessness the war creates provides cover for other drug-trafficking organizations.

Both because it drives the cocaine trade and threatens a democracy, the FARC is a threat to American security and liberal order.

In response, the Bill Clinton and Andrés Pastrana Arango administrations developed Plan Colombia, a joint campaign to combat the FARC and the drug trade and enhance Colombia's governance and professionalize its security forces.[2] Starting in the late 1990s, the United States deployed a small number of military personnel—one hundred in 2014—to train and support Colombian security forces. The United States also gave a substantial amount of foreign aid to Colombia, totaling $8.6 billion from 2003 to 2012—two-thirds of it economic assistance. The United States designated the FARC an FTO in 1997, which enhanced the United States' ability to sanction individuals and institutions that support the group. Colombia has demonstrably improved its rule of law, regulatory quality, and political stability according to the World Bank,[3] even as drug trafficking and political violence have declined and negotiations with the FARC are under way.

Plan Colombia is a model: It was a whole-of-government, civilian–military campaign; it was economical but serious, involving a sizeable investment of people and money compared with the United States' other engagements in the region, but small compared with US commitments worldwide; and it was driven and led by the host (democratic) government. There are, as always, problems. Colombia has shown some democratic backsliding in recent years; right-wing nonstate militias have had a troublingly permissive operating environment; some drug operations have simply moved across the borders to Peru and Bolivia; and, in war, there are always accusations of excess and human rights violations. No undertaking is free from unintended consequences, blowback, and some degree of moral compromise—but that should not stop policymakers from learning from the successes of Plan Colombia and applying them elsewhere. The impending end of the FARC insurgency and the inroads against the cocaine trade, at least within its borders, could free Colombia to become a model of democratic stability and success in Latin America. Colombia is already one of the United States' strongest diplomatic supporters and, in 2013, expressed interest in joining NATO. While expanding NATO out of the North Atlantic theater is a bad idea, the United States should consider designating Colombia an MNNA.

If the United States chooses to designate either Colombia or Mexico as allies, it should review Argentina's status. It is unclear why Argentina is a designated ally or what benefits the United States gets from it. Similarly, the United States should recognize that the Inter-American Treaty of Reciprocal Assistance (also known as the Rio Treaty) is effectively dead. It played no meaningful role after the terrorist attacks in 2001, Mexico withdrew in 2002, and several more states are in the process of withdrawing.[4]

Cuba and Venezuela

The only two state-centric problems in the Western Hemisphere are Cuba and Venezuela. Neither are threats to American security, and both are too weak to be a serious threat to liberal order. Cuba, which narrowly missed annexation by the United States in the mid-nineteenth century and again following the war with Spain, should have been a close partner with the United States in the twentieth century. The United States' obsessive opposition to the communist regime since 1961 has been out of proportion to the threat the island nation actually posed and was driven more by domestic politics and American diplomatic embarrassment at having been shown up by a minor dictator time and again—though John F. Kennedy was right to face down the Soviet Union over its deployment of nuclear missiles there in 1962. The embargo against Cuba has failed to serve any discernable US interest. The United States should continue to voice diplomatic opposition to Cuba's autocracy, but President Obama's moves to normalize diplomatic ties in 2014 and remove Cuba from the list of state sponsors of terrorism the following year was sensible—although he could have driven a better bargain by waiting for the drop in oil prices to start hurting Cuba's patron, Venezuela.

Venezuela is a bigger problem than Cuba because of its oil wealth and the potential for it to sponsor illiberal movements elsewhere in Latin America. Unlike other relatively young Latin American democracies, Venezuela's was established in 1958 and remained relatively robust until Hugo Chávez was elected in 1999. Venezuela is living proof, if any were needed, that democracies can die from suicide—the Weimar Republic of the twenty-first century. The 2002 coup attempt was misguided—the way to stop a demagogue is for locals to vote him out of power while the chance still exists, not to use extra-constitutional means. Instead, when Chávez's illiberalism became evident, the United States should have mounted an energetic campaign to aid civil society and independent media, empowering them for the next electoral cycle, and should have demanded international observation of Venezuelan polls. However, to be blunt, the death of Venezuelan democracy is simply not important enough to US security or world order—compared with the United States' various interests in Europe, East Asia, South Asia, and the Middle East—to expend many resources on.

Africa

Africa has traditionally been the least strategically important region to the United States. Despite much change in recent decades, Africa's relative unimportance to US security remains the same. The African states combined, excepting only Egypt, account for less than 5 percent of world GDP, less than 3 percent of world military spending, and less than 2 percent of US trade. There are no African great powers or nuclear weapons states. The United States has no important trade relationships on the continent on par with those in Europe, Asia, or Latin America. While the continent has some economic potential, its markets are underdeveloped and held back by weak infrastructure, corruption, and poor governance. There are few major buyers of American weapons (again, not counting Egypt). The major nonstate threat emanating from the region—piracy—is less urgent than that from the terrorists in South Asia and the Middle East and the drug cartels in Latin America.

However, while its *relative* importance remains low compared with other regions, it is nonetheless more important than it used to be. Some things have changed in ways that have created opportunities for the United States, while emerging threats have made it impossible for the United States to simply ignore Africa. There are a surprising number of full or partial democracies in Africa, South Africa foremost among them. Most emerged after the Cold War as civil wars petered out, socialist systems collapsed, and liberalism emerged in Africa, as elsewhere, as the default choice. The United States could encourage a network of partnerships and trade among the almost two dozen democracies in the region, which could help consolidate newer democracies, such as South Africa, Zambia, and Senegal, and help older ones, such as Botswana, emerge into new roles. Giving technical assistance, economic support, and governance aid to Tunisia's newly democratic government could help dispel the myth that Arabs, Africans, Muslims, and developing states cannot or will not succeed at democracy. So would highlighting the remarkable story of the Comoros, a tiny island nation off the eastern coast of Africa that is a member of the Arab League and that, after decades of coups and countercoups, gradually transitioned to democracy between 2002 and 2006. Greater democratic stability and better governance across Africa would help prevent its continued economic development from becoming an occasion for domestic unrest, civil war, foreign exploitation, or regional conflict that could draw in outsiders or raise calls for expensive and dangerous UN- or US-led interventions.

Unfortunately, the map of democracy in Africa does not align with the map of the United States' security interests: The democratic and partly democratic states are concentrated in the south, southeast, and west; jihadist groups, such as al-Qaida in the Islamic Maghreb and al-Shabaab, are mostly active in the north and east, and pirates operate off the northeastern coast. South Africa, the continent's largest and most powerful full democracy, might be a helpful diplomatic partner for the United States on global issues but offers little in way of cooperation against common threats. The exception is Nigeria, a semidemocracy in West Africa with oil that is combating a jihadist insurgency in its north. Nigeria would be the biggest opportunity for the United States in Africa but for its domestic problems—weak governance, corruption, and sectarian conflicts. The United States should explore low-cost engagement in Nigeria—for example, counterterrorism training for its military and police and election support—to invest in a future when Nigeria finds its way out of its current morass. Nigeria and South Africa are the likeliest African candidates for great power status.[5]

In the meantime, the United States is stuck with its current autocratic partners. Because al-Qaida is not nearing strategic defeat, the United States has little alternative but to continue its military assistance and weapon sales to Sudan and Ethiopia to improve their counterterrorism capabilities—though this should be reviewed annually to verify the need still exists. Djibouti has proven exceptionally useful to the United States as the location of its largest military facility on the continent and the headquarters for counterpiracy operations, with access to both the Gulf of Aden and the Red Sea. The Djiboutian autocracy has slightly moderated since the peaceful 1999 resignation of the longtime strongman president. The United States should look at deepening ties with Djibouti, including by naming it an MNNA, if Djiboutian policymakers show any willingness to continue liberalization. If so, the United States may have the opportunity to relocate the headquarters of Africa Command from Europe to Djibouti.

Africa provides unlimited opportunities to deploy stability operations but fewer strategic reasons to do so. Somalia, the world's most failed state, is the most obvious potential case for intervention because of pirates and al-Shabaab, but both threats appear manageable, while an effort to rebuild Somalia would be prohibitively costly and unlikely to succeed, especially while tribal and factional violence continues. If the war ebbs or the sides agree to partition, the United States should not lead, but also should not oppose, a UN intervention there or in other weak and failed African states such as Chad, the Democratic Republic of the Congo, and Côte d'Ivoire. These states' weaknesses do not currently threaten the United States or its allies, and so the United States need not lead stabilization efforts. But instability, left unaddressed, can spread, and widespread state failure can eventually become a systemic threat to liberal order. Investing in stability even in regions of peripheral strategic importance can eventually create the opportunity to invest in democracy and thus a future US partner. That is why the United States should encourage UN interventions in any state that needs international assistance, even in peripheral regions and even, if possible, support the UN with money, equipment, and trainers. Even if the specific operation is unimportant to the United States, the UN is, and supporting the UN is a cheap way for the United States to invest in stability in peripheral regions, an appropriate occasion for buck-passing.[6]

Terra Nullius

There is one more geopolitical region to consider, universally omitted from discussions of grand strategy: *terra nullius*—unclaimed regions. These include Antarctica, the Moon, Mars (and beyond), and outer space. US policymakers should begin thinking more seriously about a strategy toward these regions. This might seem fanciful—these topics are typically treated under the rubric of science policy, not foreign policy. But, as a thought experiment, imagine how history might have differed if the Spanish Empire had developed a more deliberate approach to the New World in the sixteenth or seventeenth centuries. If it had seen in those regions not simply a lode of natural resources for extraction but also a site for a future home, things may have been different.

That does not mean the United States should equip its next Mars rover with an American flag to robotically plant on the red surface. It does mean that the government should take seriously the strategic implications of permanent or semipermanent human habitation in these regions. The question is not hypothetical. There is already a permanent human presence on Antarctica—by Americans. The United States operates five facilities in Antarctica—two in the summer and three year-round, including McMurdo Station, the continent's largest. If global climate change proves as bad as the worst predictions expect, the pressure to settle and perhaps farm the outer fringe of Antarctica—and thus change its legal status—could become irresistible by century's end. Similarly, there have been humans in orbit around Earth in the International Space Station continuously since November 2000. The recent dawn of commercial spaceflight—SpaceX and the Orbital Sciences Corporation have provided launch vehicles and crew and cargo transport vehicles to active space programs—brings closer the day of space tourism and commercial development. President George W. Bush announced plans in 2006 for a permanent Moon base. The United States, Russia, China, and the EU have all undertaken planning for manned missions to Mars.

The Antarctic Treaty of 1959 and the Outer Space Treaty of 1967 prohibit territorial claims, military bases, or the deployment of weapons of mass destruction in these areas because they are classified as the "common heritage of mankind." As arms-control measures, these treaties make sense. But in resting arms control on the ambiguous and novel legal concept of the "common heritage," they have unintended consequences. Effectively removing these areas from national jurisdictions retards the development of a statutory or regulatory framework necessary for scientific and commercial development. In late 2015, the US Congress moved in the right direction with a law allowing US citizens and companies to claim property rights over resources recovered in space.

In addition, though the scientific community would strongly oppose saying so, it would be unwise to pretend that science is simply removed from the political and strategic considerations of great powers. The line between scientific exploration and military reconnaissance has always been thin. The Lewis and Clark Expedition was one of the greatest botanical, ethnographic, and geographic research expeditions in history: It was also a US Army reconnaissance operation designed to discover and outflank Spanish, French, Russian, and British designs on the continent. Much of the National Aeronautics and Space Administration's developments in rocketry overlapped with the invention of intercontinental ballistic missiles. The US military's global positioning system satellites provided a major boost to civilian industries when President Clinton allowed dual use in 1996. Several states operate reconnaissance satellites that provide crucial intelligence to their military forces, which seems to violate the spirit of the demilitarization of space.

The first state to establish itself in these regions will be in a position to set precedents, treaty interpretations, and norms for the rest of the world to follow. Because of its technological edge and more robust commercial sector, the United States is in natural position to continue leading the exploration, development, and, someday, settlement of these unpopulated regions. (For example, the United States operates 41 percent of the 1,235 satellites in orbit around earth, and a much higher percentage of its satellites are commercial compared with Russia's and China's, according to the Union of Concerned Scientists.[7]) As it does so, it will be the first to reap the benefits and the first to have an opportunity to establish the rules of the game in places of legal and political ambiguity.

Similarly, if there is one area of science and technology with potentially incalculable strategic implications, it is the development of artificial general intelligence (AGI), which some thinkers speculate may happen sometime in the twenty-first century. The creation of AGI could generate follow-on benefits but also unpredictable dangers. AGI would almost certainly be weaponized by the first country to invent it, the most significant advance in military technology since the atom bomb—a scenario so obvious it has created countless science-fictional dystopias. As with the splitting of the atom, developing AGI under American (or allied) auspices increases the chance that its shape and use would reflect liberal norms and would, initially at least, give the democracies a monopoly on one of the most significant technologies in human history. Short of actually building an AGI, research and development in the field will give the United States a strong negotiating position in AGI arms-control negotiations.

The scenarios in which farming Antarctica and colonizing Mars are national security assets are admittedly speculative and quite distant, but small investments in the present can pay off in unexpected ways over a very long time horizon. Grand strategy, after all, should be known for its grandiosity.

Notes

1. Freedom House, *Freedom in the World 2011.*
2. Crandall, "Clinton, Bush and Plan Colombia."
3. Kaufman, Kraay, and Mastruzzi, "Worldwide Governance Indicators."
4. The continued operation of the Panama Canal is a vital national security interest of the United States. However, there are no real threats to the canal. The possible creation of another canal through Nicaragua would help, not hurt, the United States by reducing its reliance on a single strategic waterway in the Western Hemisphere.
5. But probably not the Democratic Republic of the Congo, which has been one of the most persistently failed states in the world for decades. To create a more favorable environment for improved governance, it should either partition itself into smaller units or federate with neighboring states and radically decentralize.
6. See Bellamy and Williams, "West and Contemporary Peace Operations," for a discussion of the United States and the UN.
7. The Union of Concerned Scientists compiles and publishes a list of publicly observable satellites. Forty-five percent of US satellites are civil or commercial, compared with 17 percent of Russian and 12 percent of Chinese. But Russian satellites also tend to be multipurpose.

PART IV

THE NATIONAL SECURITY TOOL KIT

10

Homeland Defense

The grand strategy outlined here is ambitious and broad in scope—it amounts to sustaining and expanding the liberal order that has been developing for seventy years—but it need not break the bounds of what is fiscally possible. The next three chapters outline the implications of this grand strategy for the United States' tools of national power: its homeland security, force structure, global posture, network of bases, foreign aid priorities, diplomacy and development, trade relationships, and intelligence programs. It describes how these tools of national security might be reformed, changed, or improved for the future.

Scholars—and, too often, policymakers—sometimes skip this step on the implicit assumption that if the plan is good enough, implementation will work itself out. The assumption is wrong. More nearly the opposite is true: Implementation is where strategy goes to die. A new de facto strategy takes shape from the pattern of behavior created by bureaucratic inertia, drift, and parochialism; budget constraints; political concerns; congressional earmarking; the lack of personnel in implementing agencies with required skills; poor morale; organizational conflict; poor oversight and accountability; corruption; and limited vision. "The balance of resources, leadership structures, and organizational cultures within [a state's] bureaucracies can hinder the implementation of even a modest set of goals," according to Sarah Kreps.[1]

Others scholars focus only on the military instrument, on the assumption that it is the most important, or only, instrument for grand strategy. Robert Art, for example, explicitly excludes consideration of nonmilitary means in implementing grand strategy for definitional reasons: To include it would turn the discussion from grand strategy to foreign policy.[2] Barry Posen, similarly, spends forty pages describing America's ideal force structure and defense posture and none at all discussing its diplomacy, development, aid, trade, intelligence, or cyber instruments of national power.[3] I have taken a different approach in this book. Focusing narrowly on the military instrument is not grand strategy—it is military strategy. Grand strategy that is only applicable in war or near war is indistinguishable from a campaign plan. The implication that the military is the most important instrument for grand strategy might be true in some conditions—in wartime, during crises, or in the midst of coercive bargaining—but not in others. Attempting to use a solely military strategy for all occasions would lead to a militarized, bullying, and ineffective presence in the world.

Grand strategy integrates all instruments of national power. I briefly review the implications of US grand strategy for the most important instruments. My discussion is necessarily brief and suggestive rather than thorough because space prevents me from discussing the full history and potential of each tool of national power; the more detailed the discussion is, the more quickly it will be overtaken by changing circumstances; and some information required for a thorough discussion remains classified. I hope here to outline a useful framework that could be applied in different ways as the situation around the world merits. I begin in this chapter with a discussion of homeland defense.

Homeland Defense

Physically protecting lives and territory is the first responsibility of government. Some scholars argue that the US homeland is relatively immune from danger, which has led them to underestimate the role of homeland defense in grand strategy. Art, for example, argues that terrorism and weapons of mass destruction are the only threats to the US homeland.[4] Others, such as Posen, exclude homeland defense from discussions of grand strategy altogether, presumably in the presumption that homeland security is unconnected to foreign policy or that grand strategy should deal exclusively with external affairs. In fact, hardening the United States against physical attack is a form of internal balancing against rivals and enemies. Improving homeland security increases the United States' relative power: It raises the cost to potential enemies of inflicting direct harm on the United States, compelling them to spend more energy and effort, redirect their efforts elsewhere, or give up entirely. For example, detecting and thwarting espionage helps the United States retain its informational advantage over rivals such as Russia and China, while a missile defense system would force them to compete in a technological arena in which the United States enjoys massive superiority.

The United States has grown its homeland defense capabilities in response to specific threats it faces. While the US homeland is relatively more secure than most other states because it faces no prospect of a land invasion by a hostile power, it is vulnerable to other risks. The borders with Canada and Mexico and US ports of entry have been strengthened since 2001 but are too porous considering the possibility of intrusion by terrorists or nuclear smugglers. Missile defense is worth pursuing, if only to drive up the cost and difficulty to rivals of building effective ballistic missiles. But the most important improvements the United States should make in its homeland defense is to revamp its approach to cybersecurity and internal security, classifying the former as part of the latter, and to create a dedicated internal security and domestic intelligence agency—separate from the FBI—to combat spies, saboteurs, traitors, hackers, and domestic terrorists.

Presidents George Washington and John Adams made the creation of the first national security and homeland defense organizations a top priority for the new government, including the Department of War in 1789, the US Navy in 1797, and the Department of the Navy in 1798—and, of course, the US Army and Marine Corps predate the government itself. These organizations' roles were originally closer to what today would be called homeland defense—protecting the territorial integrity and physical safety of the United States—although even then it was taken to include American lives, property, and honor abroad. President Adams fought a quasi-war with France in 1798 to defend neutral trading rights, Presidents Thomas Jefferson and James Madison ordered attacks on the Barbary States of North Africa in 1805 and 1815 to protect American shipping, and Madison led the War of 1812 against the United Kingdom to stop the latter's impressments of American sailors.

Homeland defense continued to be relatively lax before the twentieth century because of the United States' unique geographic position, being separated by two oceans from the other major powers. Nonetheless, coastal fortifications took up a major component of US defense spending in the nineteenth century as Americans regularly feared intrusion by recidivist European imperial powers seeking to reacquire lost colonial possessions. The responsibility for homeland defense continued to lie with the military for much of the nineteenth century as, for example, the US Army–led campaigns against Native American tribes who resisted American expansion.

During World War I, the US government created, and subsequently disbanded, its first dedicated intelligence agencies and passed the Espionage Act to guard against undercover foreign agents in response to German saboteurs during World War I. The FBI assumed responsibility (sometimes abused) for investigating cases of espionage and sabotage. The United States created its first standardized passport regime during the Great War but abolished it shortly thereafter (permanently reinstating it in 1941). And in 1924 Congress established the US Border Patrol to regulate growing waves of immigration.

After World War II, homeland defense became a much greater concern, and the US military and intelligence community established a worldwide network of reconnaissance and surveillance capabilities to prevent another surprise attack like the Japanese assault on Pearl Harbor in 1941. The North American Aerospace Defense Command (NORAD) was established in 1961 to provide for "the detection, validation, and warning of attack against North America whether by aircraft, missiles, or space vehicles."[5] And President Ronald Reagan initiated efforts in 1983 to develop a ballistic missile defense system in response to the threat of nuclear attack from the Soviet Union.

The US government gave homeland security more concerted attention in the aftermath of the 2001 terrorist attacks. The Homeland Security Act of 2002 merged almost two dozen federal agencies into the new Department of Homeland Security, which a year later also assumed control of the newly created Transportation Security Administration. Further reforms in the FBI, which remained part of the Department of Justice, also added focus to homeland security—though I argue below much more is needed.

Each stage in the development of US homeland defense capabilities grew in response to specific threats against American territory and lives that emerged in different eras. Today, thanks to new technology and globalization, there are new and greater direct threats against American territory and lives than previously. While a land invasion from a hostile power is as unlikely as ever, the United States is at risk from ballistic missiles; nuclear, chemical, and biological weapons (deployed by missile or otherwise); terrorist attacks; espionage; sabotage; and, because of the increasingly network-dependent nature of much of the American economy and infrastructure, cyberattack. In response, the United States must develop capabilities to protect against each, including border security, port security, cybersecurity, counterintelligence, and missile defense.

Border and Port Security

The United States is, and should be, welcoming to immigrants, visitors, and entrepreneurs. There were 165.5 million legal nonimmigrant admissions into the United States in 2012—mostly tourists, business travelers, and international students. Just over one million legally immigrated and gained lawful permanent resident status in the United States, and more than 750,000 permanent residents became naturalized citizens, adding to the largest immigrant population in the world. Over eleven million cargo containers arrive at US seaports annually, the physical carriers of the globalized economy. The ability of US Customs and Border Protection, US Immigration and Customs

Enforcement, and US Citizenship and Immigration Services to process the annual tidal wave of people and goods safely and efficiently at America's 328 ports of entry—its land crossings, seaports, and airports—is impressive and vital not only to US national security but also to its economy, cultural vitality, and openness to the world.[6]

That said, America's borders are infamously porous. The presence of 11.5 million illegal immigrants and migrant workers and the nearly 650,000 deportations in 2012 are not in themselves national security issues, but they strongly illustrate how easily America's borders can be illegally crossed by terrorists, drug and weapon traffickers, slavers, saboteurs, and foreign intelligence agents. Customs and Border Protection seized over 1.2 million kilograms of illegal drugs in 2013 at America's ports of entry and recorded 4,600 instances of seizing illegal firearms, representing an unknown fraction of a larger movement of illegal drugs and weapons into the United States.[7] America's porous borders have also occasionally made the country vulnerable to more direct threats, although these have been rare. German agents carried out a series of sabotage operations against American munitions and arms manufacturers during World War I—including explosions and fires in Jersey City, New York City, and a navy yard in California in 1916 and 1917.[8] Similarly, in June 1942, eight Nazi saboteurs (including two American citizens) were ferried by submarine across the Atlantic and landed on the New York and Florida coasts for similar operations, though they were betrayed by one of their number.[9] That terrorists have not yet taken a similar route to attack the United States (the 9/11 hijackers entered the country legally) has resulted in border security not receiving the same level of attention as other components of homeland security. The 9/11 attacks prompted a massive upgrade to security at airports and on airplanes, but the relative lack of attention to the land border and seaports makes them attractive targets to those who are looking for a way to enter the country without notice. It is one of the last unexploited vulnerabilities in US homeland security.

The United States must protect against nonstate actors, such as al-Qaida, who seek to do immediate physical violence to Americans on American soil, by enforcing its borders, hardening its ports, and implementing reasonable immigration regulations. Doing so would also combat the scourge of slavery and raise the cost of drug smuggling and arms trafficking. Much of this has improved since the terrorist attacks of 2001. In addition to the creation of the Transportation Security Administration (TSA) in 2001 and the Department of Homeland Defense in 2002, Congress also authorized the near doubling of the size of the US Border Patrol in the Intelligence Reform and Terrorism Prevention Act of 2004. The 1,989-mile land border with Mexico has also been hardened with drone surveillance and, since 2006, over 600 miles of fencing. The FBI consolidated its counterterrorism and other programs into a National Security Branch in 2005, and its Terrorist Screening Center began compiling and disseminating the "No Fly List" and the "Terrorist Watch List." Illicit travel has been made more difficult through the widespread adoption of biometric passports by much of the world over the last decade (including the United States in 2006).

The immigration regime, however, is still in need of broad overhaul to allow the free flow of migrant labor, visiting students, and highly skilled talent while preventing illegal entry by terrorists and drug traffickers. The land borders are still porous; a combination of additional fencing, patrol personnel, and active surveillance is probably required. And port security—divided among the Coast Guard, Customs and Border Protection, and the TSA—is relatively undeveloped, with programs such as the Container Security Initiative too small compared to the mission with which they are charged.

Missile Defense and Nuclear Safety

In addition, the United States must also protect against the possibility of a rogue, accidental, or even deliberate launch of a ballistic missile with a nuclear, chemical, or biological warhead against US territory, its bases abroad, or its allies—the most likely immediate threat in case of war with one of the nuclear powers—through functional missile defense capabilities. The United States has been researching national missile defense since 1983, withdrew from the Anti-Ballistic Missile (ABM) Treaty in 2002, and in 2004 announced it had deployed the first components of an operational national missile defense—probably the only kind of missile defense the American public is aware of. With less attention and controversy but more success, the United States has also deployed theater and tactical missile defense systems, designed for defense against shorter-range, slower missiles, such as those Iran and North Korea operate.

Missile defense offers a range of benefits. National missile defense serves the basic purpose of reinforcing the physical security of American territory and lives. The advocates of restraint, such as Christopher Layne, rightly emphasize the importance of national missile defense: "Given the reality that terrorists, or hostile states like North Korea, could acquire nuclear weapons and long-range missiles, it makes sense for the United States to develop missile defenses, which potentially are a real form of insurance."[10] The same is true of US allies' physical security for theater and tactical systems deployed abroad. Because of the cost and technological sophistication of these systems, it makes sense for the US to continue sharing the burden with its allies through joint research, development, and financing.

But missile defense systems have political and strategic effects beyond their immediate military application because missile defense is not solely about homeland security. For example, theater missile defenses deployed in Europe could allay Turkish fears of Iran's nuclear capability and help persuade it not to pursue its own nuclear weapon program.[11] The same logic in East Asia would help persuade Japan and South Korea to forgo nuclear weapons. Israel's Iron Dome missile defense system, built with US help, has eroded Hezbollah's and Hamas's ability to blackmail it and may help dampen the effect of Iran's near-nuclear capability.

The benefits of missile defense are clear. Theater and tactical missile defense are not prohibitively expensive, they are militarily viable, and they deprive rivals of the ability to threaten nuclear blackmail. The United States and its allies should continue the development and deployment of such systems. Funding for strategic missile defense, on the other hand, has stagnated, technical difficulties remain formidable, and Russian diplomatic opposition is fierce.[12] Strategic missile defense may ultimately prove technically or financially infeasible, but a continued research and development program by itself produces benefits. It forces rivals into an expensive arms race in which the United States has a clear advantage, increases the technical and financial cost of threatening the United States with ballistic missiles, lessens the relative usefulness of building and maintaining such weapons in the first place, and gives the United States a valuable bargaining chip in arms-control negotiations.

Cybersecurity

The United States must also protect against cyberespionage and cyberattack. This has been a subject of considerable confusion because of the novelty and technical complexity of the subject.[13] Scholars are right to address the issue as a major concern for national security but, as I argue below, have wrongly conceptualized the problem. Cybersecurity has become a topic of study for security studies because hackers can access computers to steal information, manipulate command-and-control systems, and sabotage infrastructure, indirectly killing people. Cyber activities are different from electronic warfare. The latter uses the electromagnetic spectrum as a weapon (e.g., to jam or intercept communications or to incinerate a target with directed energy); the former uses *information* as a weapon, employing electronic means to access or manipulate data.

The distinction between cybercrime and cyberwar is uncomplicated. Computers, like guns, are tools with no inherent moral purpose: the purpose is provided by its human user. A gun can be used to commit a crime, apprehend a criminal, assassinate a political leader, instigate a war, or end one. Much the same is true of computers and the information they process. The US and NATO's doctrine of judging a cyber action by its effects, not the means of its delivery, is sound. A unique difficulty with cyber activities is that people can act with some degree of anonymity; attributing a cyber action to a person—and thus to a purpose—can be difficult (though rarely impossible). But the difficulty inheres in the attribution problem, which is solvable, not in the concept of "cyber" itself. The attribution problem also means arms control agreements for cyberweapons are unlikely to succeed.

It is unhelpful to think of "cyberspace" or to treat "cyber" as a domain of warfare, as the Department of Defense does. The Department of Defense defines cyberspace as "a global domain within the information environment consisting of the interdependent network of information technology infra-structures and resident data."[14] And the emerging scholarly view is that "a weapon traditionally had to traverse a geographic medium—land, sea, air, or outer space. . . . The cyber revolution has dramatically altered this situation."[15] But nothing about cyber requires us to think of it separately from the tradi-tional domains of air, land, water, or space. Computing takes places inside processors, located mostly on land; information is conveyed through trillions of electrons conveyed over coaxial or fiber-optic cables that travel overland or undersea or wirelessly through radio waves in air and space. There is not a dimension in which computing takes place separate from air, land, sea, or space. It is unhelpful to think of cyber activities as "intangible" and untrue that cyber is "little constrained by space" or that cyberwar "lacks a proximate cause of injury."[16] The physical infrastructure of cyberspace can be accessed, manip-ulated, disrupted, or destroyed by other physical phenomena—such as bombs, electromagnetic interference, or more computer code. Cybercrime and cyber-attacks do not take place in a borderless or transnational plane. Users make use of computers, routers, and data sources across different jurisdictions in carrying out a cyber action, but the intermediary instruments are largely inci-dental; the perpetrator and the victim live in places with governments.

Cyberthreats are real. However, the most common kinds of malicious cyber activity appear to be theft and vandalism, which do not rise to the level of national security threats. Criminals steal credit card and Social Security numbers, or other personally identifying information from the databases of large corporations; such breaches have been disclosed by Home Depot, Kmart, Target, Dairy Queen, Citibank, Merrick Bank, and the US Postal Service since 2009. Vandalism is sometimes politically motivated. Russian hackers dis-rupted Internet service in Georgia in 2008, concomitantly with the Russian military's invasion of that country, and in May 2007, Estonian government websites were shut down and online banking suspended by a significant wave of cyber vandalism linked to Russia. The Syrian Electronic Army, a pro-Assad group, hacked some Western media outlets in 2013, and a hacker collective calling itself Anonymous has periodically vandalized and stolen information from various targets, including US, Saudi, and Israeli government websites, large corporations, and some religious organizations.[17] These types of cyber activities do not cause widespread loss of life or permanent damage to property and do not rise to the level of a national security threat—although the political nature of some of them suggests that cyberthreats are "expanding the range of possible harm and outcomes between the concepts of war and peace, with important consequences for national and international security."[18]

Cyber*attacks* would rise to that level; however, they are still mostly theoretical. Hackers could access computer systems that control critical infrastructure and, for example, shut down electrical grids or the air traffic control system, sabotage a nuclear power plant, or erase financial records. "Cyberattacks offer a means for potential adversaries to overcome overwhelming US advantages in conventional military power and to do so in ways that are instantaneous and exceedingly hard to trace,"[19] according to William Lynn, former deputy secretary of defense. Similarly, Jim Clapper, the director of national intelligence, judged in early 2014 that the probability of damaging cyberattacks was rising because the tradecraft for cyberattacks was spreading.[20] Hackers linked to Russia and China have reportedly stolen information about US infrastructure and gas, energy, and chemical facilities—including the US Army Corps of Engineers' National Inventory of Dams—that could be used in future cases of sabotage.[21] In one of the few incidents of actual attack, the Stuxnet virus, allegedly engineered by the United States (possibly with help from Israel and the United Kingdom) manipulated and damaged machinery in Iran's nuclear facilities and slowed its pace of fuel enrichment.[22]

That speculation about cyberattacks has outpaced their actual occurrence suggests that such attacks may not be as easy to launch as often assumed or that early preparations have successfully hardened the most vulnerable targets. Some scholars have even argued the cyberthreat has been overblown.[23] I disagree. Strategic surprise is possible precisely when scholars and policymakers exhibit a failure of imagination regarding new developments. Cyberweapons favor the offense, their technology is volatile, attribution is difficult, and they operate much faster than conventional weapon systems.[24] The first successful large-scale cyberattack may be too costly not to take seriously.

But the focus on hypothetical cyber*attacks* has obscured the actual incidence of the greatest cyberthreat: espionage. The US military's classified Secure Internet Protocol Router Network (SIPRNet) was penetrated by malware in 2008, probably by a foreign intelligence agency, "establishing what amounted to a digital beachhead, from which data could be transferred to servers under foreign control" in "the most significant breach of US military computers ever."[25] Separately in 2012, US investigators claimed that Chinese hackers stole classified information about the design, specifications, and technology for the F-35 Joint Strike Fighter. Chinese hackers have also been implicated in breaches of NASA's Jet Propulsion Laboratory; the Office of Personnel Management's list of US government employees with top-secret security clearances; several dozen US companies in the defense and chemical industries; the Japanese Diet; the Indian Ministry of Defense, Defense Research Organization, and office of the National Security Advisor; Canada's Defense Research and Development Organization; the Australian Security Intelligence Organization; the British Foreign Office; Google; and Morgan Stanley, among others.[26] Hackers linked to Russia successfully stole diplomatic and intelligence information from NATO, the EU, and Ukraine over a period of five years, only reported in late 2014. Nonstate actors have also been active, including WikiLeaks, which describes itself as a media outlet but is essentially a nonstate espionage organization (on its website it boasts that "WikiLeaks has released more classified intelligence documents than the rest of the world press combined"[27]), and Edward Snowden, a former contractor for the NSA. Both stole and publicly released troves of US diplomatic, military, and intelligence information in recent years.[28]

Although basic cryptology has been a part of American information assurance efforts for decades—overseen by the NSA's Central Security Service since 1972—more sophisticated cyberdefense initiatives are in their infancy. President George W. Bush issued a *National Strategy to Secure Cyberspace* in 2003 and approved a Comprehensive National Cybersecurity Initiative in 2008. President Obama published a *Cyberspace Policy Review*, appointed a cybersecurity coordinator in 2009, and released an *International Strategy for Cyberspace* in 2011—the same year that both the Departments of Defense and Homeland Security issued cyberstrategy documents.[29] More substantively, the Obama administration issued an executive order in 2013, *Improving Critical Infrastructure Cybersecurity*, though most of its provisions relating to private-sector parties—for example, encouraging information sharing, industry standards, and sharing best practices—are voluntary and collaborative.[30] The US military established Cyber Command in 2009 and (unhelpfully) designated "cyberspace" a domain of warfare. Almost all NATO member states and several US Pacific allies have issued cybersecurity policies since 2011.[31]

Experts have warned that cyberdefenses are not keeping up with the rapidly evolving world of cyberthreats.[32] One of the biggest weaknesses is the increasingly outdated statutory regime governing information technology security standards. The strategy documents, the 2013 executive order, and the various organizational initiatives are useful but limited without the funding and authorization that only Congress can provide. The last statutory response to cyberthreats was the 2002 Federal Information Security Management Act. Several scholars and experts have advocated updating the statutory guidelines for cybersecurity and increasing the legal tools available to the government to mandate compliance with cybersecurity standards. Specifically, some recommend adopting automated continuous monitoring—as opposed to compliance reporting—as the standard of cybersecurity as widely as possible, noting that the State Department, which adopted the new standard in 2009, demonstrated significantly faster improvement in cybersecurity than the Defense Department, which had not.[33] The recommendation seems reasonable: better to observe the border and stop intrusions than leave it unguarded and report afterward how many intruders got in. In addition, the government could use its procurement power—the US government is the largest purchaser of information technology products—to demand better security and safeguards in software and hardware.[34] These moves, or others like them, would likely help harden the nation's cyberdefenses.

But the biggest improvement in the nation's cybersecurity would come from reconceptualizing it as a component of internal security. Internal security is rarely addressed as a component of grand strategy, often under the mistaken belief that the United States faces no serious internal threats. As I have argued above, this is untrue. Unfortunately, the US government has a long history of alternating between neglecting internal security and creating abusive, illegal, or overweening internal security programs. Spies, saboteurs, terrorists, and traitors—whether operating online or in person—are real threats, and the United States lacks adequate tools to combat them. Before we can understand the place of cybersecurity in US grand strategy, we need a brief discussion of internal security.

Internal Security

Most Americans—including, probably, an alarming number of policymakers—are generally unaware of the threat of espionage, sabotage, and treason against the United States. Indeed, warning about "the enemy within" is sometimes seen as a bigger threat than the domestic threat itself: It bespeaks a vaguely un-American concern over the loyalties, political beliefs, and civic associations of other Americans. Franklin Roosevelt's internment of Japanese and Japanese Americans during World War II, McCarthyism, the investigations of the House Un-American Activities Committee, and the abuses of the FBI's Counterintelligence Program and the CIA's Operation Chaos are still within living memory for older Americans. American schoolchildren still learn about the Alien and Sedition Acts of 1798 as an early example of how fragile American liberty can be. Many Americans are concerned that the NSA's purported Terrorist Surveillance Program is the next chapter in overbearing or unconstitutional domestic intelligence programs. Americans' natural distrust of domestic intelligence has been a great natural strength throughout history, helping protect against the creation of secret police, pervasive surveillance, and invasive government powers. This very openness is also part of what endears the American ideal to its citizens and allows the government to take a more relaxed attitude toward domestic security.

But Americans' natural distrust of internal security has blinded them to the reality of internal security threats; some Americans seem to believe that American ideals are so self-evidently good that it is impossible to willingly betray them. But traitorous Americans, terrorists operating on American soil, and foreign intelligence agencies have inflicted untold harm on the United States, and the government has been too relaxed, even derelict, in its duty to guard American security from them. This was true long before the terrorist attacks of 2001, the age of the Internet, or the rise of cyberespionage. One of the single greatest threats to the very existence of the United States in history came in the form of treason when Maj. Gen. Benedict Arnold plotted to surrender West Point to the British in 1780, which would have given to them control of the Hudson and all New York, divided the colonies, and possibly fractured the Revolutionary cause. The Civil War is obviously the biggest example of an internal security threat in US history. Facing the threat of treason behind Union lines, President Lincoln suspended the writ of habeas corpus—as explicitly permitted by the US Constitution "when in cases of rebellion or invasion the public safety may require it"—to allow for indefinite detention without trial of suspected rebels. Although it is uncomfortable to say, the greatest threats to the United States have sometimes come from Americans themselves.

Less well known is the role treason and espionage played in accelerating the Cold War's transformation into a nuclear standoff. The record of Soviet espionage on the United States has been clouded by partisan recriminations— by conservatives damning liberals and civil liberties advocates for sympathizing with the Soviet Union and underrating the internal threat, and by liberals damning conservatives for launching witch hunts, exaggerating the threat, and using scare tactics to win elections. With historical perspective, it seems clear that the information provided to the Soviet Union by American spies about the United States' nuclear weapons research and development almost certainly accelerated the Soviet Union's nuclear weapons program. "Espionage appears to have been of greater assistance to the Soviet bomb development project than we had once thought," John Lewis Gaddis judged in 1997.

The Soviets would have eventually developed the bomb on their own, but the stolen information improved the efficiency of their research and, in turn, shortened the duration of the United States' nuclear monopoly.[35] The loss of that monopoly during the highly formative postwar years meant that the United States faced constraints on its ability to foster peaceful reconstruction with soft power and thus faced pressure to reinvest in national defense when Americans hoped for continued demobilization. Soviet espionage also gave Joseph Stalin extra confidence to resist the United States during the years prior to the Soviet Union's own nuclear test. How would the Cold War have been different if the Soviet Union developed nuclear weapons in 1952 instead of 1949? Would the Korean War have happened? Would the Cold War have been militarized so thoroughly and so quickly? Would the United States have felt compelled to fight communism everywhere? Counterfactuals are impossible to answer, but it is clear that the Soviet Union's development of nuclear weapons sooner rather than later was one of the most strategically significant incidents of the early Cold War.

Espionage continued to plague the United States through the end of the Cold War and beyond, including by the John Walker spy ring, Aldrich Ames, and Robert Hanssen. While the historical record of espionage is troubling, the present day is nearly catastrophic. The digitization of information has made it easier to steal information in bulk and to do so (sometimes) without the time-consuming effort of compromising human loyalty. The present day is, in all probability, the golden age of espionage: It is now possible to steal more sensitive information, more quickly, than ever before in human history.

The Chinese cybertheft of design specifications for the F-35 fighter jet is a concrete example of how espionage damages US national security. US military power has depended, for decades, on technological superiority—especially in the air. The Chinese now have the ability to study the designs of the F-35, find its weaknesses, build a competing version, and sell the information to third parties—probably the greatest breach of a US military research and design effort since the Soviet breach of the Manhattan Project. The United States can make expensive changes to the jet or accept more risk to its pilots. Either way, retaining US air superiority in every conflict for the next several decades—which could include conflicts with North Korea or China—will be harder, more costly, or riskier than it should have been.

But even that example pales in comparison to the astonishing compromise of US intelligence capabilities by Edward Snowden. Many Americans and journalists characterized him as a "whistleblower" and describe his activities as the exercise of "free speech." Americans are right to expect oversight of sensitive intelligence programs and full protections for their privacy and civil liberties, and President Obama was right to appoint a committee to study the NSA and propose reforms. But Snowden was not a whistleblower, which is a legal designation for someone who reports wrongdoing to an inspector general or to a general counsel. Snowden deliberately sought employment in order to gain access to classified information with the intention of disclosing it to persons not authorized to have it—which is the definition of a spy.[36] That Snowden did not conduct his espionage at the behest of a specific foreign government is beside the point: His disclosures about the NSA's electronic surveillance capabilities are free to all of America's rivals and enemies to read. They can now take precautions and adjust their online security practices. For example, encryption standards have been enhanced around the world in recent years, making it significantly more difficult for the NSA to acquire information from foreign governments and terrorists.

Recommendations

Intelligence and information security gives the United States a competitive informational and decisional advantage; espionage undermines the same. That is why intelligence and counterintelligence are crucial aspects of grand strategy.[37] Spies, saboteurs, traitors, and domestic terrorists are real threats, operating online or in person. Unfortunately, the US government has bureaucratically and conceptually misplaced these problems. Spies and saboteurs can steal information and wreck infrastructure by accessing American information technology, or they can do their work the old-fashioned way, in person. It makes most sense to understand cybersecurity as part of internal security. They both seek to counter threats to US national security from within—from American computers or Americans. The United States does not need a cyberstrategy—it needs an internal security strategy.[38]

Historically, the closest thing the United States had to an internal security and domestic intelligence agency was the FBI. The bureau does not have a distinguished track record in carrying out this duty. Its authority in this field dates to 1916, when Congress authorized the Justice Department to initiate investigations unconnected to specific violations of federal statutes at the request of the State Department. This authority was invoked by Franklin Roosevelt in 1936 to initiate FBI investigations into fascist and communist subversion in the United States. "President Roosevelt used his executive authority to determine that the FBI would be the primary civilian agency responsible for carrying out domestic intelligence," a move Roosevelt would reiterate and reinforce with administrative moves in 1938, 1939, and throughout World War II.[39] However, these moves gradually expanded the FBI's role in domestic intelligence without a corresponding legislative mandate. The

National Security Act of 1947 gave congressional approval to the FBI's lead in counterespionage and counterintelligence, but "with no clear legislative or executive standards to keep it within the intended bounds, the FBI (and military intelligence in its sphere) had almost complete discretion to decide how far domestic intelligence investigations would extend," according to the Church Committee.[40]

Without clear legislative limits, the FBI expanded the scope of its activities and the targets of its investigations. For example, from 1939 to 1978, it kept a "Security Index," a list of names of Americans and resident aliens suspected of disloyalty and whom the bureau recommended for preemptive detention in time of war. In the 1950s and 1960s, it investigated the Ku Klux Klan, black nationalist groups, antiwar protesters, civil rights groups, and other "political dissidents," sometimes with justification, many times not. More troubling, under its various counterintelligence programs, the FBI went far beyond investigating and prosecuting crime; it tried to harass suspect groups, disrupt their meetings, disseminate misinformation about them, denigrate their reputations, and obstruct their messages. "The FBI continued to cast a wider and wider net in its domestic surveillance activities," according to a RAND Corporation report.[41]

In reaction to the FBI's abuses, which came to light through the Church and Pike Committee investigations in 1975–76,[42] Congress and the bureau swung to the opposite extreme with a series of reforms that erected a "wall" between intelligence and investigations from the 1970s until 2001. The FBI retained lead responsibility for counterintelligence investigations, but for seventeen years it failed to detect John Walker (who spied for Russia), for nine years Aldrich Ames, and for twenty-two years Robert Hanssen—one of its own agents. They collectively inflicted inestimable damage on the United States' intelligence posture and may have rendered useless one leg of the US nuclear triad in the 1980s. The advent of cyberespionage has taken the problem of espionage into an entirely new dimension still further removed from the FBI's competence: There is no evidence the bureau was ever even aware of the possibility of Snowden's theft and disclosures prior to his flight from the country.

Today the internal security mission is divided up among the Departments of Homeland Security, Defense, and Justice, the intelligence community, and the Office of Personnel Management (OPM). Cyber Command guards the military's information technology networks, the Department of Homeland Security oversees security for the ".com" and ".gov" civilian domains. The FBI's National Security Branch is the lead for investigating and prosecuting cases of espionage and domestic terrorism. The NSA's purported Terrorist Surveillance Program and related initiatives reportedly conducted domestic surveillance against suspected terrorists and their affiliates abroad. The newly formed National Counterintelligence and Security Center analyzes the threat from foreign intelligence agencies and develops a national counterintelligence strategy. The OPM oversees the granting of security clearances for most US agencies.

There are problems with this arrangement. Cybersecurity is mostly a matter of protecting meta-infrastructure, which aligns more with the Department of Homeland Security's core competencies than the military's—but it is also a matter of counterintelligence, which is an intelligence mission more than a military one. Domestic intelligence is currently pursued as a law enforcement mission, led by the FBI, but it is more akin to the intelligence operations conducted by the National Counterterrorism Center and the National Counterproliferation Center.

Espionage and terrorism are neither acts of war nor mere crime: Internal security is neither a fully military mission nor a law enforcement problem, which means an internal security agency should be housed in neither the Department of Defense nor the Department of Justice. The United States needs an internal security and domestic intelligence agency akin to the United Kingdom's MI5 to counter spies, saboteurs, traitors, and terrorists—operating online or in person—while respecting Americans' civil liberties and privacy. The military and the FBI should be supporting, not leading, agencies. Cyber Command should retain its role in protecting the military's own networks and conducting any offensive cyber operations. The FBI's National Security Branch should be broken up and relocated to the new agency, and the bureau should be freed to focus exclusively on domestic crime. Because the new agency could be built on the already existing National Security Branch, the net budgetary implications of a new agency would be small.

A new agency would fit most naturally in the intelligence community, working in close coordination with the Department of Homeland Security and Cyber Command. The new agency would have two primary divisions, one to combat cyberthreats and one to combat human threats; the overlap between the two is a major reason for the formation of a new agency. Instead of replicating the enormously expensive capabilities of Cyber Command and the NSA, the cyber division of the new agency would feed collection and operational capability requirements to the NSA. The other division would assume much of the FBI's former role in counterintelligence and domestic counterterrorism but with more expansive authorities. The new agency would have authority to conduct domestic surveillance against internal targets—not as a law enforcement agency, required to secure warrants, but as an intelligence agency, proactively seeking threats. Its jurisdiction, however, should be limited to foreign nationals, American citizens with security clearances, and any citizens implicated in specific plots.[43]

The creation of a domestic intelligence agency in the United States would be controversial and politically challenging because of the United States' commendable strain of civil libertarianism. Critics may wonder if greater internal security would be worth the trade-off of decreased privacy. The creation of such an agency would not be a radical departure but a responsible evolution and improvement over what has existed since the 1920s. The United States already has a domestic intelligence agency—the FBI—but it is one that has tarnished the idea of domestic intelligence with its poor performance and abuses. Policymakers should certainly strip the FBI of its role in counterintelligence and internal security—but they should not stop there, leaving the duty unassigned. Rather, they should create a dedicated domestic intelligence agency trained and equipped specifically for its mission.

Notes

1. Kreps, "American Grand Strategy after Iraq," 638.
2. Art, "Defensible Defense."
3. Posen, *Restraint*, chap. 3.
4. Art, *Grand Strategy for America*, 47.
5. North American Aerospace Defense Command, "About NORAD."
6. Zong and Batalova, *Frequently Requested Statistics*; United States Customs and Border Protection, *Performance and Accountability Report: Fiscal Year 2013*.
7. Zong and Batalova, *Frequently Requested Statistics*.
8. PBS History Detective, "Wartime Acts of Sabotage," http://www.pbs.org/opb/historydetectives/feature/wartime-acts-of-sabotage/, accessed on January 14, 2016; Warner, "Kaiser Sows Destruction."
9. Crowdy, *Enemy Within*, 290–92.
10. Layne, *Peace of Illusions*, 188.
11. Thränert, "NATO, Missile Defence and Extended Deterrence."
12. Zadra, "NATO, Russia and Missile Defence."
13. See Kello, "Meaning of the Cyber Revolution," for a helpful primer and overview.
14. US Joint Chiefs of Staff, *Joint Publication 3–13*, II-9.
15. Kello, "Meaning of the Cyber Revolution," 22.
16. Ibid., 23, 25.
17. Center for Strategic and International Studies, "Significant Cyber Incidents since 2006."
18. Kello, "Meaning of the Cyber Revolution," 8.
19. Lynn, "Defending a New Domain," 108.
20. Office of the Director of National Intelligence, *Worldwide Threat Assessment*, 1.
21. Center for Strategic and International Studies, "Significant Cyber Incidents since 2006."
22. Farwell and Rohozinski, "Stuxnet and the Future of Cyber War."

23. Thomas Mahnken, "Cyber War and Cyber Warfare," in Lord and Sharp, *America's Cyber Future*; Rid, "Cyber War Will Not Take Place"; Rid, "Cyberwar and Peace."

24. Kello, "Meaning of the Cyber Revolution," 27–37.

25. Lynn, "Defending a New Domain," 97.

26. Center for Strategic and International Studies, "Significant Cyber Incidents since 2006." See also Michael Riley and Ashlee Vance, "Inside the Chinese Boom in Corporate Espionage," *Bloomberg*, March 15, 2012, http://www.bloomberg.com /news/articles/2012-03-15/inside-the-chinese-boom-in-corporate-espionage.

27. "What Is Wikileaks?" available at https://wikileaks.org/About.html, accessed March 17, 2015.

28. WikiLeaks' and Snowden's action are only "cyber" espionage in that they stole information from computer systems. Snowden and Chelsea Manning (WikiLeaks' source for the US cables, who was known at the time as Bradley Manning) had normal access to US computer systems in the course of their duties. It does not appear that they hacked into or illegitimately accessed any of the information they stole.

29. US Department of Homeland Security, *Blueprint for a Secure Cyber Future*; US Department of Defense, *Strategy for Operating in Cyberspace*.

30. Fischer et al., *2013 Cybersecurity Executive Order*.

31. European Union Agency for Network and Information Security, "National Cyber Security Strategies in the World," https://www.enisa.europa.eu/activities/ Resilience-and-CIIP/national-cyber-security-strategies-ncsss/national-cyber -security-strategies-in-the-world, accessed January 14, 2016.

32. Lewis, *Cyber Threat and Response*.

33. Reeder et al., *Updating U.S. Federal Cybersecurity Policy*, 2012.

34. Langevin et al., *Securing Cyberspace for the 44th Presidency*.

35. Gaddis, *We Now Know*, 94, see 92–98; Crowdy, *Enemy Within*, 310ff. See also US Department of Energy, "Espionage and the Manhattan Project," which says that "Soviet espionage directed at the Manhattan Project probably hastened by at least 12–18 months the Soviet acquisition of an atomic bomb."

36. Lana Lam, "Snowden Sought Booz Allen Job to Gather Evidence on NSA Surveillance," *South China Morning Post*, June 25, 2013. It is also noteworthy that President Obama's proposed reforms to the NSA, and the recommendations of his Review Group on Intelligence and Communications Technologies, were, by comparison to the Church and Pike investigations of the 1970s, mild. The experts and policymakers who have looked closest at the NSA's activities have raised fewer concerns about them than their counterparts did in response to the large-scale and clear abuses of power in the 1970s and earlier. See President's Review Group on Intelligence and Communications Technologies, *Liberty and Security in a Changing World*.

37. Fingar, "Intelligence and Grand Strategy."

38. Jackson, *Considering the Creation* and *Challenge of Domestic Intelligence*; Jenkins, Liepman, and Willis, *Identifying Enemies among Us*; Treverton, et al., *Reorganizing U.S. Domestic Intelligence*; Masse, *Domestic Intelligence in the United*

Kingdom; Randol, *Homeland Security Intelligence*; Posner, *Remaking Domestic Intelligence*; Crowdy, *Enemy Within*.

39. Jackson, *Challenge of Domestic Intelligence*, 23ff.

40. Quoted in ibid., 26–27.

41. Ibid., 35.

42. Formally the Senate Select Committee to Study Governmental Operations with Respect to Intelligence Activities, chaired by Senator Frank Church, and the House Permanent Select Committee on Intelligence, chaired by Representative Otis Pike.

43. About five million Americans hold security clearances, of whom one and a half million are cleared for access to top-secret information. Americans with security clearances—especially those with top-secret clearances, such as this author—should not have a reasonable expectation of privacy. The government should have the right to keep them under surveillance as the price for their access to classified information. In turn, the government should abandon the polygraph as a tool of investigation for security clearances because it is unreliable and unscientific.

11

Diplomacy and Development

In this chapter I review the civilian tools of national power, including diplomacy, foreign aid, support to stability operations, and participation in international institutions and treaties. These tools have a crucial role to play in managing relations with the great powers, championing liberalism, and investing in weak states.

Guiding Principles for Diplomacy and the Great Powers

In pursuing a favorable balance of power, US policymakers must be on guard against two potential dangers: exaggerating the importance of peripheral regions and provoking the formation of an anti-American alliance. The first danger raises its head every time an American politician claims that American credibility is on the line in some distant crisis. The Munich analogy is, frankly, overused: Not every dictator is Hitler, and few aim at world conquest. The tendency to see global significance in every incident calls to mind the Fashoda Incident of 1898, in which France sought to challenge British influence in Egypt by taking control of the upper Nile River valley region in what is now South Sudan, under the theory that British control of Egypt and its Suez Canal was key to its ability to project power not only in the Mediterranean but also in India and beyond. Small British and French forces confronted each other in a tiny stretch of inland African desert thousands of miles from any place of strategic significance while politicians in London and Paris convinced themselves that the fates of both empires hung in the balance and prepared for war—perhaps the greatest example of domino-theorizing in history: As goes Fashoda, so goes the world.[1] Credibility, honor, and influence are not always at stake in every crisis everywhere in the world. (Eventually cooler heads prevailed, and no blood was shed at Fashoda.) Sometimes masterly inactivity is the best strategy. Christopher Layne rightly warns against waging needless "wars of credibility."[2] If no discernable interest is at stake *except* reputation, then noninvolvement is *better* for American credibility. Better to refrain and win the reputation for level-headedness than intervene and win the reputation for indiscriminate interventionism.

Second, American policymakers should be sensitive to the possibility of creating the very problem they seek to avert: an anti-American alliance among nuclear autocracies. A major goal of American balance-of-power efforts should be to prevent any combination of hostile powers from acquiring enough power to threaten the existence of the United States, its allies, or liberal order. In practice, that means forestalling an Axis-like alliance between Russia and China. Such a combination is the only plausible scenario that would see the revival of the age-old fear, the hostile Eurasian hegemon. While a Sino–Russian alliance is unlikely at the moment, it would seriously compromise the United States' freedom of action and threaten liberal order.

Too aggressive a posture toward the United States' rivals could push them into each other's arms.[3] For example, it is wrongheaded to argue "the ultimate aim of the American strategy is to hasten a revolution, albeit a peaceful one, that will sweep away China's one-party authoritarian state and leave a liberal democracy in its place."[4] Seeking regime change during peacetime against a nuclear power is the very definition of utopian overreach. Nuclear-armed autocracies will remain a major threat to US national security for the foreseeable future, and the only appropriate response is a series of overlapping, tailored strategies of engagement, balancing, and, where appropriate, containment—with the assistance of a global network of democratic allies.

Balancing, understood rightly, tolerates and accepts other powers' legitimate interests. American policy toward the Soviet Union, the most powerful and overtly hostile enemy the United States ever faced, never aimed at forced regime change—President Dwight Eisenhower rejected "rollback" during his Solarium strategic planning exercise—and American policymakers rightly sought to avoid war at almost all costs, not provoke it. In some cases the United States even sought productive engagement with its rivals, as when skillful American diplomacy helped peal China away from the Soviet Union and facilitate its rapprochement with the United States—an example of a classic divide-and-conquer approach to great power politics.

Today, a grand bargain with Iran in which it verifiably gave up terrorism and nuclear weapons in exchange for trade, energy assistance, and international legitimacy would be worth exploring—though it would look far different than the 2015 nuclear accord—as would a peaceful resolution with China over the status of Taiwan (accomplished with Taiwanese consent) or with Russia over Ukraine. Such bargains are unlikely—especially with North Korea, regarding whom regime change may eventually become necessary—but so are all worthwhile diplomatic breakthroughs, and American policymakers would be foolish not to be open to them should the opportunity arise.

That does not mean the United States can buy peace with the nuclear autocracies by withdrawing or retrenching, as Barry Posen suggests. He recommends a strategy of restraint but does not explain how that would either prevent or mitigate other states' balancing. In fact, the opposite would occur. Posen inadvertently gives the best possible argument for sustaining American internationalism: States will continue to balance for fear of US intentions if the United States continues to pursue hegemony—but he also argues they will balance if their relative power increases (which it would if the United States retrenches) out of hope that they stand a chance to become the leading power. According to Posen, then, other powers will balance against the United States *regardless* of whether it is rising or declining, retrenching or pursuing hegemony, so it would be odd for the United States to follow Posen's recommendation and voluntarily reduce its own power by cutting its military and reducing its overseas presence. It is only prudent for the United States to hold on to its military power and make other states' balancing as difficult and costly as possible.

Diplomacy and Democracy

Having stressed so heavily the United States' strategic interest in championing democracy abroad, I might be expected to address how the United States can do so. Few questions are so vexed. There are as many opinions about how democracy grows as there are democracies in the world. I do not propose to resolve the question in this brief section, in part because there is almost certainly no single path, and therefore no single policy solution, to the growth of democracy.

Instead, I emphasize the United States' role as "championing" liberalism. A champion holds out, celebrates, and lauds an ideal as much as he works and fights for it. That will look different in different circumstances. In some countries, such as the Philippines, Turkey, and Poland, a few well-timed, high-level phone calls from the president, secretary of state, or other officials can make the difference in preventing a coup, ensuring the fairness of an election, calming a situation, or reassuring allies.[5] Reagan's private appeal to South Korean president Chun Doo-hwan in 1987, for example, helped tip the balance in favor of democratization there.[6] Maintenance diplomacy is an overlooked but major part of implementing grand strategy—one at which, anecdotally, the United States seems to have gotten worse. A more coherent staffing and interagency coordination system, one that enforces priorities, should help with the execution of this sort of diplomatic intervention.

In addition, the United States should *always* be rhetorically on the side of democracy and democratic movements around the world. In John Quincy Adams's phrase, the United States is and should be the "well-wisher to the freedom and independence of all."[7] Support for the "captive nations" of Eastern Europe during the Cold War, for the third wave of democratization after the fall of the Iron Curtain, and for the color revolutions of the new millennium were consistent with the United States' longstanding grand strategy. The Obama administration's hesitancy to embrace the rhetoric of democracy during the Green Revolution in Iran in 2009 and the Arab Spring of 2011 was a regrettable choice, one the administration itself eventually reversed. Liberalism is the United States' "brand." As any marketing executive knows, you have to believe in your product to sell it: As the uncertain trumpet summons no rally, so uncertain salesmanship moves no product. Scholars are often embarrassed by policymakers' simple and earnest appeals to truth, justice, and the American way, but they should recognize that authentic and winning appeals to liberal ideals are strategically savvy marketing efforts. They help sustain brand awareness and keep it in circulation for each new generation. Naturally, pushiness, arrogance, and triumphalism are equally ineffective; it is a sad commentary on American diplomacy that this even needs to be said. I suspect the disappearance of the study of rhetoric and the classics from American education has created a generation of policymakers unable to weave an artful and winsome case for liberty and self-government.

To improve US diplomacy, the State Department needs an almost complete overhaul. The Foreign Service is shockingly small for the global mission of American diplomacy and also ill-equipped and poorly trained for diplomacy in the twenty-first century.[8] Increasing the size of the Foreign Service without reforming the criteria for recruitment and promotion to alter the culture of the department would be folly. The Foreign Service needs to be far more expeditionary; more steeply immersed in language, culture, history, and especially religion; more educated in the humanities than the social sciences or law; and better equipped with the tools of persuasion and argument.

Foreign Aid and Democracy Promotion

Aside from public and private diplomacy, the United States can support liberalism with cash, people, training, and expertise.[9] There are at least four major difficulties in promoting liberalism. First, promoting democracy and capitalism, especially in the aftermath of conflict, is hard and often fails.[10] UN-led attempts at postconflict democratic peace-building in Angola, Liberia, and Cambodia in the 1990s failed and, in the former two cases, probably left those countries worse off than they were. Efforts in Afghanistan have been plagued by corruption, institutional weakness, and violence, and the ultimate outcome is still uncertain. It is not at all clear that the international community has a reliable democracy-promotion doctrine—or that such a doctrine could exist even in principle. Democracy is more than a political system. It is a set of habits and beliefs, which means it is embedded in culture. Attempting to change culture with the blunt hand of government, especially when that hand is foreign, is tricky even under the best of circumstances. Good intentions do not automatically make good policy.

Second, rapid liberalization can politicize and harden sectarian tendencies, as happened when Bosnia held elections just one year after its civil war ended.[11] The process of democratization can actually be destabilizing because the introduction of political and economic liberty empowers new actors, threatens old ones, and unleashes social forces that societies may be ill-prepared to cope with, which is at least part of what happened in Iraq.[12] Alexis de Tocqueville observed long ago that "there can be no doubt that the moment when political rights are granted to a people who have till then been deprived of them is a time of crisis, a crisis which is often necessary but always dangerous."[13]

Third, outsiders' efforts to reform weak or autocratic states run the risk of appearing paternalistic, utopian, self-righteous, or simply imperialist. The US military's occupation of Iraq sparked local opposition, but it was less of an outlier than widely believed. Even the UN-administered transitional administrations in Kosovo and East Timor, which were multilateral and widely perceived to be benevolent, legitimate, and fairly successful, engendered local resentment. Similarly, US efforts to champion democracy can appear hypocritical because they are inconsistent. US ties to autocracies such as Egypt and Saudi Arabia could easily lead an Iraqi or Libyan to believe that American professions of support for democracy in their countries are insincere.

Fourth, there are serious problems specifically with the way the United States has promoted democracy. There is little evidence that the United States has sought to proactively identify where democracy would be most beneficial to US security. US administrations pursue democracy promotion haphazardly, in response to crisis, but have done little to invest in the infrastructure of democracy broadly across strategic regions.[14] The one possible exception could have been the invasion of Iraq, justified as part of an orchestrated effort to transform and democratize the Middle East—an example that highlights how troubled and uneven US democracy-promotion efforts have been. Elsewhere, some US aid programs may have helped spark the color revolutions, but those revolutions largely failed to have a lasting impact, and the United States probably missed opportunities to follow through and help consolidate those democratic transitions.

The State Department's Quadrennial Diplomacy and Development Review explicitly made democracy promotion a priority for US diplomacy and development. However, it did not offer a prioritized list of countries most important to US interests, a necessary first step for developing a plan for where and how to foster democracy most effectively and to the greatest advantage to the United States. The nation cannot afford to promote democracy everywhere simultaneously, nor does it have the opportunity to do so—but the default posture of promoting it only in response to crisis is not an effective grand strategy. In order for the democratic peace to be a hard-nosed strategy and not a vague or utopian aspiration, the United States should identify where democracy promotion is most important and achievable, given finite resources.

The problems and challenges of democracy promotion do not suggest that the United States should stop promoting democracy but that it do so more carefully and more effectively. In particular, there are three things Obama's successors should work toward. As a first step, they should recognize and embrace America's grand strategy of investing in liberal order. Simply recognizing the grand strategy will be an improvement. Critics are right that US foreign policy, including democracy-promotion efforts, has been uneven, shortsighted, and overly responsive to the latest crisis. That is what happens to foreign policy without the ballast of a strongly articulated long-term vision to help policymakers prioritize and plan for the extended future. US officials, starting with the president, should call a spade a spade and recognize that promoting democracy is a cornerstone of US foreign policy.

Clearly articulating that strategy would improve the management and coordination of democracy-promotion efforts. The fact that promoting democracy is good for American security does not excuse policymakers from the need for careful planning and execution. Contrary to what policymakers seemed to believe in the immediate aftermath of the Cold War or of Baghdad's fall, democracy does not grow automatically. There is nothing natural about it. It is one of the least efficient forms of government. Freedom may be the right of every person, as George W. Bush argued, but that does not mean it is easily or equally practicable by every person. US democracy-promotion efforts have sometimes been marked by a naive belief that just because democracy is good, it is also therefore easy.

Scholars have disagreed about whether and how strongly foreign aid contributes to democratization, in part because some studies have been broad and underspecified.[15] More narrow studies looking at recent changes in the type and delivery of aid—such as targeting aid more specifically—have found a clearer impact on democracy.[16] Aid-for-trade programs that specifically help grow target countries' export industries have also proven effective.[17] The Marshall Plan may have been successful in part because the problems it was designed to fix were relatively simple: preexisting infrastructure destroyed by war and governments lacking liquidity to finance their own reconstruction programs. By contrast, the range of problems present in many failed states today is more formidable. They need planning for new infrastructure in addition to reconstruction of old, more liquidity might simply fuel corruption instead of trade and development, and local governments' ability to plan and manage their own aid programs is limited by relatively poorer human capital.

Foreign aid is too simple a term for what is, in fact, a wide panoply of options and resources available to the United States for supporting allies, partners, and fledgling democracies abroad. Consider just the options available for support to elections. The United States can send observers to monitor transitional elections, train election workers, run workshops on campaigns and electioneering, provide equipment for voter registration, train journalists in campaign coverage and investigative reporting, physically protect candidates in conflict countries, and even, *in extremis*, simply run the entire electoral process itself. The United States has similar options for the rest of the "infrastructure of democracy": political parties, an independent judiciary, public prosecutors, basic infrastructure, literacy programs, and more.

Democratization programs have a mixed record. "Missionary zeal pervades the field, bringing with it a disinclination for self-doubt and a reflexive belief in the value of the enterprise," according to Thomas Carothers, the foremost scholar of democracy-promotion efforts. Democracy promoters sometimes assume that because America is a democracy, Americans are naturally equipped to teach democracy to others. Democracy programs often treat the task of building democracy as an apolitical, technocratic task. As a result, programs that focus on institutional reform often "treat the symptoms rather than the causes of democratic deficits." Some democracy programs still implicitly rely on the long-discredited modernization theory that underpinned the democracy and development efforts of the 1950s and 1960s.[18]

Carothers notes some signs of progress. Aid programs have started to evolve away from a one-size-fits-all template, abandon modernization theories, use non-American examples of democracy, and recognize the role of power and politics in the formation of democracy. Above all, there is no substitute for knowing the local context and tailoring programs accordingly. Effective governance assistance requires "much deeper knowledge about the recipient society" than aid programs traditionally gathered. Acquiring and using such local expertise points, once again, to the need for a larger, more professional, better-trained diplomatic corps (including aid professionals) steeped in local languages, cultures, and religions and deployed for longer tours of duty in countries of assignment. And it requires a change of culture within the US bureaucracy as well. Carothers argues that "in the US aid bureaucracy the commitment to democracy promotion is much shallower than the official strategy documents would indicate" and is located mainly in the State Department's Bureau of Democracy, Human Rights, and Labor and in USAID's Office of Transition Initiatives.[19]

Even with improvements, there is a limit to what democracy-aid programs can achieve. "Often aid cannot substantially modify an unfavorable configuration of interests or counteract a powerful contrary actor," according to Carothers, and efforts to do so risk provoking a backlash.[20] Stephen Biddle, who noted the same dynamic in Afghanistan, recommended the United States adopt a strategy of "coercive political bargaining" to accomplish effective governance reform, which turns democracy assistance into democracy compulsion.[21] That may be the best resort when the United States is forced into a democratization campaign, as it was in Afghanistan, but it is probably most effective to invest in countries that are already at least partly democratic. Regimes that are liberal or partly liberal show a willingness to tolerate the cost and disruption of liberal norms and institutions; democracy promoters are likely to find greater local support for their programs and greater support in the senior ranks of government to which they can appeal when they encounter parochial and bureaucratic obstruction. Democracy-promotion programs in Saudi Arabia and Equatorial Guinea are a waste of time and money; the same programs in the Philippines, Pakistan, Bangladesh, Mexico, Eastern Europe, Turkey, and other influential regions with a real but fragile commitment to liberalism could be the strategic investment that helps them consolidate their nascent democratic transitions.

If US presidents continue to invoke the democratic peace in their national security strategies and turn to democratization every time they face a crisis or war abroad, they need to recognize that it will require a sustained increase in aid levels. The United States has underinvested in the tools of democracy promotion and stability operations for decades. US foreign aid peaked in 1953 at 2.5 percent of GDP. Aid decreased dramatically after the Marshall Plan was disbursed, the Vietnam War ended, and the Soviet Union fell, recovering only partly each time and reaching an all-time low of about one-tenth of one percent of GDP in the 1990s. Aid increased slightly since 2001 as the United States made investments in Iraq, Afghanistan, and Pakistan, but it still constituted only one-quarter of one percent of GDP, among the lowest levels in the rich world.[22] Policymakers routinely invoke the Marshall Plan as a model for aid and bemoan the overmilitarization of US foreign policy, but their behavior speaks otherwise: The United States has almost completely disarmed itself of an entire array of foreign policy tools, simply abandoning its tools of civilian power. US foreign policy is militarized not because the military is too big but because it is the only tool of foreign policy that Congress adequately funds.

If the foreign aid budget were increased to be proportional to the size it was during the Marshall Plan as a percentage of GDP—around 2.5 percent—it would increase about tenfold from its current level, to more than $400 billion per year. Considering the number of high priorities I identified in previous chapters—Eastern Europe, India, Pakistan, Turkey, Ukraine, Mexico, Colombia, Bangladesh, the Philippines, Malaysia, Indonesia, Iraq, and Afghanistan, alongside potential stability operations in Syria and North Korea—such money could be well spent. A few factors suggest this is not as wildly implausible as it seems. First, Americans routinely overestimate how large the foreign aid budget actually is. In 2010, Americans believed that 25 percent of the federal budget went to foreign aid; in fact, the figure is closer to 1 percent. They said that a more appropriate figure would be 10 percent—which would, by happenstance, be around $400 billion.[23]

Second, many Americans, especially policymakers, may oppose foreign aid because they believe it is mostly humanitarian assistance disconnected from America's strategic interests. In fact, food aid makes up just 10 percent of all foreign aid given since 1946. Most foreign aid is economic investment in potential trading partners and security assistance to allies combating America's enemies. Policymakers should jettison the image of foreign aid as dispensable charity—it is *strategic investment*. Finally, Americans may oppose foreign aid because they believe it is wasteful and ineffective. For many years, it was. But the United States and aid organizations such as the World Bank have made improvements in aid delivery and developed a better understanding of how to use aid money effectively, as demonstrated by organizations such as the MCC.

Congress can make other improvements to diplomacy and development policy. For example, the US Information Agency, an overseas public diplomacy organization that, among other things, funded libraries of books on American history and democracy overseas, should be reconstituted (it was shuttered in 1999) and updated for the digital age. In Congress, the budget for the State Department and USAID should be lumped together with the defense and intelligence budgets into a single national security budget bill to enable more coherent interagency budgeting and programming.

In 2008, the Project for National Security Reform proposed consolidating in the State Department much of the foreign affairs and foreign assistance activities currently done by other departments and agencies. Seventy-eight US government agencies, offices, and bureaus funded foreign assistance projects in 2009, all but six of them civilian. The State Department is officially the "lead foreign affairs agency" of the US government, which gives it the responsibility for "leading interagency coordination in developing and implementing foreign policy" and "coordinating and supporting international activities of other US agencies and officials," according to its website. That puts State putatively in charge of coordinating more than seventy civilian agencies and programs involved in foreign assistance. That responsibility presumably falls to the State Department's director of foreign assistance, who is also the administrator of USAID. However, neither State nor USAID has the equivalent of the military's Joint Staff or the intelligence community's Office of the Director of National Intelligence. Without a full-time, permanent staff to enforce the State Department's leadership, there is a functional absence of coordination within the civilian foreign assistance community.

Finally, the United States should reallocate its diplomats, facilities, and foreign aid. Globally, it has the most diplomats and diplomatic facilities in Europe and the second largest number in Latin America. It spends the most foreign aid in Africa and the Middle East (see table 11.1). It should devote a larger share of its diplomatic corps and civilian aid to East and South Asia. East Asia, the second most important theater for US national security, gets less than a fifth of the US diplomatic presence and just 5 percent of its economic assistance. The proportion of diplomatic resources devoted to Africa and the Middle East are out of proportion to their importance to the United States; if any drawdowns are required, they should come from those regions. (The United States needs a relatively large diplomatic presence in Latin

Table 11.1. Distribution of US Diplomatic Resources

	Diplomatic Facilities[a]		State Dept. Personnel Abroad[b]		Economic Assistance, 2001–12[c]	
Europe	93	32%	1,961	23%	$26.3	11%
East Asia	46	16%	1,433	17%	$12.6	5%
South Asia	24	8%	941	11%	$44.5	18%
Middle East	23	8%	1,123	13%	$59.3	24%
Latin America	46	16%	1,804	21%	$27.9	11%
Africa	55	19%	1,137	14%	$73.6	30%

[a] US Department of State, "USEmbassy.gov."
[b] American Foreign Service Association, "Department of State: Full-Time Permanent Employees." The AFA's geographic breakdown of regions reflects the State Department's regional bureaus, not the regions as I have defined them elsewhere in this book. The tally of personnel abroad overcounts the Middle East and undercounts Africa.
[c] US Agency for International Development, *U.S. Overseas Loans and Grants*.

America because of its trade volume with the region and to support the large bilateral flow of citizens.)

Stability Operations

Stability operations remain a crucial instrument in the US national security tool kit. But the tool needs recalibration. Stability operations must be whole-of-government efforts, not military operations with reconstruction duties tacked on and assigned to soldiers unqualified and untrained for the task. Secretary of State Condoleezza Rice said in 2006:

> Over the past 15 years, as violent state failure has become a greater global threat, our military has borne a disproportionate share of post-conflict responsibilities because we have not had the standing civilian capability to play our part fully. This was true in Somalia and Haiti, in Bosnia, in Kosovo, and it is still partially true in Iraq and Afghanistan. These experiences have shown us the need to enhance our ability to work more effectively at the critical intersections of diplomacy, democracy promotion, economic reconstruction and military security.[24]

The United States should lead an effort in conjunction with the UN Department of Peacekeeping to develop an interagency, international field manual for democratic peace-building. The State Department's Bureau of Conflict and Stabilization Operations (CSO) has been working on pieces of that effort. In 2008, its predecessor organization crafted the Interagency Conflict Assessment Framework to "assess conflict situations systematically and collaboratively and prepare for interagency planning for conflict prevention, mitigation and stabilization." That same year it produced a planning framework for reconstruction and stabilization missions. In 2009, the United States Institute of Peace produced its *Guiding Principles for Stabilization and Reconstruction*.

The Defense Department has and should retain a major role in stability operations. The 2010 *Quadrennial Defense Review Report*, the Obama administration's first major statement of defense policy, rightly stated that the United States needed to retain a large-scale stability operations capability. "The United States must retain the capability to conduct large-scale counterinsurgency, stability, and counterterrorism operations," it said. "DoD will continue to place special emphasis on stability operations" because stability missions will be a permanent requirement of the twenty-first century environment. "Stability operations, large-scale counterinsurgency, and counterterrorism operations are not niche challenges . . . nor are these types of operations a transitory or anomalous phenomenon in the security landscape." That is why "US military forces must plan and prepare to prevail in a broad range of operations. . . . Such operations include . . . conducting large-scale stability operations."[25]

Along with doctrinal development, continued institutional reorganization would also help. Efforts in this direction have also been under way for several years. CSO's predecessor developed a deployable and expeditionary Civilian Response Corps for contingency operations. The White House issued National Security Presidential Directive 44 the same year, updating the Clinton administration's guidance on interagency efforts in reconstruction and stabilization missions. The military has also contributed. In 2005, the Department of Defense issued Directive 3000.5, making "stability operations" a core military mission, which means it will train and equip its soldiers for these missions. The next year, the US Army and Marine Corps issued *Field Manual 3–24: Counterinsurgency*, the primary objective of which is to "foster the development of effective governance by a legitimate government."

The United States could also be getting much more from the army's Civil Affairs branch, which exists to interact with civilians in a military theater. This includes "military operations that help to stabilize or to continue the operations of the governing body or civil structure of a foreign country," according to the Civil Affairs field manual. One of the five core tasks of Civil Affairs is to "support civil administration," and Civil Affairs soldiers develop expertise in one of six functional areas: rule of law, economic stability, governance, public health and welfare, infrastructure, and public education and information. Civil Affairs operations "may include performance by military forces of activities and functions normally the responsibility of local, regional, or national government." Civil Affairs soldiers bring "cultural awareness, training in military-to-host nation (HN) advisory activities, and civilian professional skills that parallel common government functions" to the United States' foreign policy tool kit.[26] This is not a new capability: It was Civil Affairs teams (under a different name) that fanned out across western Germany after World War II, first to govern the US occupation zone, then to partner with vetted anti-Nazi Germans to rebuild their institutions of government.

The UN has carried out a parallel reform effort. It formed the UN Peace-building Commission in 2005 to improve international coordination on, and heighten attention to, postconflict peace-building efforts. The UN designed integrated missions, in which civilians from all UN agencies and departments serve alongside its peacekeepers—an equivalent to the United States' whole-of-government and counterinsurgency doctrine. In 2008, the Department of Peacekeeping Operations published a new "Capstone Doctrine" for peace operations.

The Department of Defense's Office for Partnership Strategy and Stability Operations should be promoted. It is currently headed by a deputy assistant secretary of defense and subordinate to the Office for Special Operations and Low-Intensity Conflict (SO/LIC). SO/LIC has responsibility for a wide range of high-profile issues that overshadow stability operations. The Office for Partnership and Stability Operations should be pulled out of SO/LIC and given its own assistant secretary who can partner with the assistant secretary of state for conflict and stabilization operations on equal terms. And organizations like these need to be coordinated through a clear chain of command. Currently, the State Department has the formal lead for coordinating interagency work on reconstruction and stabilization operations, which simply ensures that the process will not draw in effective participation from the Defense Department. Leadership of the interagency for democratic peace-building should come from the NSC and its staff.

Unfortunately, the efforts to institutionalize and improve America's reconstruction and stability operations capabilities have atrophied in recent years. The Civilian Response Corps was dissolved; only a residual capacity was retained in USAID's Crisis Surge Support Staff.[27] CSO had a budget of less than $40 million in 2014 and 2015, essentially enough to retain a skeleton capacity but not undertake operations—and was cut entirely in the Obama administration's budget request for 2016.[28] The 2012 defense strategic guidance and 2014 *Quadrennial Defense Review Report* reversed course from earlier defense policy statements and said, "US forces will no longer be sized to conduct large-scale, prolonged stability operations."[29] The latter document pays lip service to the need to "preserve the expertise gained during the past ten years," but nothing in the Pentagon's recent budgetary or doctrinal choices suggest that is happening.[30] Astonishingly, the United States government is ensuring that it is unlearning its lessons from Iraq, Afghanistan, Bosnia, and elsewhere. The reversal of two decades' worth of investment and grinding experience in stability operations is an unfortunate risk that ignores the realities of the contemporary security environment. Cutting back on stability operations will throw away hard-fought gains and expose the United States to new risks from across the globalizing, fragile world.

Such reversals are deeply troubling. Secretary of Defense Robert Gates addressed the need for greater attention to the civilian tools of national power, especially for stability operations, at several points during his tenure. It was precisely because the United States was fighting two simultaneous wars that Gates believed it needed larger and more effective civilian tools:

> One of the most important lessons of the wars in Iraq and Afghanistan is that military success is not sufficient to win: economic development, institution-building and the rule of law, promoting internal reconciliation, good governance, providing basic services to the people, training

and equipping indigenous military and police forces, strategic communications, and more—these, along with security, are essential ingredients for long-term success. Accomplishing all of these tasks will be necessary to meet the diverse challenges I have described. . . .

What is clear to me is that there is a need for a dramatic increase in spending on the civilian instruments of national security—diplomacy, strategic communications, foreign assistance, civic action, and economic reconstruction and development.[31]

There is no evidence that policymakers have heeded Gates's warning. If the Obama administration and its successor continue current policy trends, it is overwhelmingly likely that when the United States undertakes its next stability operation, it will again do so with underfunded agencies, poor civilian capacity, and little institutional memory of the successes and failures of Iraq and Afghanistan. Such policy drift is counterproductive because it raises the cost of future interventions and lowers the likelihood of success. More important, policymakers often speak of honoring the troops' sacrifice, but their unwillingness to internalize the lessons of the wars those soldiers fought is deeply dishonorable, a dereliction of duty, and an appalling policymaking failure of the highest order.

The United States should reverse course and not only reinvest in its tools of stabilization, reconstruction, and foreign aid—it should go further. Its previous tools were underdeveloped, uncoordinated, and criticized for their unclear mission.[32] The United States needs a standing, deployable, expeditionary civilian instrument for reconstruction, stabilization, and governance assistance. It should create a permanent, professionalized cadre of civilians with a clear mission to support overseas governance in weak and failing states and be given specialized training—especially in language.[33] In other words, it needs an Overseas Civil Service, modeled on the British Overseas, Colonial, and Indian Civil Services that administered its overseas territories in the nineteenth and early twentieth centuries. Insofar as the United States is carrying on the United Kingdom's project of constructing liberal order, it should emulate some of its policy instruments—adapted, of course, for a postimperial age—for projecting civilian power abroad in the service of developing weak and fragile states.

International Institutions and Treaties

Intergovernmental institutions can be useful instruments of national power under certain conditions. For powerful states, institutions "are useful in shaping and entrenching a favorable international environment" and help "reduce its enforcement costs, foster legitimacy, and institutionalize a favor-able international order for the long term,"[34] even as they limit other states' policy autonomy and constrain their choices. There is a trade-off: To induce other states to participate in institutions, the United States has to treat them seriously. It can do so in three ways. First, "the leading state both sponsors rules and institutions of order and acts in accordance with them." Second, it "provides some array of public goods, offered in exchange for the coopera-tion of other states." Third, the leading state "provides channels and networks for reciprocal communication and influence."[35] Supporting and participating in institutions is not without cost, but, by and large, it is the cost of doing business as a great power. To the extent that American policymakers believe the United States is or will continue to be a unipolar power, they may be tempted to renegotiate institutional bargains, gain advantages or exemptions for the United States, or circumvent institutions altogether.[36] As American unipolarity wanes (or as policymakers realize it was partly illusory all along), incentives to invest in institutions rise. Investing in the maintenance of liberal order entrenches liberal norms and ensures their perpetuation independent of unipolarity.[37] That means that paying dues for membership in international organizations, abiding by their terms, and even joining some suboptimal institutions are acceptable costs of America's grand strategy.

The most important intergovernmental institution in the world is NATO, which I addressed in previous chapters. The second is probably the EU, in which the United States has no formal role. The UN, for all its flaws, prob-ably ranks alongside the World Bank and the IMF in the third rank of inter-governmental institutions in the world because of the universal forum it provides for global diplomacy. (It has also proven effective at coordinating humanitarian relief and constructing camps for refugees. Combatants still mostly respect the neutrality of UN officials.) UN peace-building efforts have improved their doctrine, coordination, and execution in recent years, and approving blue-helmet operations are a low-cost way for the United States to support other states' stability operations in peripheral regions. But the UN, and especially its Security Council, is in need of reform. Institutions succeed if and when they accurately reflect and respond to the underlying balance of power among states. The Security Council no longer reflects the world's balance of power. The aspirants to permanent seats—India, Brazil, Germany, and Japan—are great powers or, in the case of Brazil, have great power potential. President Obama was right to publicly support India's bid, and the United States would lose little if it supported all four or perhaps all but Brazil. Including other states for geographic balance or cultural diversity makes sense for other UN bodies that deal with social and cultural affairs but not the Security Council. Power, and a record of its responsible use, should be the sole criterion for that body.

If the UN proves too rigid or fades in relevance, the United States could shift its focus for multilateral diplomacy on global issues to other fora, such as the Group of Twenty major economies or the Poland-based Community of Democracies—or simply use them alongside the UN as the situation merits. Some scholars have gone further and called for the creation of a new institution, global in scope but limited to liberal democracies, for cooperative security, such as a "global NATO" or a "Concert of Democracies" to "institutionalize and 'ratify' the democratic peace" and act as an "alternative forum for liberal democracies to authorize collective action, including the use of force."[38] (The Community of Democracies, distinct from the proposed Concert of Democracies, plays no such role). The idea of a global mutual defense agreement among all liberal democracies is ambitious and seemingly consistent with America's grand strategy, amounting to the institutionalization of the Truman Doctrine. However, the idea is problematic. A global alliance is an alliance with no cohesion and no mission focus. NATO works in part because it is easier for members to form a common threat perception (even then they often differ). Regional and theater security cooperation is more effective. Forming a Concert of Democracies would be a drastic and unnecessary step unless and until the UN proves completely ineffective.

The United States is notorious for its supposed refusal to participate in international treaties and institutions, fostering the perception that American leadership is becoming more imperial and less consensual. The perception is unjustified: The United States participates in almost all of the important treaties, conventions, and institutions in the world, holding apart from only a handful. Some American refusals are justified. Withdrawing from the ABM Treaty was better than staying in and limiting missile defense or developing it covertly. It also seems wise not to accede to the International Criminal Court's jurisdiction unless and until the court demonstrates its immunity from political manipulation by America's rivals. The American military is a high-profile target for groups critical of US foreign policy; it is easy to imagine a group using or fabricating allegations of war crimes to entangle US personnel in court proceedings. But the United States' refusal to participate in other initiatives is not worth the harm done to its reputation or the health of liberal order. There is nearly unanimous, bipartisan support for acceding to the Law of the Sea Treaty. Henry Kissinger and Madeleine Albright do not agree on much, but they agree that the United States would not sacrifice its sovereignty or lose any important interest by ratifying the treaty. The United States already complies with the treaty's stipulations; acceding to the treaty is a cost-free way of bolstering the credibility of America's commitment to liberal order.[39]

The issues surrounding other major international treaties and institutions to which the United States has not acceded are more complex. Some of them are arms-control agreements to which the United States has objected on narrow, technical grounds, such as the Biological Weapons Convention's lack of meaningful enforcement mechanisms. The United States should help shape an additional protocol on enforcement and, as it did with the Chemical Weapons Convention, accede. The Clinton administration initially objected to the Anti-Personnel Mine Ban Convention because it contained no exemption for mixed antitank and antipersonnel mines, but the Obama administration indicated in 2014 that it had dropped the United States' objections and was moving toward accession, partly in recognition that the United States simply did not use antipersonnel landmines anymore despite a decade of continuous land warfare.[40] The Comprehensive Nuclear Test-Ban Treaty is a difficult case. For purely military reasons, it seems unwise to forgo the possibility of the development of future weapons, but China's signature and Russia's ratification of the treaty suggest the United States would not be placing itself at a disadvantage if it ratified. The state of technological development on nuclear weapons would be frozen in the United States' favor, and it could restart development in a position of advantage in the future if necessary.

Finally, there is a clutch of treaties and conventions on economic, social, and cultural rights, including the rights of children, women, migrant workers, and the disabled. There is some irony in the criticism against the United States for not signing these treaties. The United States led the world in developing the very concept of a civil and political right and is one of the best in the world at actually protecting such rights. When it does champion liberalism around the world, it is inevitably criticized for cultural imperialism and for trampling on other states' cultural particularity: The United States is damned when it does champion liberalism and damned all the more when it does not. Here it seems best to be damned for not. Trying to bring such sensitive subjects as women's and children's rights under the purview of international law seems foolish and bound to fail, given the vastly different ways different states handle such topics. Such treaties have no enforcement mechanisms and are largely symbolic gestures toward noble aspirations. To the extent that the United States engages with other states on these issues, quiet bilateral diplomacy and cultural exchange seems a more effective route. Not signing these treaties does not undermine liberal order. Not signing, in fact, can *strengthen* liberal order by preserving the credibility and meaningfulness of the United States' signature. Getting every state's signature on every agreement will only succeed in cheapening the currency of international treaties.

Notes

1. James, *Rise and Fall of the British Empire*, part III, chap. 7.
2. Layne, *Peace of Illusions*, e.g., 160.
3. Art, *Grand Strategy for America*, 168–70.
4. Friedberg, *Contest for Supremacy*, 184.
5. Muravchik, *Exporting Democracy*, chap. 10.
6. Carothers, *Aiding Democracy Abroad*, 38.
7. Quoted in McDougall, *Promised Land*, 36.
8. Carlucci and Brzezinski, *State Department Reform*.
9. Carothers, *Aiding Democracy Abroad* and *Critical Mission*, are the best sources on this vast subject. Cox, Bouchet, and Lynch, *US Foreign Policy and Democracy Promotion*, and Smith, *America's Mission*, offer histories of democracy promotion. Traub, *Freedom Agenda*, and McFaul, *Advancing Democracy Abroad*, are straightforward arguments in favor of democracy promotion (the former reflecting extensively on the impact of the George W. Bush administration on the democracy-promotion agenda), while Cox, Ikenberry, and Inoguchi, *American Democracy Promotion*, debates the pros and cons of supporting democracy. Muravchik, *Exporting Democracy*, both argues for democracy promotion and goes into more detail about how to do so. Schraeder, *Exporting Democracy*, takes a more international perspective.
10. Pakenham, *Liberal America and the Third World*.
11. Paris, *At War's End*.
12. Mansfield and Snyder, *Electing to Fight*.
13. Tocqueville, *Democracy in America*, 239.
14. Demirel-Pegg and Moskowitz, "US Aid Allocation," argues that economic considerations were paramount in the Cold War, while human rights have risen, slightly, in importance since then. See also Lai, "Examining the Goals."
15. Knack, "Does Foreign Aid Promote Democracy?"; Altunbaş and Thornton, "(Small) Blessing of Foreign Aid."
16. Scott and Steele, "Sponsoring Democracy."
17. Bearce et al., "Has the New Aid Been Export Effective?"
18. Carothers, *Aiding Democracy Abroad*, 8–9, chap. 5, esp. 101.
19. Ibid., 108, 47. See also McFaul, *Advancing Democracy Abroad*, chap. 5.
20. Carothers, *Aiding Democracy Abroad*, 107.
21. Biddle, "Afghanistan's Legacy."
22. Organisation for Economic Co-operation and Development data on official development assistance as a percentage of GDP goes back to 1960 (http://data .oecd.org/oda/net-oda.htm, accessed January 14, 2016). Data from 1945 to 1960 is available through the USAID Green Book.
23. "American Public Vastly Overestimates Amount of US Foreign Aid," November 29, 2010, http://www.interaction.org/sites/default/files/American%20Public%20 Vastly%20Overestimates%20Amount%20of%20US%20Foreign%20Aid.pdf, accessed March 17, 2015.

24. Rice, "Transformational Diplomacy."
25. US Department of Defense, *Quadrennial Defense Review Report: 2010*, viii, xiii, 20.
26. US Department of the Army, "FM 3-57."
27. USAID, "Office of Crisis Surge Support Staff."
28. US Department of State, *Congressional Budget Justification, Fiscal Year 2016*.
29. US Department of Defense, *Sustaining U.S. Global Leadership*, 2012.
30. US Department of Defense, *Quadrennial Defense Review Report*, 2014, 19.
31. Gates, "Landon Lecture."
32. US Department of State Office of Inspector General, *Inspection of the Bureau of Conflict*.
33. McFaul, *Advancing Democracy Abroad*, 196ff, suggests forming a Department of Development and Democracy.
34. Ikenberry, *Liberal Leviathan*, 102, 81.
35. Ibid., 71–72.
36. Monten, "Primacy and Grand Strategic Beliefs."
37. Ikenberry, *Liberal Leviathan*, 325.
38. Ikenberry and Slaughter, *Forging a World of Liberty*, 7.
39. US Department of State, "Law of the Sea Convention Supporters," http://www .state.gov/e/oes/lawofthesea/statements/index.htm, accessed March 17, 2015. See also Borgerson, *National Interest and Law of the Sea*.
40. Rick Gladstone, "US Lays Groundwork to Reduce Land Mines and Join Global Treaty," *New York Times*, June 27, 2014.

12

Military, Intelligence, and National Security Decision Making

The role and disposition of the military is often overemphasized in debates about US national security. There is a wide range of civilian tools relevant to the implementation of grand strategy. And focusing on the number of US troops deployed abroad often reinforces the unhelpfully simplistic less-versus-more view of grand strategy. The argument for restraint often boils down to an argument against sustaining a forward-deployed military presence and in favor of a smaller defense budget. These are important debates, but as important are the questions about what kind of military the United States should buy and where it should go. A chess player does not worry exclusively about how many pieces he has: He focuses on the mix of pieces, how to combine their capabilities, how best to arrange them on the board, and how to drive the game with what he has.

In practice, a work of grand strategy can only suggest general answers to these questions. Pentagon planners have a formal "troop-to-task" methodology that helps them calculate how many and what kinds of soldiers, sailors, Marines, and airmen are needed for specific kinds of missions, an analysis it would be unwise for generalists to try to replicate. Strategy can describe the mission and identify regions and states in which troops should be stationed and why, even suggesting what kind of troops might be appropriate—but little else. In this chapter I try to outline a thought process for military planners to help identify priorities. I argue that the global footprint should prioritize platforms of access and grow more widely dispersed and flexible. I have also appended brief discussions of intelligence policy and national security decision making.

Force Structure

What kind of military should the United States buy? The first step in thinking clearly about the shape of the US military in the twenty-first century security environment is to dismiss any notion that there has been a "revolution in military affairs" wrought by information technology. During the 1990s, some defense intellectuals argued that the advent of networked computers and telecommunications would enable the United States to substitute high technology for manpower and that the new forms of intelligence available to commanders would give them "information dominance."[1] They drew the wrong lessons from the 1991 Persian Gulf War. In that war, the United States effectively leveraged relatively new technologies, including precision-guided munitions, global telecommunications, and unmanned aerial vehicles, to gain an unprecedented degree of precise information about the location and disposition of an opposing conventional military force. Some analysts wrongly saw the Gulf War as a template for future conflicts.

Similarly, some scholars pointed to the initial invasion of Afghanistan as a new model of warfare, in which very few US personnel embedded with local allies, empowered by global telecommunications, US air power, and precision-guided munitions, were able to achieve military effects out of pro-portion to their numbers.[2] But Stephen Biddle has persuasively argued that the "Afghan model" is far less unique than its advocates admit. The initial phase of Operation Enduring Freedom actually played out in surprisingly conventional ways, as a sizeable, heavy land force (the Northern Alliance) with coordinated close air support (from the United States) conducted conventional operations against Taliban formations. The employment of US intelligence and Special Operations Forces as the link between the two, with reachback communications to US air assets, was an effective organiza-tional innovation that exploited current technological capabilities but not an entirely new form of warfare.[3]

The United States' superiority in military technology and conventional warfare will be helpful for some future scenarios. If, for example, the United States finds itself in a war with Russia, US military planners may finally get to wage a high-tech version of the ground offensive through the Fulda Gap they have war-gamed for two generations (with all the catastrophic results they have long expected). Similarly, a war with China would include, as a major component, conventional naval engagements. But the Gulf War is more likely to have been an aberration than a precedent for future conflicts. Iraqi leaders were probably unaware of the full extent of US technological superiority in 1991. Russia, China, and others, having seen US capabilities and Iraq's swift defeat, are unlikely to attempt to challenge the United States in conventional combat in doctrinally predictable formations. They are also likely to develop countermeasures specifically aimed at the United States' strengths, such as through cyberattacks and antisatellite ballistic missiles. China, for example, would almost certainly couple naval combat with attacks on US information systems, including, possibly, military satellites. Russia's operations in Ukraine have used an intriguing mixture of conventional and unconventional tactics. The next war will not look anything like the Gulf War.

In addition, as the last decade has more than amply attested, there is another kind of warfare altogether, one for which the US advantage in information technology is nearly useless. As H. R. McMaster has forcefully argued, the flawed conceptual groundwork of defense transformation and overreliance on technology left the military poorly prepared for stability and counterinsurgency operations in Iraq and Afghanistan: "The disconnect between the true nature of these conflicts and pre-war visions of future war helps explain the lack of planning for the aftermath of both invasions." Commanders discovered that the massive volume of data from electronic, signals, and imagery intelligence was so vast that it simply could not be processed. Paradoxically, the revolution in military affairs did not pierce the fog of war—it only made it thicker with data. Despite the experience of those wars, the military is still clinging to the theories that led to their failures. "Military forces must abandon the dangerous and seductive illusion that technology can solve the problem of future conflict."[4]

The failure, thus far, to learn the right lessons from Iraq and Afghanistan threatens to undermine the United States' ability to face future challenges. The twenty-first-century security environment is characterized, in part, by nonstate actors and failed states. The US military must be prepared to undertake a wide range of operations that will, whether policymakers like it or not, bear at least passing similarity to those in Iraq and Afghanistan (as well as Bosnia, Kosovo, and elsewhere), including counterterrorism, counterpiracy, counterinsurgency, and stability operations. As Janine Davidson, formerly the deputy assistant secretary of defense for plans in the Obama administration, argued, "history shows that such complex missions are hard to avoid—either as stand-alone interventions or as the type of operation that must be conducted in the aftermath of a major conventional war in order to consolidate the gains or 'win the peace' through the provision of law and order, reconstruction and development."[5] Libya's descent into civil war illustrates the problems of intervening without deploying a follow-on stabilization force. A Syrian intervention would obviously require a robust stabilization capability, as might a postconflict mission in Ukraine. Even potential wars with North Korea or Iran would probably end up requiring the United States to participate in large-scale stability operations in the aftermath. That is why "military forces, their governments and coalitions need to develop improved inter-departmental capabilities for planning and executing statebuilding and counter-insurgency operations."[6] For these operations, "strategy must be grounded in social and cultural realities," knowledge of which can only be gained by a substantial number of boots (both military and civilian) on the ground.

The future force structure must therefore be capable of both high-intensity, high-technology combat against a near-peer rival and counterinsurgency, counterterrorism, and stability operations in failed states. In other words, the US military needs a little bit of everything. The army must retain heavy tank and mechanized infantry brigades for conventional land warfare in Europe but also sustain light infantry and Stryker brigades and, above all, Special Operations Forces. The air force should sustain its global attack weapons platforms, such as the B-2, but also keep multipurpose tactical aircraft such as the A-10 and F/A-18. The navy should sustain its fleet of carrier strike groups and attack and ballistic missile submarines for operations in the Mediterranean, Persian Gulf, and Pacific but should continue developing its ability for stealthy delivery and support of Special Operations Forces around the world.

A critic may argue that "a little bit of everything" is not a strategy—it is a compromise designed to avoid hard decisions and minimize congressional and bureaucratic opposition. I reply that, like a broken watch, Congress and the bureaucracy are sometimes accidentally right. Pork-barrel politics, bureaucratic provincialism, and defense industry lobbying have ground out a sausage that contains a little bit of everything, which is pretty close to what the United States needs. The diffuse, variegated strategic environment of the twenty-first century demands an equally flexible and multifaceted force structure capable of a wide array of mission sets. The military would be unwise to double down exclusively on heavy, high-tech, or conventional capabilities when it faces unconventional threats such as terrorists and pirates, just as it would be unwise to focus exclusively on light forces while Russia and China field tank divisions and aircraft carriers.

Probably the best option for coping with fiscal realities while still investing in an array of capabilities is to slow the acquisition of high-tech naval and air systems such as the F-22 and F-35 fighters, *Ford*-class aircraft carriers, and *Virginia*-class submarines. The United States has broadly erred on the side of overinvesting in these systems while underinvesting in land forces and stability operations (which constituted the majority of missions it actually has undertaken since the end of the Cold War). The Bush administration temporarily reversed the drawdown of land forces and created Stryker brigade combat teams to address glaring needs in Iraq and Afghanistan, but that seems to have been an aberration. The Obama administration and congressional budget cuts are reducing the army from 540,000 at the peak of the wars in Iraq and Afghanistan to perhaps 450,000, with a parallel drawdown in the Marine Corps. But the current force of some forty-five active-duty army brigade combat teams, twenty-eight National Guard brigade combat teams, and thirteen combat aviation brigades was barely capable of sustaining the deployment of twenty-two brigades to Iraq and Afghanistan at the peak of those wars; much less will it be prepared for future contingencies with planned reductions under way.[7] Reversing the drawdown in land forces, expanding Special Operations Forces, refitting most light infantry brigades as Stryker brigades, and moving Civil Affairs into the active component would better position ground forces for future stability operations—as would ensuring that all general-purpose forces are trained for unconventional missions. Meanwhile, the United States can pay for investments in land forces by slowing its investment in air and naval forces. Its military is already far ahead of its rivals in most major categories of weapons; it can probably afford to wait a few years before moving to the next generation. The marginal net gain in combat power from the F-35 versus the F/A-18 may be tactically significant, for example, but a few years' delay would not alter the strategic balance between the United States and its rivals. It is true that the F/A-18 and other systems are more than thirty years old—but so is the M-1 Abrams tank, first designed in the 1970s, for which there is no replacement in the pipeline.

Global Posture

Where and why should the United States deploy its military forces abroad? Proposals for the global posture of the US military vary widely from retrenching and withdrawing most troops stationed overseas to reverting to the presence that the United States maintained during the Cold War. A major difficulty is "the lack of consensus on . . . how to link the number of bases and military forces overseas to specific US global security interests."[8] The absence of consensus is unsurprising: At issue is the age-old debate about how to use military power to achieve political effects, a question of art rather than science. There is no scientific answer to the question, how many troops are required in Europe to deter future Russian aggression? The answer depends on a political judgment informed by the history of US deployments, US–Russian relations, Russian security perceptions, European security perceptions, and more. Much less is there a scientific answer to the question, what global posture is required to uphold liberal order?

Historically the United States adopted a defense posture as expansive as the scope of its ambitions for liberal order. Initially US military forces concentrated on the North American continent and, subsequently, the Western Hemisphere, when the focus of American diplomacy was on continental expansion and hemispherical hegemony. In the late nineteenth and early twentieth centuries, the United States consciously evolved its defense posture with the creation of the "New Navy" and the acquisition of coaling and port facilities across the Pacific and in the Caribbean. The US defense posture expanded to a global scope and introduced permanently stationed land forces abroad in World War II and the Cold War, becoming by the late 1980s perhaps the most expansive posture of any military force in history.[9]

Our political judgment about the future US global posture must start with the recognition that while US security interests remain global in scope, the United States has been in the process of retrenching for the past quarter century, without a specific vision to guide the process. "The reorientation of the US military posture had been going on since the fall of the Berlin Wall in 1989, albeit without any clear central idea about the desired end state," according to the authors of the most comprehensive study of US overseas military bases.[10] In 1988, the United States had 356,000 troops stationed in Europe; today there are 66,000 (mostly in Germany, Italy, and the United Kingdom), an 81 percent reduction. There were also 141,000 troops stationed in East Asia; today 81,000 remain (almost entirely in Japan and South Korea), a 43 percent reduction. It even retrenched from Latin America, dropping from 25,000 troops to 1,500 today, largely because of the handover of the Panama Canal Zone in 1999. It deployed some 250,000 troops to South Asia and the Middle East after 2001 but subsequently withdrew almost all of them. In 2015, 9,800 remained in Afghanistan and were scheduled to draw down by half by the end of 2016, while 18,000 troops remained in the Middle East (mostly Bahrain and Kuwait), probably the lowest number since before the Gulf War. Defense spending fell from 5.6 percent of GDP in 1988 to 2.9 percent in 1999, before rising to 4.7 percent in 2010, according to the World Bank.[11] Total active-duty personnel fell from 2.14 million to 1.27 million, a 40 percent reduction. Today the United States has the lowest military profile abroad since 1942, a fact the advocates of retrenchment have entirely overlooked.[12]

Our political judgment must also recognize what overseas military deployments are for, something the advocates of restraint generally misunderstand. Eugene Gholz, Daryl G. Press, and Harvey M. Sapolsky believe that US military forces are only useful to deter or defeat military challenges—and since the United States faces none, they believe, it needs only deploy enough military power to the Middle East to prevent a regional hegemon from seizing oil supplies. They are wrong about the absence of military challenges to the United States abroad, but they are also wrong about what military force is for. Military force is an instrument of diplomacy as much as war. It gives weight to a nation's will, communicates seriousness of intent, provides insurance against uncertainty, deters aggressors, reassures allies, facilitates security cooperation, and affects the psychological environment in which it operates. US overseas deployments "prevent conflict, build the capacity of key partners,

Table 12.1. Distribution of US Military Power Abroad

	US Troops, 2014[a]		US Military Facilities[b]		Allies	Security Assistance, 2001–12, $bn[c]		Weapon Sales, 1950–2013, $bn[d]		Weapon Sales, 2013, $bn[e]
Europe	66,200	37%	329	57%	27	8.7	6%	$123	22%	$3.7
East Asia	81,107	46%	206	36%	6	0.9	1%	$117	21%	$6.9
South Asia	9,850	6%	1	0%	2	53.6	36%	$15.6	3%	$0.2
Middle East	18,000	10%	19	3%	5	80.1	53%	$282	51%	$10.8
Latin America	1,460	1%	19	3%	1	4.4	3%	$10.9	2%	$0.2
Africa	402	0%	2	0%	1	3.2	2%	$6.5	1%	$0.2

[a] US Department of Defense Manpower Data Center, "DoD Personnel." The Defense Department does not report the number of US military personnel in South Korea, but the number was calculated from US Department of Defense, *Base Structure Report*, PERS-17.
[b] US Department of Defense, *Base Structure Report*.
[c] US Agency for International Development, *U.S. Overseas Loans and Grants*.
[d] US Defense Security Cooperation Agency, *Historical Facts Book*.
[e] Ibid.

Table 12.2. US Military Spending as Percentage of GDP

	% GDP	Equivalent Budget in 2016 Economy ($)
Average since 1940	7.4	1,379
Average in Peacetime since 1940	6.2	1,155
Average 1992–2015	3.7	690
Average 2002–15	3.9	727
2016 Estimate	3.3	615
2020 Proposal	2.7	503

Source: Derived from Office of Management and Budget, *Historical Tables.*

maintain core alliances, and ensure the US military's ability to secure American interests in critical regions."[13] The United States' massive lead in military high technology makes it prohibitively expensive for anyone else to try to become a true rival, thereby reinforcing the United States' conventional military predominance and dampening arms races across the world (although rivals still seek advantages through cyber and unconventional capabilities). It can help deter would-be challengers but also restrain allies. A team of scholars working to rebut Gholz, Press, and Sapolsky rightly argued that "by supplying reassurance, deterrence, and active management, the United States lowers security competition in the world's key regions."[14] In turn, the stabilizing effect of the US global deployments and security guarantees fosters global economic growth, freeing the world economy from the downward pull of great power wars, regional conflicts, and arms races.[15] The United States should maintain a globally deployed military force because the world is rife with threats against the United States and liberal order but also because the military is a useful instrument for a wide range of purposes around the world.

That said, the military is not the only tool, is often not the best tool, and overseas deployments do not necessarily have to be large to generate the benefits outlined above. Gholz and other advocates of restraint have a point when they argue that US military deployments abroad are not the best tool for fostering democracy or building liberal order. It is, after all, unusual for a state to permanently station large numbers of its military forces outside of its borders, except when they are exercising imperial control over another state. Using military deployments to uphold a certain kind of culture of world order is a relatively novel concept. There is not a direct connection between the culture of liberal order and overseas US military deployments: Liberal order does not spring spontaneously from the soil wherever a uniformed American soldier has stepped.

There is, however, an *indirect* connection. US military deployments, when done right, foster stability, which is a favorable environment for vibrant markets and democratic transition. Global military deployments are best understood as a foundation on which the United States should layer all other tools of national power for the pursuit of its interests. As Henry Nau argues, military force should be employed in and with diplomacy, not afterward or instead of. Neither military deployments nor civilian aid, for example, are effective by themselves; in conjunction, they can be very powerful. That is why, as I argued in the previous chapter, a vast increase in civilian aid is probably the more pressing need for the achievement of a number of US interests around the world.

The Two-War Strategy

Much of the contemporary debate about the United States' global posture hinges on a decades-old debate about how many wars the United States needs to fight simultaneously. Since the end of the Cold War, US military planners have argued that they need to fight two major theater wars at the same time.[16] The two-war doctrine has become something like holy writ or an *idée fixe* among defense intellectuals. Though it was first put on paper after the Cold War, it clearly reflects a much earlier mind-set, when the United States plausibly could have faced simultaneous crises in, for example, Germany and Korea or in Germany and Cuba because such crises might have been deliberately fomented by a single foe, the Soviet Union. In fact, the two-war strategy is the textbook definition of fighting the last war—rather, fighting three or four wars ago. World War II was precisely the contingency during which the United States was compelled to fight two major theater wars at the same time, and notably it is also the only time in history it has been required to do so. Ever since the Pentagon won that war, it has been unable to free itself from the intellectual construct of preparing to fight it over again—it is always tempting to relive one's glory days. But World War II was unlike any war in history, so planning to refight it is unsound.

Today's security environment is dramatically different than it was during World War II or the Cold War. The United States faces the possibility of major conventional military crises against five opponents, not two, as the number of nuclear-armed authoritarian powers hostile to the United States grows each decade. In addition to however many conventional wars the United States and its allies might have to fight, they also need to prepare against the threats from failed states and armed nonstate actors. "War" is not a monolithic unit against which states can raise a predetermined number of troops.

The answer is not to concoct a five-war strategy and permanently garrison half the planet, a hopelessly expensive and utopian effort to secure absolute security. In the face of this security environment, preparing to fight a set number of conventional wars misses the point. The 2010 *Quadrennial Defense Review Report* largely got this right: "It is no longer appropriate to speak of 'major regional conflicts' as the sole or even the primary template for sizing, shaping, and evaluating US forces. Rather, US forces must be prepared to conduct a wide variety of missions under a range of different circumstances."[17] Michael O'Hanlon developed an insightful recommendation to adopt a "one plus two" strategy—that is, one major war and up to two contingencies or stability operations.[18] O'Hanlon's idea of distinguishing between different tiers or types of conflict points in the right direction because the United States needs to develop capabilities matched to the kinds of missions it is likely to face. O'Hanlon's specific suggestion, however, that the United States prepare for one major war and two smaller contingencies leaves little margin for error. It might need "two plus two," or policymakers may even want to add a third tier to make a "one plus two plus two," meaning one major land-based conventional war, one or two major air or littoral actions (e.g., bombing Iran's nuclear facilities or providing the air component of a war against North Korea), and two stability operations.

Regardless of the number, the point is that the defense strategy should be framed around the actual threats facing the United States and the actual capabilities required, rather than a template from 1942. The United States needs the ability to fight large, conventional, land wars against enemy states. It also needs the ability to execute shorter, more limited air or naval operations against specific threats (e.g., Iran's or North Korea's weapons of mass destruction programs). And it also needs the ability to support sizeable stability operations. Happily, it does not need to be prepared to do all of these missions simultaneously because the chances of all possible bad things happening at once is very small. Rather, it needs a military that is trained and equipped for both conventional and unconventional mission sets, has organizational flexibility, and is globally deployable on short notice.

Platforms of Access

In practice, this means keeping, and even expanding, forward-deployed equipment and bases, overseas infrastructure, and training capacity to rapidly raise and deploy a major land army supported by air and naval assets anywhere in the world. It means prioritizing flexible platforms of access that can receive forces deploying from the continental United States for onward deployment to conflict zones. A RAND Corporation study on the US global posture concluded that the "minimum essential posture needs" include "a global network of ports and air bases—infrastructure and access—and the air and sea lift assets to move forces through that global network," along with forward naval forces and a global communications network.[19] The United States also needs facilities to base intelligence, surveillance, and reconnaissance assets, including airstrips for drones and listening posts. Critics have rightly understood the importance of overseas facilities as concrete expressions of US grand strategy but have wrongly seen them as outposts of imperialism.[20] Bases represent deliberate choices about where to make capital investments of military and diplomatic resources for the projection of US power and influence abroad; they do not police subject populations, take the place of local political authority, enforce US territorial annexations, or otherwise do the work of empire.

For example, in Europe the United States maintains major air bases at Incirlik, Turkey; Ramstein, Germany; Aviano, Italy; and Lakenheath, United Kingdom; naval stations at Naples, Italy; and Rota, Spain; and intelligence-gathering facilities on the continent. The air and naval facilities are the means by which the United States is able to project power onto the European continent—whether in response to a crisis with Russia, for onward deployment into Africa or the Middle East, or to stabilize a collapsing state in the Balkans. And these facilities are not manpower intensive: There are fewer than 10,000 US military personnel in the United Kingdom, fewer than 11,000 in Italy, and only 1,500 each in Spain and Turkey. That means perhaps 24,000 troops (out of 66,000 in Europe) secure the most important strategic benefits of a US military presence in Europe.

The rest, constituting the majority of US troops in Europe—including the 12th Combat Aviation Brigade, the US Army NATO Brigade, and the 2nd Cavalry Regiment—are conventional maneuver units sitting in Germany. Their missions typically include participating in training exercises with European partners and being available for contingency operations. The real strategic value of their presence is simply to add heft to the American commitment to European security. That means they should be first to be redeployed if political or strategic considerations call for further cuts to the US military presence in Europe. (Fiscal considerations, however, are largely irrelevant, as it is not necessarily cheaper to house troops in the United States than in Europe.) By contrast, the naval and air facilities and the personnel who maintain and operate them should remain. The combat units are not unimportant, and allies would be justifiably nervous at the further lowering of US troop levels that are already at their lowest point since World War II. Already "Alliance exercises could be compromised, and development of joint doctrine weakened, if insufficient numbers of American forces are based in Germany in the future," according to

O'Hanlon.[21] But the combat units can be redeployed and sent back to Europe when circumstances permit more easily than the air or naval facilities could be completely shut down and then started back up again, and the strategic impact of losing the air and naval facilities would be dramatically worse.

The same strategy should apply worldwide. The United States should prioritize its platforms of access in different theaters. Air bases in Qatar and Afghanistan and naval facilities in Bahrain, Japan, South Korea, Djibouti, Cuba, Diego Garcia, and Guam, along with the navy's carrier strike groups, are the sinews of US power projection worldwide. They are the facilities the United States would need if it is forced into a major war with any of the nuclear autocracies or if it undertakes a limited strike against a regional actor. They are also the facilities from which US forces would stage when executing a targeted strike against a rogue actor or deploying into a failed state for a stability operation. The facilities are applicable to all possible mission sets. If policymakers are forced to choose, preserving the network of bases, naval stations, airfields, depots of prepositioned equipment, and intelligence facilities should take priority over the maintenance of large numbers of combat troops in Europe or East Asia.

Christopher Layne criticized this approach and suggested that the United States does not need to station troops abroad; it only needs to secure the option for future deployments in case of crisis, a common argument by advocates of restraint.[22] This is unpersuasive. Basing rights could be easily revoked or simply overridden in times of war or crisis, when the United States most needs access. Worse, because of the speed of modern combat, such bases could actually be destroyed or occupied by enemy forces before the United States has the ability to invest them with its own forces. "It takes weeks, if not months, to deploy a force of the size and strength required for some of the most likely and most dangerous scenarios the United States could face around the world," according to two Obama administration defense officials with experience actually planning for and managing the deployment of US forces overseas, an experience most scholars lack.[23] Bases must be physically occupied, supplied, and operated continuously by US personnel to be meaningful assets in the US defense posture.

The facilities are so important and useful, in fact, that policymakers should consider developing new ones. The US military's infrastructure is relatively well developed in Europe and East Asia, less so in South Asia and the Middle East, and almost nonexistent in Africa and Latin America. In this perspective, it seems clear that the Obama administration's failure to secure a SOFA allowing US troops to remain in Iraq was a serious missed opportunity, one that a future administration may want to revisit if the political situation in Iraq permits, and the withdrawal of most US forces from Afghanistan by the end of 2016 also merits reconsideration. The US–Afghan Strategic Partnership Agreement provided the groundwork for deepening ties and an enduring, mutually beneficial military partnership in South Asia.

In addition, the Defense Department should revise the Unified Command Plan to create a South Asia Command (SACOM) to manage its defense relationships on the subcontinent and the Indian Ocean. Splitting Afghanistan and Pakistan from CENTCOM and India from Pacific Command (PACOM) would relieve those commands of peripheral areas and allow them to concentrate fully on their primary concerns—Iran, and China and North Korea, respectively. Creating SACOM would also help bring more coherence and focus to US military policy in South Asia.[24]

Elsewhere, the failure to find an African country willing to host the headquarters for the US military's AFRICOM (currently headquartered in Germany) ensures that command, and US policy on the continent, will remain hamstrung unless and until US diplomats can convince African leaders of the benefit to them of a stronger US presence in their region. Djibouti is the best candidate to house the headquarters. And in Latin America, the United States might capitalize on growing US–Colombian ties over the past fifteen years to establish a more enduring presence to fight the drug trade, deliver humanitarian assistance, help stabilize fragile countries, and prevent Venezuela from trying to export its "Bolivarian revolution." For the navy, home-porting ships abroad while sea-swapping crews would sustain a more consistent naval presence in key theaters and get more use out of each ship.

Focusing on platforms of access in each theater also would help US planners tailor overseas deployments to the needs of individual regions and countries. The likeliest US military operations in Africa, for example, are humanitarian, counterterrorism, and stability operations: There is no need to plan for an armored division to deploy to Africa. By contrast, a major priority in almost every region is training local partners. The United States' various bases, ports, and airfields could be designed to accommodate joint training exercises, classrooms, war games, and simulations with local security forces. Outside of Europe and East Asia, it makes sense for the United States to focus on developing smaller and more flexible forward operating sites and cooperative security locations over large main operating bases.[25]

Covert Action

Grand strategy is incomplete without considering the tools of intelligence and covert action; a complete strategy should prescribe how each tool should be employed around the world in the same way it did for diplomacy and military power. Unfortunately, I can only offer a generic recommendation here that the intelligence posture—the basing and deployment of intelligence facilities and personnel—should broadly follow and support national priorities. The military rightly teaches its officers that intelligence drives operations, meaning that timely, accurate, and relevant information about the battlefield and the enemy creates an indispensable decisional advantage for command ers that enables them to act at the decisive point on the battlefield. In the same way, national intelligence should drive grand strategy. In the absence of information, policymakers are reduced to guesswork, opportunism, and risk mitigation rather than calculated plans. Without intelligence, grand strategy is useless. The post-9/11 reforms to the intelligence community were overdue but poorly designed, adding with the Office of the Director of National Intelligence (DNI) a layer of bureaucracy without giving it sufficient statutory authority to compel true community-wide integration. The DNI should either be empowered or abolished.

Discussions of grand strategy are particularly ill-served by a poor understanding of covert action. Sometimes the US government undertakes activities with the intention of concealing its role—what US law calls "covert action" or sometimes "special activities."[26] Covert action can be a powerful and effective instrument of national power, but my sense is that scholars have very little notion of the scope of covert action or its prominence as a tool of US national security strategy. It receives virtually no mention in theories of international relations or discussions of US grand strategy. That is, of course, by design—but it creates difficulties. Scholars and aspiring policymakers have few resources from which to gain an understanding of the capacities of covert action except by looking at declassified history. But that history is incomplete, selective, and often cannot be verified. In particular, the publicly available historical case studies of US covert action tend to be accounts of reported failure or abuse, which, in my (admittedly limited) observation, is not a representative sample of the broader universe of covert actions. There are few publicly known examples of successful covert action from which scholars and policymakers can learn positive lessons. Some recent exceptions—the initial US entry into Afghanistan immediately after 9/11 and, later, the raid on Osama bin Laden's compound[27]—are notable because they were paramilitary operations that the United States did not try to hide after the fact. In that sense, they were clandestine but not truly covert. President Obama even publicly acknowledged the drone program in January 2012 (though not any details about where it operates), and US officials apparently did not object when the media reported that the US government had coengineered the Stuxnet computer virus.[28]

Covert action is a tactic, not a strategy. It is the best tool of choice in only certain conditions—when knowledge of the United States' role in any initiative would be detrimental to its success. Its secrecy is the only unique thing about covert action: It is simply the secret implementation of initiatives that, in other circumstances, are normal foreign policy. It can include military or paramilitary operations, such as the bin Laden raid. But it can also include training for foreign security forces that secretly cooperate with the United States, support to foreign political actors and cultural elites who favor US interests and ideals, and *any* operations in areas normally denied to US personnel, like the Office of Strategic Services' operations behind enemy lines in World War II. The potential scope and range of covert action is as broad as the range of foreign policy.

Covert action is obviously relevant for combating armed nonstate groups. The extent of US counterterrorism operations worldwide, including training foreign security forces, is both impressive and probably will not be known in full for decades.[29] The alleged drone program is the most widely reported instance of covert US kinetic operations—and also the best example of why covert action is best understood as a tactic, not a strategy. According to most accounts of the program, it has kept pressure on jihadists in South Asia and the Middle East and denied them operational freedom, but few would argue that they are a definitive solution to the problems of jihadist terrorism and stability.[30] The United States has withdrawn most of its tools of national power from the regions of conflict but apparently sustained drone operations, suggesting that policymakers have drifted toward a short-term, unsustainable, and ultimately ineffective approach that feeds questions about the oversight and accountability of Washington's secret programs.[31] Covert action works best when part of a broader strategy that includes diplomacy, development, and other tools of national power.

But covert action is also an important tool for another of the United States' strategic courses of action: championing liberalism.[32] The growth of democracy in nondemocratic countries is often a dangerous and difficult business in which the normal tools of US foreign policy have limited influence. The United States could delegitimize local actors by publicly supporting them. USAID programs—such as support to civil society, journalists, and elections monitors—are often unwelcome or prohibited in closed countries. But selective support given secretly can have a strategic effect. In the 1980s, according to former CIA director Robert Gates, the United States covertly gave support to Solidarity, the Polish trade union—an important but largely untold story that played a role in ending the Cold War.[33] Today, similar support to aspiring democrats in closed countries can and should be a major part of American grand strategy.

National Security Decision Making

The last and most important resource for implementing America's grand strategy is command and control. The ability, or lack thereof, of US policy-makers to act coherently, to coordinate disparate parts of the public enterprise, to move the machinery of government with purpose, to overcome inertia and direct change in the bureaucracies—to make government *act strategically*—is a crucial grand strategic resource. Too often scholars have assumed this ability is entirely a function of presidential personality.[34] That approach is unsatisfying. There are structures and processes that can support and enable better command and control, and equally there are structures that obstruct it.[35]

The current national security decision-making system, created in 1989 by former national security adviser Brent Scowcroft, involves passing issues through a series of ascending interagency committees for staffing and development before they are considered by the cabinet secretaries in the Principals Committee and then by the full NSC with the president. The lower-level committees ostensibly weed out issues that do not merit higher-level consideration and prepare decision packages for those that do. After a decision is reached, the issue is passed back to the same committees to oversee and coordinate its implementation.

There are two problems, both of which undermine the government's ability to do strategic planning. First, the system relies on the same committees to do both strategic planning and oversight and implementation, ensuring neither is done well. Second, in practice, the system relies heavily on the overburdened Deputies Committee (DC)—an interagency committee of the deputy secretaries of state and defense and their counterparts in other agencies. The deputies routinely delegate their interagency duties downward to assistant secretaries in charge of regional desks. That means a different set of officials develop strategy and policy toward different regions or in response to different crises: There is no set of officials below the president and the NSC who integrate policy across regions, issues, and departments.

Put another way, there is no interagency body in the US government charged with developing grand strategy below the president and his immediate advisers. The president and his cabinet secretaries are the only officials who have the full picture and are able to integrate across regions and agencies. The principals are the only officials with an integrated view of the operating environment; when they make decisions and delegate implementation, they are handing issues down to subordinates who do not see the whole picture and do not understand the full context for policy decisions, which accounts for why implementation often does not follow the decision makers' intent. This is at least partly responsible for the reactive, oscillating, crisis-focus mentality of much US foreign policy.

The US government needs an integrated, interagency strategic planning committee. President Eisenhower had such a body, called the Planning Board, under his national security adviser Robert Cutler. President George W. Bush's national security adviser Stephen Hadley tried to resurrect the idea in the final months of the Bush administration without success. Instead of issues ascending through a hierarchy of interagency committees for staffing and then descending down the same chain for implementation, the next president should create two separate committee structures: the first to develop policy options for the NSC's consideration, the latter to oversee and coordinate the implementation of presidential decisions.

The reconstituted Planning Board would be the principal policy development body of the NSC, charged with writing the first draft of American grand strategy. It would comprise the strategic planners at each department and agency, such as the director of policy planning at the State Department. The strategic planners should be tasked with *interagency* strategic planning through their work on the Planning Board but also *departmental* strategic planning at their home agencies. The hybrid nature of their work would ensure that their planning at both locations would be informed by the other.

The members of today's DC cannot fulfill this duty. They have full-time responsibilities as the chief management officers of their respective agencies. By contrast, Planning Board members would have no other duties. Strategic planning at their agency and on the Planning Board would be their full-time job. The hybrid nature of the Planning Board makes it distinct from both the part-time DC and the full-time NSC staff of today. The back-and-forth between the White House and the agencies solves the problems of how to get realistic planning from the agencies that was not captive to parochial interests and how to foster a national, strategic mindset without falling prey to an ivory-tower mindset divorced from reality. The strongest endorsement comes from Zbigniew Brzezinski, President Carter's national security adviser:

> I was one of those who thought that the Eisenhower structure was over-organized, over-institutionalized, and its abolition . . . was a good idea. I changed my mind subsequently, and in light of my own experience. When I was in the White House, I had the opportunity to read the still-then-classified minutes of the Eisenhower NSC. And I came to the view that the Planning Board was a very important instrument, the elimination of which has handicapped the US government ever since then. Because the consequence is we don't have overall national security planning. We just don't.[36]

Notes

1. O'Hanlon, *Technological Change*; Mazarr, *Revolution in Military Affairs*; Metz and Kievit, *Strategy and Revolution in Military Affairs*.
2. Andres, Wills, and Griffith, "Winning with Allies."
3. Biddle, "Allies, Airpower, and Modern Warfare."
4. McMaster, "On War," 25, 26.
5. Davidson, *Retrench or Rebalance?*, 10.
6. McMaster, "On War," 27.
7. O'Hanlon, *Moderate Plan*.
8. Davis et al., *U.S. Overseas Military Presence*, 30.
9. On the history of US global deployments, see Krepinevich and Work, *New Global Defense Posture*, chaps. 3–6, and Pettyjohn, *U.S. Global Defense Posture*.
10. Krepinevich and Work, *New Global Defense Posture*, ii.
11. World Bank, *Data*. A report by Dinah Walker for the Council on Foreign Relations found different numbers but a similar trend, from about 7.5 percent in 1988 to 3.7 percent in 2000.
12. US Department of Defense, Personnel and Procurement Statistics, "Active Duty Military Personnel Strengths by Regional Area and by Country," December 31, 2014 (https://www.dmdc.osd.mil/appj/dwp/rest/download?fileName=SIAD_309 _Report_P1412.xlsx&groupName=milRegionCountry), and September 30, 1988 (https://www.dmdc.osd.mil/appj/dwp/rest/download?fileName=M05%20 Military%20Only.zip&groupName=pubGeographical), accessed March 4, 2015. Numbers for South Korea are available in the *Fiscal Year 2014 Base Report*.
13. Flournoy and Davidson, "Obama's New Global Posture," 55. See also Lostumbo et al., *Overseas Basing of U.S. Military Forces*.
14. Brooks, Ikenberry, Wohlforth, "Don't Come Home, America," 39.
15. Art, *Grand Strategy for America*, 139–45.
16. See, for example, *National Military Strategy*, February 1995.
17. US Department of Defense, *Quadrennial Defense Review Report 2010*, 42.
18. O'Hanlon, "End Two-War Planning."
19. Lostumbo et al., *Overseas Basing of U.S. Military Forces*, 287.
20. Johnson, *Sorrows of Empire*; Lutz, *Bases of Empire*.
21. O'Hanlon, *Unfinished Business*, 22–23.
22. Layne, *Peace of Illusions*, 190.
23. Flournoy and Davidson, "Obama's New Global Posture," 56.
24. It is, in fact, astonishing that for eight years the United States carried on two simultaneous wars under CENTCOM and never split the command—yet another small data point that may help explain the lack of coherence and focus in both wars.
25. Krepinevich and Work, *New Global Defense Posture*, iii.
26. See the National Security Act of 1947, Section 503, and Executive Order 12333, Section 3.4(h).
27. See Schroen, *First In*; Owen and Maurer, *No Easy Day*; and Bergen, *Manhunt*.

28. Dan Lothian and Reza Sayah, "Obama's Drone Comment Was No Slip-up, Official Says," CNN, January 31, 2012. One of the original reports on Stuxnet is David Sanger, "Obama Order Sped Up Wave of Cyberattacks against Iran," *New York Times*, June 1, 2012.

29. Sanger, *Confront and Conceal*, is probably the most mainstream attempt at publicly describing covert aspects of contemporary US foreign policy, though, of course, it cannot be corroborated.

30. Byman, "Why Drones Work"; Cronin, "Why Drones Fail"; Bergen and Tiedemann, "Washington's Phantom War."

31. Zenko, *Reforming U.S. Drone Strike Policies*.

32. Muravchik, *Exporting Democracy*, chap. 9.

33. Gates, *From the Shadows*, 237–38, 358, 450–51.

34. Neustadt, *Presidential Power*; Destler, "National Security Advice." See Zegart, *Flawed by Design*, which summarizes and criticizes this view.

35. See Miller, "Organizing the NSC," for a longer treatment of this issue.

36. Council on Foreign Relations, "The NSC at 50."

Conclusion

The history of American diplomacy is the story of American statesmen wielding American power and championing liberal ideals—never with perfect consistency, often in uneasy balance, and leavened by pragmatism and realpolitik. But American statesmen consistently believe that American security is well served when liberal ideals gain ground abroad. They are right: American security and liberal order are mutually constitutive. Liberal order is the outer perimeter of American security.

In service of this grand strategy, the United States has adopted a five-pronged approach to the world. It balances against the autocratic great powers, champions liberalism, undertakes kinetic operations against armed nonstate groups, invests in good governance abroad, and protects the homeland. This set of goals serves American security and sustains liberal order. This grand strategy is superior to restraint because it is more farsighted and morally defensible. It is superior to liberal internationalism because it is more realistic and achievable. Promoting democracy and capitalism and undertaking stability operations can be both feasible and cost-effective.

The contemporary security environment is rife with threats to American security and liberal order, including nuclear autocracies, armed nonstate groups, and jihadists. America's grand strategy needs adjustments to meet the challenges of the twenty-first century. Throughout this book, I have recommended a variety of tweaks, including a framework for better prioritizing regions, issues, and problems around the world; forming a Pacific Alliance; creating a South Asia Command; deemphasizing the Middle East; establishing an MI5-like domestic intelligence agency; institutionalizing stability operations as a core mission for the US military; and vastly increasing foreign aid. I conclude with a brief recommendation on how to tweak US grand strategy to better meet the challenge of the transnational jihadist movement. I place this discussion here not because it is the most important issue but because the issue requires the full picture of US grand strategy for perspective.

The Jihadist Insurgency

The five strategic objectives of US grand strategy complement and reinforce one another. This is nowhere more evident than in the US efforts against the transnational jihadist movement. It is crucial that the United States and its allies prevent any jihadist movement from seizing state power anywhere else in the world. Another jihadist regime—whether in Yemen, Somalia, Iraq, Syria, Afghanistan, or Pakistan—would provide additional safe haven and state resources for jihadist groups, significantly magnifying the threat they pose to the United States. Their victory in Pakistan, with its nuclear weapons, or Saudi Arabia, with its oil wealth, would be a major threat to American security and liberal order.

The United States cannot aim at the military defeat of every jihadist group worldwide, which would require US troops in combat from Morocco to Indonesia. Rather, the United States should take direct action only against actors who directly target Americans or threaten to overwhelm local security forces while, as David Kilcullen argues, seeking to "disaggregate" the collection of jihadist movements by severing the ties—fund-raising, communications, and travel—between them and supporting local counterinsurgency and counterterrorism efforts led by local governments.[1]

That suggests that the goals of US-led global efforts against jihadist movements should be, first, to thwart attacks by jihadist groups; second, to defeat central nodes, such as al-Qaida, that tie the disparate networks together or aspire to global operational reach; third, to prevent any jihadist group from seizing additional state power; fourth, to counter Iran's and Pakistan's efforts to use jihadist groups to expand their influence; fifth, to empower local security forces across the world to defeat local jihadist chapters; and sixth, where possible, to roll back the size and influence of jihadist groups and ideology.

In other words, the US strategy against the jihadist movement is simply to implement its grand strategy as a whole. It must defend the homeland by making it harder for jihadists to travel to the United States and constructing more effective internal security measures. It must take direct action against jihadist terrorist groups. It must balance against Iran and Pakistan to limit their ability to use jihadist groups. It must empower local governments through aid, assistance, and training to shrink the space in which such groups can operate. And it must champion liberalism as an alternative ideology.

The United States has made significant progress protecting the homeland through aforementioned initiatives such as the terrorist watch list and biometric passports. It has also made progress degrading al-Qaida's capabilities by evicting it from Afghanistan in 2001 and through the rumored drone program since 2004. It has also provided substantial assistance to other states, such as Pakistan, to bolster their security forces (though that should be reevaluated along with US policy toward Pakistan as a whole). Some jihadist groups, such as the Islamic Movement of Uzbekistan and the Abu Sayyaf Group in the Philippines, have been crippled perhaps beyond recovery by US and allied counterterrorism operations. In some cases the United States has successfully intervened to prevent a jihadist group from taking power, as when it reportedly aided the Ethiopian invasion of Somalia to topple the Islamic Courts Union.[2]

But the United States has suffered some significant setbacks. Homeland security still has weaknesses, as several near misses since 2001 attest. Iran has emerged strengthened by the overthrow of Iraq's regime and the 2015 nuclear deal. New jihadist movements have emerged in the Middle East, South Asia, and North Africa. In Iraq, al-Qaida and its sympathizers played a key role in plunging Iraq into chaos and civil war in 2006–7. US and Iraqi forces dealt the group a severe setback from 2007 to 2009, but after the United States' premature withdrawal in 2011, jihadists reconstituted themselves as ISIS and joined up with jihadists fighting the Assad regime in Syria. In Afghanistan, the Obama administration has largely repeated its error from Iraq, withdrawing almost all US troops before local forces are prepared to sustain the fight against the Taliban alone, ensuring continued safe haven for al-Qaida, the Taliban, and their allies in the Afghanistan–Pakistan border region. Jihadist groups have failed to mount another large-scale attack on the US homeland, but there are more groups, across a wider swath of the world, that are more capable and, possibly, more popular than they were in 2001. The United States is not winning the war.

The war against jihadist groups is not the most important issue on the national security agenda, and Americans are understandably war-weary and dispirited after setbacks in Iraq and Afghanistan. Nonetheless, the war is not over, it remains vitally important, and Americans cannot simply choose to stop fighting. It is overwhelmingly likely that jihadist groups will continue to thrive, operate, plan, train, and target US interests, bases, personnel, and the homeland. The end of the war is not in sight because the United States has not come to grips with the essential conditions of victory. It has created an impressive and efficient terrorist-killing machine in its Special Operations Forces and covert operations, but these units and tactics can only buy time for a political solution to take hold. Attempting to end the war by killing every jihadist and potential jihadist in the world misunderstands the nature of war, is unrealistic, would take decades, and is unjust. The war will continue until jihadism is discredited as an ideology—which is a political, not a military, achievement. The failure to build an alternative political order after World War I caused the Allies to lose the peace, which is why they invested a

staggering amount of time and treasure in the reconstruction of the political
and economic structures of Europe and Japan after World War II.

The United States lost the war in Iraq not because it was militarily
defeated but because it failed to build a viable political order. It is repeating
the same mistake in Afghanistan. It is as certain as anything can be in the
unpredictable world of global politics that the United States will find itself
threatened again by chaos, tyranny, and violence emanating from the Middle
East and South Asia, much of it sown by the United States' earlier missteps
and failures. The withdrawals from Iraq and Afghanistan are likely to be seen
as the Versailles of the War on Terror—catastrophic diplomatic errors that
made vain years of military sacrifice and planted the seeds for future conflict.
When the United States reengages, it is vital that it do so with the lessons of
Iraq and Afghanistan in mind: The goal in war is the construction of a better
peace. Without a plan to build a better peace, political violence will continue,
unchecked, indefinitely, to the determinant of human lives, American security, and world order.

Liberalism is key to the construction of a better peace. Despite the United
States' failures in Iraq and Afghanistan, promoting democracy should remain
a key part of the US global efforts to undermine jihadist movements. In any
conflict, a successful strategy must include an attack on the rival's ideology
and the advancement of a competing set of ideas. The United States needs
a narrative or a set of ideas that legitimizes and sells its efforts around the
world. That means the United States and, much more so, its allies and partners
across the world must engage in the war of ideas and persuade the peoples of
the world that there is an alternative to jihadist ideology. President Obama
hinted at these themes in his June 2009 Cairo speech and his May 2011 speech
about the Arab Spring, but President Bush gave the clearest expression to them
when he told the National Endowment for Democracy in late 2005 that a key
"element of our strategy in the war on terror is to deny the militants future
recruits by replacing hatred and resentment with democracy and hope across
the broader Middle East." Democracy undermines terrorism because "if the
peoples of that region are permitted to choose their own destiny, and advance
by their own energy and by their participation as free men and women, then
the extremists will be marginalized, and the flow of violent radicalism to the
rest of the world will slow, and eventually end." This, in turn, would enhance
US security: "By standing for the hope and freedom of others, we make our
own freedom more secure."[3] The controversy that attended the invasion and
occupation of Iraq should not detract from the basic validity of democratization as a component of US strategy against violent jihadist movements.[4]

Concluding with a call to use liberalism to combat jihadists may seem at
odds with the notes of moderation and pragmatism I have tried to highlight

in this book. What I have tried to illustrate is that, in the long run, it is the *most* pragmatic option, and, in the moral frameworks I have invoked, there is no alternative. Grounding foreign policy in liberal ideals, even at the expense of some hypocrisy and moral compromise, is infinitely more defensible than grounding them in no ideals at all. Reinhold Niebuhr was clear-eyed about the prospects for achieving the just, lasting, and democratic peace he wished for. It is, frankly, unlikely. And if it ever happens, it may be centuries from now and is more likely to be achieved by gradual evolution than by the orchestrated policy of a crusading democratic superpower. Global democracy is a distant dream; we dare not treat it like an objective to be pursued on a fixed timetable or to be achieved in our lifetime. But dream-inspired hopes save us from cynical acceptance of the world's present evils. That is perhaps what Niebuhr meant when he wrote, "Nothing that is worth doing can be achieved in our lifetime; therefore we must be saved by hope."[5]

Notes

1. David Kilcullen, "Countering Global Insurgency," in Mahnken and Maiolo, *Strategic Studies*, 326–41.
2. Martin Plaut, "Ethiopia in Somalia: One Year On," BBC News, December 28, 2007.
3. Bush, "Remarks to National Endowment."
4. See Gause, "Can Democracy Stop Terrorism?" and Dobriansky, Crumpton, and Gause, "Tyranny and Terror," for discussions of democracy and terrorism.
5. Niebuhr, *Irony*, 63.

BIBLIOGRAPHY

Abbas, Hassan. *Pakistan's Drift into Extremism: Allah, the Army, and America's War on Terror*. Armonk, NY: M. E. Sharpe, 2004.

Acharya, Amitav. "Power Shift or Paradigm Shift? China's Rise and Asia's Emerging Security Order." *International Studies Quarterly* 58, no. 1 (2014): 158–73. http://dx.doi.org/10.1111/isqu.12084.

Adelman, Kenneth. "Japan's Security Dilemma: An American View." *Survival* 23, no. 2 (1981): 72–79. http://dx.doi.org/10.1080/00396338108441953.

Ajami, Fouad. "The Arab Spring at One: A Year of Living Dangerously." *Foreign Affairs* 91, no. 2 (2012): 56–65.

Altunbaş, Yener, and John Thornton. "The (Small) Blessing of Foreign Aid: Further Evidence on Aid's Impact on Democracy." *Applied Economics* 46, no. 32 (2014): 3922–30. http://dx.doi.org/10.1080/00036846.2014.946186.

American Foreign Service Association. "Department of State: Full-Time Permanent Employees." http://www.afsa.org/sites/default/files/Portals/0/0313_bureau_loc.pdf. Accessed January 15, 2016.

American Petroleum Institute. *Basic Petroleum Data Book*. Washington, DC: American Petroleum Institute, 1975.

Anderson, Lisa. "Demystifying the Arab Spring: Parsing the Differences between Tunisia, Egypt, and Libya." *Foreign Affairs* 90, no. 3 (2011): 2–7.

Andres, Richard, Craig Wills, and Thomas Griffith, Jr. "Winning with Allies: The Strategic Value of the Afghan Model." *International Security* 30, no. 3 (2005): 124–60. http://dx.doi.org/10.1162/016228805775969591.

Aristotle. *Nicomachean Ethics*. Translated by Martin Ostwald. New York: Macmillan, 1962.

Art, Robert. "A Defensible Defense: America's Grand Strategy after the Cold War." *International Security* 15, no. 4 (1991): 5–53. http://dx.doi.org/10.2307/2539010.

———. *A Grand Strategy for America*. Ithaca, NY: Cornell University Press, 2013.

Art, Robert, and Kenneth Waltz, eds. *The Use of Force: Military Power and International Politics*. Lanham, MD: Rowman & Littlefield, 2009.

Babones, Salvatore. "The Middling Kingdom: The Hype and the Reality of China's Rise." *Foreign Affairs* 90, no. 5 (2011): 79–88.

Barbashin, Anton, and Hannah Thoburn. "Putin's Brain: Alexander Dugin and the Philosophy behind Putin's Invasion of Crimea." *ForeignAffairs.com*, March 31,

2014. https://www.foreignaffairs.com/articles/russia-fsu/2014-03-31/putins-brain. Accessed January 15, 2016.

Barfield, Thomas. *Afghanistan: A Cultural and Political History*. Princeton, NJ: Princeton University Press, 2010. http://dx.doi.org/10.1515/9781400834532.

Barno, David. *Responsible Transition: Securing U.S. Interests in Afghanistan beyond 2011*. Washington, DC: Center for a New American Security, 2010.

Bartlett, Christopher. *"The Special Relationship": A Political History of Anglo–American Relations since 1945*. Boston: Addison-Wesley Longman, 1992.

Bearce, David, and Sawa Omori. "How Do Commercial Institutions Promote Peace?" *Journal of Peace Research* 42, no. 6 (2005): 659–78. http://dx.doi.org/10.1177/0022343305057886.

Bearce, David, Steven E. Finkel, Anibal S. Pérez-Liñán, Juan Rodriguez-Zepeda, and Lena Surzhko-Harned. "Has the New Aid for Trade Agenda Been Export Effective?" *International Studies Quarterly* 57, no. 1 (2013): 163–70. http://dx.doi.org/10.1111/isqu.12027.

Beckley, Michael. "China's Century? Why America's Edge Will Endure." *International Security* 36, no. 3 (Winter 2011/12): 41–78. http://dx.doi.org/10.1162/ISEC_a_00066.

Behrman, Greg. *The Most Noble Adventure: The Marshall Plan and the Time When America Helped Save Europe*. New York: Simon & Schuster, 2007.

Bell, Daniel M. *Just War as Christian Discipleship*. Eugene, OR: Wipf & Stock, 2005.

Bellamy, Alex J., and Paul D. Williams. "The West and Contemporary Peace Operations." *Journal of Peace Research* 46, no. 1 (2009): 39–57. http://dx.doi.org/10.1177/0022343308098403.

Bellin, Eva. "Reconsidering the Robustness of Authoritarianism in the Middle East: Lessons from the Arab Spring." *Comparative Politics* 44, no. 2 (2012): 127–49. http://dx.doi.org/10.5129/001041512798838021.

Benjamin, Daniel, and Steven Simon. *The Age of Sacred Terror*. Vol. 14. New York: Random House, 2002.

Bergen, Peter L. *Manhunt: The Ten-Year Search for Bin Laden—from 9/11 to Abbottabad*. Toronto: Doubleday Canada, 2012.

Bergen, Peter, and Katherine Tiedemann. "Washington's Phantom War: The Effects of the US Drone Program in Pakistan." *Foreign Affairs* 90, no. 4 (2011): 12–18.

Berman, Sheri. "The Promise of the Arab Spring: In Political Development, No Gain without Pain." *Foreign Affairs* 92, no. 1 (2013): 64–74.

Betts, Richard K. "Is Strategy an Illusion?" *International Security* 25, no. 2 (2000): 5–50. http://dx.doi.org/10.1162/016228800560444.

———. "Pick Your Battles." *Foreign Affairs* 93, no. 6 (2014): 15–24.

Biddle, Stephen. "Afghanistan's Legacy: Emerging Lessons of an Ongoing War." *Washington Quarterly* 37, no. 2 (2014): 73–86. http://dx.doi.org/10.1080/0163660X.2014.926210.

Biddle, Stephen D. "Allies, Airpower, and Modern Warfare: The Afghan Model in Afghanistan and Iraq." (2006). http://dx.doi.org/10.1162/isec.2005.30.3.161.

———. *American Grand Strategy after 9/11: An Assessment*. Collingdale, PA: Diane Publishing, 2005.

Biddle, Stephen, Jeffrey A. Friedman, and Jacob N. Shapiro. "Testing the Surge: Why Did Violence Decline in Iraq in 2007?" *International Security* 37, no. 1 (2012): 7–40. http://dx.doi.org/10.1162/ISEC_a_00087.

Biddle, Stephen, Jeffrey A. Friedman, and Stephen Long. "Civil War Intervention and the Problem of Iraq." *International Studies Quarterly* 56, no. 1 (2012): 85–98. http://dx.doi.org/10.1111/j.1468-2478.2011.00705.x.

Blackwill, Robert D., Naresh Chandra, and Christopher Clary. *The United States and India: A Shared Strategic Future.* New York: Council on Foreign Relations, 2011.

Bolger, Daniel. *Why We Lost: A General's Inside Account of the Iraq and Afghanistan Wars.* Boston: Houghton Mifflin Harcourt, 2014.

Boot, Max. "More Small Wars: Counterinsurgency Is Here to Stay." *Foreign Affairs* 93, no. 6 (2014): 5–14.

Borgerson, Scott. *The National Interest and the Law of the Sea.* New York: Council on Foreign Relations, 2009.

Bouchet, Nicolas. "The Democracy Tradition in U.S. Foreign Policy and the Obama Presidency." *International Affairs* 89, no. 1 (2013): 31–51. http://dx.doi.org/10.1111/1468-2346.12003.

Bowden, Mark. *Killing Pablo: The Inside Story of the Manhunt to Bring Down the Most Powerful Criminal in History.* London: Atlantic Books, 2009.

Boyle, Michael J. "The War on Terror in American Grand Strategy." *International Affairs* 84, no. 2 (2008): 191–209. http://dx.doi.org/10.1111/j.1468-2346.2008.00699.x.

Brands, Hal. *What Good Is Grand Strategy? Power and Purpose in American Statecraft from Harry S. Truman to George W. Bush.* Ithaca, NY: Cornell University Press, 2014.

Brennan, Rick. "Withdrawal Symptoms." *Foreign Affairs* 93, no. 6 (2014): 25–36.

Breslin, Shaun. "China and the Global Order: Signaling Threat or Friendship?" *International Affairs* 89, no. 3 (2013): 615–34. http://dx.doi.org/10.1111/1468-2346.12036.

British Petroleum. *Statistical Review of the World Oil Industry, 1980.*

Brooks, Stephen G., G. John Ikenberry, and William C. Wohlforth. "Don't Come Home, America: The Case against Retrenchment." *International Security* 37, no. 3 (Winter 2012/13): 7–51. http://dx.doi.org/10.1162/ISEC_a_00107.

Brown, Michael Edward, Sean M. Lynn-Jones, and Steven E. Miller, eds. *Debating the Democratic Peace.* Cambridge, MA: MIT Press, 1996.

Brown, Seyom, and Robert H. Scales, eds. *US Policy in Afghanistan and Iraq: Lessons and Legacies.* Vol. 1. Boulder, CO: Lynne Rienner Publishers, 2012.

Bryden, Alan, and Marina Caparini. *Private Actors and Security Governance.* Münster: Lit Verlag, 2006.

Burns, Nicholas. "Passage to India: What Washington Can Do to Revive Relations with New Delhi." *Foreign Affairs* 93, no. 5 (2014): 132–41.

Bush, George W. "Remarks to the National Endowment for Democracy." October 6, 2005. *Weekly Compilation of Presidential Documents* 41, no. 40 (2005): 1502–9.

———. "Second Inaugural Address." January 20, 2005, Washington, DC.

Byman, Daniel. "An Autopsy of the Iraq Debacle: Policy Failure or Bridge Too Far?" *Security Studies* 17, no. 4 (2008): 599–643. http://dx.doi.org/10.1080/09636410802507974.

———. "Friends like These: Counterinsurgency and the War on Terrorism." *International Security* 31, no. 2 (2006): 79–115. http://dx.doi.org/10.1162/isec.2006.31.2.79.

———. "Why Drones Work: The Case for Washington's Weapon of Choice." *Foreign Affairs* 92, no. 4 (2013): 32–43.

Carlucci, Frank, and Ian Brzezinski. *State Department Reform.* New York: Council on Foreign Relations, 2001.

Carothers, Thomas. *Aiding Democracy Abroad: The Learning Curve.* Washington, DC: Carnegie Endowment for International Peace, 2011.

———. *Critical Mission: Essays on Democracy Promotion.* Washington, DC: Carnegie Endowment for International Peace, 2004.

———. "The End of the Transition Paradigm." *Journal of Democracy* 13, no. 1 (2002): 5–21. http://dx.doi.org/10.1353/jod.2002.0003.

Carter, Ashton, and William James Perry. *A New Concept of Cooperative Security.* Washington, DC: Brookings Institution Press, 1992.

Carter, Jimmy. "The State of the Union Address." January 23, 1980. Gerhard Peters and John Woolley, American Presidency Project. http://www.presidency.ucsb .edu/ws/index.php?pid=33079. Accessed on January 14, 2016.

Center for Strategic and International Studies. "Significant Cyber Incidents since 2006." http://csis.org/files/publication/140310_Significant_Cyber_Incidents_Since _2006.pdf. Accessed March 21, 2015.

Chandler, David. *Empire in Denial: The Politics of State-Building.* London: Pluto, 2006.

Chandrasekaran, Rajiv. *Little America: The War within the War for Afghanistan.* New York: Knopf, 2012.

Charap, Samuel. "The Ukraine Impasse." *Survival* 56, no. 5 (2014): 225–32. http:// dx.doi.org/10.1080/00396338.2014.962813.

Charap, Samuel, and Keith Darden. "Russia and Ukraine." *Survival* 56, no. 2 (2014): 7–14. http://dx.doi.org/10.1080/00396338.2014.901726.

Christensen, Thomas J. "Fostering Stability or Creating a Monster? The Rise of China and U.S. Policy toward East Asia." *International Security* 31, no. 1 (2006): 81–126. http://dx.doi.org/10.1162/isec.2006.31.1.81.

Clausewitz, Carl von. *On War.* Edited and translated by Michael Howard and Peter Paret. Princeton, NJ: Princeton University Press, 1984.

Cohen, Stephen. *The Idea of Pakistan.* Washington, DC: Brookings Institution Press, 2004.

Coll, Steve. *Ghost Wars: The Secret History of the CIA, Afghanistan, and Bin Laden, from the Soviet Invasion to September 10, 2001.* London: Penguin, 2004.

Collier, Paul. *Breaking the Conflict Trap: Civil War and Development Policy.* Washington, DC: World Bank Publications, 2003.

Collins, Joseph. *Understanding the War in Afghanistan: A Guide to the Land, the People, and the Conflict.* New York: Skyhorse Publishing, 2013.

Combined Maritime Forces. "CTF-151: Counter-Piracy." http://combinedmaritime-forces.com/ctf-151-counter-piracy/. Accessed March 24, 2015.

Congressional Research Service. "Direct Overt U.S. Aid Appropriations for and Military Reimbursements to Pakistan, FY2002–2016." http://www.fas.org/sgp/crs /row/pakaid.pdf. Accessed October 28, 2015.

Considerations for an American Grand Strategy: Hearings before the House Armed Service Committee, 110th Cong. (2008).

Copeland, Dale. *The Origins of Major War*. Ithaca, NY: Cornell University Press, 2000.

Cordesman, Anthony. *Afghanistan and Iraq: Learning the Lessons of Worst Case Wars*. Washington, DC: Center for Strategic and International Studies, 2014.

Council on Foreign Relations. "The NSC at 50: Past, Present, and Future." Transcript of roundtable discussion, October 31, 1997. http://www.cfr.org/history-and-theory-of-international-relations/nsc-50-past-present-future/p64. Accessed January 15, 2016.

Cox, Michael, John Ikenberry, and Takashi Inoguchi. *American Democracy Promotion*. Oxford: Oxford University Press, 2000. http://dx.doi.org/10.1093/0199240973.001.0001.

Cox, Michael, Nicolas Bouchet, and Timothy Lynch, eds. *U.S. Foreign Policy and Democracy Promotion*. London: Routledge, 2013.

Crandall, Russell. "Clinton, Bush and Plan Colombia." *Survival* 44, no. 1 (2002): 159–72. http://dx.doi.org/10.1093/survival/44.1.159.

Cronin, Audrey Kurth. "Why Drones Fail: When Tactics Drive Strategy." *Foreign Affairs* 92, no. 4 (2013): 44–54.

Cronin, Audrey Kurth, and James Ludes, eds. *Attacking Terrorism: Elements of a Grand Strategy*. Washington, DC: Georgetown University Press, 2004.

Cronin, Patrick. *Restraint: Recalibrating American Strategy*. Washington, DC: Center for a New American Security, 2010.

Crowdy, Terry. *The Enemy Within: A History of Spies, Spymasters and Espionage*. Oxford: Osprey Publishing, 2011.

Daalder, Ivo, and James Goldgeier. "Global NATO." *Foreign Affairs* 85, no. 5 (2006): 105–13. http://dx.doi.org/10.2307/20032073.

Dasgupta, Sunil, and Stephen Cohen. "Arms Sales for India: How Military Trade Could Energize U.S.–Indian Relations." *Foreign Affairs* 90, no. 2 (2011): 22–26.

Davidson, Janine. *Retrench or Rebalance? America's Evolving Defence Strategy*. Research paper. Catham House, Royal Institute of International Affairs, September 2014.

Davis, Lynn, Stacie Pettyjohn, Milanie Sisson, Stephen M. Worman, and Michael J. McNerney. *U.S. Overseas Military Presence: What Are the Strategic Choices?* Santa Monica, CA: RAND, 2012.

Demirel-Pegg, Tijen, and James Moskowitz. "U.S. Aid Allocation: The Nexus of Human Rights, Democracy, and Development." *Journal of Peace Research* 46, no. 2 (2009): 181–98. http://dx.doi.org/10.1177/0022343308100714.

Destler, I. M. "National Security Advice to U.S. Presidents: Some Lessons from Thirty Years." *World Politics* 29, no. 2 (1977): 143–76. http://dx.doi.org/10.2307/2010089.

Deudney, Daniel, and John Ikenberry. *Democratic Internationalism: An American Grand Strategy for a Post-Exceptionalist Era*. New York: Council on Foreign Relations, 2012.

Deutsch, Karl. *Political Community and the North Atlantic Area: International Organization in the Light of Historical Experience*. Princeton, NJ: Princeton University Press, 1957.

Diamond, Larry. *The Spirit of Democracy: The Struggle to Build Free Societies through-out the World*. London: Macmillan, 2008.

Dobbins, James. "War with China." *Survival* 54, no. 4 (2012): 7–24. http://dx.doi.org/10.1080/00396338.2012.709384.

Dobriansky, Paula, Henry Crumpton, and Gregory Gause. "Tyranny and Terror: Will Democracy in the Middle East Make Us Safer? Aiming High." *Foreign Affairs* 85, no. 1 (2006): 135–38. http://dx.doi.org/10.2307/20031849.

Doyle, Michael W. "Kant, Liberal Legacies, and Foreign Affairs." *Philosophy and Public Affairs* 12, no. 3 (1983): 205–35.

"Drone Wars Pakistan: Analysis." Data site and interactive Internet resource. New America Foundation. http://securitydata.newamerica.net/drones/pakistan/analysis.html. Accessed October 28, 2015.

Dueck, Colin. *Reluctant Crusaders: Power, Culture, and Change in American Grand Strategy*. Princeton, NJ: Princeton University Press, 2008. http://dx.doi.org/10.1515/9781400827220.

Dumbrell, John. *A Special Relationship: Anglo–American Relations from the Cold War to Iraq*. London: Palgrave Macmillan, 2006.

Economy, Elizabeth. "The Game Changer: Coping with China's Foreign Policy Revolution." *Foreign Affairs* 89, no. 6 (2010): 142–52.

Edelman, Eric. *Understanding America's Contested Primacy*. Washington, DC: Center for Strategic and Budgetary Assessments, 2010.

Edelman, Eric, Andrew F. Krepinevich, and Evan Montgomery. "The Dangers of a Nuclear Iran: The Limits of Containment." *Foreign Affairs* 90, no. 1 (2011): 66–81.

Elie, Paul. "A Man for All Reasons." *Atlantic Monthly* 300, no. 4 (2007): 82–96.

Elkus, Adam. "Must American Strategy Be Grand?" *Infinity Journal* 3, no. 1 (Winter 2012): 24–28.

Englehart, Neil. "State Capacity, State Failure, and Human Rights." *Journal of Peace Research* 46, no. 2 (2009): 163–80. http://dx.doi.org/10.1177/0022343308100713.

Epstein, Rachel. "NATO Enlargement and the Spread of Democracy: Evidence and Expectations." *Security Studies* 14, no. 1 (2005): 63–105. http://dx.doi.org/10.1080/09636410591002509.

Esposito, Chiarella. *America's Feeble Weapon: Funding the Marshall Plan in France and Italy, 1948–1950*. Santa Barbara, CA: Greenwood Publishing Group, 1994.

Etzioni, Amitai. "Is China a Responsible Stakeholder?" *International Affairs* 87, no. 3 (2011): 539–53. http://dx.doi.org/10.1111/j.1468-2346.2011.00989.x.

Fairweather, Jack. *The Good War: Why We Couldn't Win the War or the Peace in Afghanistan*. New York: Random House, 2014.

Farwell, James, and Rafal Rohozinski. "Stuxnet and the Future of Cyber War." *Survival* 53, no. 1 (2011): 23–40. http://dx.doi.org/10.1080/00396338.2011.555586.

Fearon, James, and David Laitin. "Neotrusteeship and the Problem of Weak States." *International Security* 28, no. 4 (2004): 5–43. http://dx.doi.org/10.1162/0162288041588296.

Feaver, Peter. "Debating American Grand Strategy after Major War." *Orbis* 53, no. 4 (2009): 547–52.

Federation of American Scientists. "Status of World Nuclear Forces." http://fas
.org/issues/nuclear-weapons/status-world-nuclear-forces/. Accessed March 19,
2015.

Ferguson, Niall. "Sinking Globalization." *Foreign Affairs* 84, no. 2 (2005): 64–77.

Fingar, Thomas. "Intelligence and Grand Strategy." *Orbis* 56, no. 1 (2012): 118–34.
http://dx.doi.org/10.1016/j.orbis.2011.10.006.

Finnemore, Martha. "Legitimacy, Hypocrisy, and the Social Structure of Unipolarity." *World Politics* 61, no. 1 (2009): 58–85. http://dx.doi.org/10.1017
/S0043887109000082.

Fischer, Eric, Edward Liu, John Rollins, and Catherine A. Theohary. *The 2013 Cybersecurity Executive Order: Overview and Considerations for Congress.* Washington,
DC: Congressional Research Service, 2013.

Fitzpatrick, Mark. "North Korea: Is Regime Change the Answer?" *Survival* 55, no. 3
(2013): 7–20. http://dx.doi.org/10.1080/00396338.2013.802848.

Flournoy, Michele, and Janine Davidson. "Obama's New Global Posture." *Foreign
Affairs* 91, no. 4 (July/August 2012): 54–63.

Forsberg, Randall. "Toward the End of War." *Boston Review* 22, no. 5 (1997): 4–9.

Franke, Volker, and Robert H. Dorff, eds. *Conflict Management and Peacebuilding:
Pillars of a New American Grand Strategy.* Carlisle, PA: Strategic Studies Institute,
2013.

Fravel, M. Taylor. "Power Shifts and Escalation: Explaining China's Use of Force in
Territorial Disputes." *International Security* 32, no. 3 (Winter 2007/8): 44–83.
http://dx.doi.org/10.1162/isec.2008.32.3.44.

Freedman, Lawrence. *Strategy: A History*. Oxford: Oxford University Press, 2013.

———. "Ukraine and the Art of Limited War." *Survival* 56, no. 6 (2014): 7–38. http://
dx.doi.org/10.1080/00396338.2014.985432.

Freedom House. *Freedom in the World 2011*. Washington, DC: Freedom House, 2011.
https://freedomhouse.org/report/freedom-world/2011/mexico. Accessed January 14, 2016.

Friedberg, Aaron. *A Contest for Supremacy: China, America, and the Struggle for Mas-
tery in Asia*. New York: Norton, 2011.

———. "The Future of U.S.–China Relations: Is Conflict Inevitable?" *International
Security* 30, no. 2 (2005): 7–45. http://dx.doi.org/10.1162/016228805775124589.

Friedman, Benjamin, Harvey Sapolsky, and Christopher Preble. *Learning the Right
Lessons from Iraq*. Washington, DC: Cato Institute, 2008.

The Fund for Peace. *Fragile States Index 2014*. Washington, DC: Fund for Peace, 2014.

Gaddis, John Lewis. *The Cold War: A New History*. New York: Penguin, 2006.

———. *George F. Kennan: An American Life*. New York: Penguin, 2011.

———. "A Grand Strategy of Transformation." *Foreign Policy*, no. 133 (2002): 50–57.
http://dx.doi.org/10.2307/3183557.

———. *Strategies of Containment: A Critical Appraisal of Postwar American National
Security Policy*. Vol. 690. Oxford: Oxford University Press, 1982.

———. *We Now Know: Rethinking Cold War History*. New York: Council on Foreign
Relations, 1997.

Galeotti, Mark, and Andrew S. Bowen. "Putin's Empire of the Mind." *Foreign Policy* 206 (2014): 16–19.

Gall, Carlotta. *The Wrong Enemy: America in Afghanistan, 2001–2014.* Boston: Houghton Mifflin Harcourt, 2014.

Gallagher, Mary. "'Reform and Openness': Why China's Economic Reforms Have Delayed Democracy." *World Politics* 54, no. 3 (2002): 338–72. http://dx.doi. org/10.1353/wp.2002.0009.

Gartzke, Erik. "The Capitalist Peace." *American Journal of Political Science* 51, no. 1 (2007): 166–91. http://dx.doi.org/10.1111/j.1540-5907.2007.00244.x.

Gates, Robert. *From the Shadows: The Ultimate Insider's Story of Five Presidents and How They Won the Cold War.* New York: Simon & Schuster, 1996.

———. "Landon Lecture." Speech at Kansas State University, Manhattan, Kansas, November 26, 2007.

Gause, F. Gregory, III. "Can Democracy Stop Terrorism?" *Foreign Affairs* 84, no. 5 (2005): 62–76. http://dx.doi.org/10.2307/20031706.

Geertz, Clifford. *The Interpretation of Cultures: Selected Essays.* New York: Basic Books, 1973.

Gentile, Gian. *Wrong Turn: America's Deadly Embrace of Counterinsurgency.* New York: The New Press, 2013.

Gentile, Gian P. "A Strategy of Tactics: Population-Centric COIN and the Army." *Parameters* 39, no. 3 (2009): 5–26.

Gholz, Eugene, Daryl G. Press, and Harvey M. Sapolsky. "Come Home, America: The Strategy of Restraint in the Face of Temptation." *International Security* 21, no. 4 (1997): 5–48. http://dx.doi.org/10.1162/isec.21.4.5.

Gibbs, Robert. "Press Briefing by Press Secretary Robert Gibbs." January 27, 2011. Gerhard Peters and John Woolley, American Presidency Project. http://www .presidency.ucsb.edu/ws/index.php?pid=88945. Accessed on January 17, 2016.

Gilman, Nils. *Mandarins of the Future: Modernization Theory in Cold War America.* Baltimore: Johns Hopkins University Press, 2003.

Gilpin, Robert. *War and Change in World Politics.* New York: Cambridge University Press, 1983.

Giustozzi, Antonio. *Koran, Kalashnikov, and Laptop: The Neo-Taliban Insurgency in Afghanistan.* New York: Columbia University Press, 2008.

Glaser, Charles. "Why NATO Is Still Best: Future Security Arrangements for Europe." *International Security* 18, no. 1 (1993): 5–50. http://dx.doi.org/10.2307/2539031.

———. "Will China's Rise Lead to War? Why Realism Does Not Mean Pessimism." *Foreign Affairs* 90, no. 2 (2011): 80–91.

Goldgeier, James. "NATO Expansion: The Anatomy of a Decision." *Washington Quarterly* 21, no. 1 (1998): 83–102. http://dx.doi.org/10.1080/01636609809550295.

Goldsmith, Arthur. "Making the World Safe for Partial Democracy? Questioning the Premises of Democracy Promotion." *International Security* 33, no. 2 (2008): 120–47. http://dx.doi.org/10.1162/isec.2008.33.2.120.

Gompert, David. "North Korea: Preparing for the End." *Survival* 55, no. 3 (2013): 21–46. http://dx.doi.org/10.1080/00396338.2013.802849.

Gordon, Michael, and Bernard E. Trainor. *Cobra II: The Inside Story of the Invasion and Occupation of Iraq*. New York: Vintage Books, 2006.

———. *The Endgame: The Inside Story of the Struggle for Iraq, from George W. Bush to Barack Obama*. New York: Pantheon, 2012.

Graham, Thomas. "The Sources of Russia's Insecurity." *Survival* 52, no. 1 (2010): 55–74. http://dx.doi.org/10.1080/00396331003612471.

Gray, Colin S. "The 21st Century Security Environment and the Future of War." *Parameters* 38, no. 4 (2008): 14–26.

Greenstein, Fred. *The Hidden-Hand Presidency: Eisenhower as Leader*. New York: Basic Books, 1982.

Grotto, Andrew. "Is Iran a Martyr State?" *Brown Journal of World Affairs* 16, no. 1 (2009): 45–58.

Gventer, Celeste Ward. "Counterinsurgency and Its Critics." *Journal of Strategic Studies* 37, no. 4 (2014): 637–63. http://dx.doi.org/10.1080/01402390.2014.944338.

Habeck, Mary. *Knowing the Enemy: Jihadist Ideology and the War on Terror*. New Haven, CT: Yale University Press, 2006.

Hallams, Ellen, and Benjamin Schreer. "Towards a 'Post-American' Alliance? NATO Burden-Sharing after Libya." *International Affairs* 88, no. 2 (2012): 313–27. http://dx.doi.org/10.1111/j.1468-2346.2012.01073.x.

Hanson, Victor. *Between War and Peace: Lessons from Afghanistan to Iraq*. New York: Random House, 2007.

Haqqani, Husain. *Pakistan: Between Mosque and Military*. Washington, DC: Carnegie Endowment for International Peace, 2010.

Hayes, Jarrod. "Identity and Securitization in the Democratic Peace: The United States and the Divergence of Response to India and Iran's Nuclear Programs." *International Studies Quarterly* 53, no. 4 (2009): 977–99. http://dx.doi.org/10.1111/j.1468-2478.2009.00565.x.

He, Kai, and Huiyun Feng. "If Not Soft Balancing, Then What? Reconsidering Soft Balancing and U.S. Policy toward China." *Security Studies* 17, no. 2 (2008): 363–95. http://dx.doi.org/10.1080/09636410802098776.

Hehir, Aidan. "The Myth of the Failed State and the War on Terror: A Challenge to the Conventional Wisdom." *Journal of Intervention and Statebuilding* 1, no. 3 (2007): 307–32. http://dx.doi.org/10.1080/17502970701592256.

The Helsinki Final Act (Final Act of the First Summit of the Commission for Security and Cooperation in Europe). Organization for Security and Cooperation in Europe, 1975.

Henderson, Phillip. "Organizing the Presidency for Effective Leadership: Lessons from the Eisenhower Years." *Presidential Studies Quarterly* 17, no 1 (1987): 43–69.

Herberg-Rothe, Andreas. "New Containment Policy: A Grand Strategy for the Twenty-First Century?" *RUSI Journal* 153, no. 2 (2008): 50–54. http://dx.doi.org/10.1080/03071840802103272.

Herring, George. *From Colony to Superpower: U.S. Foreign Relations since 1776*. Oxford: Oxford University Press, 2008.

Hill, Charles. *Grand Strategies: Literature, Statecraft, and World Order*. New Haven, CT: Yale University Press, 2010.

Hoffman, F. G. "Forward Partnership: A Sustainable American Strategy." *Orbis* 57, no. 1 (Winter 2013): 20–40. http://dx.doi.org/10.1016/j.orbis.2012.10.003.

Hogan, Michael. *The Marshall Plan: America, Britain and the Reconstruction of Western Europe, 1947–1952*. New York: Cambridge University Press, 1989.

Howard, Lise. *UN Peacekeeping in Civil Wars*. New York: Cambridge University Press, 2008.

Hughes, Christopher, and Ellis Krauss. "Japan's New Security Agenda." *Survival* 49, no. 2 (2007): 157–76. http://dx.doi.org/10.1080/00396330701437850.

Hunt, Michael. *Ideology and U.S. Foreign Policy*. New Haven, CT: Yale University Press, 2009.

Huntington, Samuel. *The Clash of Civilizations and the Remaking of World Order*. London: Penguin, 1996.

———. *Political Order in Changing Societies*. New Haven, CT: Yale University Press, 2006.

———. *The Third Wave: Democratization in the Late Twentieth Century*. Vol. 4. Norman: University of Oklahoma Press, 1993.

Ikenberry, John. *After Victory: Institutions, Strategic Restraint, and the Rebuilding of Order after Major Wars*. Princeton, NJ: Princeton University Press, 2009.

———. "American Grand Strategy in the Age of Terror." *Survival* 43, no. 4 (2001): 19–34. http://dx.doi.org/10.1080/00396330112331343105.

———. "Constitutional Politics in International Relations." *European Journal of International Relations* 4, no. 2 (1998): 147–77. http://dx.doi.org/10.1177/1354066198004002001.

———. *Liberal Leviathan: The Origins, Crisis, and Transformation of the American World Order*. Princeton, NJ: Princeton University Press, 2012.

Ikenberry, John, and Anne-Marie Slaughter. *Forging a World of Liberty under Law: U.S. National Security in the 21st Century*. Princeton Project Papers. Princeton, NJ: Woodrow Wilson School of Public and International Affairs, 2006.

International Energy Agency. *World Energy Outlook 2008*. Paris: Organization for Economic Cooperation and Development, 2008.

International Institute for Strategic Studies. *The Military Balance*. London: International Institute for Strategic Studies, 2014.

Jackson, Brian, ed. *The Challenge of Domestic Intelligence in a Free Society*. Santa Monica, CA: RAND, 2009.

———. *Considering the Creation of a Domestic Intelligence Agency in the United States: Lessons from the Experiences of Australia, Canada, France, Germany, and the United Kingdom*. Santa Monica, CA: RAND, 2009.

James, Lawrence. *The Rise and Fall of the British Empire*. London: Macmillan, 1994.

Jenkins, Brian, Andrew Liepman, and Henry Willis. *Identifying Enemies among Us*. Santa Monica, CA: RAND, 2014.

Jisi, Wang. "China's Search for a Grand Strategy: A Rising Great Power Finds Its Way." *Foreign Affairs* 90, no. 2 (2011): 68–79.

Johnson, Adrian, ed. *Wars in Peace: British Military Operations since 1991*. London: Royal United Services Institute, 2014.

Johnson, Chalmers. *The Sorrows of Empire*. London: Macmillan, 2007.

Johnston, Alastair. "Is China a Status Quo Power?" *International Security* 27, no. 4 (2003): 5–56. http://dx.doi.org/10.1162/016228803321951081.

Joint and Coalition Operational Analysis (JCOA). *Decade of War*. Vol. 1, *Enduring Lessons from the Past Decade of Operations*. Washington, DC: Department of Defense, 2012.

Jones, Seth G. *A Persistent Threat: The Evolution of Al Qa'ida and Other Salafi Jihadists*. Santa Monica, CA: Rand Corporation, 2014.

———. *In the Graveyard of Empires: America's War in Afghanistan*. New York: Norton, 2010.

———. "Mirage of the Arab Spring: Deal with the Region You Have, Not the Region You Want." *Foreign Affairs* 92, no. 1 (2013): 55–63.

———. "Syria's Growing Jihad." *Survival* 55, no. 4 (2013): 53–72. http://dx.doi.org/10.1080/00396338.2013.823034.

Kagan, Robert. *Dangerous Nation*. New York: Vintage Books, 2007.

———. *Of Paradise and Power: America and Europe in the New World Order*. New York: Vintage Books, 2007.

———. "One Year After: A Grand Strategy for the West?" *Survival* 44, no. 4 (2002): 135–39. http://dx.doi.org/10.1093/survival/44.4.135.

Kaldor, Mary. *New and Old Wars: Organized Violence in a Global Era*. Hoboken, NJ: John Wiley & Sons, 2013.

Kane, Tim. "Global U.S. Troop Deployment, 1950–2005." Heritage Foundation, Center for Data Analysis. Report #04–11. http://dx.doi.org/10.2139/ssrn.1146649.

Kang, David. "Why China's Rise Will Be Peaceful: Hierarchy and Stability in the East Asian Region." *Perspectives on Politics* 3, no. 3 (2005): 551–54. http://dx.doi.org/10.1017/S1537592705270342.

Kaplan, Robert. "The Geography of Chinese Power: How Far Can Beijing Reach on Land and at Sea?" *Foreign Affairs* 89, no. 3 (2010): 22–41.

Katzenstein, Peter, ed. *The Culture of National Security: Norms and Identity in World Politics*. New York: Columbia University Press, 1996.

Kaufman, Daniel, Aart Kraay, and Massimo Mastruzzi. "Worldwide Governance Indicators." Online data set and interactive tool. World Bank, 2015. http://info.worldbank.org/governance/wgi/index.aspx#home. Accessed October 28, 2015.

Kello, Lucas. "The Meaning of the Cyber Revolution: Perils to Theory and Statecraft." *International Security* 38, no. 2 (2013): 7–40. http://dx.doi.org/10.1162/ISEC_a_00138.

Kennedy, Paul. *The Rise and Fall of the Great Powers*. New York: Random House, 1987.

Keohane, Robert. *After Hegemony: Cooperation and Discord in the World Political Economy*. Princeton, NJ: Princeton University Press, 2005.

Khalilzad, Zalmay. "Lessons from Afghanistan and Iraq." *Journal of Democracy* 21, no. 3 (2010): 41–49. http://dx.doi.org/10.1353/jod.0.0184.

Kirkpatrick, Jeane. "NATO Enlargement." Testimony before the Senate Foreign Relations Committee, 105th Cong. (October 9, 1997).

Kissinger, Henry. *Diplomacy*. New York: Simon & Schuster, 2012.

———. "The Future of U.S.–Chinese Relations: Conflict Is a Choice, Not a Necessity." *Foreign Affairs* 91, no. 2 (2012): 44–55.

———. *On China*. New York: Penguin, 2011.

Knack, Stephen. "Does Foreign Aid Promote Democracy?" *International Studies Quarterly* 48, no. 1 (2004): 251–66. http://dx.doi.org/10.1111/j.0020-8833.2004.00299.x.

Krasner, Stephen. "The Case for Shared Sovereignty." *Journal of Democracy* 16, no. 1 (2005): 69–83. http://dx.doi.org/10.1353/jod.2005.0013.

———. "An Orienting Principle for Foreign Policy." *Policy Review* 163 (2010): 3–12.

———. "Talking Tough to Pakistan: How to End Islamabad's Defiance." *Foreign Affairs* 91, no. 1 (2012): 87–96.

Krepinevich, Andrew, Jr. *The Army and Vietnam*. Baltimore: Johns Hopkins University Press, 2009.

Krepinevich, Andrew, and Robert Work. *A New Global Defense Posture for the Second Transoceanic Era*. Washington, DC: Center for Strategic and Budgetary Assessments, 2007.

Kreps, Sarah. "American Grand Strategy after Iraq." *Orbis* 53, no. 4 (2009): 629–45. http://dx.doi.org/10.1016/j.orbis.2009.07.004.

Kroenig, Matthew. "Time to Attack Iran: Why a Strike Is the Least Bad Option." *Foreign Affairs* 91, no. 1 (2012): 76–86.

Kunz, Diane. "The Marshall Plan Reconsidered: A Complex of Motives." *Foreign Affairs* 76, no. 3 (1997): 162–70. http://dx.doi.org/10.2307/20048105.

Kupchan, Charles. "After Pax Americana: Benign Power, Regional Integration, and the Sources of a Stable Multipolarity." *International Security* 23, no. 2 (1998): 40–79. http://dx.doi.org/10.1162/isec.23.2.40.

———. *The End of the American Era: U.S. Foreign Policy and the Geopolitics of the Twenty-First Century*. New York: Vintage Books, 2007.

Kuperman, Alan. "Obama's Libya Debacle." *Foreign Affairs* 94, no. 2 (2015): 66–77.

Kydd, Andrew. "Sheep in Sheep's Clothing: Why Security Seekers Do Not Fight Each Other." *Security Studies* 7, no. 1 (1997): 114–55. http://dx.doi.org/10.1080/09636419708429336.

Lai, Brian. "Examining the Goals of U.S. Foreign Assistance in the Post–Cold War Period, 1991–96." *Journal of Peace Research* 40, no. 1 (2003): 103–28. http://dx.doi.org/10.1177/0022343303040001208.

Langevin, James R., Michael T. McCaul, Scott Charney, and Harry Raduege. *Securing Cyberspace for the 44th Presidency*. Washington, DC: Center for Strategic and International Studies, 2008.

Laqueur, Walter, ed. *Voices of Terror: Manifestos, Writings, and Manuals of Al Qaeda, Hamas, and Other Terrorists from around the World and throughout the Ages*. Naperville, IL: Sourcebooks, 2004.

Layne, Christopher. "From Preponderance to Offshore Balancing: America's Future Grand Strategy." *International Security* 22, no. 1 (1997): 86–124. http://dx.doi.org/10.1162/isec.22.1.86.

———. "Kant or Cant: The Myth of the Democratic Peace." *International Security* 19, no. 2 (1994): 5–49. http://dx.doi.org/10.2307/2539195.

———. *The Peace of Illusions: American Grand Strategy from 1940 to the Present.* Ithaca, NY: Cornell University Press, 2006.

———. "The Unipolar Illusion: Why New Great Powers Will Rise." *International Security* 17, no. 4 (1993): 5–51. http://dx.doi.org/10.2307/2539020.

Lee, Sheryn, and Benjamin Schreer. "The Taiwan Strait: Still Dangerous." *Survival* 55, no. 3 (2013): 55–62. http://dx.doi.org/10.1080/00396338.2013.802850.

Leffler, Melvyn, and Jeffrey Legro, eds. *In Uncertain Times: American Foreign Policy after the Berlin Wall and 9/11.* Ithaca, NY: Cornell University Press, 2011.

Levin, Norman. "What If North Korea Survives?" *Survival* 39, no. 4 (1997): 156–74. http://dx.doi.org/10.1080/00396339708442949.

Lewis, James Andrew. *Cyber Threat and Response: Combating Advanced Attacks and Cyber Espionage.* Washington, DC: Center for Strategic and International Studies, 2014.

Lewis, James, James R. Langevin, Michael T. McCaul, Scott Charney, and Harry Raduege. *Securing Cyberspace for the 44th Presidency: A Report of the CSIS Commission on Cybersecurity for the 44th Presidency.* Washington, DC: Center for Strategic and International Studies, 2008.

Lieven, Anatol, and John Hulsman. *Ethical Realism.* New York: Vintage Books, 2009.

Lind, Jennifer. "Democratization and Stability in East Asia." *International Studies Quarterly* 55, no. 2 (2011): 409–36. http://dx.doi.org/10.1111/j.1468-2478.2011.00652.x.

Lindsay, James, and Ray Takeyh. "After Iran Gets the Bomb: Containment and Its Complications." *Foreign Affairs* 89, no. 2 (2010): 33–49.

Lipset, Seymour Martin. *Political Man: The Social Bases of Politics.* Vol. 330. Garden City, NY: Doubleday, 1963.

Lipson, Charles. *Reliable Partners: How Democracies Have Made a Separate Peace.* Princeton, NJ: Princeton University Press, 2013. http://dx.doi.org/10.1515/9781400850723.

Lister, Charles. "Assessing Syria's Jihad." *Adelphi Papers* 54, no. 447–48 (2014): 71–98.

Lord, Kristin, and Travis Sharp, eds. *America's Cyber Future: Security and Prosperity in the Information Age.* Washington, DC: Center for a New American Security, 2011.

Lostumbo, Michael, Michael J. McNerney, Eric Peltz, Derek Eaton, David R. Frelinger, Victoria A. Greenfield, John Halliday, Patrick Mills, Bruce R. Nardulli, Stacie L. Pettyjohn, Jerry M. Sollinger, and Stephen M. Worman. *Overseas Basing of U.S. Military Forces.* Santa Monica, CA: RAND, 2013.

Louis, William Roger, and Hedley Bull. *The "Special Relationship": Anglo–American Relations since 1945.* Oxford: Oxford University Press, 1986.

Lutz, Catherine, ed. *The Bases of Empire.* New York: New York University Press, 2009.

Lynn, William. "Defending a New Domain: The Pentagon's Cyberstrategy." *Foreign Affairs* 89, no. 5 (2010): 97–108.

Lynn-Jones, Sean. "Why the United States Should Spread Democracy." ISP Discussion Paper Series, Paper 98-07. Belfer Center for Science and International Affairs, John F. Kennedy School of Government, Harvard University, 1998. http://belfer

center.ksg.harvard.edu/publication/2830/why_the_united_states_should _spread_democracy.html. Accessed on January 13, 2016.

MacDonald, Paul, and Joseph Parent. "Graceful Decline? The Surprising Success of Great Power Retrenchment." *International Security* 35, no. 4 (2011): 7–44. http:// dx.doi.org/10.1162/ISEC_a_00034.

MacMillan, Margaret. *The Rhyme of History: Lessons of the Great War.* Washington, DC: Brookings Institution Press, 2013.

Mahnken, Thomas, and Joseph Maiolo, eds. *Strategic Studies: A Reader.* London: Routledge, 2014.

Mandel, Robert. *Global Security Upheaval: Armed Non-State Groups Usurping State Stability Functions.* Redwood City, CA: Stanford University Press, 2013.

Mandiant Intelligence Center. "APT1: Exposing One of China's Cyber Espionage Units." 2013. http://intelreport.mandiant.com/Mandiant_APT1_Report.pdf. Accessed October 28, 2015.

Mansfield, Edward, and Jack Lewis Snyder. *Electing to Fight.* Cambridge, MA: MIT Press, 2005.

Markey, Daniel. *No Exit from Pakistan: America's Tortured Relationship with Islam-abad.* New York: Cambridge University Press, 2013. http://dx.doi.org/10.1017 /CBO9781107053755.

Marshall, George C. "Speech at Harvard University." Address to the Harvard Alumni Association, Cambridge, MA, June 5, 1947. http://marshallfoundation.org/mar shall/the-marshall-plan/marshall-plan-speech/. Accessed October 28, 2015.

Martel, William. "Grand Strategy of 'Restrainment.'" *Orbis* 54, no. 3 (2010): 356–73. http://dx.doi.org/10.1016/j.orbis.2010.04.003.

———. *Grand Strategy in Theory and Practice: The Need for an Effective American Foreign Policy.* New York: Cambridge University Press, 2015.

Masse, Todd. *Domestic Intelligence in the United Kingdom.* Washington, DC: Congressional Research Service, 2003.

Mastanduno, Michael. "Preserving the Unipolar Moment: Realist Theories and U.S. Grand Strategy after the Cold War." *International Security* 21, no. 4 (1997): 49–88. http://dx.doi.org/10.1162/isec.21.4.49.

Mazarr, Michael. *The Revolution in Military Affairs: A Framework for Defense Planning.* Carlisle, PA: Strategic Studies Institute, 1994.

McDougall, Walter. *Promised Land, Crusader State: The American Encounter with the World since 1776.* Boston: Houghton Mifflin Harcourt, 1997.

McFaul, Michael. *Advancing Democracy Abroad.* Lanham, MD: Rowman & Little-field, 2009.

McKinley, William. "Second Annual Message." December 5, 1898. Gerhard Peters and John Woolley, American Presidency Project. http://www.presidency.ucsb .edu/ws/index.php?pid=29539. Accessed October 28, 2015.

———. "Third Annual Message." December 5, 1899. Gerhard Peters and John Wool-ley, American Presidency Project. http://www.presidency.ucsb.edu/ws/index .php?pid=29540. Accessed January 13, 2016.

McKinney, Chris, Mark Elfendahl, and H. R. McMaster. "Why the U.S. Army Needs Armor." *Foreign Affairs* 92, no. 3 (2013): 129–36.

McMaster, Herbert. "On War: Lessons to Be Learned." *Survival* 50, no. 1 (2008): 19–30. http://dx.doi.org/10.1080/00396330801899439.

Mead, Walter Russell. *God and Gold: Britain, America, and the Making of the Modern World*. New York: Vintage Books, 2008.

———. *Special Providence: American Foreign Policy and How It Changed the World*. London: Routledge, 2013.

Mearsheimer, John. "Back to the Future: Instability in Europe after the Cold War." *International Security* 15, no. 1 (1990): 5–56. http://dx.doi.org/10.2307/2538981.

———. "The False Promise of International Institutions." *International Security* 19, no. 3 (1994): 5–49. http://dx.doi.org/10.2307/2539078.

———. *The Tragedy of Great Power Politics*. New York: Norton, 2001.

———. "Why the Ukraine Crisis Is the West's Fault: The Liberal Delusions That Provoked Putin." *Foreign Affairs* 93, no. 5 (2014): 77–89.

Mehta, Pratap Bhanu. "How India Stumbled: Can New Delhi Get Its Groove Back?" *Foreign Affairs* 91, no. 4 (2012): 64–75.

Mendelson, Sarah. "Democracy Assistance and Political Transition in Russia: Between Success and Failure." *International Security* 25, no. 4 (2001): 68–106. http://dx.doi.org/10.1162/01622880151091907.

———. "Russians' Rights Imperiled: Has Anybody Noticed?" *International Security* 26, no. 4 (2002): 39–69. http://dx.doi.org/10.1162/016228802753696762.

Menon, Rajan. "The Limits of Chinese–Russian Partnership." *Survival* 51, no. 3 (2009): 99–130. http://dx.doi.org/10.1080/00396330903011529.

———. "Reorienting Japan." *Survival* 50, no. 3 (2008): 177–90. http://dx.doi.org/10.1080/00396330802173255.

Metz, Steven, and James Kievit. *Strategy and the Revolution in Military Affairs: From Theory to Policy*. Collingdale, PA: Diane Publishing, 1995.

Miles, James. "Waiting Out North Korea." *Survival* 44, no. 2 (2002): 37–49. http://dx.doi.org/10.1080/00396330212331343322.

Milevski, Lukas. "A Collective Failure of Grand Strategy: The West's Unintended Wars of Choice." *RUSI Journal* 156, no. 1 (2011): 30–33. http://dx.doi.org/10.1080/03071847.2011.559975.

Miller, Aaron David. "The False Religion of Mideast Peace." *Foreign Policy* 179 (2010): 50–59.

Miller, Manjari Chatterjee. "India's Feeble Foreign Policy: A Would-Be Great Power Resists Its Own Rise." *Foreign Affairs* 92, no. 3 (2013): 14–19.

Miller, Paul D. "American Grand Strategy and the Democratic Peace." *Survival* 54, no. 2 (2012): 49–76.

———. *Armed State Building: Confronting State Failure, 1898–2012*. Ithaca, NY: Cornell University Press, 2013.

———. "A Bibliographic Essay on the Allied Occupation and Reconstruction of West Germany, 1945–1955." *Small Wars and Insurgencies* 24, no. 4 (2013): 751–59. http://dx.doi.org/10.1080/09592318.2013.857935.

———. "The Case for Nation-Building." *Prism* 3, no. 1 (2011): 63–74.

———. "Evangelicals, Israel and U.S. Foreign Policy." *Survival* 56, no. 1 (2014): 7–26. http://dx.doi.org/10.1080/00396338.2014.882149.

———."The Fading Arab Oil Empire." *National Interest* 120 (July–August 2012): 38–43.

———."Finish the Job." *Foreign Affairs* 91, no. 1 (2011): 51–65.

———."Five Pillars of U.S. Grand Strategy." *Survival* 54, no. 5 (2012): 7–44.

———. *Getting to Negotiations in Syria: The Shadow of the Future and the Syrian Civil War*. Santa Monica, CA: RAND, 2014.

———."Graveyard of Analogies: The Use and Abuse of History for the War in Afghanistan." Paper presented at the Clements Center Summer Seminar on History, Strategy, and Statecraft, Beaver Creek, CO, July 2014.

———."How to Exercise US Leverage over Pakistan." *Washington Quarterly* 35, no. 4 (Fall 2012): 37–52. http://dx.doi.org/10.1080/0163660X.2012.725022.

———."National Insecurity: Just How Safe Is the United States?" *Foreign Affairs* 91, no. 4 (2012): 146–51.

———."On Strategy, Grand and Mundane." *Orbis*, Spring 2016, in press.

———."Organizing the National Security Council: I Like Ike's." *Presidential Studies Quarterly* 43, no. 3 (2013): 592–606. http://dx.doi.org/10.1111/psq.12047.

———."The US and Afghanistan after 2014." *Survival* 55, no. 1 (2013): 87–102. http://dx.doi.org/10.1080/00396338.2013.767406.

Mills, Nicolaus. *Winning the Peace: The Marshall Plan and America's Coming of Age as a Superpower*. Hoboken, NJ: John Wiley & Sons, 2008.

Milward, Alan. *The Reconstruction of Western Europe, 1945–51*. London: Routledge, 2003.

———. "Was the Marshall Plan Necessary?" *Diplomatic History* 13, no. 2 (1989): 231–53. http://dx.doi.org/10.1111/j.1467-7709.1989.tb00053.x.

Monroe, James. "Seventh Annual Message," December 2, 1823. Gerhard Peters and John Woolley, American Presidency Project. http://www.presidency.ucsb.edu/ws/index.php?pid=29465. Accessed October 28, 2015.

Monten, Jonathan. "Primacy and Grand Strategic Beliefs in U.S. Unilateralism." *Global Governance* 13, no. 1 (2007): 119–38.

———. "The Roots of the Bush Doctrine: Power, Nationalism, and Democracy Promotion in U.S. Strategy." *International Security* 29, no. 4 (2005): 112–56. http://dx.doi.org/10.1162/isec.2005.29.4.112.

Morgenthau, Hans. *Politics among Nations*. Rev. ed. New York: Knopf, 1978.

Moyar, Mark. *Triumph Forsaken*. New York: Cambridge University Press, 2006. http://dx.doi.org/10.1017/CBO9780511511646.

Mueller, John Paul. *Retreat from Doomsday: The Obsolescence of Major War*. New York: Basic Books, 1989.

Mulaj, Kledja, ed. *Violent Non-State Actors in World Politics*. New York: Columbia University Press, 2010.

Muravchik, Joshua. *Exporting Democracy: Fulfilling America's Destiny*. Rev. ed. Washington, DC: American Enterprise Institute, 1992.

National Security Strategy of the United States. Washington, DC: White House, 1987, 1988, 1991, 1993–2000, 2002, 2006, 2010, 2015.

Nau, Henry. *At Home Abroad: Identity and Power in American Foreign Policy*. Ithaca, NY: Cornell University Press, 2002.

———. *Conservative Internationalism: Armed Diplomacy under Jefferson, Polk, Truman, and Reagan.* Princeton, NJ: Princeton University Press, 2013.

———. "Conservative Internationalism." *Policy Review* 150 (2008): 3–44.

Neustadt, Richard. *Presidential Power.* New York: New American Library, 1960.

Niebuhr, Reinhold. "Augustine's Political Realism." In *The Essential Reinhold Niebuhr*, edited by Robert Brown. New Haven, CT: Yale University Press, 1986.

———. *The Children of Light and the Children of Darkness: A Vindication of Democracy and a Critique of Its Traditional Defense.* Chicago: University of Chicago Press, 2011. http://dx.doi.org/10.7208/chicago/9780226584010.001.0001.

———. *The Irony of American History.* Chicago: University of Chicago Press, 2010.

Nixon, Richard. "Address to the Nation on the War in Vietnam," November 3, 1969. Gerhard Peters and John Woolley, American Presidency Project. http://www.presidency.ucsb.edu/ws/index.php?pid=2303. Accessed October 28, 2015.

Nordlinger, Eric. *Isolationism Reconfigured: American Foreign Policy for a New Century.* Princeton, NJ: Princeton University Press, 1995.

North American Aerospace Defense Command. "About NORAD." Department of Defense. http://www.norad.mil/AboutNORAD.aspx. Accessed January 14, 2016.

Obama, Barack. "Address to the Nation on the Situation in Libya." March 28, 2011. Gerhard Peters and John Woolley, American Presidency Project. http://www.presidency.ucsb.edu/ws/index.php?pid=90195. Accessed January 17, 2016.

———. "The President's News Conference." June 23, 2009. Gerhard Peters and John Woolley, *American Presidency Project.* http://www.presidency.ucsb.edu/ws/index.php?pid=86323&st=&st1=. Accessed April 12, 2016.

———. "Remarks at the State Department." May 19, 2011. Gerhard Peters and John Woolley, American Presidency Project. http://www.presidency.ucsb.edu/ws/index.php?pid=90397. Accessed January 17, 2016.

———. "Remarks in Cairo, Egypt." June 4, 2009. Gerhard Peters and John Woolley, American Presidency Project. http://www.presidency.ucsb.edu/ws/index.php?pid=86221. Accessed January 17, 2016.

———. "Remarks on the Drawdown of United States Military Personnel in Afghanistan." May 27, 2014. Gerhard Peters and John Woolley, American Presidency Project. http://www.presidency.ucsb.edu/ws/index.php?pid=105217. Accessed January 17, 2016.

———. "Remarks on United States Military and Diplomatic Strategies for Afghanistan and Pakistan." March 27, 2009. Gerhard Peters and John Woolley, American Presidency Project. http://www.presidency.ucsb.edu/ws/index.php?pid=85924. Accessed January 17, 2016.

Ochmanek, David, and Lowell H. Schwartz. *The Challenge of Nuclear-Armed Regional Adversaries.* Santa Monica, CA: RAND, 2008.

Odierno, Raymond. "The U.S. Army in a Time of Transition." *Foreign Affairs* 91, no. 3 (2012): 7–11.

Office of the Director of National Intelligence. *Worldwide Threat Assessment of the U.S. Intelligence Community.* 2013.

Office of Management and Budget. *Historical Tables: Budget of the U.S. Government.* Washington, DC: Government Printing Office, 2015. Available at https://www .whitehouse.gov/sites/default/files/omb/budget/fy2016/assets/hist.pdf. Accessed on January 13, 2016.

Office of the Secretary of Defense. *Military and Security Developments Involving the People's Republic of China.* Washington, DC: Department of Defense, 2011.

Office of the US Trade Representative. "U.S.–India Bilateral Trade and Investment." https://ustr.gov/countries-regions/south-central-asia/india. Accessed October 28, 2015.

O'Hanlon, Michael. "End Two-War Planning for U.S. Ground Forces." December 19, 2011. http://www.brookings.edu/research/opinions/2011/12/19-defense-budget -ohanlon. Accessed October 28, 2015.

———. *A Moderate Plan for Additional Defense Budget Cuts.* Washington, DC: Brookings Institution Press, February 2013.

———. *Technological Change and the Future of Warfare.* Washington, DC: Brookings Institution Press, 2011.

———. *Unfinished Business: U.S. Overseas Military Presence in the 21st Century.* Washington, DC: Center for a New American Security, 2008.

Oneal, John, and Bruce Russett. "Assessing the Liberal Peace with Alternative Specifications: Trade Still Reduces Conflict." *Journal of Peace Research* 36, no. 4 (1999): 423–42. http://dx.doi.org/10.1177/0022343399036004003.

———. "The Classical Liberals Were Right: Democracy, Interdependence, and Conflict, 1950–1985." *International Studies Quarterly* 41, no. 2 (1997): 267–94. http:// dx.doi.org/10.1111/1468-2478.00042.

One Earth Future Foundation. *The Economic Cost of Somali Piracy 2011.* Broomfield, CO: One Earth Future Foundation, 2011.

Organization for Economic Cooperation and Development. Online database.

Owen, John. *The Clash of Ideas in World Politics: Transnational Networks, States, and Regime Change, 1510–2010.* Princeton, NJ: Princeton University Press, 2010. http://dx.doi.org/10.1515/9781400836765.

———. *Liberal Peace, Liberal War: American Politics and International Security.* Ithaca, NY: Cornell University Press, 2000.

Owen, John M., IV. "The Foreign Imposition of Domestic Institutions." *International Organization* 56, no. 2 (2002): 375–409. http://dx.doi.org/10.1162/ 002081802320005513.

Owen, John, and William Inboden. "Putin, Ukraine, and the Question of Realism." *Hedgehog Review* 17, no. 1 (2015).

Owen, Mark, and Kevin Maurer. *No Easy Day: The Firsthand Account of the Mission That Killed Osama Bin Ladin.* London: Penguin, 2012.

Oye, Kenneth, ed. *Cooperation under Anarchy.* Princeton, NJ: Princeton University Press, 1986.

Pakenham, Robert. *Liberal America and the Third World.* Princeton, NJ: Princeton University Press, 1973.

Pape, Robert. *Dying to Win: The Strategic Logic of Suicide Terrorism.* New York: Random House, 2005.

———. "Soft Balancing against the United States." *International Security* 30, no. 1 (2005): 7–45. http://dx.doi.org/10.1162/0162288054894607.

Pardee Center for International Futures. *Data.* Online interactive database and tool. http://pardee.du.edu/access-ifs. Accessed October 28, 2015.

Paris, Roland. *At War's End: Building Peace after Civil Conflict.* New York: Cambridge University Press, 2004. http://dx.doi.org/10.1017/CBO9780511790836.

———. "Saving Liberal Peacebuilding." *Review of International Studies* 36, no. 2 (2010): 337–65. http://dx.doi.org/10.1017/S0260210510000057.

Paul, T. V. "Soft Balancing in the Age of U.S. Primacy." *International Security* 30, no. 1 (2005): 46–71. http://dx.doi.org/10.1162/0162288054894652.

Paul, T. V., and Mahesh Shankar. "Why the U.S.–India Nuclear Accord Is a Good Deal." *Survival* 49, no. 4 (2007): 111–22. http://dx.doi.org/10.1080/00396330701733951.

Petraeus, David. "Statement before the Senate Armed Services Committee." March 15, 2011. 112th Cong. (2011). http://www.dod.mil/dodgc/olc/docs/testPetraeus 03152011.pdf. Accessed on January 15, 2016.

Pettyjohn, Stacie. *U.S. Global Defense Posture, 1783–2011.* Santa Monica, CA: RAND, 2012.

Pew Research Center. *America's Global Image Remains More Positive than China's.* Washington, DC: Pew Research Center, 2013.

Phillips, Christopher. "Syria's Torment." *Survival* 54, no. 4 (2012): 67–82. http://dx.doi .org/10.1080/00396338.2012.709389.

Podhoretz, Norman. *World War IV: The Long Struggle against Islamofascism.* New York: Vintage Books, 2007.

Pollack, Kenneth. *A Path Out of the Desert: A Grand Strategy for America in the Middle East.* New York: Random House, 2009.

Porch, Douglas. *Counterinsurgency: Exposing the Myths of the New Way of War.* New York: Cambridge University Press, 2013. http://dx.doi.org/10.1017 /CBO9781139226301.

Porter, Patrick. *The Global Village Myth: Distance, War, and the Limits of Power.* Washington, DC: Georgetown University Press, 2015.

Porter, Wayne, and Mark Mykleby. *A National Strategic Narrative.* Washington, DC: Woodrow Wilson International Center for Scholars, 2011.

Posen, Barry. *Restraint: A New Foundation for U.S. Grand Strategy.* Ithaca, NY: Cornell University Press, 2014.

———. *The Sources of Military Doctrine: France, Britain, and Germany between the World Wars.* Ithaca, NY: Cornell University Press, 1986.

Posen, Barry, and Andrew Ross. "Competing Visions for U.S. Grand Strategy." *International Security* 21, no. 3 (1996): 5–53. http://dx.doi.org/10.2307/2539272.

Posner, Richard. *Remaking Domestic Intelligence.* Stanford, CA: Hoover Institution Press, 2011.

President's Review Group on Intelligence and Communications Technologies. *Liberty and Security in a Changing World.* 2013.

Press-Barnathan, Galia. "Managing the Hegemon: NATO under Unipolarity." *Security Studies* 15, no. 2 (2006): 271–309. http://dx.doi.org/10.1080/096364106 00829554.

Putin, Vladimir. "Prepared Remarks at 43rd Munich Conference on Security Policy." *Washington Post*, February 12, 2007.

Quinn, Adam. "Theodore Roosevelt." In *U.S. Foreign Policy and Democracy Promotion: From Theodore Roosevelt to Barack Obama*, edited by Michael Cox, Timothy Lynch, and Nicolas Bouchet. London: Routledge, 2013.

Randol, Mark. *Homeland Security Intelligence*. Collingdale, PA: Diane Publishing, 2010.

Rashid, Ahmed. *Descent into Chaos: The U.S. and the Disaster in Pakistan, Afghanistan, and Central Asia*. New York: Penguin, 2008.

Raviv, Dan, and Yossi Melman. *Spies against Armageddon*. Beirut: Levant Books, 2012.

Ray, James Lee. "War on Democratic Peace." *International Studies Quarterly* 57, no. 1 (2013): 198–200. http://dx.doi.org/10.1111/isqu.12029.

Reagan, Ronald. "Address to Members of the British Parliament," June 8, 1982. Gerhard Peters and John Woolley, American Presidency Project. http://www.presidency.ucsb.edu/ws/index.php?pid=42614. Accessed October 28, 2015.

Reeder, Franklin S., Daniel Chenok, Karen S. Evans, James A. Lewis, and Alan Paller. *Updating U.S. Federal Cybersecurity Policy and Guidance: Spending Scarce Taxpayer Dollars on Security Programs That Work*. Washington, DC: Center for Strategic and International Studies, 2012.

Reiter, Dan. "Why NATO Enlargement Does Not Spread Democracy." *International Security* 25, no. 4 (2001): 41–67. http://dx.doi.org/10.1162/01622880151091899.

Rice, Condoleezza. "Transformational Diplomacy." Speech at Georgetown University, Washington, DC, January 18, 2006.

Ricks, Thomas. *Fiasco: The American Military Adventure in Iraq*. New York: Penguin, 2006.

———. *The Gamble: General David Petraeus and the American Military Adventure in Iraq, 2006–2008*. New York: Penguin, 2009.

Rid, Thomas. "Cyberwar and Peace: Hacking Can Reduce Real-World Violence." *Foreign Affairs* 92, no. 6 (2013): 77–87.

———. "Cyber War Will Not Take Place." *Journal of Strategic Studies* 35, no. 1 (2012): 5–32. http://dx.doi.org/10.1080/01402390.2011.608939.

Riedel, Bruce. *Deadly Embrace: Pakistan, America, and the Future of the Global Jihad*. Washington, DC: Brookings Institution Press, 2012.

Robinson, Linda. *Tell Me How This Ends: General David Petraeus and the Search for a Way Out of Iraq*. New York: PublicAffairs, 2009.

Robinson, Linda, Paul D. Miller, John Gordon IV, Jeffrey Decker, Michael Schwille, and Raphael S. Cohen. *Improving Strategic Competence: Lessons from 13 Years of War*. Santa Monica, CA: RAND, 2014.

Ronis, Sheila. *Forging an American Grand Strategy: Securing a Path through a Complex Future*. Carlisle, PA: United States Army War College Press, 2013.

Roosevelt, Franklin. "Fireside Chat," December 29, 1940. Gerhard Peters and John Woolley, American Presidency Project. http://www.presidency.ucsb.edu/ws/index.php?pid=15917. Accessed October 28, 2015.

———. "Press Conference," December 17, 1940. Gerhard Peters and John Woolley, American Presidency Project. http://www.presidency.ucsb.edu/ws/index.php?pid=15913. Accessed October 28, 2015.

———. "Statement on the Atlantic Charter Meeting with Prime Minister Churchill," August 14, 1941. Gerhard Peters and John Woolley, American Presidency Project. http://www.presidency.ucsb.edu/ws/index.php?pid=16154. Accessed October 28, 2015.

Ross, Robert. "Balance of Power Politics and the Rise of China: Accommodation and Balancing in East Asia." *Security Studies* 15, no. 3 (2006): 355–95. http://dx.doi.org/10.1080/09636410601028206.

Rostow, Walt. "Lessons of the Plan: Looking Forward to the Next Century." *Foreign Affairs* 76, no. 3 (1997): 205–12. http://dx.doi.org/10.2307/20048111.

———. "The Stages of Economic Growth." *Economic History Review* 12, no. 1 (1959): 1–16. http://dx.doi.org/10.1111/j.1468-0289.1959.tb01829.x.

Rothstein, Hy, and John Arquilla, eds. *Afghan Endgames: Strategy and Policy Choices for America's Longest War.* Washington, DC: Georgetown University Press, 2012.

Roy, Denny. "Hegemon on the Horizon? China's Threat to East Asian Security." *International Security* 19, no. 1 (1994): 149–68. http://dx.doi.org/10.2307/2539151.

Ruggie, John. *Constructing the World Polity: Essays on International Institutionalisation.* London: Routledge, 2002.

Rumer, Eugene, and Angela Stent. "Russia and the West." *Survival* 51, no. 2 (2009): 91–104. http://dx.doi.org/10.1080/00396330902860835.

Runkle, Benjamin. *Wanted Dead or Alive: Manhunts from Geronimo to Bin Laden.* London: Macmillan, 2011.

Russett, Bruce. "'And Yet It Moves': A Correspondence Item." *International Security* 19, no. 4 (1995): 164–84.

Sagan, Scott, Kenneth Waltz, and Richard Betts. "A Nuclear Iran: Promoting Stability or Courting Disaster?" *Journal of International Affairs* 60, no. 2 (2007): 135–50.

Sanger, David. *Confront and Conceal: Obama's Secret Wars and Surprising Use of American Power.* New York: Crown, 2012.

Sapolsky, Harvey M., Benjamin H. Friedman, Eugene Gholz, and Daryl G. Press. "Restraining Order: For Strategic Modesty." *World Affairs* 172, no. 2 (2009): 84–94. http://dx.doi.org/10.3200/WAFS.172.2.84-94.

Sarotte, Mary. "Perpetuating U.S. Preeminence: The 1990 Deals to 'Bribe the Soviets Out' and Move NATO In." *International Security* 35, no. 1 (2010): 110–37. http://dx.doi.org/10.1162/ISEC_a_00005.

Schadlow, Nadia. "Competitive Engagement: Upgrading America's Influence." *Orbis* 57, no. 4 (2013): 501–15. http://dx.doi.org/10.1016/j.orbis.2013.08.001.

———. "War and the Art of Governance." *Parameters* 33, no. 3 (2003): 85–94.

Schain, Martin, ed. *The Marshall Plan: Fifty Years After.* London: Macmillan, 2001.

Schimmelfennig, Frank. "NATO Enlargement: A Constructivist Explanation." *Security Studies* 8, no. 2–3 (1998): 198–234. http://dx.doi.org/10.1080/09636419808429378.

Schmidt, John. *The Unraveling: Pakistan in the Age of Jihad*. London: Macmillan, 2011.

Schraeder, Peter, ed. *Exporting Democracy: Rhetoric vs. Reality*. Boulder, CO: Lynne Rienner Publishers, 2002.

Schroen, Gary. *First In: An Insider's Account of How the CIA Spearheaded the War on Terror in Afghanistan*. New York: Presidio Press, 2005.

Schultz, Kenneth. *Democracy and Coercive Diplomacy*. Vol. 76. New York: Cambridge University Press, 2001. http://dx.doi.org/10.1017/CBO9780511491658.

Schweller, Randall. "Bandwagoning for Profit: Bringing the Revisionist State Back In." *International Security* 19, no. 1 (1994): 72–107. http://dx.doi.org/10.2307/2539149.

Schweller, Randall, and Xiaoyu Pu. "After Unipolarity: China's Visions of International Order in an Era of U.S. Decline." *International Security* 36, no. 1 (2011): 41–72. http://dx.doi.org/10.1162/ISEC_a_00044.

Schwenninger, Sherle. "Revamping American Grand Strategy." *World Policy Journal* 20, no. 3 (2003): 25–44.

Scott, James, and Carie Steele. "Sponsoring Democracy: The United States and Democracy Aid to the Developing World, 1988–2001." *International Studies Quarterly* 55, no. 1 (2011): 47–69. http://dx.doi.org/10.1111/j.1468-2478.2010.00635.x.

Shambaugh, David. "The Coming Chinese Crackup." *Wall Street Journal*, March 16, 2015.

———. "Containment or Engagement of China? Calculating Beijing's Responses." *International Security* 21, no. 2 (1996): 180–209. http://dx.doi.org/10.1162/isec.21.2.180.

Shultz, Richard H., and Andrea J. Dew. *Insurgents, Terrorists, and Militias: The Warriors of Contemporary Combat*. New York: Columbia University Press, 2013.

Silove, Nina. "Beyond the Buzzword: A Theory of the Concept of Grand Strategy." Unpublished manuscript. 2014.

Simons, Anna, and David Tucker. "The Misleading Problem of Failed States: A 'Socio-Geography' of Terrorism in the Post-9/11 Era." *Third World Quarterly* 28, no. 2 (2007): 387–401. http://dx.doi.org/10.1080/01436590601153887.

Singer, J. David. "Reconstructing the Correlates of War Dataset on Material Capabilities of States, 1816–1985." *International Interactions* 14, no. 2 (1988): 115–32. http://dx.doi.org/10.1080/03050628808434695.

Sjursen, Helene. "On the Identity of NATO." *International Affairs* 80, no. 4 (2004): 687–703. http://dx.doi.org/10.1111/j.1468-2346.2004.00411.x.

Smith, Rupert. *The Utility of Force: The Art of War in the Modern World*. New York: Vintage Books, 2008.

Smith, Tony. *America's Mission: The United States and the Worldwide Struggle for Democracy*. Princeton, NJ: Princeton University Press, 2012. http://dx.doi.org/10.1515/9781400842025.

Snidal, Duncan. "The Limits of Hegemonic Stability Theory." *International Organization* 39, no. 4 (1985): 579–614. http://dx.doi.org/10.1017/S002081830002703X.

Sorley, Lewis. *A Better War: The Unexamined Victories and the Final Tragedy of America's Last Years in Vietnam*. Boston: Houghton Mifflin Harcourt, 1999.

Special Inspector General for Afghanistan Reconstruction. Quarterly Report to Congress. January 2015.

Spiro, David. "The Insignificance of the Liberal Peace." *International Security* 19, no. 2 (1994): 50–86. http://dx.doi.org/10.2307/2539196.

Stevenson, Jonathan. "The Syrian Tragedy and Precedent." *Survival* 56, no. 3 (2014): 121–40. http://dx.doi.org/10.1080/00396338.2014.920151.

Stokes, Doug. "Goodbye America? Transatlantic Grand Strategy after the Financial Crisis." *RUSI Journal* 158, no. 4 (2013): 70–75. http://dx.doi.org/10.1080/03071847 .2013.826510.

Strachan, Hew. "The Lost Meaning of Strategy." *Survival* 47, no. 3 (2005): 33–54. http://dx.doi.org/10.1080/00396330500248102.

———. "Strategy and Contingency." *International Affairs* 87, no. 6 (2011): 1281–96. http://dx.doi.org/10.1111/j.1468-2346.2011.01036.x.

Subramanian, Arvind. "The Inevitable Superpower: Why China's Dominance Is a Sure Thing." *Foreign Affairs* 90, no. 5 (2011): 66–78.

Suhrke, Astri. *When More Is Less: The International Project in Afghanistan.* New York: Columbia University Press, 2011.

Suri, Jeremi. "American Grand Strategy from the Cold War's End to 9/11." *Orbis* 53, no. 4 (2009): 611–27. http://dx.doi.org/10.1016/j.orbis.2009.07.005.

Taylor, Brendan. "Japan and South Korea: The Limits of Alliance." *Survival* 54, no. 5 (2012): 93–100. http://dx.doi.org/10.1080/00396338.2012.728346.

Thompson, Peter. *Armed Groups: The 21st Century Threat.* Lanham, MD: Rowman & Littlefield, 2014.

Thränert, Oliver. "NATO, Missile Defence and Extended Deterrence." *Survival* 51, no. 6 (2009): 63–76. http://dx.doi.org/10.1080/00396330903461674.

Tibi, Bassam. *Islamism and Islam.* New Haven, CT: Yale University Press, 2012.

Tocqueville, Alexis de. *Democracy in America.* New York: Penguin, 2003.

Transparency International. *Corruption Perceptions Index 2014.* http://www.transpar ency.org/cpi2014. Accessed October 28, 2015.

Traub, James. *The Freedom Agenda.* London: Macmillan, 2008.

Treverton, Gregory, Steven W. Popper, Steven C. Bankes, and Gerald P. Frost. *Reorganizing U.S. Domestic Intelligence.* Santa Monica, CA: RAND, 2008.

Truman, Harry. "Special Message to Congress on Greece and Turkey: The Truman Doctrine," March 12, 1947. Gerhard Peters and John Woolley, American Presidency Project. http://www.presidency.ucsb.edu/ws/index.php?pid=12846. Accessed October 28, 2015.

Tucker, Nancy Bernkopf. "China–Taiwan: U.S. Debates and Policy Choices." *Survival* 40, no. 4 (1998): 150–67. http://dx.doi.org/10.1080/713869434.

Ucko, David. "Critics Gone Wild: Counterinsurgency as the Root of All Evil." *Small Wars and Insurgencies* 25, no. 1 (2014): 161–79. http://dx.doi.org/10.1080/09592 318.2014.893972.

Union of Concerned Scientists. *Satellite Database.* http://www.ucsusa.org/nuclear -weapons/space-weapons/satellite-database#.VpnK4xGqSOA. Accessed January 15, 2016.

United Nations. "Declaration by the United Nations." January 1, 1942. http://www
.unmultimedia.org/searchers/yearbook/page.jsp?volume=1946-47&page=36&
searchType=advanced. Accessed January 13, 2016.

United Nations Office on Drugs and Crime. *Global Report on Trafficking in Persons.*
New York: United Nations Publications, 2014.

———. *World Drug Report 2010.* New York: United Nations Publications, 2010.

United States Agency for International Development. *U.S. Overseas Loans and Grants:
Obligations and Loan Authorizations, July 1, 1945–September 30, 2012* (The Green
Book). http://gbk.eads.usaidallnet.gov/.

———. "The Office of Crisis Surge Support Staff." http://www.usaid.gov/who-we-are
/organization/bureaus/bureau-democracy-conflict-and-humanitarian-assistance
/office-2. Accessed January 14, 2016.

United States Army and United States Marine Corps. *Counterinsurgency Field Manual
(FM 3-24).* Washington, DC: Department of the Army, 2007.

United States Bureau for Economic Analysis. *Interactive Data.* Online database and
tool. http://www.bea.gov/itable/index.cfm. Accessed January 15, 2016.

United States Census Bureau. "U.S. International Trade Data." Data available at http://
www.census.gov/foreign-trade/data/index.html. Accessed January 14, 2016.

United States Customs and Border Protection. *Performance and Accountability
Report: Fiscal Year 2013.*

United States Defense Security Cooperation Agency. *Historical Facts Book as of September 30, 2013.* Washington, DC: Department of Defense, 2013.

United States Department of Defense. *Base Structure Report: Fiscal Year 2014 Base-
line.* http://www.acq.osd.mil/ie/download/bsr/Base%20Structure%20Report%20
FY14.pdf. Accessed April 23, 2015.

———. *Quadrennial Defense Review Report: February 2010.*

———. *Quadrennial Defense Review Report: 2014.*

———. *National Military Strategy.* Joint Chiefs of Staff, February 1995.

———. *Report on Progress towards Security and Stability in Afghanistan.* December
2012.

———. *Strategy for Operating in Cyberspace.* 2011.

———. *Sustaining U.S. Global Leadership.* 2012.

United States Department of Defense Manpower Data Center. "DoD Personnel,
Workforce Reports and Publications." https://www.dmdc.osd.mil/appj/dwp
/dwp_reports.jsp. Accessed April 23, 2015.

United States Department of Energy. "Espionage and the Manhattan Project." Washington, DC: Office of History and Heritage Resources. https://www.osti.gov
/opennet/manhattan-project-history/Events/1942-1945/espionage.htm. Accessed
January 14, 2016.

United States Department of Homeland Security. *Blueprint for a Secure Cyber Future.*
2011.

United States Department of Justice. *Attorney General's Annual Report to Congress on U.S. Government Activities to Combat Trafficking in Persons, Fiscal Year
2005.*

United States Department of State. *Congressional Budget Justification, Fiscal Year 2016.*

———. "Foreign Terrorist Organizations." http://www.state.gov/j/ct/rls/other/des /123085.htm. Accessed October 28, 2015.

———. *Papers Relating to the Foreign Relations of the United States, 1906.* Washington, DC: Government Printing Office, 1906.

———. *Papers Relating to the Foreign Relations of the United States, 1943: Near East and Africa.* Washington, DC: Government Printing Office, 1943.

———. *Papers Relating to the Foreign Relations of the United States, 1952–1954: National Security Affairs.* Washington, DC: Government Printing Office, 1952–1954.

———. "Proliferation Security Initiative." http://www.state.gov/t/isn/c10390.htm. Accessed May 23, 2012.

———. *Treaties in Force.* Washington, DC: Department of State, 2013.

———. USEmbassy.gov. Web portal of all US embassies and consulates. http://www .usembassy.gov/index.html. Accessed April 23, 2015.

United States Department of State Office of Inspector General. *Inspection of the Bureau of Conflict and Stabilization Operation.* 2014.

United States Department of the Army. *Field Manual 3–57: Civil Affairs Operations.* Washington, DC: Department of the Army, 2014.

United States Energy Information Administration. *Annual Energy Review: 2010.* http:// www.eia.gov/totalenergy/data/annual/pdf/aer.pdf. Accessed February 9, 2012.

———. *Annual Energy Outlook: 2011.* http://www.eia.gov/forecasts/aeo/pdf/tbla21. pdf. Accessed February 27, 2012.

———. *International Energy Statistics.* http://www.eia.gov/cfapps/ipdbproject/IED Index3.cfm. Accessed October 28, 2015.

———. "Monthly Energy Review," January 2015. http://www.eia.gov/totalenergy /data/monthly/pdf/mer.pdf. Accessed October 28, 2015.

United States Institute of Peace. *Guiding Principles for Stabilization and Reconstruction.* Washington, DC: US Institute for Peace, 2009.

United States Joint Chiefs of Staff. *Joint Publication 3–0: Doctrine for Joint Operations.* Washington, DC: Department of Defense, 2011.

———. *Joint Publication 3–13: Information Operations.* Washington, DC: Department of Defense, 2014.

Van Creveld, Martin. *The Transformation of War.* New York: Simon & Schuster, 2009.

Walt, Stephen. "In the National Interest: A New Grand Strategy for American Foreign Policy." *Boston Review* 30, no. 1 (2005): 2.

———. *The Origins of Alliances.* Ithaca, NY: Cornell University Press, 1990.

Waltz, Kenneth. "The Emerging Structure of International Politics." *International Security* 18, no. 2 (1993): 44–79. http://dx.doi.org/10.2307/2539097.

———. "Structural Realism after the Cold War." *International Security* 25, no. 1 (2000): 5–41. http://dx.doi.org/10.1162/016228800560372.

———. *Theory of International Politics.* Long Grove, IL: Waveland Press, 2010.

———. "Why Iran Should Get the Bomb." *Foreign Affairs* 91, no. 4 (2012): 2–5.

Waltz, Kenneth, and Scott D. Sagan. *The Spread of Nuclear Weapons: A Debate Renewed*. New York: Norton, 2003.

Warner, Michael. "The Kaiser Sows Destruction." *Journal of the American Intelligence Professional* 46, no. 1 (2002): 3–9.

Waterman, Harvey, Dessie Zagorcheva, and Dan Reiter. "NATO and Democracy." *International Security* 26, no. 3 (2006): 221–35.

Webb, Michael, and Stephen Krasner. "Hegemonic Stability Theory: An Empirical Assessment." *Review of International Studies* 15, no. 2 (1989): 183–98. http://dx.doi.org/10.1017/S0260210500112999.

Wendt, Alexander. *Social Theory of International Politics*. New York: Cambridge University Press, 1999. http://dx.doi.org/10.1017/CBO9780511612183.

Wendt, Alexander E. "The Agent-Structure Problem in International Relations Theory." *International Organization* 41, no. 3 (1987): 335–70.

White House. *The Comprehensive National Cybersecurity Initiative*. Washington, DC: White House, 2008. https://www.whitehouse.gov/issues/foreign-policy/cybersecurity/national-initiative. Accessed January 14, 2016.

Williams, William Appleman. *The Tragedy of American Diplomacy*. New York: Norton, 1988.

Wilson, Woodrow. "Address to a Joint Session of Congress on the Conditions of Peace," January 8, 1918. Gerhard Peters and John Woolley, American Presidency Project. http://www.presidency.ucsb.edu/ws/index.php?pid=65405. Accessed October 28, 2015.

Wohlforth, William. "The Stability of a Unipolar World." *International Security* 24, no. 1 (1999): 5–41. http://dx.doi.org/10.1162/016228899560031.

Wood, Gordon S. *Empire of Liberty: A History of the Early Republic, 1789–1815*. Oxford: Oxford University Press, 2009.

Woodward, Bob. *Bush at War*. New York: Simon & Schuster, 2002.

———. *Obama's Wars*. New York: Simon & Schuster, 2011.

———. *Plan of Attack*. New York: Simon & Schuster, 2004.

———. *State of Denial*. New York: Simon & Schuster, 2006.

———. *The War Within: A Secret White House History, 2006–2008*. New York: Simon & Schuster, 2008.

Woolsey, R. James. "At War for Freedom." *World Today* 59, no. 8/9 (2003): 6–9.

World Bank. *Data*. Online database. http://data.worldbank.org. Accessed October 28, 2015.

Xiang, Lanxin. "Washington's Misguided China Policy." *Survival* 43, no. 3 (2001): 7–24. http://dx.doi.org/10.1093/survival/43.3.7.

Yost, David. "NATO's Evolving Purposes and the Next Strategic Concept." *International Affairs* 86, no. 2 (2010): 489–522. http://dx.doi.org/10.1111/j.1468-2346.2010.00893.x.

Yurgens, Igor. "A Positive Stalemate for Ukraine." *Survival* 57, no. 1 (2015): 71–77. http://dx.doi.org/10.1080/00396338.2015.1008296.

Zadra, Roberto. "NATO, Russia and Missile Defence: Towards the Lisbon Summit." *RUSI Journal* 155, no. 5 (2010): 12–16. http://dx.doi.org/10.1080/03071847.2010.530498.

Zegart, Amy. *Flawed by Design: The Evolution of the CIA, JCS, and NSC*. Redwood City, CA: Stanford University Press, 2000.

Zelikow, Philip, and Condoleezza Rice. *Germany Unified and Europe Transformed: A Study in Statecraft*. Cambridge, MA: Harvard University Press, 1995.

Zenko, Micah. *Reforming U.S. Drone Strike Policies*. New York: Council on Foreign Relations, 2013.

Zenko, Micah, and Michael Cohen. "Clear and Present Safety: The United States Is More Secure Than Washington Thinks." *Foreign Affairs* 91, no. 2 (2012): 79–91.

Zong, Jie, and Jeanne Batalova. "Frequently Requested Statistics on Immigrants and Immigration in the United States." Migration Policy Institute, 2015. http://www.migrationpolicy.org/article/frequently-requested-statistics-immigrants-and-immigration-united-states. Accessed on January 15, 2016.

INDEX

abolitionist ideology, shared Anglo-American belief, 36

Adams, John, 32, 223

Adams, John Quincy, 33, 243; restraint in different times, 128

Afghanistan, 63n71; counterterrorism against counterinsurgency, 24, 133; democratic outcome in, 53; drone program against militants, 185; failed state intervention decision, 133; government corruption and development, 187–88; illicit drug trade in, 86, 186; improved relations in strategic regions, 158; lack of resources and defeat, 59; long-term presence needed, 186–87; missteps in, 53–56, 58; nation-building and culture, 134, 188; role of technology, 261; stability operations in, 282; strategic importance, 185–86; Taliban, 54–56, 86; war on terror, 7, 50–51; war on terror and nonmilitary tools, 134–36

Africa: emerging democracies in South, 213; jihadist groups in north and east, 213; need for US military headquarters in, 271; pirates off northeastern coast, 213

al-Assad, Bashar, 73, 202–4, 281

Albright, Madeleine, 255

allies and partners abroad: reliance on, 7; strategic value of US military abroad, 269–70

al-Qaida, 133, 181, 214; and Afghanistan, 185–87, 280–81; in failed states, 87; in Iraq, 56–57; nonstate actors, 22, 91–92; and Pakistan, 178–79, 181–83; War on Terror, 6–7, 51, 54

American grand strategy, 18, 20–22, 28n49; action plan, 157–58, 279; attempts to define, xi–xiii; criteria for stronger ties, 156–57; decision-making system, 274–75; definition of terms, xiv–xv; democratic control, increase in, 18, 154–55; goals for Middle East, 192; good governance abroad, 18, 20; great power diplomacy, 18, 31; great power rivalry, 100; implementation of, 153–54, 221–22; intelligence and covert action, 271–73; liberalism, 18, 20, 45, 60, 106; liberalism and Treaty of Washington, 36; moral foundation, 101–2; objectives for South Asia, 175; power and liberty, 46–47, 68; pragmatism and ideology in, 30; prevention of hostile takeover, 67; realist and liberal inclinations, 20, 99, 119; security environment update, 22–23; terrorism, operations against, 18

American grand strategy, country plan: Afghanistan, 187–89; India, 176; Iran, 197–98; Israel, 207; Nigeria, 214; Pakistan, 180–85; Saudi Arabia, 199–200; Syria, 204–5

American hegemony, 15; erosion of, 65

American security. *See* national security

Angell, Norman, 69

anti-American alliance, Russia and China, 241

Anti-Imperialist League, 38

Arab Spring, 52, 200–201; in Tunisia, 90

Arab World, internal problems, 197–98

Argentina, status as an ally, 21

Aristide, Jean-Bertrand, 141

Arnold, Benedict, 232

Art, Robert: definition of security, 11; democracy and realpolitik, 110, 154; exclusion of nonmilitary means,

ABOUT THE AUTHOR

Paul D. Miller is the associate director of the Clements Center for National Security at the University of Texas at Austin. Dr. Miller previously served as director for Afghanistan and Pakistan on the National Security Council staff. He also served as an intelligence analyst with the Central Intelligence Agency and an intelligence officer in the US Army. He is a veteran of the war in Afghanistan and is the author of *Armed State Building* (Cornell University Press, 2013). He holds a PhD in international relations and a BA in government from Georgetown University and a master's degree in public policy from Harvard University.